TRUTH AND INTERPRETATION

TRUTH AND INTERPRETATION

AN ESSAY IN THINKING

Brayton Polka

St. Martin's Press   New York

BD
171
.P65
1990

ISBN 0-312-04218-3

Library of Congress Cataloging in Publication Data
Polka, Brayton.
Truth and interpretation: an essay in thinking/Brayton Polka.
  p. cm.
ISBN 0-312-04218-3
1. Truth. 2. Hermeneutics. 3. Thought and thinking.
4. Faith and reason. 5. Belief and doubt. I. Title.
BD171.P65   1990
121—dc20   89-49022
                          CIP

DEDICATION

Friends and students who encourage me to write as I think, to write as I teach, to write as I talk, are an inspiration: Terry Boyd, Lee Danes, Geri Das Gupta, Sydney Eisen, John Elias, Steen Halling, Grant Havers, John Hornstein, Tom Klein, Avron Kulak, Wally Kushnir, Rob Lawrence, Bernie Levinson, Bernie Lightman, Rod Macdonald, John Mahaffy, Sherlee McCuaig, Bill Showkowy, Pamela Steiner, Patrick Taylor, Tom Taylor, Anne Marie Williams, Bernie Zelechow

Even the most circumspect of philosophers think that what is known is *more easily understood* than what is strange and that proper method, for example, demands that we start from the "inner world," from "the facts of consciousness," because this world is *better known to us*. Error of errors! The known is the familiar; and the familiar is the most difficult to "know," that is, to see as a problem, that is, to see as strange, as distant, as "outside us." The great certainty of the natural sciences in comparison with psychology and the critique of the elements of consciousness—with the *unnatural* sciences, as one might almost say—rests precisely on the fact that they take *what is strange* as their object, while it is almost like something contradictory and absurd *to wish* to take what is not strange generally as an object.

Nietzsche, **The Joyful Wisdom**, V.355

All the sciences from now on have to prepare the way for the future task of the philosophers: this task meaning that the philosopher has to solve the *problem of value*, that he has to determine the rank order of values.

Nietzsche, **On the Genealogy of Morals**, I.Note

"I do not know yet," he replied, "because I have not finished telling the story." "But you know what happened," I insisted.... "No," Branly denied vehemently. "I shall not know until I tell it. That is the truth.... Everything depends on your understanding the words. You had a past, but you do not remember it. Try to recapture it in the little time you have left, or you will lose your future."

Carlos Fuentes, **Distant Relations**

The logical laws of thought do not apply in the id, and this is true above all of the law of contradiction. Contrary impulses exist side by side, without cancelling each other out or diminishing each other. There is a common saying that we should learn from our enemies. I confess I have never succeeded in doing so.

Freud, **New Introductory Lectures on Psychoanalysis**, 31 & 34

Contents

Preface

I. BEGINNING WITH THE TRUTH OF DESCARTES

I think, therefore, I am. I interpret the truth, therefore, I exist in the truth. When Descartes launches modern thinking, in his discourse on method which is at one with his meditations on first philosophy, by means of his famous formulation that I think, therefore, I am, what he shows us is that thinking expresses existence and that existence involves thinking. But what he then goes on to demonstrate to us is that the relationship between thinking and existence, the relationship of self-consciousness, proves (reveals) the existence of God. If God does not exist, Descartes holds, then we shall have no way of knowing whether or not our clear and distinct ideas are true. Descartes is the heir of scholastic thought, both philosophical and theological. Medieval and Renaissance thought is itself a complex amalgam of Greek and biblical speculation. The Greek tradition runs from the pre-Socratic philosophers through Socrates and his disciple Plato and Plato's disciple Aristotle to their Stoic, Epicurean, skeptical, and Neoplatonic heirs. Biblical speculation reflects the complex traditions of Judaism, Christianity, and Islam, including their interaction and their absorption of and not infrequent surrender to the traditions of Greek wisdom. Descartes recognizes, with an explicit awareness unknown to his predecessors, that thinking, existence, and truth are mutually related, each involving and expressing the other. Descartes recognizes that it is not the Greek logic of contradiction, which fatally opposes thinking and existence, the subject and the object of the thinker, but biblical ontology which, in binding divine and human thought and existence in the covenant of history, provides the structure of thinking whose subject and object are simultaneously the existence of truth and the truth of existence. The ontological argument for the existence of God, when truly comprehended (thought), Descartes shows, reveals the truthful existence of the thinking self. However clear and distinct ideas may be, they must exist to be true, and to be true they must exist. The only

true object of thinking is (self-) existence, and the only true subject of existence is (the) thinking (self).

I do not intend my work to be a commentary on Descartes' discourse, but I do invoke Descartes to frame my own discourse which I also
understand to be an essay in thinking, a meditation on the truth of existence, a meditation on the existence of truth. Descartes is a pioneer whose
essentially true yet not infrequently crude formulations of the problematic
of thinking offend not only his contemporaries but also his successors,
from his greatest disciple and critic, Spinoza, through Kant and Hegel,
down to Husserl, Heidegger, Wittgenstein, Dewey, and Ryle, including
Derrida and Rorty in our own time. To begin to comprehend the significance of Descartes' offence is to comprehend how truth as its own
standard, following Spinoza's ontological formulation of the truth of existence, makes its demand on us. To paraphrase Kierkegaard, himself a
defender of Cartesian doubt: either think truthfully—either think the truth
of existence—or be offended by your thoughtless lack of truthful existence.

Particularly offensive has been Descartes' beginning, his beginning
in doubt, his beginning with the ego conceived as the soul (thinking substance), as distinct from the body (extended substance). Equally offensive
has been Descartes' conclusion: that thinking (the thinking self) proves,
demonstrates, leads—therefore—to existence, the existence not only of the
self but also of God (truth). Descartes' ontological argument demonstrating
existence (the existence of both the soul and God) appears to his contemporaries—whose resistance to thinking truthfully Descartes elicits in the
Objections to his six Meditations, the Replies to which enormously assist
him in explicating the centrality of God, of existence, to his thinking—to be
both linear and circular. But Descartes knows that the claim, I think, therefore, I am, is not linear: thinking does not precede existence. The self thinking and the existing self are united in truth by the category of
"therefore"—by, in Kant's language, the categorical imperative. Equally,
Descartes' ontological demonstration of existence (of the self, of God) is not
simply circular, with the beginning merely presupposing its end. The
demonstration I think, therefore, I am is not tautological or empty, for it
demands a beginning in doubt, a fall, a testing so rigorous that the one
thing that the knight of thinking cannot doubt is that he is both the subject
and the object of doubt, simultaneously. This beginning in doubt, this
doubtful beginning, this doubting of all beginnings, Descartes recognizes,

is utterly unlike the apathy of ancient skepticism (whether in the tradition of Plato's Academy or of Pyrrho), not to mention the willfully skeptical, world-weary indifference of either the mystic or the sensualist (both equally biblical heirs). To doubt everything with the utmost rigor, to doubt something precisely because you care for it is to concentrate within your soul, within your mind or self, all possible passion. Doubting expresses the most passionate concentration, not lifeless apathy. When the beginning in doubt, when the doubtful beginning is carried all the way to its end, what it reveals, in the messianic tradition of the prophets, is that there is one thing—which is everything—which cannot be doubted: that an I exists which doubts and that something exists which the I doubts. Doubting involves no less a self which doubts (exists) than an object (existence) to be doubted. Doubting is both the alpha and the omega, both the beginning and the end, of the ontological argument for existence, proving that, insofar as I think, I exist.

The existence of the self, brought into existence through doubting, through thinking, through testing, through proving itself, is the proof that God exists. Once again, however terse or even crude is his meditation, Descartes is not arguing for a linear (finite) movement from self to God. Nor is he surreptitiously presupposing God, in circular (finite) fashion, and then claiming to prove what he has already assumed from the beginning. Rather, Descartes is profoundly aware that the consciousness that we exist (the Socratic representation of natural paganism) can become self-conscious of what existence is only if consciousness involves existence and existence expresses consciousness. The self thinking is both existing subject and the subject (object) of existence. But just as the self cannot begin doubting unless it exists, unless it is grounded in existence, so doubting leads to, demonstrates, the existence of God. God represents for Descartes the infinity of existence, consciousness, and truth. Infinity, Descartes is clear, is not the ancient Greek lack of perfection, that which lacks its end, *finis* or *telos*. Nor is infinity merely the negation of the finite in the tradition of negative theology common in the Neoplatonic currents of Judaism, Christianity, and Islam (and which is but the mirror opposite of what Hegel inimitably characterizes as the bad infinite and brilliantly deconstructs as the mindless standard of modern thinking, both philosophical and theological: the compulsively infinite replication of the finite). Infinity represents existence, perfection, and power: willing. Infinity comprehends all the attributes which theologians had traditionally ascribed to God as creator, judge, and redeemer, including omnipotence and omniscience. Infinity represents existence as created, not in the natural images of finite time and space, but in the absolute image of God.

Infinity is the representation of existence as conscious, that is, self-conscious, commitment to the truth. Descartes is traditional in conceiving of God as infinite (and it is precisely the conception of God as infinite which had allowed medieval thinkers, Jewish, Christian, and Muslim, to provide an ever-deepening critique of the finite teleology of Greek logic). He is radical, however, in recognizing the infinite implications of divine existence for thinking. The idea that God exists infinitely in and for the world—in and for the liberation of the world from the idolatry of the finite—is but to work in the tradition of the biblical God whose covenant with and incarnation in human being reveal his commitment to history, which, unlike natural space and time, is infinite. Descartes recognizes that thinking, in order to be true, must exist (it does not merely exist in the mind), that is, if ideas are to be true, they must exist. He recognizes that existence, to be true, must be thought, that is, that existence is not found separate from self-consciousness. I formulate these issues in radical terms so that we can appreciate both the difficulty which Descartes faces in articulating his project of thought and the difficulty contemporaries and successors have in comprehending it. Descartes does not hold, indeed, he totally eschews the notion, that thought exists or that ideas exist on analogy with finite things in natural space and time. Nor does he hold, rather he completely eschews the notion, that finite things depend for their natural existence upon thought. But he does hold tenaciously to the position that thought, existence, and truth, in their distinction from the body, from finite extension, involve the infinite (God). But he is untrue to his own insight when he continues to view the self (soul) as finite, for he has made clear that the self (in thinking existence as the truth) cannot be finite as natural things in space and time are finite. Existence is infinite, thought is infinite, truth is infinite, for they express human liberation, not from the world, but in the world from the world of things (idols). Existence describes not finite things but self-conscious human beings who, in order to exist, must think the truth, and who, in order to think the truth, must reveal their existence.

The legacy of Descartes is complex, for few of his successors are able to keep to his critical path of doubt, where, for thought to exist, it must be true, and where, for truth to exist, it must express the infinite existence of God. The deviations from the critical path are of two standard kinds (each reflecting Hegel's bad infinite). On the one hand, human beings are reduced to the finite. The fear and trembling involved in holding to the infinite as absolute limit, the absolute which is limited, overwhelms most thinkers. Human beings do die; death is central to human existence. Indeed, if human beings did not die, if their souls were immortal in the finite tradition of the Greeks, the infinite would not exist: there would be no thought, existence, or truth. But if humans were only finite (in the tradition of Heidegger), death would have no meaning, for it would merely reflect the pagan cycle of generation and destruction. On the other hand, truth is reduced to the finite, to certainty (in both the empiricist and the rationalist traditions). The separation of truth from God and of God from truth is one of the most characteristic features of modernity. Philosophers, holding that faith (God) is not a philosophical problem, strip truth of its relationship to God (infinite existence as the true idea of the mind) and reduce it to natural certainty (which inevitably turns into uncertainty). Theologians, holding that truth is not a philosophical problem, strip God of his relationship to truth (infinite existence as the true idea of the mind) and reduce it to supernatural certainty (which inevitably turns into uncertainty). To essay thinking, as we undertake it here, is to recognize that thinking involves the self in the existence of truth, whose theological representation is God. We can and, indeed, must vary the metaphors expressive of thinking, infinitely. But to reduce thinking to the finite or to elevate the finite to thinking is to lose both.

When Descartes claims to prove the existence of the soul and God—philosophically—what he shows, if in some sense unbeknownst even to himself, is that thinking involves the dialectic of doubt and faith. Doubt is thoughtless unless it involves faith in existence, and faith is doubtful unless it is tested by the utmost thoughtfulness. Against his critics, Descartes knows that his philosophy is grounded in the existential *logos* of biblical theology, not in the contradictory logic of Greek ontology. It is the encompassing circle of consciousness and existence, self and truth, the individual and God, not the vicious circle of the law of contradiction, which is the beginning and the end of doubt. Descartes' philosophy does not hide a ghost in the machine; its conception of the self is not solipsistic (*solus: ipse*), alone in itself; the self exists as a self only in its thinking, and it is a thinking self only because there is an object to its thought, which is existence, and existence—God—is true only insofar as it is universally true for all (thinking selves).

However inadequate may be Descartes' formulation of the relationship between thinking, existence, and truth, however inadequate has been the comprehension of Descartes by the tradition of modernity which he launches, our concern, here, is not to document the history of that inadequacy but to meditate upon ways of overcoming it. Descartes' own inadequate grasp of the relationship of thought and existence, of soul and body, is reflected in the fact, as we have indicated, that he has difficulty in conceptualizing the self, given that it cannot be directly identified with either the finite (mathematically quantifiable) existence of body or the infinite existence of God (the truth of universal existence, the universal existence of truth). He fails to see that, precisely because, as he demonstrates once and for all, the ground of the new science of nature is metaphysical (resting on the ontological argument for the existence of God), the metaphysics of thinking is fundamentally ethical. Descartes knows that, with his distinction between soul and body, between thinking and sense experience, between self-consciousness and consciousness, all action describing the ego, the self, the individual person—thinking, knowing, doubting, believing, feeling, willing, desiring, loving, hating...—belongs to the thinking self. He distinguishes truly, in other words, between emotion and sensation (just as he does between thought and sensation). Knowledge, whether cognitive or affective, is fundamentally not of things but of persons. It is one of the bitterest ironies of modernity, however, that, beginning with Descartes himself, knowledge becomes increasingly attached to things, to finite objects, while the emotions, expressing infinite passion, passion for the infinite (love, hate, joy, fear, caring...), are attached to persons who are then described in terms of the private, the subjective, and the emotional. What Descartes in fact shows, although he fails to be consistent with his own insight, is that it is natural bodies existing in (as) finite space and time, which, as the proper objects of scientific investigation, are, in themselves, private (deprived of the truth), merely subjective. On the other hand, it is thinking which, as the motive power of the individual, is truthful (objective), for it involves and expresses the infinite existence of the self (both human and divine). Still, Descartes fails abysmally in his *Passions of the Soul* to develop a coherent conception of the ethical self. He collapses into the very relativism which his dialectic of thinking and existence, grounded in the truth as the relationship of subject and object, had overcome.

The four great thinkers of modernity—Spinoza, Kant, Hegel, and Kierkegaard—elaborate their conception of the relationship of thought, existence, and truth in order to save Descartes from himself, but their work has largely fallen on deaf ears. Spinoza demonstrates in his *Ethics*, the single most concentrated work of ratiocination known to me, that the circle of existence, involving the human being and God and expressing truth as the standard of thinking, is ethics, human relatedness. But it is Kant who first, explicitly and systematically, demonstrates that the reason that both the subject and object of existence are truth is because thinking is fundamentally willing. To think—freely—is to will the good universal—true— for all. If reason is not grounded in the practice of human relations, Kant demonstrates with relentless passion from the beginning to the end of his critical philosophy, then it will inexorably divide into the thoughtless dualisms of empiricism and rationalism, skepticism and dogmatism (and Kant perspicaciously recognizes that empiricism and rationalism, in their one-sided blindness, are each equally skeptical and dogmatic). That we cannot know the thing-in-itself except as an object of possible experience, as a finite object of scientific investigation, is Kant's negative formulation for the actual practice of the thing-in-itself, the human self whose willing— thinking—the good true for all human existence is the ground of all objective knowledge.

In advancing the framework of Kantian discourse Hegel changes its terms. Consistent with the critical distinction which Kant makes between objects of possible experience and human subjects, between nature and freedom, knowledge and thinking, things and persons, price and dignity, finite means and infinite ends, Hegel elevates what he calls knowledge to the absolute—truth—(which Kant identifies as the subject and object of practical reason: will or thinking) and analyzes what Kant conceives of as the finite objects of nature in terms of immediacy. Absolute knowledge— which Descartes often calls certainty but is careful to identify with truth— belongs to spirit, whose dialectic Hegel is the first to render historical. The biblical concept of spirit now replaces the Greek term psyche as the central metaphor of the human story. The history of spirit is the spirit of history.

That history—spirit—is neither empiricist nor rationalist, neither temporal nor eternal, neither corporeal nor psychical (the Cartesian language of body and soul having been shown to be inadequate by Kant and Hegel) is the Hegelian heritage which Kierkegaard shows to express what he calls the religious. The religious stage or sphere of existence expresses for Kierkegaard the paradox that if faith (or God...) has always been in the world, then faith (God...) has never been in the world. God—truth, the individual self—comes into existence historically. Kierkegaard, following Kant and Hegel, shows that history is the domain of thought and existence, of consciousness and God, of truth. If truth has always been in the world, then it has never been in the world. Truth is historical. History is truthful. If history has always been the truth of the world, then it has never truly been in the world. If truth has always been the history of the world, then it has never existed historically in the world.

The formulation of truth in the paradoxical discourse of Kierkegaard may make it appear that we have radically diverged from the original meditation of Descartes. To thinking as the practice of willing what is the truth of existence for all human beings has been added the paradox of historical dialectic: that truth exists only insofar as it is historical and that history exists only insofar as it is truthful. Still, the basic issue of the relationship between thought and existence and their common object (subject), truth, remains. But the paradox of historical truth, of truth as history, also serves to reveal the problematic which shapes this essay in thinking, whose frame is the Cartesian *ergo* yoking together the thought and the existence of the self. If thinking has always been in the world, if the self has always existed, then self-consciousness has never existed in the world. What Kierkegaard shows us is that thoughtful existence, if it is true, occupies what he calls the religious sphere or stage of existence. He shows us that the most profound ratiocination, if it is true, is dialectical, paradoxical, faithful, and religious. He shows us equally that, if religion has always been in the world, then it has never been in the world. Kierkegaard shows us that faith is a category of existence, that existence is religious, and that the religious, as the overcoming of the one-sidedness of what he calls the aesthetic (the sensuous: body) and the ethical (the psychical: soul), is the historical: it comes into existence, freely, as history. But Kierkegaard's demonstration of the religious grounds of thought presupposes the liberation of thought, on the part of Descartes, Spinoza, Kant, and Hegel, from its pagan bondage to Plato and Aristotle, their teachers and heirs, and their heirs include the philosophers and theologians of what Kierkegaard calls Christendom, that state (church) of mind, the bad faith, represented by the idolatrous rationalization of paganism in the terms of faithful thinking, as distinct from what he calls Christianity: the purity of heart in willing one thing.

We intend our essay in thinking to occupy the framework which Descartes establishes as involving the truth of God's existence and which Kierkegaard shows to express the paradox (dialectic) of history. We cannot go further than thinking—to paraphrase Kierkegaard's pseudonymous author in *Fear and Trembling* who shows that, although we cannot go further than Abraham, although we cannot go further than faith, we surely do have the responsibility of not standing still, let alone of not going backward: we do have the responsibility of going eternally at least as far as faith, of ever becoming the knight of faith. Although we cannot go further than thinking, surely we do have the responsibility, at least once in our lives, to begin thinking, which brings us to the issue shaping this work. So far we have indicated some of the implications involved when thinking is understood to express truth and existence. To think is to exist in the truth. But it is equally important to recognize that thinking is expressly interpretation. To think is to interpret. To think is to recognize, in the fullness of self-consciousness, that truth does not exist outside its interpretations and that interpretation does not exist outside its truth. In this essay in thinking my concern is to show that thinking expresses the dialectic of truth and interpretation.

II. TRUTH AND INTERPRETATION

In my previous book, *The Dialectic of Biblical Critique: Interpretation and Existence*, I establish the groundwork of the critique I continue here. Above all, in my work I want to show that we can develop an adequate conception of what I am here calling thinking—thinking the truth of interpretation and the interpretation of truth—only if we come to understand, once and for all, that, yet again to invoke Kierkegaard's knight of faith, if thinking has always been in the world, then it has never been in the world. Neither truth nor interpretation is something given, universally, in the nature of being human. Truth and interpretation are the universal to be established through human thinking: willing, action, love.

Thinking the dialectic of truth and interpretation is to understand, for example, how Rousseau's claim that human beings are naturally good is consistent with Pascal's claim that human beings naturally hate one another and Hegel's claim that human beings are naturally evil. All three thinkers presuppose what I call the dialectic of infinite and finite, which emerges in Rousseau's discourse as the recognition that truth, when properly interpreted, embodies the argument from right to fact, not from fact to right. The existence of slaves, for example, testifies to their oppression, to their unjust, unnatural existence. Slaves are not rightfully born into slavery; unjustly they are made and/or make themselves slaves. That they are slaves, in fact, violates their natural right of existing as human beings. Whereas Rousseau understands nature as expressing the (infinitely) human right of subjects, Pascal and Hegel view nature as the realm of finite objects. For Rousseau, the facts of (finite) social existence contradict the natural right of being human. For Pascal, human beings can overcome their natural (finite) opposition or hatred only through the good faith of infinitely loving their neighbor. Pascal's distinction between natural hatred, based on the finite laws of nature, and human love, based on good faith in the infinite, is consistent with Hobbes' distinction between the state of nature and the political realm. For Hobbes, human life in the finite state of nature is nasty, brutish, and short; it is based on fear, on the fear of finite contradiction, on the fear of being contradicted by the finite; for not only can the finite always be taken away (by somebody whose strength rests on possessing a greater quantity of finite things), but the finite will ultimately be taken away from everyone—in and through death. In the political realm, in contrast to the state of nature, human life is (infinitely) based on the mutual respect of the golden rule. As Hegel demonstrates time and again, the finite is contradictory; it contradicts the (infinite) spirit of self-consciousness. Human beings are evil precisely because they contradict the infinite spirit of humanity by reducing it to the finite state of nature, making it subserve the flesh, to recall the language of Paul.

If humanity (human nature) has always been in the world, then it has never been in the world. If we are to develop consistent, comprehensive, and coherent—what Spinoza calls adequate—conceptions of truth and interpretation, they must be grounded in an idea of nature as right, not factual (empirical); in an idea of history as infinite, not finite (natural); in an idea of thinking as rational and faithful, not skeptical or dogmatic (dualistic).... I show in my *Dialectic of Biblical Critique* that the position whereby we establish, evaluate, and narrate the facts of human history in light of human right is uniquely—universally—biblical. The Bible is the first (and the last) book which shows, from beginning to end, that, if it has always been in the world, then it has never been in the world. The Bible comes into the world—of nature and civilization—showing that in the beginning God creates the heavens and the earth and all their creatures, both natural and sentient, both sentient and human, both pagan and thoughtful (those who providentially choose the life of right), both thoughtful (adherents of the covenant) and thoughtless (idolaters). The Bible reveals that creation is *ex nihilo*—from nothing that is not creative. The Bible distinguishes the creative God (the God of creation) in all space and for all time from the gods of generation (the gods of the generations), whose finite representations in space and time are now revealed as contradictory and whose natural similitudes are the idols against which patriarchs, prophets, psalmists, Jesus, and the apostles constantly oppose the metaphors of creation.

It is not nature in itself, understood as the finite realm of spatial and temporal objects, whose generation the Bible celebrates, whatever the deceptive appearances of the beginning of Genesis, but nature interpreted as spirit, miracle, right, freedom, grace, and creation. Yet it is precisely the distinction between finite and infinite nature, between generation and creation, between finite objects and infinite subjects, between things and persons which the Bible reveals as the creation of God from nothing, for there is nothing in the world of nature, in the cosmos, as such, which bespeaks the creative nature of being human. Creation is not grounded in nature, in generation; natural (creative) right is not grounded in the mere facts of nature. Rather it is creation which is its own ground, the ground on which we establish priorities among the facts of natural generation.

What I undertake to show in *The Dialectic of Biblical Critique* is that it is the critical distinction between creation and generation, between natural right and natural fact, between the infinite and the finite which introduces a crisis into the world, a crisis of conscience, a crisis of thought, a crisis of choice. For, if the creation of thought (creative thought, the thought of creation) has not always been in the world, how does it enter the world, what is its relationship to the world, what happens to the world which it enters? The Bible relates the story of how the creation of man and woman, of humanity, from nothing (pagan) involves their fall, their expulsion from the paradisiacal innocence of natural fact, into the critical consciousness of living thoughtfully on the basis of right. I show in my previous book that, when we ground our thinking in the dialectic of biblical critique, in biblical dialectic—than which there is no other—we discover that, to use the terms of the present essay, there is no thinking in the Greek or extra-biblical world. In my previous book I show that the Greeks have no conception of either existence or interpretation. In the strong language forcing upon us anew the crisis of recognition, the Greeks do not exist, and Greek texts cannot be interpreted. Interpretation and existence are not natural terms applying immediately, without the critical awareness that all discourse, all narrative, all demonstration makes the eternal transition from right to fact. Rather, interpretation and existence are concepts which, like all concepts, as distinct from mere terms (words), involve and express communication. I devote the central, major section of my previous book to what is, so far as I know (with the exception of works like those by Miranda and Eidelberg), the first, exacting demonstration that Greek texts, because they are grounded in images of natural generation (fate), have no conception of, in the terms of the present essay, truth or interpretation. The reason that I emphasize the importance of recognizing that thinking—the dialectic of truth and interpretation—is unknown to or absent from the world of the Greeks is that their civilization has been and remains so influential for us moderns, the heirs of the Bible. That the Greeks, for all their sophistication, do not differ in kind from so-called primitive peoples, all of whom have or are capable of having sophisticated cultures, both verbal (if not literate) and material, or from the sophisticated civilizations of the East, may, at first, appear preposterous. But the Greeks do not, any more than other extra-biblical peoples, conceive of right—freedom, equality, and solidarity—as the basis of truthful interpretation (of the interpretation of truth). There is no interpretation outside of the truth of existence, and to exist is to interpret the truth: I think, therefore, I am. Thinking is not a natural faculty, in Pascal or Hegel's terms. Thinking is, however, the natural right of humankind, in Rousseau's terms, and there is only one, true object of interpretation: the rightful thought and existence of the human subject.

In the present book I continue the discourse initiated in my *Dialectic of Biblical Critique*. I shall not repeat here but presuppose the detailed critique of Greek texts provided there. But, in order to establish our conception of thinking as the dialectic of truth and interpretation, it is critically important to grasp the contradiction of Greek life as lacking any conception of thinking, any conception of either truth or interpretation. Here I shall outline the consequences for the Greeks (as for all extra-biblical peoples) of holding to the law of contradiction (and to its sister laws of identity and the excluded middle) as the indemonstrable beginning and end of life and then briefly show the reflection of the law of contradiction in the lives of typically Greek heroes: Oedipus, Socrates, and Pentheus.

III. THE GREEKS AND THE LAW OF CONTRADICTION

When Greek authors acknowledge ignorance of their premises, stating that first principles cannot be demonstrated, they say what they mean and they mean what they say. In other words, they mean it when they say that they are blind to and are blinded by the appearances of life which contradict the law of contradiction, that which Aristotle calls the first, indemonstrable principle of logical demonstration. That the law of contradiction underlies Greek life as the first principle of demonstration which cannot be demonstrated means that every additional or subsequent principle or premise is equally indemonstrable and unknown. A blind beginning inexorably leads to a blind ending, as Oedipus discovers, to his horror. The law of contradiction is the indemonstrable basis of demonstration precisely because it applies solely to the finite realm of nature. That which is finite or natural is, for the Greeks (as for all extra-biblical peoples), at its end (*finis* or *telos*). It is finished, perfect, immortal, and unchanging, known only in itself (and not to us). It is precisely because the finite (that which is at, or identical with, its end) is dead to appearances, to life, that it is consistent with the law of contradiction for which something cannot both be and not be in the same space at the same time. Only that which is finite, perfect, immortal, unknowable, and dead to the life of appearances abides by the law of contradiction. Life in the body, including political life, in contrast, is fatally associated with that which is unfinished, imperfect, mortal, and changing; it is in-finite, lacking its end. The lack of an end is precisely what characterizes life for the Greeks; it is equally what characterizes appearances whose infinite metamorphoses show that they are always other than (or different from) what they are in themselves, which is their end. Life, as appearance, is inexorably fated to contradict its end, whose first premise is indemonstrable. The ultimate contradiction of Greek life is that you cannot reach your end, beyond all contradiction, in death, without first beginning in life; but to begin in life is to be fated, from the beginning, to contradict your end.

Even the immortal gods of the Greeks do not escape the fatal logic of the law of contradiction, for, being no less contradictory in appearance, as Socrates reminds his listeners, than their mortal imitators, they are no less blind to and ignorant of the first indemonstrable principle of demonstration, whose logic they contradict unceasingly. It is equally true that, although Plato and Aristotle invert the distinction between mortal humans and immortal gods by imputing immortality to the soul (Plato) or mind (Aristotle), they are no less fated than are their fellow Greeks to maintain the fatal distinction between (infinite) appearance and (finite) reality. It is only when the soul is dead to appearances, dead to life, and when the mind thinks only its own thoughts, separate from the appearances of life, that they can adhere to the fatal logic of contradiction. But again, soul or mind, as the indemonstrable first principle of life whose end is perfect and complete only separate from life (in death), has to begin in a human (bodily and political) life in order to arrive at its end. To begin, however, is but to unleash the revenge of the law of contradiction, which demonstrates, on the basis of its own blind beginnings, that to begin is to lack all principle (origin) of demonstration. To begin is to lack, to be the opposite of, to be opposed to and by your end. Unlike the ancient Hebrews, for whom thought and existence are grounded, not in the natural (contradictory) images of space and time but in the infinite image (metaphor) of God (truth), the Greeks, like all extra-biblical peoples, view themselves in the finite images of nature, whose appearances, in being opposed to or the opposite of each other, ineluctably contradict one another.

The law of contradiction is the *logos* of Greek life. Since something cannot both be and not be in the same space at the same time and since being is defined by (as) its end (*finis* or *telos*), there is fatal and unending opposition between finite (that is, perfect, immortal, and unchanging) being, which is at its end, dead to the appearances of life, and the infinite (that is, imperfect, mortal, and metamorphosing) appearances of being which, contradicting its end, show its life to be one of ignorance. The law of contradiction is fatal to the Greeks (as to all extra-biblical peoples) and baffles moderns (above all, philosophers) because, according to the law of contradiction, for something to be known (to be), it must appear, yet, according to the same contradictory law, appearances, because they are in-finite, lacking a *telos,* do not exist, that is, they lack being. The secret hidden within the fatal *logos* of contradiction is revealed only within the biblical tradition (and thus Kant exposes the antinomies of pure reason by demonstrating that their contradiction can be penetrated only on the basis of a conception of reason not grounded in the law of contradiction: the two opposites in each of the first two pairs of antinomies are both false, while the two opposites in each of the second two pairs of antinomies are both true). When thought and existence are grounded in finite conceptions of nature, in finite space and time, then everything which is and which is thought is always opposite (opposed) to itself, unknowingly. If I base my identity on the finite objects of nature, I—both my thought and my exist-ence—vanish into them. I am—always other than what I am; for, in ig-norantly (blindly) identifying my being with finite nature, I identify it with that which, because it can and will be taken away from me, is fatally op-posed to me. Immediate identity with nature fatally leads, inexorably, by the law of contradiction, to contradiction by nature. The Cretan liar al-ways/never tells a lie: it is true that he lies, and it is a lie that he tells the truth. The Cretan liar is opposed to, the opposite of, himself, but his self-contradiction remains a mystery to him, a mystery into which he unknow-ingly (blindly) vanishes, because, although he knows that he lies, he remains ignorant of what his lie is. It is characteristic of the Greeks, as of all extra-biblical peoples, that they have a Cretan liar but no Cretan truth-teller. It is only in willing the truth—of thought and existence—that we can account for our lies, that we can know what our lies are, that they are a denial, evasion... of the truth. It is only in recognizing that we cannot will that lying be made into a universal principle of existence that we can truth-fully account for the fact that we lie, that we are liars.

For the Greeks, to know the good is to be the good; to be identical with the good is to be dead to the life of appearances. The good must be identical with itself, not subject to change, and immortal in order to abide by the law of contradiction. The good is indeed the law of contradiction, it-self, which, the very instant it appears, contradicts itself by showing that it is other than what it is in itself. To seek knowledge of the good, on the other hand, is to be blind to and ignorant of the good, for you can seek only what you do not know. To seek the good is to lack knowledge of what you are seeking. All seeking in the Greek world—all desiring, willing, loving, hoping, aspiring: all action, all life—is vain, merely apparent, empty. What seeking knowledge of the good demonstrates, by the fatal *logos* of contradiction, is that the subject seeking knowledge and the object to be known, what Plato calls appearance and Form and Aristotle things (the good) known relative to us and things (the good) known in themselves, are fatally opposed to each other. Socrates knows THAT he is ignorant of the good, but he has no idea WHAT the good is of which he is ignorant. The fatal opposition between the relative that and the absolute what (the thing-in-itself) is precisely what Descartes, in embodying the *logos* of the Bible in his discourse, overcomes by identifying thought (the self), existence (the self and God), and truth (God), all representing the idea (Hegel's *Idee*).

The hard lesson for us moderns to learn from Greek texts is that, when saying and meaning are ignorantly, or fatally, identified as natural (finite), then they possess neither truth nor interpretation. Greek texts are not, in truth, texts. Texts as things existing naturally in the interpretation of themselves, as things whose interpretation naturally exists in itself, can, as Kant would say, be known only as the natural objects of possible experience appearing in finite space and time and, in order to be interpreted as in truth existing, must be thought (willed) as subjects of practical experience by a community of persons, that which Kant calls the kingdom of ends and Rousseau the social contract. Greek texts have neither surface nor depth, neither letter nor spirit, neither language nor communication, except in appearance, whose endless metamorphoses reflect the law of contradiction, showing that the only happy text, one for which knowledge of the good is to be the good, is a dead text, dead to the contradictory appearances of life. Surface or literal facts do not truly exist outside their interpretation by the right of spirit. There is only a veritable sense of the literal when we locate the letter within the priority of spirit, when we argue, not from fact to right, but from the right of spirit to literal fact. All natural languages are perfect, but they communicate nothing, they have nothing to communicate outside the dialectic of truth and interpretation.

But there the Greek text is—read for over two millennia; our libraries house millions upon millions of editions and translations of Greek texts; our university scholars turn out endless commentaries on them; the public, both sophisticated and popular, is insatiable in its appetite for the glory that is Greece; our schools continue to teach our children that the origin of democracy is the fatal Greek rule of one, some, or many over others and not the Hebrew law freely recognizing the right of all: the right of the covenant, the right of the poor and the dispossessed, the right of truth, the right of interpretation, the right to think and to exist freely, the right of God and neighbor: the golden rule. The texts of the Greeks, as of all extra-biblical peoples, must be read, thought about, and doubted so passionately until we realize, finally, at least once in our life, with Descartes, that we must turn ourselves around and be converted to the truth about them. We traditionally say that the reason we study the works of the Greeks, as of all extra-biblical peoples, is because they are part of our universally human heritage. But the concept of what constitutes the universality of human history traditionally remains uncritical, without a sufficient sense of the crisis that we must suffer in learning to read what we must learn cannot be read. We must read, think through, and doubt all the way to the ground the works of the Greeks so that we come, finally, to realize that that which can, must be, doubted in truth is precisely (only) that which reflects, self-critically, our doubt. We can doubt only that which exists in the truth, only that which interprets us as we will to interpret it. Greek texts do not sustain our doubt—our thinking freely and creatively—for their words but reflect appearances whose contradictions mirror the images of natural blindness, ignorance and death. We need but think of the typically Greek heroes: Oedipus, Socrates, and Pentheus.

Oedipus the king blinds himself once he learns that, before he is born, he is fated to violate the most sacred taboos of his society: to kill his father and to sleep with and to have children by his mother. His act of self-blinding reflects the horror of his discovery that he knows nothing. He learns that he is fatally ignorant, that he is ignorant of life from the beginning, that all beginnings are in ignorance. To begin in the Greek world is inexorably to find yourself at your contradictory end, reversed by, blind to, and ignorant of your beginning. Eying King Oedipus led blind into exile from the *polis* by his daughter Antigone, who is also his sister, the chorus sings at the end of *Oedipus the King*: count no man happy until he is dead, dead to the contradictory appearances of life. The only happy man is a dead man. In the *Poetics* Aristotle identifies the hero's reversal from "philosopher," the lover of or seeker after wisdom, to one who is blinded by his ignorance of fate with the catharsis of pity and fear experienced by the play's spectators. The spectators experience ignorance of fate—that they, too, are ignorant, from the beginning, of their beginnings, of the principles of life—as the purgation of pity and fear. They see that all principles are indemonstrable; they see that, from the beginning, they are no less blind to their fate, that they are no less dead to life, than the heroic Oedipus. Catharsis of pity and fear reflects fatal ignorance. Nothing substantial remains. The law of contradiction's indemonstrable rule over the appearances of life is fatally triumphant.

But reversals, following the pagan doctrine of opposites whose metamorphosis is endless, know no *telos*. When the unheroic Oedipus—blind, exiled, and stripped of honor—is found aged at Colonus (in Sophocles' play by that name), his position is reversed yet again. He now rails against his unlucky fate for having given him no chance in life: don't blame me, he says; blame the gods; it's not my fault. *Oedipus at Colonus* concludes with the mysterious disappearance of its hero, whose end is observed only by Theseus. All that those who had been in attendance upon Oedipus and the audience learn is that Oedipus' end is a secret which Theseus is never to reveal. Oedipus' secret fate is complete. He begins in complete ignorance of his beginning, and he ends with his ending a total secret which Theseus is to tell nobody. Theseus' secret is the secret of Oedipus, the secret of the play, the secret of the Greeks. The secret of Oedipus is his apotheosis, his reception, in the end, into the circle of the very gods the violation of whose sacred taboos had fatally reversed the wise king in the beginning. Oedipus' life is fatally suspended between his beginning in ignorance and his secret end. The secret of Oedipus in the end is that he is ignorant of his fate from the beginning. The secret of his end is the purgation of pity and fear, leaving nothing at all, except natural ignorance, blindness, and death, a fate no different from that of Damocles or Sisyphus. The secret of the Greeks is that they have no secret. Their lives are empty, futile, blind, ignorant, and dead, fated, from the beginning, to follow to the end the law of contradiction, with whose fatal secret they then vanish in ignorance from life.

Like Oedipus, Socrates receives a devastating message from the Delphic Oracle. But, whereas the oracle which Oedipus obtains from Apollo leads to the king's reversal, showing that, whatever the appearances of his beginning in wisdom, he learns in the end the secret that all beginnings are fatally unknown, Socrates learns in the beginning that he is the wisest man in Greece because he, at least, knows that in the end he knows nothing. Socrates knows that he is ignorant, unlike the politicians, poets, and rhetors of Greece who, in seeking wisdom, are ignorant, like Oedipus, of the fact that they cannot seek, except in ignorance, what they do not know.

The Delphic Oracle of Apollo, the omphalos of Greek life, bears the fatal inscriptions *know thyself* (the unexamined life is not worth living) and *nothing in excess*. Oedipus shows that the search for self-knowledge reveals the most terrible excesses, the secret of which is the fate that brackets the appearances of life between non-existence before birth and non-existence after death, this bracketing of life being indistinguishable from Plato's theory of the naturally immortal soul, whose birth announces its suspension of life and whose death releases it from life's suspense (and which skeptics later call the *epoché*: suspension of judgment as the epoch of life). In reversing the image of heroic honor central to epic and tragedy, in holding (in the *Gorgias*) that it is better to suffer wrong (in having wrong done to you) than to do wrong (to others), Socrates is no less fatally excessive or reversed than is Oedipus or all Greek heroes (those whose honor compels them to rule over others as victims in order to avoid being dishonored or victimized by the rule of others). In holding that it is better to suffer wrong (done to you by others) than to do wrong (to others)—instead of willing, with others, to do the good universally true for all, as commanded by the biblical covenant—Socrates is, however, no less canny than Achilles or Odysseus in reversing his apparent position as victim by victimizing his opponent. In the *Iliad* Achilles sulks in his tent, the apparent victim of Agamemnon's rule, until the fortunes of the Greeks are reduced (by the gods, in the favor they show the Trojans) to the point that it is he alone who can reverse Greek losses by defeating Hector, whose spectacular death leads (beyond the actual narrative of the *Iliad*) to the deception of the Trojan Horse (and Helen's complicity) and the destruction of Troy: the slaughter of its heroic men and the enslavement of its women and children. Odysseus, the apparent victim of the gods, is long delayed on his way home to Ithaca from the rape of Troy to reclaim his natural position from the suitors striving to usurp his board and bed. But in the end he turns the tables on the suitors and slaughters them. It is better to do wrong (to others) than to suffer wrong (from others).

Socrates stands accused of the contradictory crimes of impiety and introducing new gods into the *polis*. According to his accusers, not only does Socrates demonstrate maieutically to the heroic young men of Athens that to seek knowledge of the gods is to lack or to be ignorant of it, but he also claims to follow the oracular warnings of a *daimon* (a standard Greek word for god along with *theos*) about what he should avoid doing. Socrates' ignorance of the traditional gods of the *polis* is repeated in his daimonic ignorance; for, in warning him against action, his *daimon* shows him that he is ignorant of what he does. We should note that what the *daimon* tells Socrates is always what not to do, never what to do. Not to act is always to be in ignorance of the good and never to be in the wrong. To act, however, is, in contrast, always to seek the good in ignorance and thus always to be in the wrong (about knowing the good.) Socrates' *apologia* for his theological and daimonic ignorance rests on the oracle which he receives from Delphic Apollo: that he is the wisest man in Greece because he, at least, knows that he knows nothing. He is ignorant of the god Apollo himself. The oracle which Socrates receives from Apollo is no different from the secret which Oedipus carries beyond this life. Precisely because we are ignorant of our beginnings, the principles of life, our life ends in total ignorance.

Socrates' dependence on oracular and daimonic ignorance is closely connected with his claim that it is better to suffer wrong than to do wrong. Socrates can show that it is better to suffer wrong from others than to do wrong to others only if somebody does wrong to him. For Socrates to be right somebody else (the party opposite or opposed to him) must be wrong. Socrates' position that he is right (in being ignorant) blindly depends on the opposite position, that somebody is wrong (in ignorantly claiming to possess knowledge). His right (ignorance) depends directly on the wrong (knowledge) of others. That ignorance and knowledge, right and wrong, depend blindly on each other is precisely what Socrates, in Plato's dialogues, demonstrates to the Sophists, to their apparent bewilderment (not to mention to the utter bafflement of modern commentators). Sophists can wrongly claim that wrong (from the point of view of others) is right (from their own point of view)—that to live by wrong or crime is right (might is right)—only if the power to which they are opposed or by which they are opposed (that is, Socrates) can rightly claim that right (from Socrates' point of view) is wrong (from the point of view of others: right is might). Socrates' claim in the *Republic* that there is "one change," the identity of philosopher and king, which would make possible the just *polis*, at least, in unchanging (immortal) *logos* (logic or discourse), if not in changing (mortal) appearance, reflects the same contradictory position. Just as "one" and "change" are immortally opposed to each other (for each is defined through its opposite: *one* is that which does not change, while *change* is that which lacks unity), so wisdom (known only in itself, in the soul) and politics (known only relative to us, in life) are eternally opposed to each other and thus are blindly dependent on each other. Socrates claims, in the persuasive fashion of *sophia*, that the rule of the philosopher-kings is just for all, but all we need do is to play the gadfly to his own Trojan horse in order to show that his *logos* is hollow in its sophistry. Those over whom rule is to be established for their own good are defined by their opposite: the ruled are ignorant that they are ignorant of the good. But what, we ask, is the meaning of the good, in whose name the ruled are ruled, when they are ruled, it is said precisely, because they are ignorant of it? Indeed, the rule of the philosopher-kings, which is utterly contradictory in itself (for the immortal one and mortal change are fatally opposed to each other), is contradicted by those over whom they rule. For the rule of the good is fatally dependent on ruling over those who are ignorant of the good. The good is good for others only insofar as they are not good, that is, insofar as they are ignorant of the good. Victim and vanquisher, slave and master, ruled and ruler are fatally opposed to each other. Each of the opposites in the pair of opposites, in being unknowingly dependent upon the contradiction of the other, is thus dependent upon its own contradiction to which it is blind and by which it is blinded. The circle of fate is closed, known only in itself. The secret of oracular and daimonic wisdom of which Socrates, the wisest man in Greece, is ignorant, he no less, that is, no more, than others, is the law of contradiction, which is itself blindly dependent on that to which it is fatally opposed, its contradictory appearances in and as Greek life.

Contradiction makes its appearance directly on stage in the guise of the god Dionysus in *The Bacchae* of Euripides, the last of the great fifth century tragedies written by Aeschylus, Sophocles, and Euripides. Pentheus, the young, heroic king who champions the virtues of wisdom (know thyself) and moderation (nothing in excess), is upset to find his just rule contradicted by the god Dionysus, under whose Bacchic inspiration the people of Pentheus, above all, the women (including his mother) and the old men (including his grandfather), now live. Ultimately unable to resist the Dionysian frenzy himself, Pentheus dons what at first he had called the effeminately unheroic dress of the bacchants in order to spy on their secret

celebrations. But the bacchants descry Pentheus and, enraged with the en-
thusiasm of revenge, rend him limb by limb. His mother, in perfect contradiction of both herself and her son, triumphantly carries the sacrificial
victim to Dionysus into the city, ignorant that it is Pentheus' head which
she bears so proudly. The mother opens her eyes to discover that, victimized by the god, the god's victim is her own son whom she has en-
thusiastically killed with her own hands, under divine inspiration. The
contradictory appearances of the god reverse the heroic appearances of
wisdom and moderation, showing them to reflect the ignorance, blindness,
and death of the victim. Count no Greek (or extra-biblical) individual
happy, wise, or just until he is dead, dead to the appearances of life.

We must read the Greeks so that we experience the severe limits of
thinking, of willing, of being. We must learn the hard lesson that the
Greeks cannot be read, that it is an essential reading experience to discover
that reading is limited by what cannot be read, that something can be read
only if you read it as you will to be read by it. The Greeks, or at least the
Greek elite, were literate by the fifth century. But the literacy of classical
Greece is not to be substantially distinguished from the orality of Homer
and his heroic audience, for the critical difference marking the thought and
existence of truth and interpretation is not that between literacy and
orality, between the written word and the spoken word, between writing
and speaking. The difference that counts is not *that* we write or speak but
what we write and speak and *how* we write and speak it. What we write
and speak expresses the truth of thought and existence and how we write
and speak it involves interpretation as the thought and existence of truth.

It is a strange business, this elaborate demonstration that Greek texts
are not texts, that they do not exist in the truth and cannot be interpreted.
But it is only when we experience the absolute limit of reading—of thinking—that we learn that reading (thinking) involves the principle of the absolute, the absolute principle of right. The principle of right, the right of
thinking the truth as interpretation and interpretation as truthful, is not an
indemonstrable first principle that leaves its adherents in contradiction,
their (finite) thought fatally opposed to their (finite) existence. To think is
to recognize that our beginning, our principle of existence, expresses our
absolute commitment to right and involves the absolute right of interpretation. Only when we come to this recognition do we learn to give up reversing the biblical command that we must lose our lives in order to save them

by claiming to find the principles, the origins, the beginnings of our thought and existence in the Greeks, with the result that, in projecting our identity upon the Greeks and then in reflecting that identity back upon ourselves, we lose both the Greeks as different from ourselves and ourselves as different from the Greeks.

IV. THE PROBLEMS OF MODERNITY

I should point out that my *Dialectic of Biblical Critique* is itself grounded upon an unpublished five-volume study, which I entitle "Dialectic and Interpretation," of which Volume I is devoted to a detailed study of the major texts of Plato and Aristotle (and their predecessors). In Volumes II-V I undertake to show that those whom I consider to be the major thinkers of modernity—beginning with Descartes but, above all, Spinoza, Kant, Hegel, and Kierkegaard—provide an ever deeper reading of, to use the terms of the present essay in thinking, truth and interpretation, by grounding (although often not explicitly) thinking—self-conscious human existence—in the Bible. I show in these volumes that, in order to provide an adequate reading of Spinoza, Kant, Hegel, and Kierkegaard (to whom one could also add Marx and Nietzsche, the other two giants of nineteenth century thought), the reader must develop a comprehensive conception of reading, of thinking, as the dialectic of truth and interpretation. It is precisely these four thinkers, above all, who demand from the reader an adequate conception of thinking and provide the reader the context in which to develop an adequate conception of truth and interpretation.

In the present essay I propose to continue this thinking, presupposing here my detailed exegesis of the Greek texts and of the texts of the four major, modern thinkers. I want now to indicate that systematic examination of thinking as the dialectic of truth and interpretation engages consideration of four problems which are fundamental to modern thought and existence, four problems which, indeed, constitute modernity. So long as these problems are not even articulated, let alone treated adequately, it will be impossible to develop a comprehensive conception of thinking. All four of these problems have already been adumbrated, in one way or another, in the discussion up to this point. They are (a) the relationship between the religious and the secular (faith and reason); (b) the relationship between the Hebrew and Christian Bibles (Judaism and Christianity); (c) the relationship between the Bible and universal world culture; and (d) the relationship between paganism and idolatry (Socratic ignorance and Satanic knowledge).

A. THE RELATIONSHIP BETWEEN FAITH AND REASON

The first issue central to the very constitution of modernity involves the relationship between religious and secular values, the relationship between theology and philosophy, between faith and reason. As Dewey indicates so vividly in his major works, dualism vitiates both the life of the mind and our human practice (and it is important to remark that the very distinction between mind and practice threatens to multiply the dualisms which we undertake to overcome dialectically, for, as Kant demonstrates, to be mindful is categorically to will the end universally true, in practice, for all). But, because Dewey himself does not firmly grasp the difference which the creation of the Bible (biblical creation) makes between paganism (for example, the Greeks) and the chosen people, between ignorance and sin (the knowledge of good and evil), he is unable either to articulate clearly or to treat comprehensively the problem of dualism in modern life. What we must begin to grasp as an adequate idea, in Spinoza's discourse, is that the only way in which we can overcome the dualism between the religious and the secular, between spirit and the world, between theology and philosophy, between faith and reason is to understand that each of the two elements in these pairs of opposites is true only and insofar as the other is true. That the spirit of dialectic—the reconciliation, the interpretation, of opposites (the *coincidentia oppositorum*) through recognition of their common ground in the truth of interpretation and in the interpretation of truth—is itself identical with dialogue, that is, with the golden rule, is a truth which not even Hegel or Kierkegaard systematically and explicitly acknowledges, for they, too, are wont to maintain the superiority of philosophy to religion (Hegel) or the superiority of religious to rational speculation (Kierkegaard), although the very structure of their dialectical thinking, when comprehended, deconstructs all hierarchical dualisms.

In simple terms we must learn that both the religious and the secular, both theology and philosophy, both faith and reason are grounded in the Bible. The faith of the Bible is not blindness or ignorance but the most discerning, the most challenging, the most embracing, the most demanding conception of life, notwithstanding the generations of superstition, both learned and popular, resulting from the spiritless admixture of biblical revelation with the immediacies of seeing and knowing (what Kierkegaard calls immediate sensation and immediate cognition). Biblical revelation of the truth demands or presupposes not blind, unthinking obedience on the part of the faithful, for that would but leave them enslaved to authoritarian rule from which the God of Exodus liberates them. Revelation demands, on the part of those who have eyes to see and ears to hear, the most profound concentration, the fullest attentiveness, the greatest patience, the most passionate involvement—*fides quaerens intellec-tum*—in order to choose life: to choose life eternally, to choose eternal life. But the Bible, from the patriarchs to Jesus, never claims that the way of life, life in the covenant, is easy, except in the profound sense that adherence to the truth has an infinite ease about it that finite lying—losing one's way among the finite idols of soul and body—never has, with all its anxiety, repression, and fear, the fear of the truth, the fear of being revealed for what one is, the fear that it is precisely the finite which can be taken away from one (by others who possess a yet greater number of finite things) and which finally will be taken away from one by that to which all finitude is subject: death. It is equally the case that, because truth is found only in its interpretations, the constitution of truth is the joyous task ever to be under-taken by the faithful. Abraham is tested by God precisely because it is truth which constantly demands faithful interpretation (interpretation of faith).

Just as the biblical conception of faith—of the faithful people who choose the way of life, not death—reveals the truth of thought and exist-ence, the thought and existence of truth, so the Bible is no less rational than it is faithful. The people of the Book live in the natural world of space and time, of finite sensibility and finite understanding, but not of that world, for they are created in the image of God, who, as the exemplar of true life, following Spinoza, demands that the natural facts of the finite world be judged by the infinite right of human thought and existence. The reason of biblical thought and existence is critical judgment, judgment of what is right and true. To be rational is to will to do unto others as you would have them do unto you. Reason, no less than faith, when properly conceived, embodies the categorical imperative of the golden rule. According to the golden rule of dialectic, faith and reason, religion and philosophy can each be true only and insofar as the other is true. Neither is true in itself; neither is true in finite (dualistic) opposition to the other. Neither is true in its rule over the other. Each is true only as it does unto the other as it would have the other do unto it.

B. THE RELATIONSHIP BETWEEN THE HEBREW AND CHRISTIAN BIBLES

Just as it is likely very difficult, if not a practical impossibility, for most thoughtful persons to comprehend how the difference between faith and reason can be grounded in the dialectic of biblical truth without coming to see that neither faith nor reason is found in the Greek (pagan or extra-biblical) world, so it is also likely—and this is the second problem whose engagement is presupposed in this essay in thinking—that the biblical origins of both faith and reason will be practically an impossibility to comprehend unless we establish an adequate idea of the relationship between the Hebrew and Christian Bibles, between Judaism and Christianity. I speak normally of the Bible (and not of the Old and New Testaments or of Judaism and Christianity) in order to outflank, yet also to encompass, the issue of that peculiar book which Jews create and which in turns creates Christians, the book which, for Jews, is their testament to life and the book which, for Christians, contains two testaments to life, Old and New, the first life leading to the second, yet the second life presupposing and grounded in the first. For Christians, the New Testament fulfills the promise of the Old, yet Jesus as the Christ, the principle of Christianity, knows, as he makes clear in the Gospels, only the Scriptures common to his fellow Jews. He comes, he says, not to abolish but to fulfill Scripture; but surely that is the task, too, of every reader of the Bible, Jewish and Christian, religious and secular, faithful and rational. For Jews, the Bible is complete. The dialectic of old and new, the historical dialectic of beginning and beginning ever anew, is complete without the addition of the New Testament. Yet the New Testament—the four Gospels (each telling in different fashion the story of Jesus), the divers epistles, and the Apocalypse of John—emerges in Greek, the universal language of the eastern Mediterranean world, uniquely from the Hebrew traditions of Aramaic Palestine (we must not forget that at the time of Jesus, that is, well before the destruction of the Second Temple in 70 C.E. by the Roman legions and the resultant diaspora of the Jews, there are large Jewish communities living outside Palestine in Babylon and Alexandria). It is simply evasion of the truth for (by) either Jews or Christians to view the New Testament as rooted in the traditions of Hellenism and not in Jewish orthodoxy (faith in the straight or right way, the way of life). Christians find in Judaism a parent whom they claim to outgrow. Jews find in Christianity a child whom they refuse to acknowledge as their own. These family differences must be understood, however, not to reflect the fatal relativism of natural, that is, blind and ignorant, opposition but, rather, to embody the spirit common to the unique choice of universal life.

The most thoughtful, both the most faithful and the most rational, consideration of the Bible, Jewish and Christian, reveals, as we shall see, the very principle of dialectic which we have already encountered in these prefatory remarks and which is the ground of this study. Just as the Bible reveals the very difference between paganism (for example, the Greeks) and the choice of life, between the ignorance of the law of contradiction and revelation of the truth of thought and existence, so it reveals a second dialectical principle of difference: differences are true only insofar as they are grounded in the truth (identity) of differences. The Hebrew Bible and the Christian Bible (Judaism and Christianity) are true only insofar as the other is, as their differences are, true. If either the Hebrew Bible or the New Testament is false, or, insofar as the Hebrew Bible or the Christian Bible is false, then the other is equally false. They stand on the common ground of truth and interpretation both in their difference from paganism (ignorant opposition to the thought and existence of truth and interpretation) and in their determined resistance to idolatry (consciously willful negation of truth and interpretation).

C. THE RELATIONSHIP BETWEEN THE BIBLE AND UNIVERSAL WORLD HISTORY

We have seen that the dialectic of truth and interpretation—that truth is found only in its interpretations and that interpretation involves and expresses truth—raises the fundamental issues of the relationship between faith and reason, the religious and the secular, and of the dialectical structure of the Bible, the relationship between Judaism and Christianity. If the Bible is no more (less) religious than it is secular, if the principles (origins as the ends) of life involve good faith no more (less) than the rational good, then a third problem emerges as fundamental to comprehending the dialectic of truth and interpretation, that of world history. How it is that truth is historical interpretation and history truthful interpretation is rendered yet more problematic when we view the world as one action, to invoke Macmurray's providential formulation of the relationship of human action and world history. The notion that action is not one or complete or that no action will ever be one or complete until it encompasses the entire world, that action is both unique and universal, raises the question of how the countlessly diverse, human experience of the planet—past, present, and future—much of it utterly contradictory, can be accounted for as belonging to one action, to universal history. The history of human thinking—the history of the utter diversity of human thought as embodied in the most divergent sexual, social, and cultural ways and their vastly diverse material and spiritual foundations, from the earliest representations of ritual and myth to the atom bomb—is, to paraphrase Hegel, to think human history, to think humanity historically. To think humanity as historical and to think history as human—I (being human) think, therefore, I am (historical)—is to think world history as one action, to view human history *sub specie aeternitatis,* under the form of eternity, under the eternal species of humankind, as distinct from viewing human beings as teleological, their *telos* or end identified with natural space and time whose finite differences generate opposed traditions of rulers and ruled.

In order to comprehend truth as the history of its interpretations and interpretation as the truth of history, we must develop a conception of thinking (and existence) which identifies differences with their truth and truth with its differences. Differences (different interpretations) are true only insofar as they recognize the truth of the differences opposite them and do not undertake to enjoy (defend) their differences at the expense of others. Truth is its own standard, the standard of both true and false differences, insofar as it distinguishes between differences which express the truth of others and differences which discriminate against others. Differences are not true (or false) in themselves, just as there is no truth (known) only in itself apart from its differences. The differences of being human, of the human species, of human history must be liberated from both mastery over and enslavement to others. For differences to be discriminating, but not discriminatory, they must express the dialectical truth of unique and universal. If, as Kierkegaard says, purity of heart is to will one thing—the unique truth universal for all—and not doublemindedly to obey two different masters, then I must will my unique differences to be universally true to all others as I will all others to will their universal differences to be uniquely true to me. Differences not disciplined by the truth either vanish into indifference (relativism) or become intolerant of difference (totalitarianism). Truth not disciplined by differences either disappears into opinion (the indifference of interpretation) or becomes intolerant of different interpretations (totalitarianism). Interpretation is infinite, and there are infinite interpretations. But there are also false interpretations, those which falsify (evade or deny) the truth of difference.

It is the Bible which uniquely provides the universal framework of history, of identity and difference, of truth and interpretation. In coming into thought and existence, in the midst of pagan differences, the Bible creates the difference which truth makes historically: either think differently or be offended by the difference which thinking makes. The Bible demands—commands—that difference, that one's choice of difference, be true, true for all, and not merely one more difference which either strives to rule over other differences, reducing the differences of others to indifference, or succumbs indifferently to the rule of others' difference. For the Bible, paganism is the difference which cannot account for itself. Paganism is in itself without either faith or reason; it is neither religious nor secular. It possesses no will to truth whose interpretations embody the world as one action. Paganism is lost in the infinitely pullulating oppositions of finite rulers and ruled until it is interpreted as the unaccountable difference by the biblical account of the truth.

Once the Bible comes into thought and existence, creating humankind from nothing, from nothing pagan, paganism is revealed, however, to be not only extra-biblical—as found in both the vast civilizations of antiquity and so-called primitive cultures which exist prior to their creation in and through the Bible by thousands of years—but also post-biblical—as found in cultures both grandiose and tribal, which exist posterior to their creation in and through the Bible for more than, now, three millennia. Since a fundamental feature of modernity is universal world culture, which, however, is characterized by the most enormous and often contradictory differences, the relationship between the Bible, as the principle of human right, as the universal principle of thinking, and the vastly diverse peoples of the earth becomes particularly acute. That the world is one action is revealed in the revolutionary efforts of global democratization to replace the tyrannical rule of natural fact (the rule of some natural facts over other natural facts) by the radical rule of right (freedom, equality, and solidarity for all). But then it appears that the democratization of life is directly implicated in the dehumanization of human beings as a central feature of modernity (post-modernism), for it involves the eclipse of God, the loss of faith, the relativism of values, the subversion of human ends by technological means, ultimately, totalitarianism. Humanity is eclipsed by the untold suffering which poverty, disease, hunger, and exploitation bring to millions, especially, although not by any means exclusively, in the third world (for women, above all), reflecting the vast disparities between rich and poor; by the tyranny, imperialism, racism, and terrorism which gravely menace human freedom; and by the nuclear arms race, the population explosion, the unrelenting destruction of the natural environment, and AIDS which threaten the very existence of life on the planet. How we are to think the future of humanity is truly an awesome problem for those committed to the democratic rule of right.

Our task here is to reflect upon modernity, to address the contemporary reader, and to think through, to think beyond, the standard divisions, dualisms, and distinctions riving modern life. We must learn to articulate a conception of democracy as historical difference that liberates it both from relativity and from totalitarianism, which result—to put the issue in the conceptual terms of this essay—from, on the one hand, the skeptical reduction of all differences to indifferent opinion, and, on the other, the dogmatic reduction of all differences to one opinion indifferent to others. We undertake to develop a conception of truth which liberates its interpretations from relativism and a conception of interpretation which redeems its truth from dogmatism (and, as always, these formulas can be reversed). Truth and interpretation embody the principle of dialectic such that neither can be thought and neither can exist without the other.

D. THE RELATIONSHIP BETWEEN PAGANISM AND IDOLATRY

We shall be able to account, faithfully and rationally, for difference only on the basis of the difference created by the Bible between paganism and the chosen people. But the crucial difference established by the Bible is not that between paganism and the people of the Book, not even in the beginning, although it is essential. The crucial difference, as the Bible makes clear from beginning to end, is that between heartfelt obedience to the covenant and idolatrous subversion of the covenant. The difference between paganism and idolatry is the fourth problem which emerges when we undertake to comprehend the dialectic of truth and interpretation, how truth is found only in its interpretations and how interpretation embodies truth. The difference between paganism and idolatry is grounded in the difference between arguing from right to fact and arguing from fact to right. To judge the different facts in light of the right true for all is to discriminate between truth and falsehood. To judge right on the basis of factual differences is to identify truth with differences which falsely discriminate against the differences of others.

Extra-biblical pagans have no choice of difference(s); like Socrates, they are ignorant (unconscious) of the difference which choice makes. Members of the biblical covenant are in a totally different position, for, like Abraham, they have the responsibility of hearing the different call of right, the call to judge the finite facts of natural thought and existence by the infinite rights of being human. Ignorance is no longer an excuse before the law. Although the Bible shows the holy people of God bringing terrible devastation upon the pagan inhabitants of ancient Israel, their real enemy is not paganism, as such, but idolatry. The enemy is not otherness, pagan differences which do not embody a self-conscious conception of difference as relationship. The polemic of the Bible is aimed not at pagans but at the people of the law, at the adherents of the covenant themselves. It is aimed against the different people, the people of difference, the people who make the difference in the world, the people who make the world different by their difference from the world. To be different, to differentiate yourselves from others such that your unique difference is accessible to all people universally, notwithstanding their natural differences, is to constitute the golden rule as the different law which is common to all, not to lose your differences among the pagan or natural gods which are indifferent to the contradictory fate of being human. It is not those outside the biblical covenant (pagans) but those to whom the covenant has been revealed, the people who have the responsibility of constituting the difference which truth (the truth which difference) makes, who constantly run the risk of either losing truth among its differences (interpretations) or of losing differences within the truth. Idolatry concerns either reducing the God whose truth involves interpretation to the finite differences of natural space and time or elevating the finite differences of natural space and time to the God whose interpretation expresses truth. The result of the direct identity between divinity and differences is not only the proliferation of gods (polytheism), whose natural rivalries reflect worldly opposition, but equally the rationalization of the *status quo* of power for both ruler and ruled.

One cannot become a pagan, for one is born a pagan, and the one thing that a pagan cannot become is what he naturally is. But one becomes an idolater by rationalizing paganism in bad faith, by claiming that (a) finite difference is absolute or that the absolute is (a) finite difference. Only those who recognize the difference which truth and interpretation make in the world constantly risk seduction by the idolatry of becoming pagans, as the Bible shows us from beginning to end. The dualistic (conscious) opposite of the biblical commitment to right is not paganism but idolatry, the idolization of finite facts as the truth beyond interpretation or as the interpretation beyond truth, something unthinkable to Socrates.

The distinction between (extra-biblical) paganism and (biblical) idolatry I typify by the distinction between Socrates and Satan. Socrates knows that he is ignorant. To will—to act, to seek the good—is to reflect ignorance of your end which, from the beginning, fatally (blindly) compels you to violate the law of contradiction: either you are at your end, dead to the life of appearances (and your apparent life is not); or the appearances of your life lack their end (and you are not—dead, at your end). The Satanic position is utterly different from that of Socrates. Whereas Socrates knows that he knows nothing, Satan wills to reduce knowledge to nothing. Satanic consciousness is uniquely (universally) biblical (or modern): it is conscious of its ignorance; it does not merely know *that* it is ignorant but it knows, that is, it wills to know, *what* it is ignorant of. Satanic consciousness is outraged by the limit to its will to knowledge (power), that what it knows involves and expresses its ignorance, its difference from others; for what it knows embodies its relationships to others, what others who are different know. Because Satanic consciousness can never possess certain (finite) knowledge in itself but only absolute (infinite) truth in and through its relationship with others (including itself), its impulse is to subvert (negate) the golden rule by reducing to nothing the truth of its relationship to the other, by reducing its limitation to the other to nothing. Whereas God creates humankind from nothing, from nothing natural or pagan, from nothing which is not creative, Satan undertakes to pervert creation by reducing it to the nothing whence it comes. Since creation rests on nothing prior to itself, for it is its own priority, the cause of itself, following Spinoza, its perversion through Satanic will is to reduce thought and existence to nothing, to the natural space and time of paganism, something inconceivable to Socrates. Divine creativity and Satanic nihilism represent the two poles of the biblical drama of human history. Idolatry is the sin against the spirit of truth and interpretation which cannot be forgiven, for it undertakes to reduce to nothing, to annihilate, the very difference which creates truth and interpretation from nothing.

The distinction between extra-biblical and biblical paganism, between paganism and idolatry, between Socrates and Satan allows us to formulate the third principle of dialectic which is central to this essay in thinking. Whereas the first principle of dialectic distinguishes between the Bible and paganism (between both Judaism and Christianity, on the one hand, and paganism, on the other) and the second principle of dialectic distinguishes between the Hebrew and Christian Bibles such that each can be no less (or more) true to its interpretations and the interpretation of the truth than the other, the third dialectical principle of truth and interpretation involves a distinction within a distinction, a distinction which creates the most critical difference which is also the most subtle and the most difficult to articulate and to grasp. It may have appeared that the difference between arguing from right to fact and arguing from fact to right is the difference between biblical revelation and pagan ignorance of the truth. But it is Satan, not Socrates, who subverts the biblical principle of right, not by simply reversing fact and right, in the tradition of the pagan doctrine of opposites, but by rationalizing (totalizing) fact as right.

In the pagan (or extra-biblical) world, what I claim to be my right by nature reflects my ignorance of your natural right, and thus my right is blindly dependent on your right (as yours is on mine). Mastery and slavery, both mental and material, are found everywhere in the pagan world. Both are natural. Masters naturally lose out to others and find their position reversed into that of slavery. Slaves naturally revolt and become natural masters over those whom they reduce to slavery. Through the vicissitudes of revolt, civil war, and conquest the opposed positions of masters and slaves (rulers and ruled) metamorphose endlessly into their opposite; and the manumission of slaves is also common. But, as Aristotle makes clear, how one thing changes its nature into its opposite, how things which are opposite in nature become naturally their opposite, how slaves (whose end is their master, for whom they are but tools, lacking a human soul) become masters and how masters (by finding that their end is the tool, the slave, over whom they had earlier ruled) become slaves is unknowable. Nature is precisely that which, being born as finite, is identical with (is already at) its end. It is little wonder that Aristotle locates the beginning of *philosophia* (the contradictory opposition between love as seeking, that is, lack, and wisdom) in the wonder of ignorance. For to begin in wonder is to begin with the indemonstrable, first principle of beginning, the law of contradiction, whose maieutic fatally demonstrates that to seek (desire or love) wisdom is to lack wisdom, to seek in ignorance of its beginning (to begin in ignorance). That finite nature is always blind to and ignorant of its beginnings is reflected in the countless metamorphoses (reversals) which it is fated to undergo. That nature, as finite, is perfect yet is reversed without ever attaining its end is precisely the fate which blinds the Greeks (and all extra-biblical pagans) to ignorance of their beginnings (principles). Because it is the nature of masters to rule over others and the nature of slaves to be ruled by others, each is blindly dependent on its opposite.

That masters can exist without slaves or that slaves can exist without masters is unthinkable in the pagan world. Indeed, the very principle of Greek honor (*arete*) presupposes the natural opposition between ruler and ruled, master and slave. Heroic honor depends directly (blindly) on one hero's stripping the honor from the hero opposite (opposed to) him, and thus honor is immediately (blindly) dependent on dishonor, on dishonoring another. Plato's conception of the body as the prison (slave) of the soul and the Stoics' conception of the passions as the slave (prison) of the soul are but another reflection of pagan enslavement to their ultimate master, the unchanging law of contradiction (fate), which is itself blindly dependent on its opposite, the endless metamorphosis of appearances (chance). That in the pagan world blind, immutable fate, finite and determinate in oracular pronouncement, is ever experienced by individuals as mutable chance, infinite and indeterminate in oracular reception, itself but reflects the unending progress (the infinite regress) of the pagan doctrine of natural opposites.

In the pagan or extra-biblical world there is argument from neither right to fact nor from fact to right. There is in truth no (faithful or reasoned) argument at all but only endless opposition between the parties, each blindly dependent on its opposite, each constantly displacing the other by exchanging places with it. In the world of biblical paganism or idolatry, however, there is argument from fact to right, argument whose bad faith rationalization is decked out in the principles of right (whether theological or philosophical, whether religious or secular, or both). In the modern (that is, biblical) world, idolatrous or Satanic dualism replaces the pagan or Socratic doctrine of opposites of the extra-biblical world. The true enemy of dialectic is Satanic dualism, not the pagan doctrine of opposites. But the reason that it is so essential to become clear about the extra-biblical doctrine of opposites is that, when it is confused with either faith or reason, and thus with both, it then becomes impossible to distinguish, rigorously and systematically, between dialectic and dualism, between the argument from the right of human thought and existence to the facts contradicting this right and the argument from the facts which are used to rationalize, in bad faith, a version of right not democratic in its principles of equality, freedom, and solidarity.

V. CONCLUSION

In this Preface I have wanted to indicate the fundamental issues which an essay in thinking must comprehend. The intellectual program that lies before us is formidable. To think, we find, implicates us in the most search-ing examination of truth and interpretation. Thinking (existence) embodies a conception of truth which involves us in interpretation and a conception of interpretation which expresses the truth. Indeed, we undertake to show that, following Spinoza, truth is its own standard—of interpretation—and interpretation is its own standard—of truth. It is precisely because truth and interpretation are each sovereign, autonomous, absolute, and infinite that the one can be thought (willed) only in, as, and through the other. The dualisms paralyzing modern thought and existence can be overcome only when we develop a conception of thinking which is grounded in ideas of truth and interpretation, each of which, when taken together, embodies the absolute right of men and women to think and to exist in equality, freedom, and solidarity with all.

To say with Descartes—I think, therefore, I am—is to involve myself in both *what* I think I am, which is the truth of interpretation, and *how* I think I am, which is the interpretation of truth. To hold that truth is its own standard, to bear witness to the truth, to will to be truthful in deceiving not even myself, following Nietzsche, is always to face the responsibility that truth is to be found only in its interpretations and that interpretations are to be found only in their truth. It is radically to eschew any notion that truth can be found in itself without relationship to interpretation (without

the relationship of interpretation). It is no less radically to eschew any notion that truth is lost, beyond retrieval, in interpretations which are endlessly relative. It is equally the case that we must radically eschew any
notion that interpretation can be found in itself without relationship to
truth (without the relationship of truth). It is no less the case that we must
radically eschew any notion that the endless proliferation of interpretations
reduces truth to the relativity of interpretation. Thinking involves the activity of interpretation and interpretation expresses commitment to the
truth.

　　　Our program of developing a comprehensive conception of truth
and interpretation will engage us, as we have seen, in thinking through issues that involve four problems fundamental to modern thought. What all
four problems reveal to us, however, is the paradox that they have defied
solution and will continue to defy solution until and unless it is recognized
that thinking, the dialectic of truth and interpretation, is grounded in the
Bible. It is only when we (1) show that faith and reason are both grounded
in the Bible, (2) demonstrate the dialectical unity of the Bible (Jewish and
Christian), (3) comprehend the relationship between the Bible (the chosen
people) and the peoples of the world (history), and (4) distinguish systematically between paganism (as exemplified by the Greeks) and idolatry
(the subversion of the covenantal rights of humanity) that we shall be able
to develop an adequate conception of thinking. It is only when we come to
see that the Bible creates the very conditions of thinking—whose unique
subject is the unconditional (absolute, infinite, sovereign, and universal)
existence of human beings—that we shall be able to comprehend the
relationship between truth and interpretation. It is the Bible, and it can
only be the Bible, which comprehends and is comprehended by the dialectic of truth and interpretation.

PART I
INTRODUCTION

1

What is Truth?

I. TRUTH AS ITS OWN STANDARD

When Jesus tells Pilate that he has come to bear witness to the truth, Pilate asks Jesus: what is truth? Jesus answers, in silence: truth is its own standard, the standard of both itself and the false. The *index* of truth is the *index* no less of what is false. That Pilate, the imperial representative of pagan certainty, is clearly uncertain before this Jew who bespeaks the prophetic authority of truth yet is viewed by Jewish officials as a false prophet reveals the paradox of truth whose sovereignty is silent in the world. Render unto Caesar that which is Caesar's and unto God that which is God's. Render unto Caesar that which is Caesar's—nothing truthful—and unto God that which is God's—everything truthful. The truth to which Jesus has come to bear witness is the absolute standard of the world, the standard of justice no less for Caesar than for Jesus. The revelation of truth is in the world, but the world knows it not. The light of truth shines in the darkness, and the darkness does not overcome it.

What is surprising to Pilate is that Jesus does not appeal to common sense as a means of supporting his claim that he has come to bear witness to the truth. Pilate knows that common sense, the *consensus omnium gentium*, the consent of all the people, is the imperial trunk which rests upon two massive legs, sensible experience (inductive logic) and abstract reasoning (deductive logic), that which Kant and Hegel call sensibility and understanding and Kierkegaard immediate sensation and immediate cognition. As a disciple of Greek sophistication, Pilate also knows that the common sense of empiricism and rationalism rests on premises or first principles which are indemonstrable; they rest on the law of contradiction. What, indeed, is the truth when either I, on the basis of premises unknown to me, contradict you, or you, on the basis of premises unknown to you, contradict me? When there is no mind or thinking beyond immediate sensation and cognition—not Aristotle's *nous* but Hegel's biblical spirit (*Geist*)—when there is no third position to reconcile the gentile opposites by showing that each is true only insofar as all are true, then the headless torso of the mighty Ozymandias, the king of kings of Shelley's famous sonnet whose visage lies shattered upon the shifting sands of paganism, rules as the contradictory fate of which all are ignorant. Before the contradictory law of Pilate Jesus is silent, in truth. He knows that Pilate, in undertaking to contradict his interlocutor by asking him, what is truth?, but contradicts himself, for to contradict another is but to be blindly dependent, in the tradition of Socrates, on the contradictory law of the other, on the law of contradiction which fatally opposes self and other. Unlike Pilate, who, being immediately or ignorantly (blindly) self-contradictory, knows that he is contradictory but does not know what his contradiction is, Jesus recognizes the imperial law of contradiction for what it is. Because the law of contradiction is indemonstrable, ignorant of its own premises or beginnings, its rule is completely contradictory or arbitrary. When the consent of the people is based on the contradictions of common sense, on the commonality of sense experience and abstract understanding, then blind imperialism is inexorably the result. For, in the absence of truth as its own standard, the standard of both itself and everything different from or opposed to itself, differences, being irreconcilable, can only blindly contradict or oppose each other.

Precisely because, as Aristotle holds, there must be one, first, indemonstrable, autocratic principle to bring to a halt the infinite regress (progress) of all those *gentes* claiming to be first (whether in the guise of one, several, or many: autocracy, aristocracy, or democracy), so Pilate knows that there must be an autocrat (whether embodied in one, several, or many rulers) whose rule over others is indemonstrable. The autocracy of the law of contradiction is reflected in Pilate's questioning response to Jesus: what is truth? How is Jesus to respond to autocracy? How are we? The issue is not whether we speak or remain silent, not whether we speak or act. Since we have no choice but to communicate, the issue is how we communicate, not whether our communication as such takes the form of speech or silence, the form of speech or action. But how do we establish communication with one who is ignorant (unconscious) of or blind to the truth of communication, the truth that communication is its own standard, the standard for all speakers? Is there any alternative to autocracy other than the authority of truth as its own standard, for both interlocutors? Jesus recognizes that the contradictory law of autocracy is blind to and ignorant of its own premises. The secret of its ignorance is precisely that it possesses no secret for those who have ears to hear and eyes to see. The secret of paganism, the secret of Oedipus, is itself auto-cratic, for, since self and authority are immediately identified with each other, they are also immediately contradictory (opposed to each other). Jesus knows that his task in life, in coming to bear witness to the truth, is to submit to the passion of distinguishing between God and Caesar, between truth and autocracy, between the covenant and the *consensus gentium*, between love of neighbor (even when the neighbor is the enemy) and gentile opposition, between the golden rule and the golden mean. But Jesus is also silently prescient (providential), knowing that Caesar's rule will collapse once its secret is revealed by truth as its own standard to be contradictory. It is the case that Jesus suffers gentile contradiction, crucifixion, at the hand of the Romans and that, in the face of continuing Jewish resistance to the contradictory rule of Caesar, the Roman legions conquer Jerusalem, raze the Temple, and exile the Jews from the holy city. Still, Jewish law proves, unlike the contradictory rule of Roman imperialism, to be indomitable to the end; and Christian faith ultimately proves that the ground of Rome's indemonstrable, unknown, blind, contradictory, and autocratic beginnings is truth as its own standard.

What the translation of the philosophical fragment of conversation between Pilate and Jesus into the paradoxical discourse of Spinoza shows us is that we have to distinguish between autocracy and truth as its own standard. But the real enemy is not pagan autocracy—might is right (or right is might)—notwithstanding the appearances. Once we see that the secret of the indemonstrable beginning of the law of contradiction can be revealed by the light of truth to be what it is—nothing—and can become what it is not—which is something—only by consciously undertaking to prove, thoughtfully, the truth of its existence (the existence of its truth)—I think, therefore, I am—the contradictions of pagan autocracy become powerless before truth as its own standard. As I indicated in my prefatory remarks, it is not paganism but idolatry which is the determined opponent of truth as its own standard. That paganism oscillates between certainty and uncertainty, that my being a certain one depends on your being a certain other, each blind to and ignorant of the certainty which the other claims, is the contradictory fate of origins lacking all power (will) of demonstration. Jesus is silent before Pilate's contradictory question—what is truth?—because he recognizes that it is the fate of the pagan world to lack a point of view, a perspective, a ground which unites the interlocutors. The autocrat—and each individual (and any particular combination of individuals, that is, of atoms) in the pagan world is autocratic, in that autocracy involves the immediate identity of self and authority—is blindly opposed to the autocrat opposite him. In contradicting the other he is no less self-contradictory. It is precisely the law of contradiction which rules that any appearance of unity—the relationship of self and other, the relationship of the self with itself, the relationship which is the self—is contradictory. The only unity which escapes the fatal logic of the law of contradiction is the unity dead to appearances. In his silence Jesus reveals his understanding of pagan logic: that, by the law of contradiction, he is condemned to death by Pilate, and that Pilate, too, is dead to life, being blindly dependent on the very death to which he has consigned the other.

Although the confrontation between Pilate and Jesus is that between paganism and faith, between the law of contradiction and truth as its own standard, it foreshadows a future fraught with the dark possibilities of persecution in the name of truth as its own standard, something unthinkable to either Socrates or Pilate. From the point of view of the law of contradiction, precisely because it has no point of view, the notion of truth as its own standard for me no less than for you is unthinkable (the concept of truth does not exist in the pagan world). From the point of view of truth as its own standard, precisely because it is the perspective no less true for me than it is for you, because it can be true for me only insofar as it is true for you, truth is constantly subject to falsification. The real enemy for Jesus and his biblical predecessors is not paganism, not even when paganism is represented in so formidable an opponent as Pharaoh, Goliath, Nebuchadnezzar, or Caesar. The real enemy is idolatry. The ancient, pagan kings are ruthless, it is true. In ruling by the law of contradiction, they hold that it is better to do evil (to others) than to suffer evil (from others). The Romans, for example, are violent in their conquest of Jerusalem and in their suppression of Jewish revolt in the second century C.E., not to mention in their cruel treatment of Christians. Still, long before the destruction of the Second Temple, Jews flourish in Babylon (where they were exiled after the destruction of the First Temple by the Babylonian king and where they produce centuries later one of their two great versions of the Talmud) and in Alexandria (in the land of their original exile where they produce long before the time of Jesus their Greek translation of Scripture). Paul of Tarsus, the Greek-speaking Jew who proclaims Jesus as the risen lord of the world, the world Jewish and gentile, free and enslaved, male and female, claims his right as a Roman citizen and appeals his arrest to the emperor in Rome. But what is ominous in the confrontation between Pilate and Jesus is that Pilate washes his hands of the matter, unlike Lady Macbeth who is unable to free herself from the stain of corruption. Pilate releases Jesus into the hands of his fellow Jews, for whom Jesus' crime is infinitely worse than finite opposition to Caesar, for which the punishment is finite destruction of the body. Jesus, who has taught that there is one sin which can never be forgiven, the sin against the spirit, has blasphemed the spirit. He has identified himself with God, with truth as its own standard, a claim inconceivable to Pilate—what is truth?—but one central to the Bible and its revelation of truth to the world. The biblical position that truth is its own standard, the standard of the true no less than of the false, introduces not only truth but also the falsification of truth—idolatry, and thus persecution of the truth—into the world. Indeed, the Bible is fundamentally concerned not with paganism but with idolatry, false prophecy, and Antichrists, from beginning to end. The moment that truth as its own standard enters the world, the moment that truth is revealed to and in the world as the world's standard, the issue of how this standard is to be lived—in human thought and existence—becomes the central problem facing humankind.

For Pilate, as for the Greeks (and all extra-biblical pagans), sin (wrongdoing) is ignorance. One cannot knowingly do wrong (evil). All wrong is done in ignorance of the good, of what the good is. By the law of contradiction, knowledge and ignorance, good and evil (wrongdoing), are forever opposed to each other. There is no common position—no rule or standard of truth for all—whereby individuals can be held responsible for wrongdoing through knowing what it is that they have done wrong (for knowing evil). It is the case that all extra-biblical societies punish wrongdoing; all establish codes for what constitutes acceptable and unacceptable behavior (articulated through myth and ritual, whether oral or written); all elaborate laws, in general and/or specific terms, regulating behavior, punishing the unacceptable, and rewarding the acceptable. But punishment in the extra-biblical world of paganism is always based on ignorance of the good. No one knowingly does wrong. To know the good is to be (identical with) the good. Because there is no notion of willing the good universally true for all, there is no notion at all of will in the pagan world, no notion of will as its own standard. Because there is no notion of will in the pagan world, there is no concept of responsibility, of knowing (of accepting responsibility for) what one has done wrong. Punishment, like all pagan experience, fatally presupposes the law of contradiction, whereby, according to the doctrine of opposites, my good depends directly (blindly and ignorantly) on your wrong. Indeed, I can be right—because it is better to do evil than to suffer evil (or vice versa)—only at your expense, only if you are wrong. But then my good directly depends on your wrongdoing.

We may, indeed, recall the protest of Protagoras, in Plato's dialogue of that name, against Socrates' demonstration that virtue (justice, wisdom, the good...) cannot be taught or learned (which will later become the Stoic *topos* that virtue is its own reward). Protagoras points out to Socrates, reasonably enough, it seems, that the only rationale in punishing individuals for wrongdoing is so that they will learn from their mistakes and not repeat them in the future. Socrates has no difficulty, however, in suspending Protagoras on the contradictory horns of his dilemma. In holding that man is the measure of all things, insofar as they appear to him (we find the classic exposition of Protagoras' famous claim in Plato's *Thaeatetus*), Protagoras is one with Socrates in adhering to the law of contradiction as the indemonstrable first principle of life. What is good is good insofar as it appears good to me. Whatever appears, insofar as it appears to me, is the good. Because the good and its appearances to me are identical, there is no possible way for me either to know or to do the wrong. The only wrong is appearances as they appear (good) to you. To know the good is to be the good. To do something wrong is to do it in ignorance of the good. What Socrates demonstrates to Protagoras—but it is important to note that Socrates' demonstration of *sophia* is no less sophistical than the sophistry of Protagoras which it exposes as ignorant of its contradiction—is that punishment, like all action (including speech itself) in the Greek world, is blind, for it is done in ignorance of the good. Punishment is fatal ignorance, blindness, ultimately death.

That punishment reflects contradictory ignorance of the good, that one is punished precisely as the fatality which blinds one to the truth of one's beginning, is brilliantly evident in the fates of Oedipus, Socrates, and Pentheus, as we have seen. For the Greeks, punishment is blind fate, and fate is blind punishment. The close connection in the Greek world of punishment, fate, ignorance of beginnings, the law of contradiction, and death is made particularly clear in the *Republic*, traditionally viewed as the greatest or most characteristic work of Greek intellect. Once Socrates explains, at the end of Book IX of the *Republic*, that the just individual can be at home only in a heavenly, not an earthly, *polis*, he then goes on in the tenth and final book to impute immortality to the soul in its separation at death from the body and to show how the Greek poets from Homer through his heirs the tragedians, with their depiction of how very mortal the gods are and how immoral their human imitators are, have no place within the just, that is, the immortal, separate, and divine *polis*. Because the *polis* is good in itself—to know the good is to be the good—it is finite, at its end, and dead to the contradictory appearances of life. That the only happy man is finite—perfect, immortal, unchanging, at his end: dead to the life of appearances—is then reflected in the myth of punishment with which the *Republic* concludes. Socrates repeats for the benefit of his interlocutors the myth of heroic Er who, it is said, returned to earth from the kingdom of the dead with his vision of the cosmic machinery of fate whereby the gods punish those whose earthly lives have been unjust and reward those whose earthly lives have been just, precisely like, Socrates points out, runners in the games who are either humiliated in defeat or crowned in triumph. That Plato gives us here his version of the *deus ex machina*, the god manifesting himself at the end of the human drama as the fatal machination which shows human heroes to be ignorant of and blind to their beginnings, is made clear by the cosmic punishment to which mortals are subject. Human beings are punished precisely because they are ignorant and blind, from the beginning. Since no one knowingly does anything wrong, since wrong is done only in ignorance of the good, since wrong is ignorance (of the good), the unjust are punished only because they are ignorant. Indeed, punishment itself is ignorance, which is the very position which Socrates demonstrates with such effect to Protagoras (although Protagoras' notion that man is the measure of all things as they appear to him no less embodies the law of contradiction than does Socrates' position). In precisely the same sense that the unjust are punished, after death, for being ignorant of justice in life, so the just are rewarded, after death, for knowing justice in life. But then we realize that the notion that justice (virtue) is its own reward is the contradictory secret of the Greeks. If to know the good is to be the good, if the identity between the subject knowing the good and the good known by the subject is finite—complete, perfect, immortal, at its end, dead to appearances—then justice (along with all the other virtues) will be no less lifeless. If virtue is its own reward, then nothing will be gained by heaping rewards upon the virtuous (philosophers or runners) once they have completed the race of life. But that the victory is not complete without additional rewards, just as Aristotle cannot conceive of virtue, in the *Nicomachean Ethics*, without what he calls the external attributes of wealth, status, children, good fortune, and friends, shows that virtue identical with itself, virtue as its own reward, remains blindly dependent on appearances which then show it to be completely contradictory. After death the unjust are punished for being ignorant of the good in life, while the just are rewarded for being dead to the contradictory appearances of the good in life. The secret of the Greeks, as of all extra-biblical pagans, is that the law of contradiction shows all humans to be ignorant of and blind to the appearances of life. Virtue is its own reward for life's punishment, for the life of contradictory punishment. To know the good is to be dead to the contradictions of life. To be ignorant of the good is to be alive to the deadly law of contradiction.

That we learn that virtue, for the Greeks as for all extra-biblical peoples, is its own fatal reward for living dead to the contradictory appearances of life reminds us, yet again, that we must consciously expose the limitations of the law of contradiction to the light of truth if we are to be in a position to comprehend truth as its own standard. Truth is the standard not only of what is true but equally of what is contradictory, of what contradicts the truth. The law of contradiction, in its finitude, in being identical with its end, in being perfect, immortal, and unchanging, is itself blind to and ignorant of its own contradictions. The law of finite contradiction is found only in its infinite appearances, and yet it is precisely the appearances of life which, in lacking or in being opposed to their end, contradict the law of contradiction. The law of contradiction, which is but the *logos* of fate, is blind to its own contradictions. From the point of view of truth as its own standard, however, we can say that, for the Greeks, truth is its own contradiction (or contradiction is its own truth). Virtue is contradiction. Virtue is its own contradictory reward. Oedipus seeks the truth of the terrible plague ravaging Thebes only to discover that he is his own contradictory truth. It is the crimes of the king, whose fatal beginnings are unknown to him, which constitute the plague. The king gouges out his eyes and suffers exile from the *polis* as punishment for his ignorance which, from its blind beginning, was fated to contradict him. That Oedipus blindly suffers punishment for the fatally destructive deeds which he performed in ignorance—for no one can knowingly do wrong—is reflected in his secret disappearance from Colonus: virtue is its own reward, the reward for being dead to the appearances of contradiction.

There is a world of difference, however, between truth as its own (Socratic) contradiction and the falsification of truth as its own standard. It is the difference between extra-biblical paganism and biblical idolatry, between ignorance of the good (virtue is its own reward) and falsification of the good (the denial that virtue is the reward of all). Within the pagan doctrine of opposites certainty and uncertainty are fatally opposed to each other. My certainty (whether the heroic claim that it is better to do than to suffer wrong or the Socratic claim that it is better to suffer than to do wrong) is opposed (from my point of view) to your uncertainty. But, since the only thing of which I am certain is that you are uncertain, my certainty is blindly dependent on your uncertainty which is opposite it. Neither of the two opposites reflecting the law of contradiction has any conception of truth reconciling them, nor does either of them have any conception of falsehood according to which one knowingly (purposely) falsifies the truth of the other by undertaking to reduce it to merely finite uncertainty. The distinction between paganism and idolatry is precisely that between, on the one hand, the natural (irreconcilable) opposition between certainty and uncertainty and, on the other, falsification, the latter involving the active (conscious) will of so subverting the truth that it is reduced to certainty, to that which is finite, to nature, to a thing or an object. The difference between paganism and idolatry is that, whereas paganism oscillates between that which is finite (perfect, identical with its end, knowable only within itself, immortal, and dead) and that which is in-finite (imperfect, opposed to its end, knowable only as contradictory appearance, mortal, and living), each blindly dependent on the other, idolatry involves the falsification of truth as its own infinite standard by undertaking to reduce it to this or that finite idol.

That truth is its own standard, the standard of both itself and the false, indicates that truth is neither certain nor uncertain. But it also indicates that the truth can be falsified (perverted, denied, oppressed, evaded...). Falsification, that is, knowledge of doing wrong, the will to subvert the truth, is absent from the pagan world. It cannot be thought (willed), and it does not exist outside the concept of truth as its own standard. Truth as the universal standard for all does not exist within the pagan doctrine of opposites. Truth as its own standard does not rest upon the law of contradiction for its existence, for it is precisely truth as its own standard which creates the premises, the priorities, the demonstrable beginnings, the principles of demonstration for classical logic (which is to be infinitely distinguished from the dialectical logic of, say, Spinoza, Kant, Hegel, and Kierkegaard). What defines the fatal *telos* of the law of contradiction is that it is logic without reason (thinking), whereas reason is the standard of thinking truthfully. Reason is its own standard, its own priority, its own principle or beginning. The law of logical contradiction is indemonstrable for the precise reason that it has no power (thought or will) to create its own starting point, its priorities or principles. Logic can prove any position right or wrong, depending on where it starts. But where it starts is completely arbitrary, and what Socrates, along with the sophists and tragedians, points out is that, in being ignorant of its beginning, *logos* is no less ignorant of its end. It is in-finite, uncertain in appearance, lacking the finite end of certainty, and contradictory. From the point of view of the law of contradiction (which is no point of view because it is always the opposite of that on which it is blindly dependent), one can lack *logos* or be illogical, but one can be neither rational nor irrational. Indeed, every hero opposite me lacks, from my point of view, certain (finite) *logos*, for there is no logic—speech, discourse, argumentation...—which is common to the two of us. The only way in which I can demonstrate the certainty of my logic, which rests on the indemonstrable, first principle of contradiction, is to show that it is better for me to rule over you with my contradictory logic than for me to suffer the contradictory rule of your logic (or vice versa, following the Socratic *logos* inverting and thus blindly following the law of contradiction).

When reason becomes the standard of truth, two radically new consequences follow, however. First, the reasonable person cannot be illogical. Precisely because reason is grounded, not in logical operations displaying the interconnections of premises which have been blindly presupposed, but in premises whose truth it is its task to demonstrate, from beginning to end, reason is in no way opposed to logic, nor is it illogical. Reason is concerned with demonstrating the truth of its premises. The logical operations it employs may be more or less clear and distinct, but the truth (or falsity) of our premises, as Descartes makes perspicuous, is not dependent on clarity or distinctiveness as such. What counts is the absolute distinction (clarity) between truth and its falsifications, and this distinction is not merely one more logical distinction. Rather, it is the standard for all distinctions. The distinction between truth and falsity can be established only on the authority of truth as its own distinct standard. It is the case, however, that, precisely because reason is not bound by logical form, it often appears illogical to those who are habituated to viewing the priorities of life within the forms of traditional logic. Reason is no less the motif (standard) of, say, art, religion, conversation, love-making, or politics than it is of philosophy.

The second consequence to follow from the critical distinction between logic and reason (rationality) is that, although reason cannot be illogical, it can be, is, and becomes irrational. In demonstrating to his fellow Greeks that to hold to the law of contradiction as the *logos* of life involves one in ignorance of the good, from the beginning to the end of one's life, what Socrates shows us is that irrationality is inconceivable in the Greek world. Irrationality is founded, not on the logic of ignorance, not on logic blind to its own indemonstrable, first principles, but on knowledge of the good, on thinking, on willing truth as its own standard of rationality. The stakes in life are infinitely raised once truth becomes its own standard. Although truth cannot be either certain or uncertain, it can be falsified (denied...). Although truth is its own infinite standard, it is constantly subject to partisan or ideological (idolatrous) reduction to finite interests. Although truth as its own standard makes the principle of reason, and not the logic of contradiction, the demonstrable beginning of life, it also introduces irrationality, the willful (thoughtless) contradiction of reason, into the world.

Idolatry, not paganism, is the enemy of truth as its own standard for the paradoxical reason that it is uniquely those who are subject to the universal authority of truth who undertake to subvert it by reducing it to this or that finite interest. The reason that it is so critically important to distinguish between paganism and truth, between the law of contradiction and truth as its own standard, is to allow us to constitute the critical distinction between truth and idol. It is only when we distinguish between truth and certainty, or between falsity and uncertainty, that we are then in a position to distinguish between truth and falsity. The paradox that we elaborate throughout this work, in one way and another, is that it is only those to whom the truth is revealed who can willfully distort it by reducing it either to a certain, finite version of the truth (dogmatism) or to an uncertain, finite version of the truth (skepticism). Our disagreement is not with Socrates; we do not polemicize against paganism. Rather, our polemic is aimed at those who, in failing to distinguish between Socratic ignorance and Cartesian doubting of truth, obfuscate or inhibit proper discussion and comprehension of truth and its endless falsifications. Relativism and dogmatism are each a species of authoritarianism, as distinct from the authority of truth as its own standard; and there is neither authoritarianism (whether relativistic or dogmatic) nor true authority (sovereignty) in the Greek (extra-biblical) world. Relativism reduces truth to the authoritarianism of private opinion (solipsism), while dogmatism elevates private opinion to authoritarian truth (totalitarianism). Relativism and dogmatism can both be perfectly logical, if their irrational principles are granted. Indeed, they often thrive on contradiction, on holding fanatically to the position that the more they contradict the truth the more profound they are, something inconceivable to the Greeks. But both relativism and dogmatism are profoundly irrational, for they substitute their own arbitrary (or finite) authority for truth (reason) as its own authoritative standard.

I suspect that the reader has been offended by Spinoza's dogmatic formulation of truth as its own standard. One of the themes which we shall be exploring later in this essay in thinking involves the fact that the opposed rhetorics (languages) of dogmatism and skepticism, idealism and materialism, soul and body, spirit and nature, thought and action, reason and emotion (will) can be liberated from falsifying dualisms only through the dialectic of metaphor as its own standard, the standard of both dogmatic and skeptical *topoi*, of both sensuous and psychic images. Because all natural languages are perfect (finite), they are inherently (innately) contradictory, their deep structures of grammar and syntax fatally contradicted by the surface (superficial) images in which they appear. Although natural languages are identical with their end—they finitely say what they mean, and they mean finitely what they say—their meaning and saying are found only in the naturally opposed images of body and soul, which fatally contradict each other. There is nothing inherently (innately) communicable in and through language, although everything communicable (truthful) can be communicated, in principle, in every natural language. Communication as its own infinite standard—the communication of truth, truth as communication—is unthinkable and cannot exist without natural language, but finite language does not thoughtfully exist in and of itself. Communication is its own standard, the standard of both communication and what is not communication, that is, language.

I originally found Spinoza's dogmatic formulation of truth as its own standard to be impenetrable and a rude shock to my new world pragmatism (individualism, liberalism, utilitarianism, empiricism, skepticism, secularism...). I knew that individualism was meaningless if it could not be preserved from relativism (solipsism: the problem of "other minds"), but I continued to have difficulty in distinguishing between dogma and dogmatism, between truth and an uncritical way (method) of appropriating truth (to recall Kant's critical distinction). But I now find the dogmatic formula of truth as its own standard, precisely because it appears to lack any self-conscious appropriation consistent with the Cartesian formula of self-consciousness with which we initiated this essay—I think, therefore, I am—to be an invaluable check on thoughtless individualism. I now see that truth is its own standard for each individual, precisely as each individual is his (her) own standard of truth. This statement can in truth be uttered by, to, and for the individual, but it is critically true, however, only insofar as (*quatenus*: one of the miraculous terms central to Spinoza's discourse) it is uttered by, to, and for all individuals and thus throws all individuals into crisis, confronting them with rendering their existence thoughtful, their thought existential. The only way in which individualism can be preserved from the authoritarianism of private opinion (whether skeptical or dogmatic) is through a concept of authority (sovereignty) common to all. Truth as its own standard embodies the authority of all over all (as distinct from the pagan opposition of one, some, or many ruling over others). Truth as its own standard is profoundly democratic and communal. Truth as its own standard is the standard both for what constitutes community and for what subverts community. There is no truth outside its communication (outside its embodiment in community); and there is no communication outside truth (outside the community of truth). Once again, when we apply the critical distinction between paganism and idolatry, we see that the Greek (and the entire extra-biblical) world lacks both truth and communication (community) and that idolatry is the subversion of not only truth but equally communication.

One of the advantages of the dogmatic formulation of truth as its own standard is that, in appearing to be self-contained without embodiment in the history of an individual ego, it is not easily reducible to the egoism of historicism. On the other hand, it is only when we show, in the following two sections of this chapter, that if truth as its own standard has always been in the world, then it has never been in the world (truth as history: Section ii) and that truth embodies the dialectic that for one position to be true the position opposite it must also be true (truth as relationship: Section iii), that Spinoza's dogma will be preserved from dogmatism. But here we must first examine the structure of the relationship between truth and falsehood and how it is that truth as it own standard is the principle, the priority, the beginning of demonstration, as distinct from the law of contradiction which, for the Greeks (not to mention their benighted followers), identifies demonstration with arbitrary beginnings ignorant of and blind to their priorities.

There is a profound relationship between truth as its own standard, the standard of both itself and the false, and demonstration (proof, argumentation...). That the Greeks begin with lack of demonstration, that, for them, demonstration rests on that which cannot be demonstrated, the law of contradiction, is intimately bound up with the fact that for them falsity (wrong) is ignorance. What we must come to appreciate is the infinite difference between the good (truth) known in itself, whether Plato's Form of the good or Aristotle's *nous* (mind: the unmoved mover, thought thinking itself), and Spinoza's truth (good) as its own standard. But, as always, the distinction between the doctrine of opposites and the dialectic of truth as its own standard, between paganism and truth (the Bible), is not the critical difference. This difference is but the heuristic which enables us to constitute the properly critical distinction between truth and idolatry, between truth and its falsifications.

When seen in the light of the law of contradiction, the concept of truth as its own standard is clearly paradoxical. Indeed, we shall discover that truth as its own standard eternally confronts us with the paradox of either/or, the either/or of paradox, what Kant constitutes as the leap of reason (the *a priori* synthetic judgment) and Kierkegaard calls the leap of faith. Either choose the paradox, either choose paradoxically, or be offended by your own self-contradiction in and through the paradox of truth as its own standard. But, again, the critical distinction is not between paradox and contradiction but between the paradox of truth and its idolatrous falsifications. Whereas the law of contradiction renders the natural world of paganism ignorant of and blind to its own beginnings, idolatry undertakes to reduce others to contradiction. The paradox captured in the formulation of truth as its own standard is that truth (or any value commitment) can be falsified (evaded, corrupted, oppressed...) only when it is known (revealed) to all. Only when everyone is responsible to and for the truth does the (idolatrous) possibility of its falsification (sin) erupt into the world. In the Greek world, the world of natural paganism, the world based on nature as the truth (good) known in itself, precisely because there is no concept of truth (or good) universally accessible to all, there is equally no concept of its falsification, its willful perversion. Again, we see that it is idolatry, the idolization of finite (natural) facts as infinitely true, which is the determined enemy of truth. It is Satanic perversion of the truth, not Socratic ignorance of the truth, which stalks the world, although one of the favorite means of subverting the truth, at least on the part of philosophers, both academic and popular, is to hide their idols of truth beneath the mantle of Socratic ignorance.

Truth as its own standard means that truth can be demonstrated only insofar as it is accessible to all. Truth can be falsified only insofar as individuals (groups of individuals), in claiming to represent it for all, reduce it to some finite version of what constitutes existence. Truth is its own standard, both of what is true for all and of what is not true for all (what is false), precisely because it is only the truth which constitutes the beginning of humanity, the principle of human right, the ground of demonstration. What is uniquely paradoxical about Spinoza's dogmatic formulation of the truth is that one cannot begin outside it and then arrive at it. One cannot begin separate from the truth and then discover the truth. One cannot begin in some neutral (natural) space and time and then begin thinking (willing) the truth of existence (the existence of truth). One is born, as a human being, not into nature but into the truth. Our birth is not natural but human. One begins, and this beginning is the conscious creation of the only, the universal way in which this beginning can make sense, that this beginning is principled, that it begins with the principle of recognizing the truthful existence of the other as he (she) recognizes the truth of your existence. All beginning is in and with the truth. The only argument worthy of human beings is the argument that begins with (from) the truth as its own standard. One cannot argue to the truth from some putative point of view outside the truth. That this demonstration of the truth—that one can argue only from and not to the truth—is identical with the ontological argument for existence, both divine and human, that one argues not to but from God's existence, will become increasingly evident in this essay. Truth—humanity, freedom, God, natural right, love...—is its own standard (ground), the standard (ground) of demonstration and of what is not truly demonstration.

The paradox reemerges, then, when we think about the Greek beginning in ignorance. There are only two positions possible: the blind beginning in nature (truth is innate); the thoughtful beginning in truth (truth is its own standard). Either/or. There is, however, no choice between nature (truth as innate) and truth (truth as its own standard). Choice, the choice of truth, is not natural; it is not based on nature; it is not innately blind to or ignorant of its own free beginnings, its principles of freedom. Choice, the choice of truth, is its own standard, the standard of both freedom and what is not freedom; but what is not freedom, the willful perversion of the choice of truth, freedom as its own standard recognizes as choice. One is not free not to be free. Not to be free belongs to freedom as its own standard of what constitutes freedom, including the denial of freedom. One cannot choose to be untruthful. One does not have the right to evade or to deny the truth. The denial of truth belongs to truth as its own standard. Demonstration—demonstration of the truth and truthful demonstration—begins and ends with the truth. Because there is no truth outside its demonstration(s) and demonstration does not exist outside the truth, we see that, in the truly simple sense, all thought, all existence is demonstration—of the truth. To exist as a human being is to think, and to think involves and expresses the truth, for there is only one object (subject) of thoughtful existence, and that is the truth (of human being[s]). All thoughtful existence involves demonstration from, in Rousseau's terms, right (truth) to fact. The finite facts of nature are not their own standard, for they are fatally opposed to each other. The innate, that is, the apparent, oppositions of the world can be saved from contradiction only through a conception of human nature based on right as its own standard, as the standard right for all, without discrimination based on natural differences.

What is truth? Truth is its own standard, the standard of dogma which is not dogmatic and the standard of doubt which is not skeptical. Truth as its own standard is the universal point of view, the universal perspective which is accessible, known, and demonstrable to (by) all. Truth as its own standard must be infinitely distinguished from paganism whose appearances have their indemonstrable beginnings in the law of contradiction. Paganism is fatally subject to the rule of opposites, wherein every beginning, every point of view, because it is blind to its own contradictory logic, ineluctably contradicts the other, on which it thus remains ignorantly dependent. Following the doctrine of opposites, every position is blindly opposed to (the opposite of) both itself and its other. Every position is ignorant of its oscillation between certainty and uncertainty, between determinate fate and indeterminate chance. What the concept of truth as its own standard reveals to us is that its opposite is not the doctrine of opposites. The opposite of truth is neither certainty nor uncertainty but falsity (evil, sin...). The opposition between certainty and uncertainty, between finite perfection, knowable only in itself and dead to appearances, and its infinite appearances, knowable only relative to the apparently living individual, bears no relationship to the opposition between truth and its falsifications (there is no analogy between these two "opposites," notwithstanding the identity of their terms).

The distinction between paganism and truth as its own standard serves the heuristic purpose of allowing us to grasp, truly, the only distinction which counts, the distinction between truth and idolatry, which is the distinction which truth as its own standard introduces into the world, the distinction between truth and the reduction of the standard of truth for all to this or that private interest or idol. In paganism, things are (naturally) certain or (unnaturally) uncertain, each but the blind reflection of the other. Things cannot become certain or uncertain except through natural metamorphosis. But, in the world for which truth is its own standard, certainty or uncertainty always involves falsification, reification, the reduction of infinite truth, the truth universal for all individuals, to the interests of some individuals, to the exclusion of the interests of other individuals. In the world for which truth is its own standard human beings are infinite, neither certain (finite) nor uncertain (in-finite: lacking the finite perfection of nature); they are born into the truth. But it is precisely because all human beings possess the natural right of distinguishing between the right of demonstration and the facts of nature (whether one is born, say, black or white, male or female, Jew or Christian, rich or poor, straight or gay...) that the possibility of subverting the truth enters the world. Whereas, in the pagan world, because the truth is that which is blindly contradicted, there is no truth to be contradicted, that is, the truth is contradiction (but not contradictory), in the world for which truth is its own standard the truth is constantly contradicted (perverted, oppressed, evaded...). Truth is contradictory, that is, the standard universal for all is subverted in making it contradict the thought and existence of particular individuals (or groups of individuals). It is precisely truth as its own standard which introduces the notion of false truth—something inconceivable to Plato, to the extra-biblical world, generally—into the world and which creates the task of ever overcoming the falsifications of truth in the name of truth as its own standard, the standard of the true as well as of the false. Only if truth is its own standard can it be responsible for its falsifications, can it comprehend as its own the errors which are committed in its name, which it commits in its own name. Either/or. Either truth is blind to its own contradictions, from the beginning. Or truth, from the beginning, in principle, is its own standard, the standard both of itself and of its contradictions. But the either/or of choosing truth as its own standard is not the choice between choosing truth, which is demonstrable to all, and indemonstrable contradiction, which is blind to all beginnings. The either/or of choosing the truth is grounded in truth as its own standard, for choice (freedom) is its own standard, the standard of both choosing freedom and falsifying freedom, that is, not choosing freely.

II. TRUTH AS THE NECESSARY EXISTENCE OF HISTORY

When Jesus tells the uncertain Pilate that he comes to bear witness to the truth as its own standard, the standard no less true for Pilate than for Jesus, the standard universally true for all human beings, notwithstanding their certain oppositions, it is critically important to see that we are in the presence of two utterly different conceptions of what constitutes human thought and existence, two completely different notions of space and time. The pagan notion of space and time, as represented by Pilate's Roman imperialism, is based on nature whose logic of contradiction fatally demonstrates that whatever *is* may *not be*, to invoke Hume's argument at the end of his *Enquiry Concerning Human Understanding* against the ontological argument for the prior necessity, the necessary priority, of existence. Whatever *is* may *not be*. According to the law of contradiction, whatever is natural occupies a certain space and time and may not occupy another space at the same time. Pilate is perplexed by one who is not moved by the imperial representative of natural law, the unmoved mover, who, in moving others (in providing them their blind *telos*), is not moved by others. Jesus, however, has come to bear witness to the truth that whatever is must be. There is one truth whose existence involves necessity and whose necessity expresses existence. Truth is the necessary standard of existence precisely because it brings to light the secret contradiction hidden within the dark law of contradiction, that of the unmoved mover, that my being depends on my contradicting you, showing you that whatever is (from my natural position in space and time) may not (need not) involve the nature of your position in space and time. The truth whose existence involves necessity and whose necessity expresses existence is the revelation that human being is not located in the contradictory nature of space and time, where, for one to move others, it must deny that it is moved by others, holding that whatever *is* may *not be*. The truth linking necessity and existence, to which Jesus, the heir of the patriarchs and the prophets, bears witness is the priority of human being to the natural law of spatial and temporal contradictions. To move others as you would have them move you is the truth which shines in the darkness of pagan contradiction, and pagan contradiction does not overcome it.

But what is even more perplexing to not only Pilate but especially his modern avatars like Hume is that the truth, to which Jesus comes to bear witness, is historical. If truth has always been in the world, then it has never been in the world. If truth has always belonged to the world of natural space and time, then it is fatally lost in the unearthly secret of the law of contradiction whose opposites undergo the metamorphosis of generation and destruction without end. The perplexing condition of truth as its own standard is that it can exist in the world only if it is not of the world of natural space and time. Truth is its own condition precisely because it does not belong to the natural conditions of space and time. For truth to be its own condition, the unconditional standard not only for itself but for all conditions, then it must come into existence from nothing, from nothing which is conditioned by the nature of space and time. With the uncritical distinction which he effects between matters of fact and relations of ideas, Hume finds himself forced to reduce existence to the natural facts of space and time (the empirical realm of sensation), while relegating necessity (or thought) to the ideal realm of the association of ideas (the rational realm of understanding). It is little wonder, then, that, when Hume reflects autobiographically in the Conclusion of Book I of his *A Treatise of Human Nature*, he expresses melancholy that he finds that the only choice which he has left himself is that betwixt, as he puts it, a false reason and no reason at all.

Hume has shown that, within the empirical realm of natural facts, there is no necessary existence—whatever *is* may *not be*. Within the realm of natural space and time there is no necessity. No causal connection can be established between empirical facts such that their effects could not be (explained) otherwise. If P, then Q. But the customary colligation of effect Q with cause P does not prove, with binding necessity, that effect Q could not also be caused by A, B, or... or that P could not cause effects Z, Y, or.... There is no necessary proof, but only customary expectation, that the sun will rise tomorrow. There is no logical contradiction involved in denying the existence of a natural fact. It can always be other than it is. Hume equally shows that personal identity is an idea whose necessity is a tautology lacking existence in nature. In other words, the mind is constituted by ideas whose logic of necessity has no bearing on existence and whose content reflects the existence of natural facts which bear no necessity. Hume finds himself betwixt a false reason and no reason at all because he shows that reason can claim to discern neither necessity in things that exist (in natural space and time) nor existence in the necessary (tautological) relationship of ideas. To claim that existence is necessary is to reason falsely. To claim that the idea of necessity (personal identity) does not exist is to have no reason at all. Existence and thought are without necessary relationship. Their relationship is purely arbitrary, contingent, conditional, and customary. Thus Hume's very claim itself—that whatever *is* may *not be*, that there is no contradiction in denying the existence of a natural fact—itself either exists without necessity or is necessary without existing.

What Hume fails to recognize, however, is that there is one fact whose existence is necessary, one fact whose necessity exists. There is one fact whose contradiction itself is contradictory: his own necessary existence as a human being. Human being reveals the necessary bond of thought and existence—I think, therefore, I am—to those who have ears to hear and eyes to see. In making the necessity of human reason depend blindly, or thoughtlessly, on the natural existence of space and time and the natural facts of human existence depend ignorantly, or irrationally, on mental necessity, Hume is without a critical path by which to distinguish between nature and custom. That which is natural in space and time is reflected as custom in the mind, while that which is natural to the mind but reflects human custom. The closed circle, the circle closed to its own contradictions, is complete. In denying necessity to (human) existence, in failing to distinguish between human existence and things existing in natural space and time, Hume secretly supports the *status quo*, the position which argues from the unnecessary, but presently established, facts of human existence to what is customarily legitimate. He argues from natural facts to rights which have no basis in human nature, no basis in the necessity of being human. To argue from the natural facts of space and time which may *not be* to that which constitutes human nature is to find oneself ineluctably suspended betwixt a false reason and no reason at all. Hume fails to recognize that the only argument worthy of being human, the only argument which liberates human beings from the irrationality of the choice between false reason and no reason at all, is the one that begins with the necessary existence of human beings. To be human is to argue with Rousseau from the necessary existence of right to the right constitution of facts. Human being is that existence whose thoughtful constitution must be necessary.

Pascal had already observed in his *Pensées* that natural opposition between human beings is indistinguishable from opposition based on custom. The hatred with which human beings naturally oppose each other is indistinguishable from the hatred generated by human opposition based on custom. We blindly rationalize custom by calling it natural, just as we ignorantly rationalize our conception of nature by decking it out as custom. The choice between finite nature and finite custom, where nature constantly becomes the primacy of custom and custom constantly becomes second nature, is no choice at all. It leaves us, as Hume impotently recognizes, betwixt a false reason and no reason at all, between falsely imputing necessity to naturally existing facts and truly imputing necessity to a mind which does not exist. Hume makes the existence of natural facts depend blindly on ideas whose necessity is arbitrary (customary), in that they have no existence, while he makes the necessity of mind depend ignorantly on facts of nature whose necessary existence is irrational (natural). What is customary (human) has necessity without existence, while what exists (naturally) is without necessity. Human nature is an oxymoron which Hume is powerless to explicate, as he himself, in his melancholy, laments. So long as existence is reduced to the nature of finite space and time and necessity is reduced to the tautology of finite ideas, human nature remains ignorant of and blind to its own contradictions. Thought remains ignorant of existence, and existence remains blind to thought. Hume is unable to grasp the foolhardiness of his own claim that whatever *is* may *not be*. For there is one being whose existence involves necessity, not on the model of natural space and time, it is true, and one being whose necessity expresses existence, not on the model of the relationship of tautological ideas, it is equally true. That being is *l'homme* to whom Rousseau passionately addresses his *Discourse on the Origins of Inequality*, where he notes that human nature involves the freedom and perfectibility of arguing from (natural) right to (human) fact. The human being is the oxymoron who, self-consciously foolish, challenges, with Paul, the arbitrary wisdom of the world, whether called natural or customary, in the name of the necessity of thoughtful existence (existing ideas). The self-contradictory claim of fools—that whatever *is* may *not be*—gives way to the self-conscious fooling of human beings—that whatever is must be. Whatever is human has the right to exist. Whatever is human exists necessarily.

We may recall, however, that Kant tells us that it was precisely Hume's melancholic recognition that he was suspended between a false reason, which exists without necessity, and no reason at all, reason whose necessary tautologies do not exist, which roused him from the somnolence of German idealism in the tradition of Leibniz. Whereas Leibniz argues that sense experience is but the faulty reflection of ideas whose necessary existence as monads constitutes with sufficient reason the best of all possible worlds, Hume demonstrates that the colligation of necessity and existence is purely arbitrary: it can be demonstrated neither empirically nor rationally. Although Kant wakes up to what he calls the subreption of the hypostatized consciousness, in the tradition of Leibniz, thanks to Hume's demonstration that facts either exist (naturally) without necessity or are (ideally) necessary without existence, he turns his critique of pure reason against Hume no less than against Leibniz. To Leibniz' uncritical repetition of the law of identity—whatever is, is—Hume responds, no less uncritically, with the law of contradiction—whatever *is* may *not be.* Kant recognizes in Hume's melancholy a subreption of consciousness no less critical than in Leibniz' theodicy reflecting the best of all possible worlds. Whereas Leibniz hypostatizes consciousness, treating it as a thing necessarily existing in space and time, Hume makes consciousness impotent, its ideas bearing no necessary relation to existence. Both Leibniz and Hume surreptitiously introduce into their arguments the very opposite of what they claim, Leibniz, the necessary existence of space and time, and Hume, the necessary existence of ideas. Each is the mirror opposite of the other, their arguments involving custom and nature, empiricism and rationalism, skepticism and rationalism, the law of contradiction and the law of identity each blind to and thus ignorantly dependent on, as it inexorably metamorphoses into, its opposite.

Leibniz, on the one hand, wants to preserve the existence of necessary ideas. But his concept of existence remains attached to objects, to things, as they exist in space and time. Sense experience, based on natural space and time, is but confused or contradictory reason; or, in other words, reason but reflects the confusions or contradictions of sense experience. Leibniz cannot say with Descartes—I think, therefore, I am—for, in continuing to adhere to the law of identity as the law of truth, he cannot so doubt the necessity of existence and the existence of necessity that he makes the Cartesian discovery that the one thing which he cannot doubt is the necessary existence of doubt, the oxymoron, the self-conscious foolishness of consciousness. Because consciousness (thinking, ideas, mind, reason), for Leibniz, is not separated from but remains the reflection of sensation, of which it is but the clarification, the clear and distinct idea, he is unable to develop a critique of pure reason. Leibniz knows that reason must involve the idea of necessary existence, but his idea of necessity remains attached to the law of identity precisely because he cannot conceive of existence other than through the images of natural space and time.

Hume, on the other hand, wants to preserve the contingency of things naturally existing in space and time. But, because the idea of necessity remains that of logical contradiction without existence and the mind has no existential content outside sense data, reason constantly finds itself to be impotent: whatever *is* may *not be*. Reason has no way in which to establish priority (causal connections or personal identity) among its sense data. The only basis for natural priority is the force of arbitrary custom. The only basis for the priority of ideas, whose logic is tautological, is uncritical acceptance of the customary colligation of natural facts. Hume cannot say with Descartes—I think, therefore, I am—for, in continuing to adhere to the law of contradiction as the law of truth, he cannot so doubt the necessity of existence and the existence of necessity that he makes the Cartesian discovery that the one thing which he cannot doubt is the necessary existence of doubt, the oxymoron, the self-conscious foolishness of consciousness. Because consciousness (thinking, ideas, mind, reason), for Hume, is not separated from but remains the reflection of sensation, of which it is but the clarification, the clear and distinct idea, he is unable to develop a critique of pure reason. Hume knows that reason must involve the idea of necessary existence, but his idea of necessity remains attached to the law of contradiction precisely because he cannot conceive of existence other than through the images of natural space and time.

It is important to note that Hume's melancholy, in reflecting the best of all possible Leibnizian worlds, is altogether different from Pilate's perplexity before Jesus' claim that he comes to bear witness to truth as its own standard. It is the case that both Pilate and Hume presuppose the law of contradiction, whose necessity is without existence, whose necessity contradicts all existence. Pilate, however, would have found Hume's melancholic suspense between a false reason and no reason at all to be absolutely inconceivable. The very notion of a false reason or of a reason whose existence is its non-existence cannot be conceived on the basis of the extra-biblical doctrine of opposites, where reason (truth as certainty) is fatally opposed to unreason (falsity as uncertainty), where that which is (superior) is opposed to (rules over) that which (as inferior) is not. Pilate is perplexed by Jesus because he cannot conceive of the human being opposite him as his equal, as the neighbor whom he must love as himself. He views reason as the rule of one over others. For Pilate, his own reason can be certain (true) only if the reason opposite him is uncertain (false), or if, following the fatal metamorphosis of natural opposites, the one opposite him falsifies his (Pilate's) reason by establishing the rule of its reason over him. Pilate knows (unconsciously), therefore, that, ultimately, the greatest of rulers, even Caesar himself, notwithstanding his divinization, rules impotently over others. Precisely because Caesar's rule exists only through those over whom he rules, his rule depends blindly on those who, as ruled, are ignorant of his rule. All rule, not only human but also divine, including the rule of the gods over humans, reflects the fatal doctrines of opposites, where the ruler is blindly dependent on that over which he rules, this other representing, ultimately, the faceless visage of fate.

Melancholy, the melancholy of a Hume suspended by the double oxymora of a false reason—a reason which knows itself to be false—and of the existence of a non-existing reason, is unthinkable in the pagan world. Melancholy, not the black bile flowing in natural space and time but the metaphor reflecting the dread of necessary existence, enters the world with the conception of truth as its own standard of existence, the standard of both existence and non-existence. Hume's melancholy is generated by his conscious recognition that it is necessary for him to continue, that he wills to continue, his treatise on human nature beyond Book I, notwithstanding the fact that he has shown that his understanding, the subject of the first book of his treatise which he now contemplates in his melancholy, is either false or non-existent and that it is on the basis of this false or non-existent understanding that he will continue to philosophize on human passions (in Book II) and on human morals (in Book III). What, we ask, is the nature of this will to knowledge, now working in the tradition of Francis Bacon for whom knowledge is power, which is consciously, willfully, false or non-existent? Whereas Pilate is perplexed by Jesus, who, in coming to bear witness to the truth of scripture, does not express fear before the contradictory law of Caesar, Hume experiences melancholy before the self-contradiction of his own reason.

The notion that reason, or truth, is contradictory would have been inconceivable to Pilate, as to any pagan. Reason (truth), in paganism, is that by which I contradict you or you contradict me. It is inconceivable that I could contradict myself or that reason could be self-contradictory. The conception of truth held by Pilate is always that represented by Socratic ignorance or the Cretan liar. Because one can never knowingly do evil, Pilate is surprised by Jesus. From Pilate's point of view Jesus cannot be anything other than ignorant of any wrong-doing. But this does not suggest to Pilate that Jesus, as one rebelling against the rule of Caesar, should not be punished, for it is precisely those who are ignorant of justice, not those who are just in ruling over the ignorant, who justly undergo punishment. It is better to do evil to others than to suffer evil from others. Pilate represents the position of the Cretan liar, who, in saying that he lies, knows that he lies and lies that he knows. But the Cretan liar does not know what his lie is. He has no conception of what it is that constitutes his lie. He can neither imagine nor conceive of Hume's notion of a false reason or of a reason existing in its non-existence. It is inconceivable to the Cretan liar that he could know his lie, that he could possess his lie, that he could become responsible for his lying. He has no way of knowing that his lie would be exposed for what it is—that it expresses his failure to will the good true for all human beings—only in light of truth as its own standard, the standard of both the truth and its deceptions. Reason, in the pagan world, encloses the fatal secret whereby contradiction always remains blind to its own contradictions. Pilate is perplexed by Jesus, for he can only imagine those opposite him in the likeness of the Cretan liar. Just as the Cretan liar can only imagine himself in opposition to himself, deceived by his own deception, Pilate can only imagine the one opposed to him as deceiving him, in ignorance of the justice of imperial rule. But thus Caesar's justice (truth) remains blindly dependent on the deception opposite it, which is precisely what Jesus exposes to the light of truth as its own standard. The Cretan liar of paganism is replaced by the truth bringer of the Bible. It is precisely because the pagan Pilate cannot imagine the one opposite him to be other than a deceiver that he himself remains blindly dependent on the lie which he imputes to the other and for which he cannot, therefore, assume responsibility. The conception of truth as its own standard, the standard uniting all opposites, is absent from the pagan world. It is the Cretan liar, hidden within his own self-contradiction, not the prophet bearing witness to the truth of self-contradictory lies, who rules paganism.

Melancholy, of which Hume's vividly expresses the type characteristic of modern intellectuals, is the pathology of spirit that enters the world as the claim that contradiction exists, that false reason exists, that I exist in the non-existence of my reason. Whereas it is inconceivable to Socrates, Pilate, or any pagan that truth is contradictory, for the contradiction of truth is always the secret which cannot be told, since its truth is always the fatal opposite of itself, the conception of a false conception, the conception of falsity, of error—of sin, as the falsification of thought and existence—enters the world with truth as its own standard, the standard of both truth and its contradictions. The world knows three conceptions of truth: (1) truth blind to its own contradictions (the Socratic ignorance of Pilate); (2) truth consciously self-contradictory (Hume's melancholy); and (3) truth as its own standard (as expressed by Jesus or Spinoza). The first is represented through the doctrine of opposites, which shapes all extra-biblical thought. The second is identical with idolatry, the conscious (willful) falsification of the truth of thought and existence (the thought and existence of truth) by reducing the necessity of human thought and existence to the contradictory images of space and time. The third expresses the dialectic of thought and existence, of truth and interpretation. Once again, we emphasize the importance of distinguishing between Jesus and Pilate, between the biblical conception of truth as its own standard and the pagan conception of truth as blind to its own contradiction (the pagan conception of contradiction as blind to its own truth), so that we can properly distinguish between the prophetic truth of contradiction and the idolatrous contradiction of truth.

To hold that whatever *is* may *not be* reveals the law of contradiction to be contradictory, something inconceivable to Socrates and the world of paganism, generally. Hume's melancholy reflects his self-contradiction, his inability either to ground his thought and existence in necessity or to ground his necessity in thought and existence. He fails to see that the law of contradiction applies only to the natural (finite) realm of space and time and that, in order to develop a consistent conception of either existence or necessary ideas, he must distinguish systematically between nature and freedom, fact and right, between, on the one hand, space and time and, on the other, the historical thought and existence of human beings. What is particularly pathetic about Hume's melancholic recognition that he finds himself betwixt a false reason and no reason at all is that he knows that he is in error, yet he cannot conceive of what his error is. Unlike Socrates, for whom error is always ignorance of the good (lack of the good in the Neoplatonic tradition), for whom error is inconceivable, Hume knows that he is in error, yet he cannot develop a conception of what that error is. With his attachment to the law of contradiction and its reflection in the natural images of space and time, error for Hume either exists but is unnecessary or is necessary but does not exist. Hume is unable to recognize that the only basis for conceiving of error, for comprehending error, for recognizing that one is in error is the revelation to all of truth as its own standard. His error, his sin of melancholy, his inability to conceive of (his) error as both necessary and existing, as the product itself of conscious, thinking (willing) existence, is grounded in a double failure. First, error becomes comprehensible only when we conceive of thought and existence (divine and human) as necessary and of necessity (the self-determination of God or human beings) as involving both thought and existence. Second, in order to detach thought and existence from the contradictory images of natural space and time and necessity from the blind logic of contradiction, we must develop a conception of both thought and existence as historical. It is true that neither Descartes nor Spinoza has an explicit conception of history. But, in their determination to bear witness to thinking existence as the standard of truth, Descartes and Spinoza overcome the melancholy entailed by the idolatrization of the law of contradiction and its reflection in the images of natural space and time through their conception of the necessary existence of being self-consciously human.

What is so enormously difficult for most thinkers (and by that term I mean to include all those who express consciousness of their existence, whatever the medium) to realize is that the only way in which thought and existence can be bound together is to conceive (live) each as necessary. To invoke the theme of the next section of this chapter, neither thought nor existence can be necessary unless both are necessary. But both can be necessary only if each, thoughtful existence and the existence of thought, is distinguished no less from the finite space and time of nature than from the natural logic of finite contradiction. The necessity binding thought and existence is freedom, not fate, freedom from both the logical determinism of the law of contradiction and from the natural determinism of space and time. The necessity freely binding thought and existence is, finally, history. History is not grounded in the empiricist (conditional or contingent) necessity of space and time, for, as Hume correctly discerns, there is no absolute, but only relative, necessity in causal connections, only customary or utilitarian colligation (that which has become in our century statistical probability). Although Hume correctly observes that causal links connecting natural phenomena cannot be held to be necessary (they could be otherwise), he fails to recognize that truth is not a matter of more or less empirical certainty, of more or less contingency or probability. Truth is historical, not empirical. Truth does not belong to the space and time of nature. Truth is historical, not logical. Truth does not belong to the logic of contradiction. Truth is historical precisely because it is its own standard of thoughtful existence. If truth has always been in the world, in the world of natural space and time, then it has never been in the world. If the necessary existence of thought or the necessary thought of existence has always been in the world, then it has never been in the world. Necessity worthy of human beings must come freely into historical existence from nothing, from nothing that is fated to be blind to and ignorant of its thought and existence.

The necessity of arguing from right to fact, the necessity of truth as its own standard is the necessity binding thought and existence, the necessity of history. Historical necessity, the realization that if history has always existed then it has never existed, expresses freedom from the contradictory law governing the natural world of space and time. History, understood as the necessity of determining human right, always involves the argument from right to fact. What is right for human beings, truth as its own standard, comes freely into existence from nothing, from nothing which is not worthy of being human. Truth as its own standard, the standard of both the true and the false, is historical and thus neither empiricist, subject to the contingencies of cause and effect, nor logical, subject to the fatal necessity of contradiction. Truth is given not in the natural conditions of space and time but in the unconditioned, the absolute, the necessary existence of thought and the necessary thought of existence. Truth is given in and as history. The ontological argument for existence itself comes into historical existence, into history, as the thought whose doubt is so profound that it discovers that there is one being which it cannot doubt—the absolute existence of the historical other whom it can think only as its own history. Truth is not contradictory, for it comes into existence as the self-conscious oxymoron whose necessity is its freedom. In its freedom from the logic of contradiction dominating the space and time of nature, it is free, that is, it is obligated, to hold all persons to history as its own absolute standard, than which there is no more perfect or other. Truth is the paradox that as soon as it is—as soon as it comes into existence—it must have been, historically. Truth is the recognition that once it comes freely into existence—from nothing—it is historical. If truth has always been in the world, then it has never been historically in the world. Truth is its own standard, the absolute standard of both what constitutes historical existence—the ontological argument from right to fact—and what falsifies the existence of history—the empirico-logical argument from fact to right.

III. TRUTH AS HISTORICAL RELATIONSHIP

The truth to which Jesus comes to bear witness is its own standard, the standard whose existence involves necessity and whose necessity expresses existence. Truth is the absolute standard, the standard of both what is absolutely true and what absolutely falsifies the truth. Truth, Jesus silently reveals to Pilate, is the standard no less for the exalted Roman than for the lowly Jew. If truth has always been in the world, then it has never been in the world. If truth has always been in the world, then it will have lain fatally hidden in the dark contradictions of natural space and time whose images reflect human ignorance and blindness. If truth has always been in the world, then its necessity will contradict its existence and its existence will contradict its necessity. The truth which has always been in the world, the truth which lies hidden in nature, is the law of contradiction whose finite logic is indistinguishable from the myth of the finite. That something (or some things) cannot both be and not be in the same space at the same time is fatally reflected in myth as ignorance of and blindness to the nature of its beginnings. Just as the law of contradiction is the first, indemonstrable principle of demonstration, of *logos*, so myth is the narrative structure, or *logos*, which remains ignorant of and blind to its own principles, its own beginnings. Aristotle's logic (in his *Organon*) is consistent with his *Poetics*. Just as syllogistic logic is endlessly concerned with the metamorphosis of terms, being powerless to establish, to demonstrate, its own premises or priorities, so the narrative of myth, mythical narrative, endlessly describes the metamorphoses of the images of natural space and time without beginning. Everything can and does turn into everything else, gods into humans, humans into plants and animals and even inanimate objects, and inanimate objects, plants and animals, and humans into each other and into gods. All pagan mythology operates in this fashion, from, for example, ancient Hinduism to Ovid's *Metamorphoses* to the pre-Columbian civilizations of the New World. But mythical metamorphosis, in knowing no beginning or end, reflects the law of contradiction by being ignorant of and blind to its own contradictions. The logic of contradiction blindly supplies the structure of the binary oppositions which shape pagan mythology, while mythical narrative ignorantly supplies the content, the indemonstrable beginnings or principles, of the law of contradiction.

The contradictory law dictating that no two persons can occupy the same space at the same time naturally generates opposition between them, with neither party being able to communicate (explain...demonstrate) why its occupation in a given space at a particular time takes precedence over the occupation of another. Precisely because the law of contradiction is the indemonstrable, first principle of life, of narrative, of the myths of space and time, every beginning is indemonstrable and contradicts every other beginning. Every party knows that for its occupation to be true (certain) the occupation of the other must be contradicted as untrue (uncertain). The occupation of the same space at the same time by two (or more) parties is possible only when one party rules over (or is ruled over by) the other. All pagan myth is based on the natural strife of elements, on the natural enmity between individuals modeled on Democritus' atoms whose blindness to and ignorance of the other are represented by the endless metamorphoses through which they inexorably pass. Truces, based on momentary or apparent equality between the opposing forces or on their mutual exhaustion, are common. One need but think of the ten-year Trojan War. But peace, the peaceable kingdom, is unimaginable within the natural strife of opposing elements occupying the same space and time. Nature provides no images of the lion lying down peaceably with the lamb. To use natural images to express, to communicate, to reveal truth as its own standard, the standard both of itself and the natural similes of space and time, involves metaphor, oxymoron, paradox... interpretation. Peace, as the absolute condition allowing human beings to occupy unconditionally, to share, the same space at the same time, without natural enmity or strife, is no less inconceivable than unimaginable within paganism.

To conceive of peace, to think (of) peace as the standard for all humans, is to employ not the syllogistic logic of contradiction, which always opposes one party to the other, but the dialectical logic of paradox, which unites both (all) parties within the priority of beginning with the principle of human right. Just as imagination, based on the natural images of space and time, fatally involves human beings in blind opposition to each other, so logic, based on the law of contradiction, always reflects ignorance of the other. There is a strict parallelism between the logic of contradiction and its reflection in natural similes which constitute the binary oppositions of myth. Both the law of contradiction and simile, the mirror image of each other, reflect their blindness to and ignorance of their indemonstrable beginnings. There is equally a strict parallelism between the logic of dialectic and its embodiment in metaphors which constitute the union of opposites within the absolute standard of truth. The logic of both dialectic and metaphor, each embodying truth as its own standard, provides the ground of demonstration, of principle, of beginning, of right. Whereas extra-biblical paganism reflects the relativism of natural images, in which, for my point of view to be right (true), I must contradict your point of view as wrong (false), the peaceable kingdom embodies the metaphor of relationship which is its own concept, the conception of necessary existence, the conception of existence which is necessary for all human beings and for which there is no analogue, no simile, no natural image in space and time. The peaceable kingdom is its own standard, its own absolute perspective, the perspective which saves the appearances, the images of space and time, by grounding them in history as the narrative revealing the truth of all. That all human beings are equally related to the truth, that all human beings belong to a common history, that all human beings occupy or share the same common space and time as history reveals the fundamental distinction between relationship and relativism. Relationship is its own standard, the standard of both what constitutes and what falsifies relationship, the standard both of relationship and relativism. Truth is relative—not to me or to you but to us: it establishes our relationship. Truth is that which constitutes our relatedness. Truth is our relationship. Truth as relationship is absolute, yet it is neither certain nor uncertain. Truth is historical, yet it is neither empiricist nor rationalist. Truth is the relationship of subjects, yet it is neither subjective (merely relative to the individual) nor objective (it does not involve objects as finite things in space and time). Truth is both necessary and existent. But it is neither logically necessary nor empirically existent. Truth is the relationship that for one position (party) to be true the position (party) opposite it must equally be true. Truth is dialectic, the dialectical relationship that one is true only if and as the other is true.

The dialectic of relationship that neither the one nor the other can be true within itself establishes the common space and time for all human beings as history. My space and time cannot be mine unless I recognize your space and time as equally yours. Different spaces and times either violate the law of contradictory logic or reveal the truth of dialectical logic. Truth as relationship involves the relationship of existence and necessity, their dialectic, such that each involves and expresses the other. For one to exist it is necessary for both to exist. For one to be necessary the existence of the other must be necessary. Neither existence nor necessity can be true unless both are equally true. The principle, the beginning, the origin of both existence and necessity is their relationship. Neither is prior to the other. Both existence and necessity, in their dialectical relation, come into existence, from non-existence, from nothing, necessarily. As soon as they exist, they must have been necessary. There is no first history in the nature of time and space. There is no way in which to arrive at that which is first within nature, except by ruling over that which is then viewed as secondary. That which is first, or prior, in history is always the paradox of relationship, that, as soon as it comes into existence, necessarily, it is historical. History always expresses the relationship of past, present, and future, each embodying the presence of relationship, the relationship of self and other, of thought and existence, of existence and necessity: I think, therefore, I am. The very necessity of history demands that it exist both prior to and posterior to its presence. The future of history always presupposes a historical past, while past history equally presupposes a historical future. It is only because history is not grounded in the contradictory images of natural space and time that it is both prior to and posterior to itself. History is, in Kant's paradoxical language, the *a priori* synthetic judgment, the prior judgment which has both a past and a future, the judgment whose priority it is to establish the synthesis of ends worthy of being human: the peaceable kingdom, or what Kant calls perpetual peace.

All peoples naturally have a past and a future. Plato certainly recalls today that some years ago he saw his master Socrates in the agora exposing the ideas brought forth by his eager, young interlocutors to contradiction and that tomorrow he will go to the Academy to meet his disciple Aristotle whose peripatetic way reflects cosmic contradiction as the god, the unmoved mover. But to claim to move others while denying that you are moved by others is to claim that your position in space and time is unmovable, opposed to the position in space and time of the other which, from your point of view, is moving, that is, moved by you. From your position the position opposed to yours is without its own *telos*, for it is you who, in moving the other, supply (you claim) the *telos* for it. It is little wonder, then, that the Greeks, and all extra-biblical peoples, logically understand time (including space as cosmic process) to be circular while mythically experiencing it as linear. The fatal circle which, in being unmoved by others, moves others is experienced by those who are moved by it as chance, as the fortuitous movement between past and future. Neither the past nor the future exists with necessity, for each is the contradictory opposite of the other. Existence is attached to the moving images of past and future, to the metamorphosis of endless generation and corruption, while necessity is attached to the immobile present, to that which does not change, to the immortal, the perfect, the finite, to the mover which, in moving others between past and future, remains unmoved by others in the immortal present. It is precisely the law of contradiction which, in claiming to move others between past and future, without being moved by others from its natural position (secretly hidden) in space and time, shows that past and future constantly contradict each other in their endless oppositions. The contradiction hidden within the recesses of extra-biblical logic is that, in identifying necessity and existence with natural space and time, it exposes as contradictory all appearances of past and future.

But to view past and future, not as linear, metamorphosing images which contradict an unmoving, eternal present whose closed circle is its own fatal secret, but as history, as historical presence, is to make truth its own standard. It is to imagine, to conceive of, all human beings as figures in one narrative whose principle of history, whose historical beginning, demonstrates that the whole of humanity begins with or moves from the conception of right true for all to the facts which presently contradict the necessary existence of humankind. History is the dialectical relationship that for the past or the future to be true both must be true. The past and the future can be true only in and through (as) the other. To view—to imagine and to conceive—the past as future and the future as past, to view the past and future as equally historical, is to recognize the paradox, the oxymoron, which is history. History is the relatedness of all human beings to a common space and time, to a community, which is true for all. When past and future contradict each other, as in the case of extra-biblical paganism, and when past and future are laden with lying, deception, hypocrisy, double standards, two masters, oppression..., as in the case of idolatry, then both past and future, if they are to be historically true for all human beings, will involve nothing less than the exposure of the law of contradiction to the light of revelation and the systematic overcoming of oppression and discrimination in light of truth as its own standard. History involves the future no less than the past. History is found equally in utopia, no place (in space and time), and in *topoi*, commonplaces (whose beginnings are hidden in space and time). The only thing upon which I want to insist at this point in my essay in thinking is the importance of distinguishing between the relationship of past and future as history, their reciprocity, their mediation, their dialectic, and the notions of past and future which, in their opposition, reflect the contradictory images of natural space and time.

Having earlier seen that truth as its own standard involves our comprehending truth as history, we now see that history involves the conception of relationship, the dialectic that for one position to be true the position opposite it, the other, must be equally true. History as relationship, the relationship of history, means that no one enjoys, by right, a natural privilege in space and time, that we are all equally related to truth as its own standard, the standard both of history and of what is not history. What is not historical is precisely a notion of a privileged past or future, a privileged space or time such that it contradicts the space and time of other positions. History is the relationship that for one position to be true the position opposite it must also be true. History is the common story establishing the mutual relationship of all in space and time. But the ground for common, or universal, relationship is not the space and time of nature, where my position ineluctably involves your contradictory opposition. The only common ground whereupon we are equally, freely, and communally related is history. The conception of truth as historical relationship involves the very structure of dialectic where for one to be true two must be true. Neither the one nor the other (nor any combination of ones or others) can be true either within itself or without itself. The very dialectic of self and other expresses truth as its own standard. Truth is its own standard, not for me, as such, and not for you, as such, but for us, when we recognize, embrace, and live the relationship that truth is my standard only insofar as it expresses your standard and that it is your standard only insofar as it involves my standard.

That truth constitutes the standard of relationship—the dialectic that for one to be true the other must be equally true—shows that relationship is what is absolutely true for all. Absolute truth is relationship, that all humans are equally, freely, and communally related to the truth. The absolute is historical, the relationship of past and future such that the present is common to all. The absolute is my relationship to the truth so long as it is equally your relationship to the truth. The absolute is no more to be identified with (or reduced to) certainty than relationship is to be identified with (or reduced to) uncertainty. Truth is its own absolute relationship precisely because it is neither certain nor uncertain. Insofar as certainty designates finite particularity—this or that particular item, to which one can point with certainty—it adheres to natural space and time and is subject to the logic of contradiction. But, insofar as certainty involves space and time, it is indistinguishable from uncertainty. What is certain from my perspective is always uncertain from the perspective opposed to it. Certainty (like uncertainty) oscillates between skepticism (empiricism) and dogmatism (rationalism), always contradicting its opposite but never revealing itself for what it is, except to one whose perspective is that of the absolute truth of relationship, for what it is is that it is blind to and ignorant of its own contradictions. To hold that one can be true only in and as—through—the other is to recognize that truth as its own absolute standard is neither certain nor uncertain. The person who is true (honest, just, fair, loving...) is not a certain individual relative to other certain individuals, their certainty being indistinguishable from their uncertainty. Rather, the person who is true... recognizes that one is related to the other, and the other to the one, in that absolute relationship which is true for all. Precisely because truth involves the relationship of persons, not a congeries of things in the space and time of nature, it is absolute for both, but never for the one in opposition to the other.

Although truth as its own absolute standard is never certain or uncertain, it is constantly falsified by becoming what is certain for me in opposition to what I judge to be your uncertainty. Truth is never certain or uncertain in itself, for it is its own standard, the absolute standard of both the truth and its falsifications. Truth is falsified, however, when I, in identifying truth with what is certain to me, reduce you to contradictory uncertainty, to uncertain contradiction. Truth is the relationship whereby both you and I—we—are the absolute standard. Truth is not certain or uncertain; it is not this certain thing opposed to that certain thing, which, in not possessing my certainty, is uncertain. But truth is constantly distorted, perverted, denied, enslaved... in becoming what is certain in opposition to what is (from the point of view of certainty) lacking in certainty, that is, to what is uncertain.

Just as absolute truth is the relationship in which both the one and the other are absolute, but neither certain nor uncertain, so absolute truth is always limited. The concept of absolute limit—the limit of the absolute—is unimaginable and inconceivable in paganism, for which both absolute and limit are viewed in terms of the images of natural space and time whose contradictions generate opposition between certainty and uncertainty. Absolute limit is the oxymoron whose dialectic holds that for one to be true the other must also and equally be true. The absolute is true only insofar as (its) limit is true. The limit is true only insofar as it is absolute. The absolute is truly limited only insofar as the limit is truly absolute. The absolute is truly limited to the absolute only insofar as the limit is absolutely its own limit. I indulge in this painful exercise of dialectical rhetoric (the rhetoric of dialectic) in order to free ourselves from the ingrained habits of thinking within the sterile opposition between certainty and uncertainty, within the standard dualistic modes of dogmatism and skepticism (rationalism and empiricism). The absolute is limited—absolute truth is its own limit—not because truth is to be understood either as an ideally certain goal for which we empirically strive, but which always remains beyond our uncertain or limited grasp, or as an ideally subjective (inner) certainty, whose full possession is limited by the (external) uncertainties of the body, the senses, politics, language.... Absolute truth is limited, absolute truth is our limit, precisely because it limits us—human beings—to the absolute. The only limit worthy of being human is limitation to the absolute. The only absolute worthy of being human is absolutely limited. The concept of truth as its own standard, the standard which is true for both you and me only insofar as it is equally true for us both, is absolutely limited to itself. It is the absolute limit of itself.

Absolute truth as its own limit expresses neither certain (or empirical) correspondence to something outside itself nor certain (or rational) coherence with something internal to itself, to recall the standard one-sided and dualistic conceptions of truth. The correspondence and coherence theories of truth are revealed by truth as its own historical standard of relationship to be self-contradictory, for they are unable either to limit themselves to the absolute or to view the absolute as their limit. The theory of empirical correspondence, in presupposing a relationship between one thing (the mind) and that which is opposed to it, an object in space and time, is always subject to Hume's contradictory law that whatever *is* may *not be*. The theory of rational coherence, in presupposing a relationship wherein the mind is identical with itself, is always subject to Leibniz' tautological law of identity that whatever is, is. Both, in failing to think through the relationship of existence and necessity such that each is the absolute limit of the other, blindly reflect the melancholy of living in the world of nature (custom) as the best of all possible human (natural) worlds, something simply inconceivable to Socrates and altogether unprincipled to Rousseau. With his correspondence theory, which shows that, because there is no certain correspondence between reason and the world, he is betwixt a false reason and no reason at all, Hume remains blindly dependent on the coherence of an uncertain world whose nature he ignorantly reflects as customary. With his coherence theory of the most certain of all possible worlds, Leibniz remains blindly dependent on his correspondence to an uncertain world whose customs he ignorantly reflects as natural. Although correspondence as the external standard of truth and coherence as the internal standard of truth are each championed, in opposition to the other, as the certain bulwark against skepticism and dogmatism, they ineluctably give way to their uncertain opposite. In finding that our correspondence to the external world involves the melancholy of being betwixt a false reason and no reason at all, we reflect the inner coherence of the best of all possible worlds.

Truth as its own standard, the standard whose absoluteness is limited to the dialectic that for one to be true the other (opposite it) must be equally true, both involves correspondence and expresses coherence. Neither correspondence nor coherence can be true unless both are true. Both correspondence and coherence are true as the absolute whose limit embodies the dialectic of correspondence and coherence. The relationship of absolute limit is such that my absolute must always involve your limit and your absolute must always express my limit. My absolute is limited by (to) you, and your absolute is limited by (to) me. My limit is your absolute, and your limit is my absolute. Absolute truth, the relationship which is absolute truth, is not founded on the images of natural space and time. Neither absolute nor limit corresponds to or coheres with space and time. But it is true that, although the correspondence and coherence expressive of absolute limit do not involve the natural images of space and time, human relationship as its own standard, the standard of both historical life and natural death, does recognize its absolute limit in nature, in death. Correspondence and coherence embody the eternal dialectic of history, whose absolute limit is nature. If the absolute limit has always been in the world, then it has never been in the world. If the absolute limit does not die, then it has always been dead (hidden in the pagan secret of the law of contradiction for which the only happy man is a dead man). We shall return to the problematic of death in later chapters, but here, in our introductory discussion, what we want to establish is the preliminary notion that truth as its own absolute standard, the relationship of human beings, entails the standard for, the relationship to, death. Truth as its own standard is the standard of both the living and the dead. Truth as history is the eternal calling of the dead to life. If life has always been in the world, then it has never been in the world: it has always been dead to life. The absolute limit of human relationship, such that for individuals to correspond to each other they must cohere together, involves their mutual recognition of death as the limit whose absolute (absolution) is life.

Truth as relationship embodies the dialectic that for either of two opposing positions to be true each must be true. Each must recognize the other as its absolute standard of truth, its limit to absolute truth. Truth is not relative either to me or to you. Truth is the relationship in and through which we are related in and to the truth, in and through which we are truthful in our relationships. Just as truth is not relative to one or the other of us, so truth as the relationship absolutely binding on the two of us is not an absolute thing for me to possess or an absolute space for me to occupy in opposition to your possession or occupation. The relationship that we both possess or occupy in the absolute is our limit, our limit to willing to do unto others as we would have them do unto us, our limit to and in the other. Our limit to the absolute other also involves our recognition that there is no proper analogue for the truth of relationship within the natural images of space and time whose oppositions are subject to the blind logic of contradiction. Truth as relationship embodies thinking whose imagination expresses not the images of natural space and time but the oxymoron of absolute limit and whose reason involves not the logic of contradiction but the dialectic of paradox. Truth is the relationship whose peaceable kingdom is constituted by those who recognize that for one to be true the other must be equally, freely, and communally true. Truth is the relationship whose absolute standard is the limit for all.

IV. CONCLUSION

When Pilate asks Jesus—what is truth?—he silently invokes the logic of contradiction whereby whatever Jesus says (or does) will be seen to oppose, to contradict, the rule of Caesar. From the certain position of imperial rule, the other as ruled is always shown to be the uncertain one whose spatial and temporal appearance is contradicted by the imperial one, the god who, in moving the other, is unmoved by the other. Pilate naturally expects Jesus to acknowledge the contradictory rule of his master, through reflecting ignorance of and blindness to the truth. It is naturally possible, Pilate recognizes, that Jesus will invert or reverse his relationship to the imperial heir of the Greek *polis* by imitating Socrates, who shows that at least he knows that he is ignorant of the truth of contradictory logic, unlike all rulers, be they rulers over others in politics (autocrats, whether tyrannical, oligarchic, or democratic), in rhetoric (sophists), or in mythology (poets). By appealing to the ruler-ruled logic of contradiction, whereby for me to be certain you must be shown to be uncertain, since it is unimaginable and inconceivable that two (or more) opposite positions could occupy the same space at the same time, Pilate silently acknowledges that imperial rule, rule over others, is doomed to reversal. The unmoving position of fate, which moves all others to their blind end, is always experienced by the individual as the wheel of fortune whose metamorphoses in natural space and time constantly involve the reversal of opposed positions. Precisely because you contradict that which is your opposite—for two cannot occupy the same space at the same time—you are no less contradicted by your opposite (from his point of view which is opposite to, which opposes, you). The law of contradiction is its own standard of contradiction, contradicting whatever appears in space and time. Pilate knows, in his fatal ignorance, that Caesar no less violates the law of contradiction than does Socrates.

Pilate is perplexed, however, when Jesus no more acknowledges the contradictory rule of Caesar than he contradicts imperial rule in the guise of Socratic ignorance. Having come to bear witness to the truth, to truth as its own standard, Jesus silently reveals to Pilate the truth that ruler and ruled, gentile and Jew, free individual and slave, male and female, self and other can be liberated from the contradictory logic of fate only when each of the opposites in such pairings recognizes that one can be true only insofar as both are true. Truth is its own standard, the standard—for all—of both what is true and what is false. Truth is history, the common space and time whose location is not in nature, which always divides human beings against each other, but in the peaceable kingdom whose dialectic of space and time as history unites beginning and end, alpha and omega. Truth is history only when past and future are so related that each is true only insofar as both are true as the presence in which all can dwell at peace. Truth is relationship, not my truth or your truth, but our truth whose history is our absolute limit.

Truth as its own standard is history, the relationship that comes into existence from nothing, from nothing that is naturally spatial or temporal. If truth as the relationship which is history has always been naturally in the world, then it has never been in the world. Truth, as historical relationship, is its own standard or ground. It adheres to the law of dialectical logic that for one to be true the other must be true. Truth does not adhere to the law of contradictory logic where for one to be true (certain) the other must be contradicted as untrue (uncertain). Truth is neither absolutely certain nor relatively uncertain. But truth, as the standard whose own relationship is history, is the absolute limit. As absolute limit truth is neither certain nor uncertain; it is neither dogmatic nor skeptical; it reflects neither correspondence with others nor coherence with itself. Truth as its own absolute limit shows that absolute and limit can be true only insofar as both are true. The identity which is absolute limit is grounded not in the contradictory images of natural space and time, where the truth of the one depends directly, that is blindly, on the falsity of the other, but in truth as the absolute standard to (and by) which all are limited. The nature of the identity uniting absolute and limit is the noncontradictory, if paradoxical, dialectic of arguing from right, whose relation to all is universal, to facts whose oscillation between the opposites of custom and nature contradict the necessary existence of being human. Truth is its own standard precisely because it bears the revelation that the relationship true for all is their common history.

2

The Structure of Interpretation

I. INTRODUCTION

Just as we outlined, in Chapter 1, basic elements constituting the concept of truth, in this chapter we want to complete our introduction to the dialectic of truth and interpretation by sketching the basic structure of interpretation. In the present, as in the previous, chapter, however, we shall not yet be confronting directly the dialectic of truth and interpretation, whereby truth involves interpretation and interpretation expresses truth, which is the subject to be taken up in Part II of our essay in thinking. Rather, here we want to reflect upon concepts central to interpretation as a propaedeutic to our later discussion. We want to show that interpretation—insofar as it is truthful—expresses a concept of identity or universality which involves three different notions of difference. First, there is the difference which is ignorant (or unconscious) of interpretation. This is the difference of the extra-biblical world which cannot account for its differences, where one difference is always opposed to and other than the difference over which it rules or by which it is ruled. This is the difference which cannot be interpreted. Second, there is the difference which acknowledges interpretation as its own standard. This is the difference of the Bible which recognizes that difference, in order to be different, must embrace interpretation as the standard of difference. Third, there is the difference which represses or denies interpretation. This is the difference of idolatry which falsely interprets other differences, the difference which reduces other differences to falsity. Interpretation, like truth, is its own standard, the standard both of interpretation and of what falsifies or is not interpretation. Interpretation sharply distinguishes itself from extra-biblical difference so that it can preserve the truth of difference from its idolatrous falsification.

If, like truth, interpretation as its own standard has always been in the world, then it has never been in the world. Interpretation is historical, for it comes into existence from nothing, from nothing which is natural in space and time. The interpretation of history is the history of interpretation. Like truth, interpretation expresses the dialectical relationship that for one position to be interpreted the position opposite it must equally be subject to interpretation. The structure of interpretation, like that of truth, is dialogue, in which one person interprets the other as that person wills to be interpreted by the other. Self and other, I and thou, reader and text, God and humankind, the relationship of persons, the covenant of the golden rule, love of neighbor, the social contract of democracy... all expressly involve the dialogue of interpretation. But interpretation as its own historical standard of dialogue, wherein for one difference to be true the difference opposite it must equally be true, involves both difference ignorant of interpretation—extra-biblical paganism—and difference which represses or suppresses the differences of others—idolatry. In order to provide a conception of interpretation whose standard is truth (and a conception of truth whose standard is interpretation) we must show that interpretation involves both ignorance of and denial of interpretation. In extra-biblical paganism there is no concept of, no will to, interpretation, while in idolatry the concept of interpretation is willfully denied.

Our desire in this essay in thinking is to show how critically important it is to comprehend interpretation (and truth) in the widest and deepest possible way. Our particular perspective involves the interpretation of texts, but the text, because it is structured by the dialectic of author and reader, self and other, is a metaphor simultaneously for the subject and the object of thinking: I think, therefore, I am. The text—reading, interpretation...—is not something given naturally or innately in space and time. The text does not reflect a neutral position, a positivist stance whose methods of verification and falsification are not subject to interpretation as its own standard. Interpretation, as we shall increasingly see, is ontological—theological—involving a comprehensive conception of aesthetics, ethics, and politics, a universal conception of human culture and society.

There is no alternative strategy of interpretation to Hegel's systematic demonstration (system of demonstration) that the concept is the content. The concept of life expresses and is expressed by the content of life. How a people conceives of itself—as determined through its texts, both cultural and social, both verbal and nonverbal, both personal and collective, both conscious and unconscious, embodying not only aesthetic ideals but also the matter of political economy—involves and expresses the content of its life. The concept is the content (the rational is the actual), and the content is the concept (the actual is the rational). Hegel's demonstration that Spirit, the identity of concept and content for a given people, means viewing all the possible social and cultural elements of their life within a structure of totality embodies two general principles of interpretation (truth). First, however divergent (trivial, irrelevant, aberrant or abhorrent...) the different manifestations of the society and culture of a given people may appear (to us) to be, we presuppose that all these differences are related to, that they express, the Spirit of that people as a whole. Second—and here the radical implications of Hegel's strategy of the interpretative explication of difference begin to emerge more clearly—the Spirit of a particular people's society and culture relates to, or expresses, the very Spirit of humanity. In order for the various peoples on earth to be different, in truth and interpretation, they must belong to, they must be part of, what Hegel calls world-historical Spirit. Difference, in order to be interpreted as different, must adhere to the identity of Spirit as its own standard. Hegel's notion of Spirit as the identity of concept and content indicates that there is nothing in human history which is not meaningful, nothing which cannot be interpreted, nothing which does not belong to Spirit, to the universal truth of world-historical Spirit.

The radical step which Freud appears to take beyond Hegel to the interpretation of dreams as the universal hermeneutic whose consciousness penetrates the differences common to the unconscious life of all humankind is actually not a new step at all. Rather, Freud deepens our recognition, consistent with Hegel, that there are no manifestations of human life, including repressed content expressed through dream fragments, which are not interpretable. Everything is meaningful—to Spirit. Nothing—in itself—is taboo. I invoke Freud in support of my general hermeneutical reflections for three reasons. First, Freud reminds us that the unconscious belongs to the structure of consciousness, that the irrational (repressed content resulting in neurosis) belongs to the rational, that libido (sexuality) belongs to love. If the client, who suffers from neurosis, is to do significant work with a therapist, dialogue must be established between them; and dialogue presupposes meaningful communication as the standard common to the two parties (although it does not guarantee its actuality). The very concept of neurosis or repression embodies the paradox that neurotic suffering, in waking and/or dream life, bespeaks a consciousness divided against, evading, or denying itself. How consciousness can be simultaneously conscious and not conscious of itself expresses both the miracle and the degradation of Spirit. What distinguishes neurosis from psychosis, in principle (however difficult it may be to articulate the difference in practice), is that the neurotic sufferer wills to comprehend his suffering, to liberate himself from neurotic compulsion, to become responsible for his unconscious, to render the repressed content of his life historical. He wills to make the lost content of his life a meaningful part of his history. The psychotic sufferer, in contrast, has lost his will of interpreting the disparate or divided (different or opposed) elements of his life within a meaningful story. It is we—spouse, family member, friend, therapist, lawyer, judge... society—not the one suffering psychosis, however, who can speak—sanely—about losing the will of interpretation. For, in bespeaking the loss of will, we presuppose that it can never be lost, in totality. The will to interpret is its own standard, the standard of both the will to interpret and the loss of the will to interpret. To paraphrase Lincoln's magisterial rule of interpretation: all of one's personality may be psychotic some of the time, and some of one's personality may be psychotic all of the time, but not all of one's personality can be psychotic all of the time. Interpretation is its own universal standard, the standard of both what is meaningful and what is not meaningful. What is not meaningful in itself belongs, therefore, to the standard of interpretation.

Freud also reminds us, secondly, that any proper concept of Spirit (for example, Hegel's) as the totality or the identity of concept and content, involves the unconscious, the irrational, the unfree, the neurotic, the unhistorical, all the content which is repressed through the structures of false consciousness and bad faith. Marx's concept of false consciousness presupposes a concept of consciousness which overcomes its own deceptions, and Sartre's concept of bad faith presupposes a concept of faith which comprehends its own sinfulness. Hegel's dialectical notion (argument) that the rational is the actual and the actual is the rational—that neither the rational nor the actual can be true unless both are true, without any hierarchical dependence of one on the other—does not mean that the identity of rationality and actuality, of concept and content, is given immediately in our lives. Rather, their identity is the project of Spirit, the task of humankind. We must constantly strive to make the rational actual—to think our necessity as existing—and to make the actual rational—to think our existence as necessary. A radically Hegelian interpretation of Freud would bring to mind the fact that our task is not only to render the unconscious conscious but equally to render the conscious unconscious. Hegel shows us that the conscious must become other than it is, in actuality, if it is to become what, in truth, it is, if it is actually to become true to its concept.

The third reason for invoking Freud, in the present prolegomenon to our introductory discussion of interpretation, is to remark briefly on the implications of his interpretative stance that nothing (in itself) is taboo. That nothing is taboo, that there is nothing which is other than Spirit, that everything belongs to Spirit recapitulates the biblical position that there is nothing idolatrous in itself, that idols are not created in the spirit of God. To hold that there is nothing for Spirit which is taboo is to hear, in the spirit of Abraham, the call of interpretation, the call which provides the key of interpretation to the dreams of humankind by locating their fragments within a universal history of meaning, and to respond: Here I am, therefore, I think, I interpret.... To recognize that there are no taboos is to recognize that the taboos of paganism have been revealed in the light of truth as the innate secrets naturally hidden within space and time and fatally subject to the law of contradiction. To recognize that there are no taboos is both to declare one's independence from paganism and to acknowledge the eternal task of interpretation, which is ever to overcome the idols, the taboos, the repressions of spirit. To recognize that nothing is taboo is to acknowledge the enormous role that taboos or idols (repressions, reifications, ideologies, mythologies...) play in our life. It is to acknowledge that, although for Spirit, there is nothing idolatrous in itself (for that is the non-interpretative way of extra-biblical paganism), we humans, in our neurotic compulsions, constantly deny our freedom through the worship of idols (enslavement to taboos). Freud shows us that all the elements of personal psychology, however disparate or even abhorrent their apparent differences may be, truly belong to the total structure of personality, just as Hegel shows us that all the elements of what we may call a historical psychology, however disparate or even abhorrent their apparent differences may be, truly belong to the total structure of Spirit. Freud equally shows us (even if he was not fully conscious of the fact) that the interpretative strategy whereby the Spirit of the individual is interpretable only as a totality presupposes the concept of person as its own standard, the standard both of itself and of its taboos. For one person to be analyzed, all persons must be analyzable. For one person to be interpreted, all persons must be interpretable. Freud's interpretative stance, like Hegel's, is universal; it claims universal applicability; it denies that there is anything hidden or innate which is not accessible to interpretation; it shows that there is no taboo which cannot be revealed in the light of the interpretation of human dreams.

I conjoin Freud and Hegel, in these brief remarks introducing interpretation, to indicate that interpretation knows no bounds or limits—for everything is revealed in the light of its truth—except that which knows no interpretation. I equally conjoin them to suggest that any proper notion of interpretation, in being its own universal standard, the standard of equally what is interpretation and what is not interpretation, must embrace both the rational and the irrational, both the conscious and the unconscious (it being understood that how this relationship is to be conceived must be carefully articulated). Interpretation as its own standard is the absolute limit. In being absolutely limited to that which can be interpreted, interpretation must be carefully delimited from both that which is ignorant of interpretation and from that which represses or denies (enslaves) interpretation. The notion that interpretation is its own standard, the standard of both interpretation and what is not interpretation, involves, therefore, the two notions of (1) ignorance of interpretation and (2) repression (denial) of interpretation. The second notion, repression of interpretation, belongs to interpretation as sin belongs to faith, irrationality (error) to reason, the unconscious to (self-) consciousness, and idolatry (taboo) to revelation. But here in this chapter we shall be primarily concerned with the difference between interpretation and that which is ignorant of and blind to interpretation, as in our introductory chapter on truth we were primarily concerned with the difference between Jesus and Pilate, between truth as the revelation binding on all humankind and extra-biblical blindness to truth. Interpretation, like thinking (feeling, being...), tends for us to become so habitual, so ingrained, so innate that we fail to recognize—we forget—that it is not given in the nature of things, in natural space and time, but must, like thinking, like love, be learned. Interpretation involves learning, education, thinking, practice, loving... for which interpretation is its own standard. But to comprehend interpretation as its own standard means that we have to grasp the paradox—what Kierkegaard calls the sword whose two-edged blade is without a hilt—that, insofar as Spirit (person or people) views itself as natural, as founded on the in-demonstrable logic of contradiction, it is without interpretation and cannot be interpreted. The two-edged blade of paradox cuts in two directions. It shows not only that interpretation as its own absolute limit is limited to the absolute standard of interpretation but also that it must recognize its own absolute limit. The limit of interpretation is that which is ignorant of and blind to interpretation. To wield the paradoxical sword of interpretation is not to cut the Gordian knot, making the finite yield to a superior, finite force, but to experience the pain of being unable to penetrate that which has no conception of interpretation. Once again, we undertake to expose the fundamental difference between the dialectical structure of interpreta-tion and the doctrine of opposites shaping extra-biblical paganism so that we shall then be in a position to distinguish between interpretation and that which is not interpretation. What is not interpretation involves two ut-terly different notions—ignorance and sin (repression), the doctrine of op-posites and dualism, extra-biblical paganism and idolatry; and, until and unless we truly distinguish, once and for all, between ignorance of inter-pretation (extra-biblical paganism) and interpretation as the revelation in-volving all humankind, we shall have no way of truly interpreting the dreams of humankind as the phenomenology of spirit overcoming its repressions as taboos.

We shall organize these introductory reflections on interpretation around three critical distinctions: (1) the distinction between simile and metaphor; (2) the distinction between contradiction and paradox; and (3) the distinction between language and communication. We emphasize, once again, that the critical distinction, the distinction that brings our thinking into crisis, is ultimately the distinction, not between the metaphor of spirit and simile as the image of nature, as such, but between metaphor as its own standard and that which undertakes to repress, deny, subvert, or enslave metaphor to a standard other than itself. As always, our polemic is against not simile, contradiction, and language, as found within extra-biblical paganism, but against the idolatry of spirit both in failing to distinguish critically between simile and metaphor, between contradiction and paradox, and between language and communication, and in undertaking to subvert the spirit of interpretation by reducing metaphor to simile, paradox to contradiction, and communication to language. The terms which we use in making critically conceptual distinctions are not, in themselves, important. But, in order to make critical distinctions, the discriminations which make all the critical difference between interpretation and its subversions, we must carefully distinguish between terms and concepts (or their equivalents). We think in terms, but thinking involves and expresses concepts. We communicate in words, but communication involves and is expressed through sentences whose standard is truth and interpretation, not proper grammar and syntax. The natural order of grammar and syntax is subject to the law of contradiction, but the meaning of a sentence involves interpretation and expresses truth. Sentences which communicate (the truth) and which possess a structure of interpretation owe their meaning to their conceptual framework, not to their terms. Thinking involves concepts expressed in sentences, which, although they need not involve grammatical or syntactical closure (perfection) or even words in order to express meaning, must embody communication, what the Bible conceives of as the Word become covenant, the flesh of humankind. The concept—of truth and interpretation: thinking—is its own standard, the standard both of itself and of the words or terms in and through which it is expressed. Our terms or words are subject to the logic of contradiction, for two terms or words cannot occupy the same space in a sentence at the same time. But our thinking, our communication, our concept adheres to truth and interpretation as their own standard. We undertake here to distinguish critically between interpretation as its own standard and that which is ignorant of the standard of interpretation—between metaphor and simile, paradox and contradiction, and communication and language—so that we shall be able to face the crisis which interpretation as its own standard creates by distinguishing between the truth of its interpretations and its taboos.

II. SIMILE AND METAPHOR

When Pilate undertakes to confute Jesus, who tells the emperor's representative that he comes to bear witness to the truth, with the question, what is truth?, we ourselves are present at the confrontation between simile and metaphor (as between contradiction and paradox and between language and communication). It is the confrontation between imperial likeness and biblical identity, between similitude and bearing witness to that which translates you into, which carries you across the gap separating you from, the standard of your own identity (*meta-pherein*, like *transferre*, means to bear or to carry across). For Pilate, as for Socrates and the entire tradition of extra-biblical paganism, questions seeking to know what something is, questions asking for the identity of an individual (thing)—what is truth? what is virtue? what is justice? who is the wisest man in Greece? what is the cause of the plague ravaging Thebes? who is the god Dionysus? what causes things to change? what is the end of life? what brings things to their end?—are questions seeking to establish the nature or substance, the end (*telos*), the finitude, perfection, and immortality of a thing. But what is important to observe is that teleological questions always involve both questioner and respondent in comparisons, likenesses, or similitudes, in similes. Seeking to fix Jesus' identity through simile, Pilate is perplexed by Jesus' silently bearing witness to metaphor as the identity transferring him to a kingdom which is the standard of both his and Caesar's identity. For Pilate, his end, the end of Jesus, the end of all those subject to imperial rule lies beyond each and every one of them in the emperor. The identity of anything, what anything is, can only be established by its end; but the end of what something is always rests on comparison with something else which lies either outside itself (as in the case of political rule over others) or inside itself (as in the case of the self's rule over itself, as we see, for example, in Socrates and his heirs the Epicureans, skeptics, and Stoics).

But Pilate also knows—and this, too, is part of his perplexity before Jesus—that the end of Caesar is not his own identity, that the end of Caesar, the end of the Roman Empire, even the end of extra-biblical paganism itself (we could say on Pilate's behalf) lies outside (or inside) itself. The end, the nature, the substance of anything, that which defines it, that which brings it to its end, that which shows it to be finite, immortal, perfect, unchanging, and one, is always a likeness or comparison with something without (or within) itself. To seek one's end always involves one in comparisons, in similes, that demonstrate, with the inexorable logic of contradiction, that one is in opposition to one's end, that one's end is in opposition to oneself. To seek your end is always to be like, and thus not to be (like), your end. To be identical with your end, to bring all comparisons, all similes, to their end in nature, is to be dead to all comparisons. Count no man happy until he is beyond all comparisons, until he is dead to all similes. The incomparable individual, the nonpareil, is he who is either god or monster, as Socrates says about himself, but not a human being. To be human is to find yourself imprisoned within corporeal similitudes, appearances which are always like something else but never like, that is, never identical with, themselves. Pilate knows that ultimately even Caesar, the Roman Empire itself, has an end whose likeness will never be known, whose simile will always remain other than and opposed to itself. The ultimate simile in extra-biblical paganism is ineluctable fate, that which, known in itself as finite, as immortal, is knowable only relative to or compared with us mortals in the infinite appearances of simile.

Simile, in the classical sense, is not merely a category of rhetoric, as if the rhetoric we use does not embody the content of our lives. Simile reflects, in precise fashion, the kind of identity, the conception of identity, which structures Roman and Greek life, as it does the life of all extra-biblical peoples. Simile bespeaks the nature of identity of the individual, of all individuals (and thus of all collectivities of individuals, for example, the *polis*), whether the individual is thing, animate object, human being, or god. Given the metamorphosis, within extra-biblical paganism, of all things (both inanimate and animate), human beings, and gods into each other, their complete interchangeability, we are indeed led to see that the differences separating things, human beings, and gods are themselves but similes whose identity is yet other similes. The regress of finite similes into an impenetrable past and the progress of finite similes into an impenetrable future are infinite. Oedipus seeks to learn the cause of the plague devastating Thebes, only to discover that his end (as king) lies in a beginning prior to his birth and that his beginning (as god) lies in an end posterior to his death. Compared to the gods whose fate blinds him to his beginning (and against whom, in the end, he rails as a blind exile), Oedipus is an incestuous parricide. Compared to the man whose fatal secret is his reception in the end by the gods (who, in the beginning, had fated him to his end), Oedipus vanishes from mortal sight: he is immortal

god. Simile is not only a figure of speech, although naturally it is that.
Simile bespeaks the very figure, the figuration in terms of which individuals, all individuals, view themselves in the totality of their manifestations. Oedipus reflects the very structure of simile. He is always other
than, or opposed to, himself, always other than what he is in himself. What
he is in himself is always simile, a likeness buried in an impenetrable past
and projected into an unforeseeable future. As mortal man he is abhorrent
to the gods. As immortal god, he is unknown to humans. The secret of his
immortal end is reflected in the secret of his beginning, that he is fated to
murder his father and to sleep with and to have children by his mother.

Simile—as individual likeness which is always other than or opposed to, the opposite of, itself—reflects, as we have indicated, the very
structure of fate. Just as simile, as finite comparison, reflects without exception a teleological notion of reality, so simile, as the figure through and in
which individuals view their identity, is fatalistic in structure. Simile, *telos*,
and fate are inextricably bound together in the cultures of all extra-biblical
peoples, from both so-called primitive cultures and the great civilizations
of Asia to the sophisticated culture of the Greeks. Extra-biblical peoples
live by what I call the doctrine of finite opposites, whose cultural con-
figurations ramify in infinitely diverse similes. This diversity characteristically confuses both academic anthropologists, including those who
seek to ground this diversity within some notion of the universally human,
and professional students of comparative religion, especially those who, in
acknowledging their own biblical origins, desire to free their study from
ethnocentric bias. The diversity of human culture, the diversity of the
dreams by which human beings conjure up their identities, typically confuses even those students of anthropology and comparative religion who
are right to seek for what is universally human and properly want to
liberate their studies from ethnocentric bias, precisely because this diversity is based on the doctrine of opposites whose appearances are always
similes.

Comprehension of diversity or difference defeats even the best-in-
tentioned anthropologists and comparative religionists for two reasons, in
addition to the enormous discipline required to obtain accurate knowledge
of human cultures whose diversity is both highly complex and extremely
subtle in its endless manifestations. First, the fact that binary oppositions
constitute extra-biblical cultures means that their diversity ramifies end-

lessly. The attempt by scholars to find some universal constant within this binary opposition is vain. Second, what scholarly students of culture fail to understand is that the doctrine of opposites, according to which extra-biblical cultures are endlessly other than and opposed to themselves, cannot be grasped from within the doctrine of opposites, which fatally condemns its adherents to blindness and ignorance (and their modern students to methodological confusion), for it can be comprehended only from the point of view of what I am calling here in my essay in thinking the dialectic of truth and interpretation. It is precisely because a given culture, whose binary opposites rest on simile, *telos*, and fate, is both infinitely open to finite change—by becoming yet again opposite to itself—and yet never changes infinitely—for it remains bound to the doctrine of opposites—that it is impossible to understand it on its own terms. The primary (primitive!) rule of cultural hermeneutics, of interpretation, is that that which does not (cannot) comprehend or interpret itself cannot, as such, be comprehended or interpreted by another. Extra-biblical cultures never claim to comprehend (or to interpret) themselves (or others). But this ignorance of and blindness to fate, based on a *telos* whose similes are constantly other than or opposed to it, are practically impossible for professional students of culture to comprehend (or to interpret), for they fail to distinguish between the ignorance of interpretation (on the part of the culture which they are studying) and the interpretation of ignorance (on their part), with the result that, in conflating both, they understand neither the culture they are studying nor themselves, neither the ignorance of the culture being studied nor their own ignorance.

We may think, for example, of the Aztecs who, when they are confronted with something new, with the appearance, from the east, of white men (in 1519 C. E.), are increasing the frenzy with which they are ripping the hearts out of living maidens as sacrifice to their blood-thirsty gods, thus guaranteeing their certain immortality (which otherwise seems uncertain). The Aztecs characteristically assimilate the different (the unknown white men) to the same, to a likeness, which, as unknown, as gods, demands new human sacrifice. But these white gods, who appear in the guise, it turns out, of bloody-minded *conquistadores*, bring with them a god and his virginal mother (of whom, by the way, he is also the father—as the son of god he is also the father of both himself and his mother—thus placing in question the notion that human culture is universally based on the taboo against incest) who demand that human sacrifice based on divine simile be replaced by divine sacrifice based on human metaphor.

To be like gods who, themselves, are imagined to be like finite nature in its self-opposition as both generator and destroyer, is always to find yourself opposed to and by the end whose likeness you seek. The demand of the god whose end is a simile providing an identity fatally opposed to your own is completely different from the paradoxical command of the god of the New World conquerors to become like god knowing good and evil, knowing that metaphor is its own standard, the standard both of itself and of its endless ramifications in simile. Because simile is always based on an end which is immediately beyond (or immediately identical with) it and because that end is itself always but another likeness whose end can never be identified except through still another simile, the demand for yet more sacrifices (including the sacrifice of human beings), in the vain and thus frenzied attempt to close the gap between simile and that which it is like, is endless.

The Socratic diagnosis of the contradiction involved in all seeking of likeness—in simile—applies universally to extra-biblical paganism. Precisely because the end which simile seeks is itself subject to the doctrine of opposites, to the logic of contradiction, it is always itself its own blind, ignorant, opposition: it is opposed to itself. Everything which is simile divides into that which is knowable relative to us and into that which is knowable in (that is, relative to) itself. Either it is like something else (the seeking of which is always in vain); or it is like itself (the seeking of which is equally in vain). In either case, because it involves infinite regress (which is indistinguishable from infinite progress: the infinite repetition of the finite), it is incomprehensible, for knowledge of it is itself likeness, demanding yet more similes. Socratic ignorance is the blind recognition that divine oracles, whether of the external Apollo or of the internal *daimon*, always appear in similes: they are both like and not like themselves simultaneously, thus subjecting the recipient of the oracular message to the logic of contradiction, to a life whose contradictions in and through simile only reach their end (reach their only end) in death. The sole end to the blind repetition of similes is death, sacrifice to the god, for the only happy individual, the one possessing *eudaimonia,* a good *daimon* (or god), is the one who is dead to similes, who has himself become a likeness, a sacrifice, unto the god. To be like the god is either to be a living contradiction, in opposition to the god, or to be the death of contradiction, a sacrifice to the god. Ultimately, however, even the dead themselves do not remain dead, for they can attain their end only in a likeness which itself is subject to the contradictory doctrine of opposites. They continue to haunt the living with the contradictory demands of sacrificial simile. Human sacrifice to the likeness of the god, to the god of likeness, is never ending.

Simile, in reflecting the doctrine of opposites, is always changing, for there is nothing opposed to itself of which it is not a simile. There is nothing of which it is not like, except itself and all others. Thus simile, in constantly passing through the cycle of generation and destruction, is unchanging; it cannot conceive of any change which is not its opposite. It is unable to conceive of itself as changing, for it is endlessly like and thus endlessly unlike itself, opposed to itself. Its end is always its fatal opposition, demanding its sacrifice. Simile is always subject to the god as the unmoved mover, the likeness which, in viewing all others in its likeness, denies that it is like any other. But, since all beings (mortal and immortal, animate and inanimate) possess souls based on the notion of moving others while not being moved by others, they are all similes which, in denying likeness to others, view others in their own likeness. Change, therefore, is always other than, opposed to, or different from myself. Change is always what happens to you, over whom I rule, not to myself, who rule over (move) you. Change is always the state of those who are ruled, of those who are opposed to or other than their end. Change is always destructive, reflecting time in the simile of the scythe cutting down the field of grain (not embodying time in the metaphor of fulfillment through the harvest of souls). But, just as human identity is understood in terms of the simile between rulers and ruled—so Caesar's identity is constituted by his rule over the diverse peoples of the Roman Empire, including the Jews—human beings are themselves subject to rule by those who are other than themselves, by the gods. The gods, like their human likenesses, are envisaged as unmoved movers, the simile which, in thinking only itself as like itself, subjects humans to a fatal end which is opposed to them, by which they are moved, and which they never move, notwithstanding, indeed, precisely because of, the unending sacrifice they are blindly moved to provide. Thus the Aztecs attempt to accommodate themselves to their changed situation by assimilating the white men from the east to gods who never change in their demand of human sacrifice. They have no way of imagining or conceptualizing change such that the newly arrived Spaniards can be viewed neither as human beings to be ruled over nor as gods by whom to be ruled. The changed situation for them is but another simile demanding unchanging human sacrifice.

Simile is always incomprehensible to (in) itself, for, in being like another (the god), it is always opposed to and by the god; and, in being like itself, it finds itself in opposition to itself. To seek knowledge whose likeness is simile is always to seek what you do not know and thus to seek in vain, to be ignorant of what you are seeking. Simile is the contradiction which is its own secret, the thing-in-itself, which is known only in its finite and thus contradictory likenesses. As thought thinking itself, as the unmoved mover, the thing-in-itself is known only in its similes which, because they are like and thus not like what they are in themselves, fatally contradict the thing-in-itself. Thus similes constantly show themselves to be contradictory, for that which they are like, the thing-in-itself, or their *telos*, is always that which they are unlike. Similes thus reflect Socratic ignorance of and Oedipal blindness to their own end. They are incomprehensible in and to themselves, and, because they are incomprehensible in and to themselves, they will always remain incomprehensible to us, to us modern students of extra-biblical cultures who are zealous to probe the most mysterious, the uncanniest, the most contradictory, the most profoundly occluded of human arcana. But there's the rub. What is eclipsed by its own simile to the sun (as the god), what is blinded by seeking knowledge in the likeness of natural light which is always fatally other than what it is in itself, for it is no less darkness than it is light, is, although always predictable, never comprehensible.

Similes are comprehensible neither to those who generate (and who are destroyed by) them nor to modern scholars who study them. More precisely, because similes are incomprehensible to and for those who generate them, and who are equally destroyed by them, they must remain incomprehensible to us. Otherwise, we shall find ourselves turning similes into idols, something unthinkable to extra-biblical pagans (and a theme which we shall not take up comprehensively until Part II of our essay in thinking). Life—culture and society—based on simile has no conception of interpretation and no idea of the image which is central to interpretation, which is metaphor, the image which eschews all claims to be like natural images based on space and time. Where there is simile, interpretation is absent. Where there is metaphor, interpretation is present. When interpretation is absent, simile is always present; when interpretation is present, metaphor is never absent. These juxtapositions, however jejune, will be useful if they serve our present purpose, which is that of riveting attention on the subject of this essay, thinking as the dialectic of truth and interpretation. Interpretation is always found in its metaphors; and metaphors, like similes, represent, it is true, things-in-themselves, but, unlike similes, what metaphors are in themselves is not to be sought in or to be identified with the natural likenesses of space and time.

Metaphor in modern (that is, biblical) times is known under many names and can be descried under many guises. Particularly beguiling is Kant's presentation of metaphor as the *ding-an-sich*, the thing-in-itself. Few, if any, of the successors to Kant's critique of pure reason are prepared, however, to recognize the thing-in-itself as metaphor, given their ingrained habit of opposing, in dualistic fashion, truth (philosophy) and interpretation (metaphor), thus leaving entrenched the dualistic opposition between philosophy and art, which itself but reflects the inveterate dualism between philosophy (reason) and religion (faith). But it is precisely Kant's recognition of a third faculty of mind—reason—as simultaneously the ground, the principle (beginning), the appropriation (end), the culmination, and the mediation of the two faculties of mind known to the Greeks, as to all extra-biblical pagans, sensibility (immediate sensation: body) and understanding (immediate cognition: soul), which leads him to posit the thing-in-itself as the subject (the metaphor) of reason. Although Kant, like Hegel or even Kierkegaard and Nietzsche, is not altogether clear (or is not clearly willing to admit) that this third category of mind is absent from or unknown to the Greek (extra-biblical) world, he recognizes the utter futility of seeking to identify reason with objects either as they are known in space and time (the proper realm of natural science) or as they are known outside space and time (sheer illusion). Either similes belong to the objective science of natural appearance—what things are like in their appearances but not in themselves. Or they vanish into sheer illusion—what things are like in themselves apart from their appearances in natural space and time. Reason recognizes that what things are in themselves can never be rationally construed in terms of natural similes. Similes belong to natural science or to illusion, while reason itself is metaphor, that identity with itself which can never be constituted on the basis of objective knowledge of things.

Kant demonstrates that the only way in which we can overcome the dualisms of Hume and Leibniz, those of skepticism (empiricism) and dogmatism (rationalism), is to show both that they involve the attempt to reduce the thing-in-itself to a natural object either known in space and time (empiricism) or known outside space and time (rationalism) and that this attempt is always destructive of the very end which it seeks to attain. What is arresting about Kant's demonstration is that it shows us that it is the very structure of simile which is reflected in the vain attempt to reduce the thing-in-itself to an object either natural or supernatural. To claim to know something in itself as an object either natural or supernatural is always to find yourself reflected in its likeness and thus to be eternally opposed to (by) it. To claim to know an object either natural or supernatural in itself means either that its image is reflected in me or that I am reflected in its image. Either its image is myself (its object) or I am myself its object (its image). Kant thus explicates philosophically the revolution which Copernicus initiates by showing that, just as Copernicus denies the likeness between the celestial spheres (including the earth) and their appearances, so we must equally show, against all common sense (based on Aristotle's cosmology), that, instead of viewing the celestial spheres as objects circulating around us, we must view ourselves (the thing-in-itself) as circulating around the objects as appearances in natural space and time. It is precisely the simile between the (inferior or ruled) earth and the (superior or ruling) sun, between the changing earth and the immortal cosmos, which Copernicus implicitly rejects in his astronomy and which Kant (in systematizing the work of his predecessors in the early modern period) then explicates as the critique of pure reason.

In contrast to the cliché still beloved by textbook accounts in their continuing bias towards Aristotelian common sense—according to which Copernicus introduces modernism by displacing man from the center of the universe—Kant sees that the truth of the Copernican revolution, of the very idea of modern revolution, is the replacement of simile by metaphor, the replacement of the natural (geometrical) circle forever oblivious of its beginnings and ends by the human circle incorporating the beginning and ends of reality. Kant shows that the center of the universe is not to be comprehended according to the similes of natural space and time. Our opposition to Aristotle does not lead us to conclude that the center of our planetary system, what we today call the solar system, is the sun, except in appearance. The replacement of geocentric cosmology by heliocentric science is not the replacement of one cosmic hypothesis or simile by another. It is, rather, a revolutionary change, transforming our understanding from simile to metaphor. The center of the universe is no longer that which we see, by analogy (simile) with the objects seen. The center of the universe is that by which we see, that according to which we interpret. That by which we see is not the sun, reflecting, in its opposition to us, our dark ignorance, but human self-consciousness: I think, therefore, I am. The center of the universe is metaphor, the thing-in-itself, reason, the human being, human practice as willing the good universally true for all.

The Greek notion of center, the Delphic omphalos, endlessly reflects human beings as ruled by that which they are like, the cosmos—the sun (Plato), the unmoved mover (Aristotle)...—and thus ultimately by that which they are unlike, by that which is other than and opposed to them as human beings. To be the center, to be like the cosmos, is always, with Socrates, to find that it is better to suffer evil (from others: the cosmos) than to do evil to others (the cosmos). The center is always outside (inside) itself and thus fatally opposed to itself. The Greek notion of center reflects the structure of simile based on direct (immediate) comparison with the nature (end) of things, with natural space and time. For something to be like something always reflects its fatal unlikeness, its ignorance of its likeness, its blindness to that with which it is compared. The ruler-ruled structure of simile, reflecting the doctrine of opposites, the endless opposition between like and unlike, between generation and destruction, has its fatal end in the unmoved mover—perfect, circular motion—which, unmoved in itself, moves the erring planets (*planetai*: wanderers) blindly and ignorantly to their immortal end.

The secret of this unmoved movement, based on the similes of the nature of things, whereby the mortal (like Oedipus) vanishes into the immortal, notwithstanding the fact that one cannot step even once into the same (unmoving) stream of life, is revealed by Copernicus and his successors for the blind simile it is. The secret of simile revealed is metaphor, the comprehension of motion, the understanding that the moving power of the universe is not itself, which, in comparison with itself, is always other than and thus a secret to itself, but what Kant calls rational will (the will of God and human beings). Kant demonstrates in *The Critique of Pure Reason* and in its completion and fulfillment, *The Critique of Practical Reason*, that the Ar-

chimedean lever by which the universe is moved cannot be identified with
the universe itself, with an unmoved mover which, as its own finite end, is
fatally blind to and ignorant of itself as simile. Kant demonstrates that it is
human reason as practice, as will whose ground is freedom, which is the
motive power of universal reality. Reason is in truth practical when it
revolts against enslavement to all powers, whether scientific or political,
which maintain their authority on the basis of a hierarchy of nature as constituted by the ruler-ruled simile: rulers who are like the ruled in being opposed to them. There is no simile in nature which reveals the equality,
freedom, and solidarity of the moving powers of the universe, which are
all human beings. Revolution is not perfectly or immortally circular motion, ruling over the irregular appearances of others. Revolution, rather, is
the radical replacement of simile as a naturally known center with
metaphor as a freely willed center.

It is not enough to save the appearances, to formulate hypotheses
which explain the observable (mathematically quantifiable) appearances of
nature but do not transform the categories of human life. When Newton
exclaims—in opposition to hypotheses which are repetitively generated, he
finds, not to explain natural phenomena but to save dogmas whose
desuetude has already been amply demonstrated—*hypotheses non fingo*, he
properly recognizes that natural science is not an enterprise whose appearances and hypotheses are based on unreal fictions. What Newton fails
to recognize, however, is that, for the hypothetical reality of natural science
(simile) to be truly distinguished from unreal fiction (illusion), it must be
shown to rest on the categorical, the metaphorical, reality of the thing-in-itself. What Kant demonstrates through his critique of pure reason is that we
can properly claim our scientific hypotheses to be not hypothetical (illusory) fictions but real similes only if we distinguish categorically between
the motions of natural appearances and the motives of human beings, between nature and freedom, between natural objects and human subjects,
between what Rousseau calls fact and right. If scientific hypotheses are not
to be mere fictions saving the appearances of nature from one likeness as
opposed to another, they must be shown to presuppose the critique of
natural objects as similes. Kant demonstrates that, if we are to obtain reliably certain knowledge of nature, a critical distinction must be made between
knowing things-in-themselves as objects of possible appearance, the objects
of scientific explanation, and willing or thinking things-in-themselves as

human beings, the subjects who collectively constitute the kingdom of ends. Kant shows that only if we distinguish systematically between knowing objects as natural appearances and thinking (willing) subjects whose unique object is universal freedom for all can we obtain objectively certain knowledge, knowledge of natural objects, which does not collapse into either one-sided skepticism or one-sided dogmatism. The center of nature is not the Delphic omphalos whose reflection in the cosmic motion of the unmoved mover fatally reduces human beings to knowledge of similes which are, in their likeness to their natural end, always unlike and opposed to their nature. The center of nature is human freedom—the freedom to think and to will; it is the metaphor of the thing-in-itself binding human beings within the kingdom of ends. Kant shows that the hypothetical appearances of nature can be saved from vanishing into illusion only if they are grounded in the metaphoric center of humanity. Nature is real, as appearance (as distinct from illusion), only if it is centered in the metaphoric reality of the thing-in-itself which, although it is known as the objects of possible appearance, must be willed as the practice of actual human subjects in order to be made real, truly metaphoric.

Whereas, in the extra-biblical world of the Greeks, the doctrine of opposites involves the unending oscillation between the one and the many, ruler and ruled, reality and appearance, the unmoved and the moved, immortal (soul or *nous*) and mortal (body), new stakes appear in the modern (biblical) world. In finding himself betwixt a false reason and no reason at all, Hume, as we have seen, generates a dualism unthinkable to Plato and Aristotle, as to all extra-biblical paganism. Kant shows that unless we ground nature in freedom, the appearances of natural space and time in human practice (the thinking and willing of subjects as things-in-themselves as distinct from knowing objects as possible appearance), then not only scientific knowledge but also the freedom of human beings to think and to will become indistinguishable from illusion, whose biblical name is idolatry and which is unknown to extra-biblical paganism. Kant recognizes that, unless we limit scientific knowledge to objects of possible (natural) experience, we shall have to give up both natural science and human freedom. The critique of pure reason emerges—reason becomes conscious of its own crisis—precisely in and as it recognizes that its center (ground, principle, priority, end...) is ultimately the metaphoric practice of liberating human beings from idolatry, from imagining and conceiving of the thing-in-itself as natural simile.

Kant's critique of the thing-in-itself is particularly beguiling because it expresses the poetic act of transferring the language of natural simile into the metaphor of human communication. The thing-in-itself is precisely that which, as thing, can be known only in its natural similitudes, but which, in itself, as no thing, can and must be willed and thought solely as and for persons. Nothing can be known in itself, for all scientific knowledge involves hypotheses (theories) whose likenesses engender, through the scientific process of observation and experimentation, new unlikenesses (anomalies, perturbations...) requiring modified or more comprehensive theories or even new theories. But the fundamental thing to be noted is that the thing is not, in itself, a thing; it is metaphor; it is express recognition that human thought and will are not based on the natural similitudes of space and time and that, if humans are to acquire reliably certain knowledge of nature, this scientific knowledge has to be consciously (thoughtfully) distinguished from the thinking of human beings whose freedom from natural simile is the thing which they must constantly strive to embody in the kingdom of ends. The kingdom of human ends, whose identity is grounded in metaphor as the thing-in-itself, must be distinguished from the natural kingdom of means, the kingdom of similes which, the moment they are known as the thing-in-itself, become illusory idols.

Utterly false, therefore, are the traditional claims that Kant rationalizes the Newtonian world system, which, in its vulgar manifestations, turns nature, including human beings, into a gigantesque, mechanistic simile whose perfect likeness is deism, than which there is nothing more faithless or thoughtless. For Kant, philosophy is not the rationalization of science. Indeed, the critique of pure reason involves and expresses the very distinction between science and morality, between nature and freedom, between simile and metaphor. In order for reason to become self-critical, it must distinguish between the thing-in-itself as it is known—as simile—in the possible appearances of natural space and time and the thing-in-itself as it is freely willed and thought—as metaphor—in actual human practice. Kant recognizes, and demonstrates, with incomparable lucidity that the hypothetical appearances of natural science can be saved from reification as illusory fictions only when philosophy, human thinking, is understood to be fundamentally poetic and not scientific. He shows that the freedom of human beings to will (to imagine) the kingdom of ends rests on sharply distinguishing between the similes of nature and the metaphors of human dignity. The critique of pure reason involves reason in the crisis whereby it critically distinguishes between the thing-in-itself as known in the possible appearances of space and time, the similes of natural science, and the thing-in-itself as willing to build, in human practice, the kingdom of ends, the metaphors of human freedom. In showing itself to be revealed in and through the thing-in-itself, philosophy shares metaphor with poetry, with upbuilding human communication, not simile with natural science. Both philosophy and poetry belong to human practice, to the freedom of human beings to think, to conceive, to imagine, to will the kingdom of ends, the kingdom worthy of human beings. The concepts of truth and interpretation central to philosophy are identical with the image of metaphor central to poetry. They represent a making whose metaphoric fictions express, not likeness to nature, but human identity, the solidarity of human freedom and equality.

Modern (biblical) philosophy and poetry, in their identity as the metaphoric thing-in-itself, stand together in their absolute difference from ancient (extra-biblical) philosophy and poetry whose identity is reflected in the natural similitudes of space and time. Just as philosophy, in its modern practice, is not a simile of (it bears no relationship to) Greek *philosophia*, the love of wisdom, except in language, so poetry, in its modern practice, is not a simile of (it bears no relationship to) Greek *poiesis*, making or poetry, except in language. Greek philosophy and poetry both reflect, like all extra-biblical self-expression, the doctrine of opposites. The conventional, scholarly view that Plato and Aristotle hold irreconcilable positions on poetry reflects the equally conventional difficulty which students of Greek thought then have in reconciling this opposition with the texts. It seems inexplicable that the poetic Plato rejects poetry, while the common sense Aristotle defends poetry. What is not grasped, however, is that Plato and Aristotle, in holding consistently to the doctrine of opposites, to simile, to the law of contradiction, are consistent with each other in their opposition. We have already seen that consistency in the Greek world, as in all extra-biblical paganism, is inherently contradictory, for it is simultaneously both like and not like itself, both certain relative to human beings (in the actual *logos* of the *polis*) and certain relative to itself (in the possible *logos* of the unmoved mover). Every point of view (or perspective) in the Greek (and extra-biblical) world is fatally opposed to itself: it is both (like) itself and not (like) itself, simultaneously (but unbeknownst to itself). We have already seen that the law of contradiction is itself blindly contradictory; for, in order to exist, that is, to appear, the law of contradiction must contradict itself, for all appearances violate the contradictory law that no thing can occupy the same space at the same time, including the law of contradiction itself. To exist, to act, to speak in the Greek world—whether philosophically or poetically—is, ineluctably, to violate the law of contradictory fate.

Scholars duly note that, in the *Republic*, Plato expels the actual poets (above all, Homer and his heirs, the tragedians) from the *logos* of political possibility whose identity (simile) reflects the "one change" of contradiction (the rule of the philosopher-kings), while Aristotle, in the *Poetics*, includes the actual poets, epic and dramatic, within the logical practice of the *polis*, where the "one change" of contradiction engenders the political reverses of one and many, rulers and ruled. What the writings of Plato and Aristotle alike show us, however, is that philosophy—thought thinking itself separate from actual human discourse—and poetry—the speech of contradiction—are opposed to each other as immortal soul (or *nous*) is opposed to mortal body.

When Aristotle demonstrates to us that the discourse of actual mortals, that found in politics, ethics, poetics, and rhetoric, exhibits the reversals to which life in the *polis*, because it is based on the simile of one change fatally metamorphosing into its opposite, is blindly subject, he but maintains the opposition between the contradiction of actual poetic speech (speech in the *polis*) and the contradiction of philosophic *logos* (found in the soul or *nous*) which he shares with Plato. When Plato, in rejecting the discourse of all poets, sophists, rhetors, and politicians—the totality of speech found in the *polis*—as ignorant of its end, as known only relative to us, opposes to it the discourse of pure form, of pure possibility, which is known only in itself as its own end, he only shows us that the poetry he expels from the republic is that which Aristotle shows to be contradictory of *nous*. We should not be surprised to discover, therefore, that Aristotle's conception of mind engenders opposition or contradiction in no way fundamentally different from the way in which Plato's conception of soul engenders opposition or contradiction. For Aristotle, mind as *nous*, as that which, in being separated from the vitally ensouled body, thinks its own thoughts, is the mover which, in moving all, is moved by none. That which is knowable and sayable only within itself, within *nous* (separated from the *polis*), is opposed to the discourse of the *polis* which is knowable only relative to us but not in itself (within *nous*). Aristotle is thus in complete accord with Plato who expels the contradictory *logos* of poets, where one is always changing (moved), from the *polis* of the contradictory *logos* of the philosopher-kings who claim to rule, as the contradictory identity of one change, over poetic speech whose unity is contradicted by change. Aristotle no less than Plato assumes a ruler-ruled opposition between the thinking or discourse of *nous* which is known only in itself (but not by us [including Aristotle] who live in the *polis*) and the thinking or discourse of the *polis* which is known only relative to us (but not in itself, in *nous*).

Once our eyes have been opened to the inherently contradictory nature of speech (as of all action or existence) within the Greek world, we see that Plato and Aristotle, in their very opposition, reflect common adherence to the law of contradictory simile. Poetic speech and philosophic speech equally reflect the contradictory nature of one change. Given that one is immortal and unchanging and that change is mortal and changing, each is blindly opposed to and thus ignorantly dependent on its opposite. Poetry—the actual, changing speech of the *polis*—shows that one is endlessly contradicted by what changes—for whatever changes is not one but many, while philosophy—the possible, logical speech of the philosopher-king ruling over others—shows that change is endlessly contradicted by that which is one, for whatever is one is unchanging. In Plato and Aristotle, as in Greek and extra-biblical thought, generally, simile based on the natural appearances of space and time fatally engenders endless opposition between the poet and the philosopher; between that which is relatively human and changing and that which is in itself the immortally one, unchanging good; between the good known relative to us and the good known in itself; and between life (changing existence without knowledge of the one good) and death (the one good without the existence of change)....

In Greek and extra-biblical thought, generally, philosophy and poetry alike are subject to the doctrine of opposites whose similes are endlessly like and not like themselves, both opposed to and other than what they are in themselves. Modern philosophy and poetry are thus presented with a situation totally unlike that known to the Greeks. Either they embrace metaphor, which is grounded not in nature but in thought and existence, both divine and human, as we shall see in Part II of our essay in thinking, or they are faced with the dilemma of establishing their identity through simile, which either gives us scientific knowledge of objects as they appear in natural space and time or vanishes into sheer illusion, that which, as we shall also see in Part II, is what the Bible identifies as idolatry. The false and falsifying antinomy between modern philosophy and modern poetry can be overcome only when metaphor is conceived or imagined in the likeness of the thing-in-itself as that which, although it can be known scientifically through its natural similes in space and time, can be made real only as it is thought or willed as the kingdom of ends truly worthy of human beings.

When Pilate asks Jesus, what is truth?, he expects Jesus to reflect his enslavement to the universal ruler by locating himself within simile as that which, relative to himself, as human being, is opposed both to and by that which is knowable in itself, the human being as the god, the Roman Emperor. Jesus responds, however, with the thing-in-itself, with metaphor. In eschewing the idolatry of natural simile as metamorphosing between the opposites of what is knowable relative to us humans and what is knowable in itself, the opposites of moved and mover which reflect the god as its own contradictory opposite, the unmoved mover, Jesus claims identity with his enemy. Jesus loves simile. He loves his opposite. He loves his neighbor as himself. He loves his enemy, the one opposite him, the one who identifies both his interlocutor and himself in terms of simile, as metaphor. The likeness which Jesus, in coming to bear witness to the truth, establishes with his interlocutor is their common identity, their universal humanity in which neither is to rule or to be ruled by the other as the god. Rather, both are to submit lovingly—freely, thoughtfully—to the common rule of God as metaphor. To view the one opposite you as your neighbor is to love him, not insofar as he continues to live by simile, which relegates both him and you to ignorance of and blindness to one another, but as the metaphoric thing-in-itself. To love your opposite as your neighbor is to treat him, not as a natural means, a simile whose standard is always fate, that which is other than himself, but as one whose end you share in love, justice, and freedom.

That the extra-biblical doctrine of opposites, whose representation is found in ever-metamorphosing similes, is replaced by biblical metaphor expressing love of enemy indicates, once again, that the real enemy to be overcome is not the opposite as simile (extra-biblical paganism) but the one who opposes you in the name of metaphor (truth, love, freedom...) while reducing you to simile, to natural means other than the truth of yourself (biblical idolatry). When Kant shows that the thing-in-itself, precisely because it cannot be known outside its possible appearances in natural space and time, must be willed (thought) as the kingdom of ends actually true for all human beings, the object of his attack is simile as the structure of idolatry. Simile provides reliably scientific knowledge so long as it is limited to the certain appearances of space and time. But, if we claim to know human beings (both others and ourselves) as things natural in themselves, as things whose likeness is based on the characteristics of space and time (involving discrimination based on race, gender, and class), then we lose both the reliability of relatively certain scientific knowledge and the trustworthiness of absolutely true human relationship. The critique of pure reason involves reason in the crisis of recognition that it is its own standard, the standard of both metaphor and simile. Reason shows that, in creating the very distinction between metaphor and simile, it must choose, not between metaphor and simile, but the critical distinction between them. The categorical imperative of reason expresses the either/or structure of freedom as its own standard: either choose the truthful metaphor of the thing-in-itself, or be offended by the similes which generate your self-contradictory melancholy of finding yourself, willy-nilly, betwixt a false reason and no reason at all.

III. CONTRADICTION AND PARADOX

Just as Pilate treats Jesus as one whose likeness with imperial rule serves to demonstrate his utter opposition to, and thus his total opposition by, the Roman ruler, so Pilate equally undertakes to show to Jesus that, in claiming to bear witness to the truth, he is contradicted by the universal truth of the emperor. In adhering to the tradition of Socrates, to the tradition of extra-biblical paganism, generally, Pilate knows that to speak—to act, indeed, to be or to exist—is to invoke a likeness which contradicts or is contradicted by the interlocutor opposite you. Following the imperial law of contradiction, a likeness cannot naturally both be and not be in the same space at the same time. To claim to be like yourself, to claim likeness with yourself, is to deny likeness with the one opposite you who no less himself (herself) claims to occupy the same natural space and time. (What constitutes the like or same natural space and time, how much quantity of space and time is involved, etc., is equally subject to the contradictory law of likeness. Contradictory likenesses ramify endlessly.) Pilate knows that, because all claims to likeness involve contradiction, they depend on imperial rule whose likeness with all others is reflected in their unlikeness with, their opposition to, the emperor. To oppose the emperor, to be unlike him, to contradict or to gainsay the emperor is, as Socrates demonstrates so brilliantly against the sophists, but to unleash the contradictory law of likeness which I call the extra-biblical doctrine of opposites.

For Jesus to oppose the emperor, Pilate holds, is to reflect imperial opposition to himself. To claim likeness for yourself in your speech (action or being) is to oppose, to contradict, the claim of likeness which is equally found in the speech of the interlocutor opposite you. Pilate has no doubt that the truth whose likeness Jesus invokes will contradict imperial rule and thus reflect its dependence on that rule. Might is—like—right, and right is—like—might. Since might and right cannot occupy the same space at the same time, one can be—like—the other only in its opposition to it. The "one change" which is required to identify (the likenesses of) might and right is either the unchanging one, which, in opposition to that which changes and thus is not one, rules over all that changes as its unity (the wisdom of imperial rule rules over others as change lacking unity), or the changing one, which, in opposition to that which is one and unchanging, rules over all that which is one as its change (the wisdom of democratic rule over others as unity lacking change). Every speaker in the tradition of Socrates, Pilate knows, invokes the notion of "one change" in his discourse. But, since one change is precisely a contradictory likeness, like all similes within extra-biblical discourse, it always involves opposition between the one who contradicts the other as changing and thus is not one and the one whose change contradicts the unchanging one.

Pilate is certain that Jesus will adhere to the structure of Socratic discourse whereby it is better to suffer evil (from the one ruling over you) than to do evil (to the one over whom you rule). It is always possible, Pilate recognizes, that Jesus might take the opposite tack, for you can never predict where the categorical adherence of Jews to the law of their god will take them. However, should Jesus proclaim, in the name of his tribal god, that it is better to do evil to, than to suffer evil from, others—might is right—then he would no less contradict himself than he would contradict the emperor, the king of kings, whose likeness with the god is proclaimed throughout the empire. Anyone so foolish as to oppose the emperor on the basis of contradictory likeness will only find himself subjected to the ultimate contradiction, crucifixion. This Pilate knows. This Jesus also knows. But Pilate does not know what Jesus knows.

What is perplexing to Pilate is that Jesus does not respond in the contradictory discourse of simile which, in order to be like itself, must rule over others, or, in order to be like others, must be subject to their rule. Jesus makes no attempt to contradict imperial rule by arguing that it is better to suffer unlike rule than to rule over unlike suffering (or the reverse). He recognizes that the law of contradiction reflects the fate in store for those who seek to establish their identity through the natural appearances of space and time. To claim likeness on the basis of the images of nature is always to find yourself in opposition to those who claim to occupy the same space and time, whose likeness is grounded in similes. To adhere to the law of contradiction as the law of truth ineluctably puts you in opposition not only to others but equally to yourself, as Socrates so persuasively demonstrates. To be—like—yourself is to discover that you are ignorant of and blind to your end, which is always a likeness whose changing appearances contradict its oneness and whose oneness contradicts its changing appearances. To be is to be subject to the contradictory law of simile according to which that which you are like is the one which is dead to changing appearances and equally that which you are like is the appearance of change which does not exist as one. To be is to find yourself subject to the contradictory law of generation and destruction, in which being and non-being are opposites whose blind dependence on the other is unknown to each. All this Jesus knows.

All this Pilate equally knows, as we have indicated. Pilate knows that, given the contradictory doctrine of opposites, according to which any likeness metamorphoses into its opposite, any ruler can be reversed into (by) the position of the ruled. Pilate knows that not only the slavish Jew before him but equally his master, the Roman emperor, even he whose likeness reflects the divine cosmos, is fated to be destroyed. What is born of or generated from the appearances of natural space and time is subject to natural change, corruption, destruction, and death. For, according to one of the standard Greek versions of the doctrine of opposites, nothing can come from nothing. When nothing comes from nothing, then everything comes from everything. Everything is both like and not like everything else (including itself); but, as always, it is blind to and ignorant of the contradictory fate which adherence to natural simile involves. Pilate knows that all life, all being, all speech is subject to the law of contradictory fate. He knows that he, Jesus, all subjects of the emperor, and, ultimately, the emperor himself are ruled by a law which contradicts all human beings through the reversals of nature, whose end is always other than itself. He knows that this law is blind fate and that all human beings, even the gods themselves, are ignorant of it. He knows that the fatal law of contradictory likeness reverses all human beings, showing them, as Stoics, Epicureans, and skeptics in the Socratic tradition, that it is better to suffer fatal reversal from others than fatally to reverse the suffering of others.

Pilate also knows, in the ignorance of what he knows, that the two opposing positions are indistinguishable from each other in their opposition; but he equally knows that he is blind to what the distinction is which unites the opposites in their eternal opposition to each other. Although these two opposites are the same, in their opposition, Pilate knows them only as opposites. Likeness inexorably divides into unlikeness, for one can be like another (ultimately, fate, to which nothing is like, for nothing like comes from nothing like) only in its rule over others (or in its being ruled by others) who are like it in its opposition to them. Pilate knows that fate is the ultimate representation of nature whose end is unknowable precisely because it can be known only in its contradictory opposites. Pilate knows that fate is that which, in reflecting the law of contradiction, is both like and not like itself. Precisely because fate is destined to appear in the natural appearances of space and time, its appearances are always contradictory. Fate is thus both always other than itself in its chance appearances and always identical with itself outside its appearances. Fate, as the mortal and immortal reflection of the doctrine of opposites, is both life and death, both appearance and reality, both change and one, both unlikeness and likeness, both ignorance and knowledge, both the good relative to us and the good relative to itself. But fate is never these opposites from a common perspective which embraces them both. Rather, fate reflects that point of view which is unlike itself in its rule over (or in its being ruled over by) others in its opposition to them. Pilate knows that he is subject to fate as the unmoved one which moves him blindly to the end of knowledge of which he is ignorant. Pilate, like Socrates, knows that he is ignorant, that he is ignorant of fate.

Unthinkable—inconceivable and unimaginable—to Pilate, however, is what he is ignorant of. To know what he is ignorant of would be to know fate, to know his opposite, to view his destiny as, in the hard saying of Nietzsche, *amor fati*. To love his fate, to love his opposite, to love his enemy as himself would be to give up the pagan opposites of Eros and civilization. Both Pilate and Jesus know that fate is the deadly attraction of blind Eros which, in moving others to the contradictory end of which they are ignorant, is unmoved by the fate of others' contradiction. But Jesus knows what Pilate does not know, which is that the contradiction of Eros (erotic contradiction) can in truth be opposed, not by continuing to contradict Eros, and thus once again be contradicted oneself by Eros, but by knowing what contradiction, fate, Eros... are. To know what fate is, to love fate, to comprehend fate is to think fate so profoundly that its doubt does not reflect mere chance or occasion but rather embodies the moment in which the truth of existence is revealed for what it is. What fate is is the paradox of the thing-in-itself. What Jesus knows about fate—what he knows as (his) fate—and what Pilate does not know in his blind opposition to fate is the paradox that, if he seeks to know fate as the thing-in-itself outside its appearances in natural space and time, then it ineluctably reduces his knowledge to blindness, to ignorance, to chance occasion. Fate is precisely the lethal contradiction hidden within the appearances of the thing-in-itself. When Narcissus sees himself reflected in the surface of the water opposite him, he plunges into it to unite himself with his natural simile, only to drown in, to be contradicted by, its unknown depths, the thing-in-itself. To know that fate is contradictory or that contradiction is fatal is totally different from knowing what contradictory fate is, the paradox that, although the thing-in-itself can be known in the contradictory opposites of its natural appearances in space and time, this knowledge is not what constitutes the thing-in-itself. What constitutes the thing-in-itself is the paradox that, although it can be known through its appearances in space and time, it is not grounded in those appearances. Rather, it is itself the ground, the constitution, of those appearances in natural space and time.

To know that something (yourself) is contradictory but not to know what the contradiction is is to reflect the ignorance of and blindness to fate which characterizes extra-biblical paganism. To know not merely that life is contradictory but also what the contradiction of life is, to know what it is that contradicts life, it is this which constitutes paradox. Paradox is the recognition that the law of contradiction is not its own standard, that it is the standard neither of what is contradictory nor of what is not contradictory. The contradictory thing about the law of contradiction is that it is determined by the doctrine of contradictory opposites. Because the law of contradiction contradicts everything, including itself, because the law of contradiction is always the opposite of or opposed to itself, it inexorably blinds its subjects to the very fact of their contradiction. The law of contradiction is the logical determination of fate which, since it is always other than itself, since it is always opposed to those opposite it, is knowable only in itself. But then the paradox (for us) reemerges. For that which is knowable in itself, within a structure of fatal contradiction, is precisely that which is selfless, indeterminate, thought thinking itself without a thinker, Aristotle's *nous*. The law of fatal contradiction inexorably splits human beings into the opposites of existence and logic, self and knowledge, life and death, the contradiction of law and the law of contradiction, the good known relative to ourselves in its contradictory appearances and the good known relative to itself in the law of contradiction. Whatever we are or do or think or feel or speak—our human existence—is always other than, opposed to, and the opposite of what it is in itself. For what it is in itself is the law of contradiction which, the instant it appears (to be), appears the opposite of itself.

The Greeks, in the tradition of extra-biblical paganism, are commanded, by the law of the contradictory oracle of Delphi, the omphalos of Greek life, to know themselves, to know what they are in themselves. But to know themselves, to know the thing-in-itself, is always to discover, with Socrates, Oedipus, and Pentheus, that, since they cannot be in the same space at the same time as the god, their appearance is the reversal or the opposite of what the god is fatally in himself (herself). To seek to know what you are in yourself is to be blinded by the knowledge that before you are born you are fated to be ignorant of the contradictory reversals to which your life of human mortality is inexorably subject and that after you die your immortal fate is to be identical with the contradictory law of opposites whose reversals are immortally reflected in the endless generation and destruction of nature.

Paradox is the recognition that what something is cannot be known in itself outside its appearances in natural space and time, that to know the thing-in-itself as an object of possible natural experience is not to know what it is in itself. Paradox is the recognition that, in order for us humans to know ourselves, we must give up knowing ourselves as objects of possible appearance, as similes of natural space and time. The paradox of knowledge is that we must give up seeking objective knowledge— knowledge based on objects (either outside or inside us)—if we are not only to know ourselves as subjects but also to possess reliably certain knowledge of the objects of nature. Contradiction is not its own standard, for it is fatally ignorant of what it is in itself, of what it is that constitutes its own standard. Fate is not its own standard, for what it is in itself is precisely the fatal secret of extra-biblical paganism, that it is always opposed to or other than itself. The standard of contradiction, the standard of fate is paradox, the recognition that, in order to know what something is in itself, we must give up seeking to know what it is by analogy with the similitudes of natural space and time.

When Pilate asks Jesus, what is truth?, he seeks, in Socratic fashion, to bind both his Jewish interlocutor and his Roman master to the law of contradictory logic. To seek to know what something is is to show yourself reversed by that which cannot be known in itself by us mortals. Were Jesus to answer Pilate in the tradition of Socratic opposition, he would reflect his ignorance of his end, which Pilate intends to identify with his ruler, the Roman emperor. But Jesus responds, in his silence, that paradox is its own standard of truth and interpretation, the standard of both itself and its contradictions. The point is not that Jesus as such is silent—for, as the Preacher says, there is a time to speak and a time to remain silent. The issue is not that we speak or remain silent. The issue is what we speak or remain silent about. What Jesus chooses to remain silent about is the truth to which, he says, he comes to bear witness. Truth is the paradox, the paradox that, in order to be revealed for what it is in itself, what is true must be true no less for me than it is for you. Truth is not based on the contradictory images of natural space and time. Rather, truth is based on what we are in ourselves, and Jesus, in the tradition of the law and prophets, conceives of and imagines that what we are in ourselves is the neighbor whom we are to love as ourselves. The paradox that each of us is the neighbor, not in himself (herself), but in and through, as, the neighbor, is what we are in ourselves.

The paradox that we can be like the neighbor only in and through the neighbor's likeness with us indicates that paradox is that likeness which, like metaphor, is identical with the thing-in-itself, not with the appearances of things in natural space and time. Neighbors are the paradox precisely because they occupy the same space and time, not in nature, but in history. Their priority as neighbors is not spatial or temporal in nature but categorical in spirit.

Contradiction must be given up as that which is true in itself if truth and interpretation are to live in the world as their own standard. The doctrine of fatal opposites that lies unknown and unknowable at the heart of the law of contradiction is that no one can be counted on to live consistently by the law of contradiction unless he is dead, dead to the contradictory appearances of life. Count no one logical, count no one happy in his *logos*, until he is dead, until he is dead to the contradictory logic of contradiction. The law of contradiction is the fate that lethally conjures up the appearances of life only to show that they are untrue to the logic ruling over life until they return to the very nature whose endless generation is the destruction of life. The truth revealed by paradox is that the thing-in-itself is not fatal otherness known only in the death of contradiction (the contradiction of death). Paradox reveals the thing-in-itself to be life, existence, the recognition that I think, therefore, I am. Paradox is the commitment to life in which thinking and existence are true only insofar as each is true. Although or, rather, precisely because knowledge of the thing-in-itself outside its appearance in the objects of the possible experience of natural space and time must be given up as fatally contradictory of both thought and existence, thought and existence constitute the truth of the thing in itself. Whereas the law of contradiction inexorably opposes thought and existence to each other as knowledge of the thing-in-itself and its contradictory appearances, the law of paradox shows that for either thought or existence to be true both must be true. When we acknowledge that neither thought nor existence can be true in itself unless both are true in themselves, we realize that paradox is but another name for dialectic, for which the content (the existence of thought) is the concept (the thought of existence). Contradiction always involves the blind sacrifice of life to thought (knowledge) and the ignorant sacrifice of thought to life (appearance). For one to be true (certain)—as ruler—the other must always be false (uncertain)—as ruled. It is unthinkable—inconceivable and unimaginable—to the law of contradiction that two beings could both occupy the same space at the same time as equally rulers and ruled enjoying the rule of all, without one being compelled to impose its ignorant rule on the other in the name of blind fate, the ultimate *telos* of the universe whose immortal rule reflects the endless opposition between thought (consciousness) and existence.

Whereas contradiction forces human beings to oppose thought (knowledge) and existence, paradox demands that thought and existence be viewed as the very categories which constitute life. Life is the paradox. The paradox is to be lived. The paradox is not to be surrendered to the fatal law of contradiction which renders thought dead to existence and existence dead to thought. The paradox is that the only joy for the individual is to live the paradox as its own standard, the standard of both what constitutes life and what contradicts life. What constitutes life is precisely what is unknown to the blind law of contradiction, the paradox that thought and existence are true only insofar as each is true to life.

What the paradox is is that the contradictions of life can and must be lived and not be surrendered to one-sided opposition. The paradox of life is that, if we are to live and not succumb to the oppositions which constitute life, then we must recognize that, precisely because both thought and existence must be true for either to be true, there are no similes with nature as something known in the possible appearances of space and time in which either thought or existence is embodied. It is precisely because we must live thoughtfully, because we must exist in our thought, that there are no similes with nature which can indicate to us the nature of either thought or existence. Thought and existence gain their identity through each other, in what they are in themselves, not through their appearances in space and time. Thought and existence are like each other; indeed, they are, they must be each other, but their identity is such that for one to be true the other must be equally true; and thus their identity through the other is not to be understood according to either of the two opposed versions of the law of contradiction, the laws of identity and the excluded middle. Ineluctably, whenever thought and existence (in whatever versions) are opposed, in one-sided fashion, to each other, the one championed always claims both to be natural and to oppose, that is, to contradict the other as unnatural. It is equally ineluctable that, whenever the law of contradiction is held up as the law of truth and interpretation, thought and existence are opposed to each other as contradictory. When Pilate asks Jesus, what is truth?, he seeks to show his interlocutor that, if truth exists, it cannot be true, and, if existence is true, it cannot exist. Truth cannot both exist and exist as known. Truth cannot both be known and be known to exist. Either truth is known and thus does not exist. Or truth exists and thus is not known. Truth can only be known not to exist. Truth can only exist as unknown. But the truth to which Jesus comes to bear witness is not known in itself—except as it appears in the objects of possible experience; but it both is thought (willed) and exists in and through—as—the neighbor. Truth, to be thought, must exist; and truth, to exist, must be thought. Truth overcomes the contradictions opposing thought and existence by embracing the paradox that each can be true only insofar as it is the metaphor of the other. Neither thought nor existence can truly gain its identity through the natural similes of space and time. Each can be truly itself only insofar as it is like the other, and this mutual likeness is itself the paradoxical expression of the relationship of thought and existence.

The paradox is the recognition that we shall always be contradicted if we seek to know the thing-in-itself outside its possible appearances in natural space and time. The paradox is thus the recognition that contradiction is blinded by and ignorant of its own contradiction when, on the basis of the law of contradiction, we seek to obtain knowledge outside of its appearances in natural similes. Within the extra-biblical world of paganism, human beings, in seeking knowledge through likeness to its opposite, nature, are always blinded by that which is opposed to them, by nature. To seek to know your end in nature, to seek your likeness in nature is always to experience your natural end as impenetrable fate which, in your blindness and ignorance, reverses you. The juxtaposition between Pilate and Jesus is the juxtaposition between contradiction and paradox, between contradiction, which ineluctably subjects the individual to ignorance of and blindness to fatal opposition, and paradox, which reveals to the individual the truth and interpretation of thoughtful existence. Pilate knows that he is ignorant, that, like all others, including Jesus, he is subject to the blind rule of fatal opposition. Pilate knows that life is contradictory. Jesus knows what Pilate is ignorant of, what it is that contradicts Pilate. He knows that ignorance of the fatal thing-in-itself is revealed as the truth of otherness when its likeness with the natural appearances of space and time is given up for the truthful relationship of thought and existence. Jesus know that life is paradox, that life is the paradox, revealing the truth of contradiction. The juxtaposition of Pilate and Jesus is the juxtaposition between extra-biblical contradiction and biblical paradox.

In insisting upon the importance of discerning perspicuously the fundamental difference between pagan contradiction and biblical paradox, we emphasize, yet again, that our real aim is to lay the groundwork for a proper analysis, in Part II of our essay in thinking, of the distinction between, not extra-biblical paganism and the Bible as such, but between biblical revelation of the truth and interpretation of thought and existence and idolatry. Pilate knows that he is ignorant. He knows that all movement, including all human moves (motives, emotions...), is contradictory, fatally subject to the cosmic law of the unmoved mover, for which thought is always other than and opposed to existence. He knows—following Socrates, himself the oracular disciple of Delphic Apollo—that the unexamined life is not worth living, and that, when life is examined, it endlessly appears in opposites reflecting fatal opposition between thought (knowledge, self-consciousness, comprehension...) and existence. He knows that to seek knowledge of life as the thing-in-itself is to find that what life is, in itself, is always other than and opposed to its contradictory appearances in natural space and time. He knows that, in the end, life is blind, ignorant fate. But what Pilate does not know and what Jesus, following the patriarchs and the prophets, does know, in fear and trembling, is that the revelation of truth and interpretation as its own standard of both thought and existence also introduces the contradictions of truth and interpretation into the world. In knowing that he is ignorant, Pilate does not know what he is ignorant of, and what he is ignorant of is no less paradox as its own standard than the contradiction of paradox as idolatry. Modern (that is, biblical) idolatry is the claim that the thing-in-itself can be known, without contradiction, as an object either natural or supernatural, something unthinkable, both inconceivable and unimaginable, in the extra-biblical paganism of Pilate. Idolatry represents the reduction of paradox to contradiction. To reduce what we know to knowledge of objects, whether natural or supernatural, is to reduce the life of human beings to the contradictions between thought and existence, the dualisms of dogmatism and skepticism, to the self-conscious melancholy of finding yourself betwixt a false reason and no reason at all. To know that one is contradicted by the thing-in-itself is one thing, the one thing that Pilate, in the tradition of extra-biblical paganism, knows in his ignorance. But to claim that the thing-in-itself is reducible to knowledge of contradictory objects, whether natural or supernatural, is something completely unknown to Pilate and the tradition of extra-biblical paganism and something which the Bible reveals as the idolatrous contradiction of truth and interpretation as their own paradox. In the extra-biblical tradition, the law of contradiction always makes that which is knowable in itself, the thing-in-itself, opposed to or other than, that is, the contradiction of, either its thought or its existence. But in the tradition of modern (that is, biblical) idolatry the law of contradiction is identified with the truth of thought and existence through comparison with either the natural objects of space and time or supernatural objects. To claim to know the thing-in-itself as exclusively either natural or supernatural simile is to reduce human beings to contradictory objects whose ends are known to violate the law of contradiction, something unthinkable in the pagan tradition of Socratic ignorance. We point out once again that, here in this preliminary chapter on interpretation, we are concerned to establish the structure of the utter difference between contradiction and paradox so that, in Part II of our essay in thinking, we can properly distinguish between paradox and its contradictory, that is, idolatrous, perversions.

Pilate, at least, in his contradictory ignorance, never claims to possess contradictory knowledge, knowledge of contradiction. He never claims to know the contradictory nature of his opponent. He never claims to know the thing-in-itself as that which contradicts the nature of his opponent. In their endless oppositions the facts of nature and right (might and right) are immortally opposed to each other. But, once the paradox—knowledge that what constitutes human right is not based on the contradictory facts of nature and that the nature of facts is based on the human right of constituting itself as the thing-in-itself—is revealed to the world, then that which is unthinkable, both inconceivable and unimaginable, to extra-biblical paganism appears in the world: the reduction of human beings to the contradiction of natural facts. If contradiction has always been in the world (of nature), then it has never been in the world, and the incomprehensibly blind contradiction of paganism bursts upon us again. But, if contradiction has not always been in the world but is brought into the world by the paradox of truth and interpretation, then the world becomes contradictory, something unthinkable to extra-biblical paganism for which the world is contradictory. It is only in distinguishing systematically between contradiction and paradox that we shall be in a position to comprehend that paradox as its own standard is the standard of both itself and its idolatrous contradictions and thus to establish a comprehensive conception of truth and interpretation.

IV. LANGUAGE AND COMMUNICATION

The distinction between language and communication is the third distinction, in addition to the distinctions between simile and metaphor and between contradiction and paradox, that I want to establish in the prolegomenon to the future of interpretation in Part II of my essay in thinking. My aim here, as in the earlier sections of this chapter, is to introduce critical distinctions which interpretation as its own standard, the standard of both what is interpretation and what is not interpretation, brings into thought and existence. Interpretation as the universal standard of humanity is given not immediately but mediately in the natural images of space and time. The medium of nature, nature as mediation, is the thing-in-itself which, although it can be known in the language of nature, can be interpreted only in and as what Kant calls the kingdom of ends, in and as communication (community). If interpretation has always been in the world of nature, then it has never been in the natural world. Interpretation is given not in the nature of language itself but in the medium of communication, in the mediation of those who communicate.

The distinction between language and communication is doubtless both closer to us than the distinctions between simile and metaphor and between contradiction and paradox and more remote from us. It is familiar to us, for we constantly experience the fact that there is much that we say, both verbally and non-verbally, which fails to communicate what we mean or indeed distorts, consciously and/or unconsciously, not only our meaning but also the meaning of others. We commonly experience the feeling that we do not say what we mean and that we do not mean what we say. We typically say that the language in and through which we communicate is not adequate to our thoughts and feelings, that words cannot express our inner world. We are familiar, then, with the gap between language (both verbal and non-verbal) and communication.

But the gap between language and communication, precisely because we live within it, is also extremely difficult for us to comprehend and to articulate. We are all language users, from birth, for, although infants do not articulate themselves in words (*in-fans*: non-speaking), their nonverbal language is understood by their adult guardians to communicate fundamental ways of thought and existence (hunger, discomfort, anger, pleasure, satisfaction, want, interest, eagerness, curiosity...). We all become natural users of language, assuming there is no physical impairment (or mistreatment). There is clearly no more amazing phenomenon on earth than the extraordinary diversity of languages which human beings learn naturally to speak as small children; yet, it is this very linguistic diversity which serves to isolate, indeed, to alienate, human beings, as groups, from each other. Language becomes intimately bound up with the social and cultural identity of groups, and this is especially evident in the modern world of imperialism, nationalism, and revolution. How language, verbal and nonverbal, is related to social and cultural expression becomes a central object of anthropological and psychological investigation in the nineteenth century and remains a topic of fundamental interest to philosophers today. That all human beings use speech would appear to distinguish human animals from non-human animals, but what it is that is common to human language, as distinct from the diverse languages of animals, has generally defied both anthropologists and psychologists to describe, except for the obvious cliché that human beings are language-using animals, which but repeats millennia-long attempts to define the universally human in terms of language.

In more recent years, ethologists have reported what they have often claimed and what have often been accepted to be startling results in teaching the great primates, our closest living relatives, the use of signing. It would appear that, if a meaningful distinction between human beings and other animals such as the great apes is to be made, it cannot be based on the use of language. But the impressive range of signs that researchers have succeeded in teaching great apes may reflect more on the ingenuity of the human communicators than on the quasi-human or indeed human capacities of their animal counterparts. It seems likely—given the distinction which, as I shall show, it is critically important to establish between language and communication—that the claims based on the teaching of extensive signing to individual apes (even if one is prepared to accept the further claim that these apes occasionally teach the signs they have learned to fellow adults and to offspring) are but one more instance of the naturalistic or romantic fallacy (which itself represents but another version of the intentional fallacy). In the hands of mature thinkers—literary and/or philosophical—our relationship to nature, including that to our fellow primates, is comprehended as fruitful metaphor or paradox. We project into nature our ideas and feelings such that nature becomes a mirror in which we see ourselves. But when we look into the mirror of nature, it is we ourselves whom we see—in new and different ways. It is not nature as the thing-in-itself which we encounter or gain insight into. Rather, it is we who, as the thing-in-itself, view nature as a metaphor which evokes, yet again, the paradoxical relationship which the human being is as the thing-in-itself. If we are to overcome viewing literature or philosophy as the mirror of nature, whether internal (subjective) or external (objective), we must recognize that the naturalistic fallacy emerges as the false claim that we can have immediate insight into or direct knowledge of nature as the thing-in-itself. The naturalistic fallacy is without exception based on similes whose contradictions are evaded through viewing natural language as human communication, through holding that there is a likeness in nature in terms of which we can communicate with, say, animals and they with us.

Nature is too important—to us humans—to be left to its specialists, whether animal or human. Nature belongs to us humans: it is our flesh, our body, our life. We are accountable for all the animals, for all the plants, for all of nature down to the least snail darter or the most astonishing quark. Nature is our accounting, our account, our *conte*. But, in viewing ourselves in the mirror of nature, in viewing nature as our own self-accounting, we must be aware of the enormous dangers of the naturalistic fallacy, which is but another term for idolatry. When we look into the mirror of nature (external or internal), we must disparage neither human being (by losing the human in its natural reflection) nor natural being (by losing nature in its reflection in us). In our accounts of nature—from a poem on daffodils to the scientific theory of evolution—we must constantly live the paradox that we know nature in itself only as similes (appearances) and that what we are in ourselves we shall never know on the basis of naturalistic similes but only as the paradox that nature is human metaphor.

When the naturalistic fallacy is understood as human fantasy, as the paradox of metaphor, and not as simile contradicting human nature, then we recognize, for example, that the one thing which the theory of evolution, that great mirror in which we contemplate our evolving animal nature, cannot explain, on its own terms of natural selection and the survival of the fittest, is the theory of evolution. The theory of evolution does not give and (in the hands of a great scientist like Darwin) does not purport to give an account of itself. The theory of evolution gives no explanation of, it remains silent about, how it is that the "theory of evolution," understood as the self-conscious reflection of human beings in the mirror of nature, evolves from, that is, relates to, the evolution of natural life. The theory of evolution does not provide an account of history, of the history (development) of theories and ideas, of human consciousness, of thought and existence, of communication. The theory of evolution, as the explanation of the origin (and development) of natural species, does not explain how the thing-in-itself is the self-conscious recognition of "I think, therefore, I am." The theory of evolution is itself a metaphor in which we see nature as the natural selection of similes of which the fittest survive. But we who contemplate nature have the responsibility of recognizing that "natural selection" and "survival of the fittest" function totally differently whether taken as natural simile (contradiction) or human metaphor (paradox).

The naturalistic fallacy emerges when the critical distinction between natural being and human being, between language and communication, is effaced. The fallacy of our nature appears when we think that the theory of evolution (like any scientific theory) gives us direct contact with, immediate knowledge of, or unmediated insight into nature. Nature is the great mirror of humanity insofar as we do not confuse the metaphor of creation with the simile of generation. Theology must not pretend to dogmatic literalism by reducing its metaphors of truth and interpretation to naturalistic similes, and science must not pretend to literal dogmatism by elevating its similitudes reflecting the appearances of natural space and time to the truth and interpretation of metaphor. Science must remain eternally vigilant, however, and never flag in demonstrating that the claims of creationism are utterly bogus as science (or theology). But it is no less important that all of us—lay people, in addition to scientists and theologians—remain eternally vigilant in ensuring that the truth which creationism strives properly to defend but surrenders in its vain attempts to turn theology into science not be lost in celebrating the victory of science over creationism. The truth which creationism possesses but which it loses in its idolatrous attempt to turn the account of human creation into a rival science which accounts for natural generation (and destruction) is the freedom of human beings to communicate with each other, notwithstanding their natural oppositions. The biblical book of Genesis gives an account of—it accounts for—human creation. Genesis does not provide a scientific account of nature, except negatively, in the sense that it limits science to obtaining reliably certain and objective knowledge of the creative thing-in-itself solely through its appearances in the natural similes of spatial and temporal objects. Science gives us knowledge of objects of possible experience; it does not give us insight into its own subject, that of science. The objective knowledge which science provides is not of the thing-in-itself but of its appearances in space and time. Science *qua* science does not study subjects who, as scientists, are not the object of scientific study but the subject of science, the creative thing-in-itself. The origin or generation of species, as an object of natural science, is a study very different from the origin of the species as the study of that which is originally and creatively human. The first reflects generation and destruction (biology); the second involves and expresses creation: life and death—metaphor, paradox, and communication.

Evolution is a mirror in which we see ourselves contemplating our natural origins, our beginnings in nature. But the mirror of evolution does not directly reveal the nature of the thing-in-itself as nature's original creation. The mirror of evolution does not reveal its own creative origins. The mirror, as natural simile, is not the self whose thinking expresses existence and whose existence involves thinking. The natural mirror of simile is finite reflection, mirroring blindly and ignorantly the thing-in-itself, until and unless the thing-in-itself contemplates itself as its own infinite standard, the standard both of infinite (self-) reflection and of the mirror of finite reflection. The naturalistic fallacy emerges when the human mind as infinite self-reflection, the thing-in-itself, confuses itself with finite reflection, with its appearances in natural space and time. The naturalistic fallacy confuses the mind as the metaphoric mirror of nature with the mirror as a naturalistic simile endlessly reflecting yet additional similes.

The point of this excursus on the naturalistic fallacy is to help us understand the conclusion at which linguistic anthropologists like Sapir arrived in the heyday of their work some two generations ago. Overcoming imperialistic claims of the natural superiority of one language (or race) over another, their work shows that all natural languages are perfect. Whatever the vast differences of natural language in syntax, grammar, and vocabulary, they are all naturally complete. All languages, whether written or unwritten, have the capacity to express what is human. There is nothing in the languages which have appeared naturally on earth, there is nothing in languages themselves, to distinguish one from another except on the basis of comparative linguistics, the science which catalogues similitudes in their multifarious appearances. There is nothing which we can know of the nature of languages, understood as things-in-themselves, which would make one essentially inferior or superior to another. But, since it is true that we do not learn and encounter natural languages except as they are deeply embedded in social and cultural contexts, we constantly confuse language with culture. For this reason, sound, scientific knowledge of languages, as of nature, generally, is always sobering. Consider, for example, the language of the Mongols, who, as east central Asian nomads, once ruled over China, not to mention Muscovy, and who, in this century, underwent the first socialist revolution after the Soviet Union. That the language of the Mongols was originally written in an alphabet deriving from Aramaic, a Semitic language, and that, today, in the Mongolian People's Republic (as distinct from the Inner Mongolian Autonomous Region of the People's Republic of China), it is written in the Cyrillic alphabet, which is typically the alphabet of a Slavic group of Indo-European languages, may tell us a lot about Mongol history. But it also exposes the naturalistic fallacy involved in any attempt to connect the natural language of a people, that is, the nature of language, directly with its history and culture.

Reference to the Mongol language serves to exemplify the principle that culture and, above all, communication, are not grounded in language, although they are not found separate from language. It may be useful to employ the term "language" as widely as we do behavior and thus to speak not only of human but also of animal behavior and language. From the detailed and patient study which ethnologists have devoted to gorillas, wolves, honey bees, lions, geese, cats, etc., our understanding of the complex behavior and "language" of various animal groups, of the roles which members play within their groups, and how, at least in some instances, individuals perform their roles, is immeasurably enriched. It is clear that such study enlarges and enhances our human understanding (I am myself a natural history buff); but it is equally clear that we must be circumspect in claiming that such study enlarges or enhances the understanding on the part of the animals themselves. Again, what is important is that we not fall into the naturalistic fallacy of claiming to understand animals in themselves when it is ultimately ourselves whom we contemplate in the mirror of our animal nature.

Consideration of nature, the naturalistic fallacy, and the natural languages of human beings allows us to focus on two distinctions which are constantly conflated or confused. First, there is the common sense distinction between human language and the languages of animals which the scientific study of animal behavior and language tends to efface. Second, there is the critical distinction between natural language—human, but also animal—and communication—which is exclusively human and includes all human beings. In the first place, common sense suggests to all peoples that, although they are intimately related to animals (and to other natural creatures and elements), as their ritual, myth, and art so richly indicate, they also differ from the animals owing to their possession of such features as manual dexterity, tool-making capacity, speech, mind (culture: religion, art, etc.), upright carriage, vulnerability (due to the long period of child-dependency and to the absence of offensive or defensive attributes like fangs, claws, wings, carapace, or speed in running), lack of estrus, non-specific dependency on the environment, substitution of learned for instinctual behavior, capacity for transforming the environment, free will, progressive development (*perfectibilité*), complex social relations.... But common sense, precisely because it fails to distinguish between itself and its reflection in nature, locates its origins in the contradictions of nature which shows humans and animals (and the other natural creatures and elements) constantly metamorphosing into each other. The reflection which truly reflects human self-reflexivity is the paradox that nature is not its own reflection. Human beings can reflect nature in truth only if they recognize that nature is not its own standard of reflection. It is only when, therefore, in the second place, we distinguish between language and communication, as between natural simile and metaphor and between the law of contradiction as based on the nature of space and time and paradox, that we are able to save the appearances of common sense based on the images of nature.

If we are to develop a properly sophisticated conception of interpretation as its own standard, the standard of both what is interpretation and what is not interpretation, we must distinguish systematically between language and communication. As always, our ultimate concern is not to distinguish between natural language and human communication, as such, but between communication and its idolatrous distortions, evasions, cor-

ruptions, repressions.... But we can begin to account for failure in communication only when we are clear, in principle, as to what constitutes
communication, and we can become clear about the constitution of communication only when we distinguish it rigorously from its natural appearances in and as language. When Pilate asks Jesus, what is truth?, he
appears to communicate. Indeed, it is likely that the appearances of what
he says bear the structure of communication even more persuasively than
the speech of his extra-biblical predecessor, Socrates; for, since they are embedded in the discourse of the Bible, the book whose *raison d'être*, as we
shall see, is communication (community), they beguile us into thinking
that Pilate knows (that we know) what he is saying (as distinct from the
mere fact that he speaks). Nevertheless, when Pilate asks Jesus, what is
truth?, he does not communicate a conception of truth. Rather, in the tradition of Socrates, as of all extra-biblical peoples, he reflects, as we have seen
in Sections II and III of this chapter, ignorance of and blindness to what he
communicates. It is not that Pilate fails to communicate, or that his communication is incomplete, or, finally, that he simply represents a tradition
of communication different from that of Jesus. Rather, Pilate is without any
conception of communication, whatsoever. The very possibility of communication (which we know must be actual in order to be possible) is unthinkable, both inconceivable and unimaginable, to Pilate.

Where speech is based on natural simile and contradiction, as we
have shown in the earlier sections of this chapter, then its language is
without any conception of communication. If language has always been in
the world of nature, then it has never naturally been in the world as communication. When language, as is universally the case in extra-biblical
paganism, is understood to reflect the natural space and time in which we
live, then human speech but reflects the self as contradictory appearance
which is fatally subject to endless generation and destruction. The contradiction to which language, when it is based on the images of nature, is
subject is that to which all nature is subject. It cannot, in itself, conceive of
or imagine itself to be. Nature is not its own concept or image. When we
seek to grasp language in the similes of natural space and time, we find not
only that it always appears to be opposed to or other than what it is in itself
but also that it is fatally ignorant of and blind to what it is in itself. Language possesses no idea or image of what it is in itself, for the other, to
which it is eternally opposed, is fate, which, as the reflection of the law of

contradictory nature, is always endlessly other than itself. For either native-born users or scientific observers to view communication as natural is blindly to subject communication to the eternal metamorphosis of the generation and destruction of nature. When Pilate asks Jesus, what is truth?, he seeks to imprison Jesus in the contradictory nature of language, just as he (unconsciously) assumes that Jesus, as the interlocutor opposite him, will seek to imprison him in the natural contradictions of language. Pilate has no conception of language as communication whereby he would communicate truthfully with others as he would want others to communicate truthfully with him. For Pilate, the truth is precisely that certainty which fatally contradicts its speaker, showing him, in his uncertainty, to be ruled by that which is opposite him, the Roman emperor, and, ultimately, fate, which blinds all humans to their natural ignorance of certainty as that which is inexorably opposed to them.

Natural language reflects the contradiction that, in order to be itself, it is always other than or opposed to itself. If nature has always been in the world, then it has never been in the world. Communication embodies the paradox that it can save nature from its otherness or self-estrangement precisely because, since it has never been naturally in the world, it comes historically into thought and existence as nature's self-reflection. To come historically into thought and existence from nothing, from nothing which is natural, is to conceive of and imagine ourselves as other than nature, as that which is nature's other, as the mirror of self-reflection in which we see ourselves as natural but in which nature remains blind to and ignorant of its otherness. It is not language which communicates; and, if we say that it is language by means of which human beings communicate, we must understand this to mean that it is human beings who have the responsibility of providing the communicative ends to the enormous variety of linguistic means that are available for their use. There is no communication in extra-biblical language for the precise reason that extra-biblical speech universally views itself in the contradictory similes of natural space and time. For extra-biblical peoples, words, along with their grammatical and syntactical arrangements, ultimately reflect the ignorance and blindness to which nature, in its endless metamorphoses, is eternally subject. It is not words as language but words as communicating truth as its own standard which Jesus, in his silence, addresses to Pilate. He comes to bear witness to, to communicate, the truth, to reveal truth as the communication binding interlocutors, in their natural opposition (difference), into a community in which words are not mere terms whose appearances naturally contradict—or are ignorant of and blind to—what they mean in themselves. For Jesus, bespeaking the tradition of the law and the prophets, the word is made flesh, our very nature; words incarnate the truth. The content is the concept, simile is metaphor, contradiction is paradox, language is communication. The mirror reflection of nature is made the self-reflection of being human: I think, therefore, I am. But this making, this *poiesis*, this communication shows that, in presupposing nature, it is the origin of nature. It makes nature original, it creates nature, something inconceivable and unimaginable to nature always other than, blind to, and ignorant of its own self-contradiction. To communicate is always to begin, to begin anew, to reveal, to both self and other, the liberation from the contradictory images of space and time and their creation, their possession, as the paradox of metaphor. To communicate is to recognize that communication is its own standard, the standard both of what truly constitutes communication and of its false and falsifying natural similitudes. We distinguish once and for all between communication—the ground underlying all human opposition—and language—the groundless opposition in which all humans are naturally born—as central to comprehending interpretation as the critical distinction between self-conscious reflection and the mirror of nature.

V. CONCLUSION

Interpretation as its own standard, the standard both of itself and of what is not interpretation, involves making a critical distinction between simile and metaphor, between contradiction and paradox, and between language and communication. We emphasize, once again, that it is not the terms in which we make our distinctions which count in themselves; what counts is the conceptual distinctions which we make through the terms we use. But the very distinction between concept and term, between the term as concept (the conceptual significance of a term) and the concept as term (the dictionary definition of a term), indicates that, although concepts do not depend directly on the terms in which they are expressed, a conceptually sophisticated presentation, whether literary or philosophical, depends on the delicate precision of the terms in which it is expressed. Great works of the spirit—whether in music, the visual arts, literature, philosophy, or religion—are rigorously systematic in their conceptual framework, however informal, aphoristic, fragmented, or unsystematic the terms of their presentation may appear to be. Weak works are precisely those which cannot bear the terms of their own concept. It is the case that there are no terms which cannot be conceptually significant, but it is equally the case that terms are significant only in and through the concepts they bear. Once we become conscious of the dialectic of concept and term, it is no longer puzzling that a concept is both itself and its term. "Concept," for instance, is both concept and term. The concept is its own standard, the standard both of itself and of the terms in which it is expressed. We think (feel, believe, reason...) in and through terms, but our thinking (emotion, belief, rationality...) is not to be located, as such, in the terms we use, in the appearances of our self-expression, but in our concepts. Concepts can be naturally known, not in themselves but only in their similitudes to the flesh, in the possible experience of natural space and time. But concepts as the thing-in-itself are the paradox whose communication is always expressly metaphorical.

Interpretation is in itself the concept—the concept of the thing-in-itself bears the structure of interpretation—precisely because it rigorously distinguishes between interpretation and that which is without the concept of interpretation. Interpretation does not involve, as such, the manipulation of the terms of simile, contradiction, and language, although the very paradox in presenting the conceptual framework of interpretation involves us in recognizing a vast world of human nature, that of extra-biblical paganism, which has no concept of interpretation. We find ourselves struggling with an analysis in which we say that the Greeks, like all-extra biblical peoples, lack the concept of interpretation, that is, they are ignorant of and blind to the concept (but not the term) of concept. We have no choice but—we are not free not—to conceptualize, to render meaningful, to put into the terms of (conceptual) meaning that which whose terms are ignorant of and blind to, opposed to and other than, their concept. The concept which is endlessly other than itself in the extra-biblical world of paganism is interpretation. The concept which, in its ignorance of and blindness to being a concept, is always the opposite of and opposed to itself is nothing less than fate itself. Fate reflects that structure of reality whose terms are endlessly opposed to and other than their concept. Precisely because the concept of interpretation, the interpretative concept, always appears, within the Greek world, in the language of contradictory similes and thus is always fatally other than itself, it ineluctably divides into the opposites of that which is known relative to our ignorance and that which is known relative to its own blindness. Language, which rests on the law of contradiction whose appearances are blind to and ignorant of their own contradiction, is always other than its own concept. It bears no concept; it possesses no consciousness, no interpretation, of itself as communication.

The reason that there is no point of view, no universality, no interpretative perspective, no history, no communication in the Greek world, as in the world of extra-biblical peoples, generally, is that what is (in the same space and time) is not (in the same space and time). Whatever is (in itself), according to the contradictory *logos* shaping all discourse, appears; yet appearance is precisely that which is other than itself. For something to be, it must not violate the law of contradiction by both being and not being in the same space at the same time. Nevertheless, for something to be, it must appear, and appearance is precisely that which, violating the contradictory *logos* of being, both is and is not in the same space at the same time. Being, therefore, is never what it is in itself; it is immortally opposed to and other than itself. To be born in the Greek world, to live—to sense, to act, to speak, to seek, to desire, to think, to will...—is to undergo the fate of discovering that the contradictory appearances of one's life blind one both to one's beginning and to one's end. It is the fatal discovery that the contradictions of life can be terminated only in death, in the death of contradictory appearance. To be born—to live—is to discover that your point of view is the reversal of what it appears to be, that there is no point of view which does not divide, ineluctably, between ruler and ruled, master and slave, one and many. To live according to the contradictory images of space and time is ultimately to reflect fate as the unmoved mover which, in moving human beings blindly to their end, is unmoved by human beings in ignorance of their end. That mover and moved, self and other, are endlessly opposed to and other than each other reflects the fate that no point of view can be established which comprehends the opposites within a universal community of human discourse, within a common framework of history, of communication, of interpretation.

The paradox of communication is that the opposites of *logos* can be comprehended within a common framework, a point of view which, in being common to both, cannot be directly identified with or reduced to either, only if each of the opposite interlocutors is equally (and freely, lovingly...) the other. Each of the speakers must, to articulate the concept in awkward terms, be the other to the other; each speaker must be the other's other. Neither can be what is other in itself; but, as the thing-in-itself, each is the other which, although it can be known in the similes of natural appearances, can be interpreted only in and through—as—the metaphors which identify the concept of other with each. The paradox in which each is (metaphorically the) other is true only if it is universally true for all human beings. The paradox of otherness excludes all who do not will to view the other as themselves and includes all who view themselves as the other. The dialectic of exclusion and inclusion is precisely that of interpretation, which distinguishes between the terms of simile, contradiction, and language, in which there is no consciousness of interpretation as the truth of the other, and the concepts of metaphor, paradox, and communication, which constitute the structure of interpretation as otherness revealed through the truth of each.

In discussing truth and interpretation in Part I of my essay in thinking, which serves as an introduction to an examination of their dialectic in Part II, I have wanted to propose two basic principles for consideration. First, it is critically important to recognize that truth and interpretation are both their own standard, the standard not only of what in itself is truth or interpretation but equally of what in itself is not truth or interpretation. Second, it becomes evident that, when the concepts of truth and interpretation are critically examined, even in an introductory way, they bear the same conceptual structure. The concepts of truth and interpretation involve us in the dialectic of exclusion and inclusion, of distinguishing between what the concepts of truth and interpretation exclude and what they include. If we fail to distinguish critically between what truth and interpretation include and exclude, between what is knowingly inclusive of truth and interpretation and what unknowingly excludes them (and what they must then knowingly exclude as unknowable), then we shall never be in a position to develop a comprehensive conception of truth and interpretation as involving that which knowingly undertakes to exclude them. It is crucial to recognize that thinking—which must never be dualistically opposed to action, speech, emotion, belief, reason...—always involves interpretation and expresses truth, which is not to deny that we constantly lose ourselves in both partial (false) interpretations and partial truths (falsehoods), etc.

Thinking, as the truth of interpretation and the interpretation of truth, is not given in the nature of things but comes into thought and existence from nothing, from nothing which can be known in and through the appearances of natural space and time.

In Part II of my essay in thinking I shall take up the dialectic of truth and interpretation. To comprehend that neither truth as its own standard, history, and relationship nor interpretation as communication through metaphor and paradox can be thought unless both are thought equally is to realize the thought that there is no truth outside (its) interpretation and that there is no interpretation outside (its) truth. In Part I, I have wanted to emphasize the critical distinction between truth and interpretation, on the one hand, and, on the other, that which is blind to and ignorant of both truth and interpretation. It is only when we make this critical distinction, the distinction between the Bible and what I call extra-biblical paganism, that we are in a position to become properly responsible for the awesome distinction for which we must eternally account, the distinction between truth and interpretation, on the one hand, and their idolatrous perversions, on the other. The option of innocence, the option of extra-biblical paganism blind to and ignorant of truth and interpretation: this option, which is not conscious of being an option, is not an option for human beings in the (post-biblical) world today. It has never been an option. The coming into thought and existence—the revelation—of truth and interpretation brings to an end the ignorance of good and evil. The new era begins with the original fall from contradictory innocence into the dialectic of truth and interpretation knowing good and evil. With the termination of the distinction which is blind to and ignorant of its distinction from truth and interpretation—except as the non-existent limit of that of which we must be conscious of not being able to comprehend in its unconsciousness—an infinitely more terrible distinction, however, bursts upon the world. This is the distinction between truth and interpretation, on the one hand, and, on the other, the reduction of truth and interpretation to the language of simile and contradiction, something completely inconceivable and unimaginable to extra-biblical paganism. Not merely to rule over the other in blindness to and ignorance of what constitutes otherness, but knowingly to reduce the other, as the thing-in-itself, to a thing which contradicts the nature of things is to replace Socratic ignorance with Satanic perversion of knowledge.

The paradox which constitutes truth and interpretation as their own standard is precisely that it also brings into thought and existence such contradictory notions as lying, deception, and false interpretation which are inconceivable and unimaginable to Socrates but which the Bible knows as sin: the reduction of truth and interpretation to idols, false prophets, and Antichrists. When Jesus tells Pilate that he comes to bear witness to the truth, he knows that he knows what Pilate does not know, which is that, in bearing witness to the truth, one must always bear witness against the enemy of truth. The enemy of truth, Jesus knows, is not Pilate, the pagan representative of the Roman Empire ignorant of and blind to truth and interpretation, but himself, in his very comprehension of truth and interpretation. If one is not one's own opposition—if one fails to comprehend the commandment of loving one's enemy—then the dialectic of truth and interpretation will be unable to comprehend its own sinning; it will be unable to comprehend, as its own, either the perversions of truth or perverted interpretations. It is only when we recognize that truth and interpretation as their own standard are also the standard of their false and falsifying oppositions that we shall be in a position to comprehend the dialectic of truth and interpretation.

PART II

TRUTH AND INTERPRETATION AS THE DIALECTIC OF THOUGHT AND EXISTENCE

3

Introduction: Human Existence, Natural Teleology, and the Question Why?

Cur deus homo? Why did God become man? Anselm asks, in about 1100, as he initiates, at the beginning of the medieval awakening, the great tradition of speculative investigation into the origins of human thought and existence to which the present essay in thinking itself belongs. Why has God become human being? Why does God become human being? Why will God become human being? Why is God becoming human being? Why does God exist as human being? Why—to acknowledge the stylish way in which Anselm's supple Latin captures the paradox of thought and existence—did human being become God? Why has human being become God? Why does human being become God? Why is human being becoming God? Why will human being become God? Why does God become human being? Why is human being becoming God? Why does human being exist as God? Why, to paraphrase Anselm in an age in which speculative interest has shifted from the God of the text to the text of the God, is the Bible—the Bible of both Jews and Christians (and we may note that the Bible is also sacred to Muslims)—the truth of interpretation and the interpretation of truth? *Cur biblia interpretationis veritas et veritatis interpretatio?* I initiate my presentation of the dialectic of truth and interpretation with meditation upon the title of one of Anselm's celebrated works not only to mark the distance which we have travelled in the nine hundred years separating us from our speculative beginnings in the Middle Ages, the so-called Age of Faith, but also to indicate the continuity of modernism, indeed, of post-modernism, the age of the so-called death of God, with biblical thinking. Our question—the very structure of the questions we ask—is grounded in a nexus of values which are consonant with Anselm's question and which are unthinkable—inconceivable and unimaginable—to any extra-biblical tradition.

Anselm, it is true, is concerned with meditating on the Incarnation: why did God become man? Why did God become a particular human being, Jesus, as the Christ, as the God/man? But the structure of Anselm's Latin question has an elasticity, a suppleness, a depth which are unknown in classical Latin. The lissomeness of Anselm's expression does not reflect great knowledge of or control over the vast grammatical and syntactical resources of classical Latin (the barbarisms of Anselm's restricted Latin style would upset not only his classical forebears in Rome but even more his idolatrous successors in the new Rome of the nineteenth century British Empire). The depth of Anselm's expression embodies—incarnates—the very content the truth of which is inseparable from his interpretation of it. Anselm is concerned to analyze why God became human being. How, in other words, are we to understand the incarnation of God in human being? Not only, however, do he and his reader know that he is thus equally concerned with the divinization of human being (God becomes human being [so that] human being becomes God), but we (author and reader) know that, if what Anselm writes is true, then its truth will be embodied in the words in which he expresses this truth. As Anselm explores the meaning of the Incarnation, of why God became human being, his very question, his analysis, implicates him not only in the truth of its answer but also in the interpretation of that truth. The point which I want to make here is that Anselm's question involves us—as the question I pose about the Bible, truth, and interpretation equally involves us—author and reader, in recognizing the mutual interrelation of the question in its form (why?) and the question in its content (why God man?) and that both the form and the content of the question why? equally involve the interrelation of truth and interpretation.

But what happens to my claim that the question why? involves both author and reader in its answer if the reader—any reader—denies (as Jews, Muslims, and various Christians, not to mention atheists and those outside the biblical tradition, deny) that God becomes human being (or that human being becomes God) or, at the very least, claims to have no interest in the question? The only possible answer, I think, is that we (readers, the heirs of the past) have an obligation to our history, to ourselves, to become responsible for the traditions which our forebears have passed on to us, neither rejecting nor accepting them uncritically. In other words, denial or disinterest, if they are not to be a matter of mere taste, not to mention simple ignorance, themselves involve, no less than acknowledgement or acceptance, the articulation of criteria involving truth and interpretation. In order to deny something (to say no) or to declare something to be without interest, we have to articulate, beyond mere taste or simple ignorance, what it is that we believe or find interesting.

It is critical to note that Anselm does not ask—did (or has) God become human being? (did or has human being become God?)—as if one were free to answer in the negative, dismissing the question as irrelevant. Anselm so positions the reader within his question that the reader must either accept its premises—and be interested in exploring why God became human being—or deny its premises, deny, in other words, not just the fact that God became human being (etc.) but the very question why? itself. But how could one deny the validity of the question why?, assuming that one's denial were not due to mere ignorance or lack of interest? Surely, the only way in which one could truly deny Anselm's question of why God became human being would be to replace it with another question asking why? One might ask: why did God establish a covenant with human beings? why did God establish a covenant with a particular people, the ancient Israelites? One might (today) deny the significance of the word "God" and ask: *cur homo homo*? and mean: why did and/or why does and/or why will wo/man become wo/man, or why did/does/will (a) human being become (a) human being? One might ask more briefly, yet: *cur homo*? or, with ultimate brevity, *cur*? One might, one supposes, finally remain silent:? But can one, in good faith, stop asking the question why? Can one refuse to ask, or to answer: *cur homo*? What does one answer in response to Anselm's question—*cur deus homo*?—if "God" is understood to be either the truth of human interpretation or the interpretation of human truth or if "man" is understood to be either the divine truth of interpretation or the divine interpretation of truth?

Reflection on why we ask questions, on the nature of the question why?, on what constitutes the very structure of questioning itself brings to light two fundamental points, each intimately interwoven with the other such that each is profoundly dependent on the other. The first point is that there is one, and only one, significant question which we can ask, and this is the question why?, although it has infinitely many legitimate (and also infinitely many illegitimate) versions. To pose a question, seriously, is to think; it is to be conscious of implicating everyone involved in what I am calling, in this essay in thinking, the dialectic of truth and interpretation. The second point to note is that, in the history of the world, notwithstanding the infinite variety of human experience, there have been two, and only two, traditions of asking why? The first, revealing the dialectic of truth and interpretation, bears the structure of Anselm's question: *cur deus homo*? The second, reflecting ignorance of and blindness to the dialectic of truth and interpretation, bears the structure of Aristotle's teleology. Why do things move? What is the end which, unmoving, moves things blindly and ignorantly to their end? The utter difference or incompatibility between these two genres of questions, between the two ways in which to ask why?, is nearly always obfuscated or indeed repressed through confusion between the infinite versions of each.

In the tradition of the Greeks, as of all extra-biblical peoples, to ask why is, as we have already seen, to show yourself to be ignorant of and blind to, to be other than and opposed to, the putative end or *telos* of your question. To ask why is to discover that your end is fated to reverse you before you are born and that your beginning is fated to reverse you in the end at your death. All extra-biblical life is teleological in structure; and teleology, as the *logos* which locates its *telos* in nature, ineluctably divides individuals (and groups) from their question. To ask a question—to ask why?—is to discover that the end of your question is the other whose contradictory appearances in nature condemn you to ignorance of your question. The structure of questioning in the Greek world reflects the contradictory logic of seeking (being, living...) which Socrates exposes so brilliantly. To ask why—to seek your end—is always to show that you ask in vain. To ask, for example, why Thebes is suffering a devastating plague (or what is truth?, that is, what is the *telos* or end of truth?) is to ask (or to seek the truth) in ignorance of your end. All questions in the extra-biblical world are teleological, and all teleological questions show the question to be ignorant of and blind to its answer, its end, which, as fate, is always other than and opposed to what the questioner seeks. In the extra-biblical world to ask why?, to ask questions, to seek answers is, without exception, to show yourself to be opposed to and other than your answer. It no less follows that, just as questions are always contradicted by their answers, so answers, that is, claims to possess the end or good, are no less contradictory. For even the gods, notwithstanding their vaunted immortality, not to mention the unmoved mover, are subject to fate; and fate is itself the mirror in which nature or reality is reflected as the doctrine of opposites, the ineluctable division between self and other, between ruler and ruled, between being and its appearances, between question and answer. The only end to the infinite regress of finite questions and to the infinite progress of finite answers is fate, that structure of otherness or opposition which is always blindly other than and ignorantly opposed to itself.

The recognition, on our part, that the Greeks, like all extra-biblical peoples, are endlessly ignorant of the questions they ask and endlessly blinded by the responses they receive is not to deny that they possess rich and diverse information—natural, ethnic, mathematical...—based on sharp observation and mental acuity. Indeed, it has often been remarked that "primitive" peoples are much better observers of their immediate environment than we who today live in the industrial and post-industrial age, in part, of course, because they are so dependent on it. (A native inhabitant of the forested mountains of New Guinea knows well, for example, the avifauna which surround him insofar as they bear directly on his life, above all, on his needs for food and ritual, to which now science and tourism have recently been added. But he is no match for the professional, field ornithologist or even the experienced, amateur bird watcher whose seeing and hearing are not primarily guided by the *telos* of utility.) How sense data and mental terms (a particular bird of paradise and "bird") are understood depends ultimately on the question why? which is addressed to them. Are they understood to relate to human thought and existence or to be subject to natural teleology?

Although the questions asked—and the responses given—in extra-biblical life possess the terms of the question, they lack, they are ignorant of and blind to, the concept of the question. To question meaningfully, to find that, in asking why?, you are not opposed to but united with your question, is to find that the one thing which you can question is the concept. To ask—what is truth?—is to ask, for instance, why the truth is important—to you, to me, to us. Neither you nor I can ask meaningful questions about truth (or anything else) except truthfully. To ask—what is truth?—is to submit oneself to the truth, to being questioned by the truth itself. To ask about truth, to seek the truth, is to presuppose the presence of truth, its thought and existence, its framework, its point of view, its perspective, its history.... As the reader will have anticipated, I associate this second genre of questions, of asking why?, with the Bible. In utter contrast to the tradition of extra-biblical paganism, in which question and answer, question and questioner, are fatally opposed to and the opposite of each other, the biblical tradition of asking questions—*cur deus homo*?—unites the question with its answer, questioners with their questions. The questioner cannot begin, he cannot seek, to answer his question unless he already knows the answer. This stark assertion, although true, needs amplification, but let me merely note at present that even when we make serendipitous discoveries, we can recognize something as involving serendipity only because we know what to expect even if we did not expect it. More generally, we can recognize something to be true, we can use the term "true" meaningfully or truthfully, only because, from the beginning, we know what truth is. Truth does not emerge from either empirical experience (induction) or mental reflection (deduction); for no number of discrete facts or reasons will add up to the truth, yet truth is not something innate, for it is found only in our experience. In contrast with the extra-biblical tradition, questions in the biblical tradition bind us to their answers. To ask a question, meaningfully (and not merely verbally or formally), is to bind oneself to knowing, that is, to analyzing, working out, living, embodying, revealing, developing... its answer. We thus learn to take with a grain of salt the skeptical rhetoric typical of individualistic North America whereby it is habitually said that what counts is, not obtaining the right answers but asking the right questions (as if those who ask the right questions were not committed to providing, to proving, to living by the right answers).

It is important to note here that the main reason that Anselm's question—*cur deus homo*?—today appears remote or, indeed, alien to us is because of the misappropriation, on the part of us moderns, of the rightful claim of natural science to have replaced the teleological question why? (why do things fall towards the earth? why do things move?) with the descriptive question how? The greatest scientists and philosophers of the seventeenth century—Bacon, Galileo, Descartes, Pascal, Huygens, Newton, Spinoza—reject root and branch the teleology of Aristotle, although it is only Spinoza who systematically eliminates Greek teleology not only from science but also from ethics, politics, logic, psychology, and metaphysics (both philosophy and theology). In part, because of the immense success of the scientific revolution, in part, because medieval philosophy and theology (largely after Anselm) had been so deeply compromised by its conflation with Aristotelian teleology, the elimination of the teleological "why?" becomes, in the modern world, nearly universally equated with the elimination of all questions asking why? There are only a very few thinkers before the Protestant Reformation—William of Occam, Marsilius of Padua, Nicholas of Cusa—who subject Greek teleology to searching critique on the basis of the very issue shaping Anselm's question, *cur deus homo*? We may recall that Luther publicly burns the works of Aristotle as a protest, not against paganism but against Rome's idolatry in reducing the revelation of why God became man to natural ignorance and blindness of why things are as they are—this book burning darkly portending the partisan ideology of modernity. But the Reformation, both Protestant and Roman Catholic, remains, like the scholastic tradition before it, deeply complicit with Aristotelian teleology.

The brilliantly successful Protestant reformers soon discover that Aristotelianism serves their interests no less urgently than it does those of their Catholic opponents, both past and present. Although Luther and other mainline reformers accuse Rome of reducing the Bible to Aristotle, they, in turn, find themselves blamed for a radical assault on the traditional social and political hierarchies whose only defense, they discover, is a notion of finite, teleological nature, stemming from Aristotle, not a concept of infinite existence, grounded in the Bible. The Protestant reformers continue the medieval tradition of using Aristotelian teleology as a means of hiding God's revelation of the truth of politics and society under a bushel to protect themselves against both radical reformers on their left and Catholic apologists on their right. Whereas they are attacked by their radical opponents for failing to use the good news of biblical freedom, equality, and solidarity to subvert the teleological bias of social and political hierarchy, they are attacked by their Catholic opponents for transforming the Bible into a revolutionary document which undermines the stability of social and political hierarchy. When the defenders of the Roman Church, for their part, find their conception of both the Bible and Aristotle under severe attack, they reaffirm the medieval subordination of not only faith but also reason to teleological hierarchy (which will lead directly to catastrophic events reflecting an anti-intellectualism unknown in the Middle Ages: the burning of Giordano Bruno and the imprisonment and silencing of Galileo). We can well understand why the two greatest philosophers of the seventeenth century, Descartes and Spinoza, are extremely cautious in arranging for both the setting of their life's work and the publication of their devastating critique of teleology and their radical transformation of the understanding of both faith and reason. Descartes chooses to pass most of his mature philosophical life in Holland so as to be beyond the reach of both the French monarchy and the Sorbonne, the theological faculty of the University of Paris. Spinoza, even though he had been excommunicated from the Jewish community in Amsterdam because of his radical critique of religion and philosophy, chooses to remain in Holland where, notwithstanding the violence of the clashes among Protestant sects and between Protestants and Catholics, there is no dominant, orthodox hierarchy, either religious or political. Spinoza selects *caute* (cautiously!) as the device with which to adorn his writings, and, of his two major works, he publishes one anonymously, and the other is published posthumously.

It is little wonder then that, in the revolutionary world of the seventeenth century, the emergence of the new science as liberation from the teleological ignorance and blindness of Aristotle generates the most profound repugnance for everything associated with medieval obscurantism and superstition. The Age of Enlightenment, in which Leibniz will proclaim that whatever is, is (the best of all possible worlds) and Hume will show that whatever *is* (the best of all possible worlds) may *not be*, lies just ahead. It is widely recognized—then and now—that the success of the new science rests on its elimination of Aristotelian teleology, of asking why things are as they are, of the very question why? But it is recognized by very few thinkers (whether literary or philosophical) that to criticize Aristotelian teleology involves not eliminating the question why?, as such, but replacing it with, by grounding it in, another conception of why? which, although it is secular, is not scientific, and which, precisely because it is modern, is biblical. But the prestige of science is—then and now—such that the aims, methods, and content of science become the dominant model for epistemology, ethics, and politics. It is true that the humanities have traditionally remained resistant to the elimination of the question why? from their agenda, but often at the expense of resigning themselves to the status of belles-lettres without either serious social meaning or significant epistemological or moral concerns. That the sciences of man, the so-called social sciences, have largely achieved academic success, especially in North America, by eliminating the question why? through basing their positivistic conceptions of method on mechanistic versions of science reflects the enormous difficulty that even the most sophisticated thinkers have in developing a conception of thinking which, in encompassing the natural sciences, is not to be either reduced or opposed to them.

Even Descartes holds that, since he has demonstrated, once and for all, the metaphysical foundations of physics, future thinkers can dispense with any further metaphysical speculation and apply themselves to what counts, to science. Having shown definitively that science is grounded in the self whose thought expresses existence and whose existence involves thinking, scientists can forget the thinking self, its thought and existence, and concentrate on studying the objects of nature. Spinoza claims in the *Ethics* that his demonstration of ethical truth is geometrical in method. His demonstration is exact and exacting and, in my judgment, true. But the truth of Spinoza's philosophy, his very claim that truth is its own standard, the standard both of itself and of the false, has nothing as such to do with that branch of mathematics called geometry (whether Euclidian or Cartesian). That even thinkers of the first magnitude like Descartes and Spinoza, than whom there is none greater, can misconceive or at least misconstrue the thinking enterprise shows how difficult it is and remains since their time to develop a conception of truth which is not reducible to scientific certainty, and, I should add, to develop a conception of interpretation which is not reducible to the unscientific, subjective uncertainty to which the humanities, including religion, commonly resign themselves.

To liberate thinking from the blindness and ignorance of Aristotelian teleology is not only to eliminate the question why? from the investigation of nature, but it is also to reveal the question why?—the same question in form but an utterly different question in concept and content—as the very constitution of thinking. Actually, this formulation, although historically sound, is not ontologically accurate. It is the revelation of the question why? in the world which both eliminates the blindness and ignorance of pagan teleology and constitutes truth as its own standard. But the revelation of truth—in the world of the Bible—creates enormous resistance, conflict, tergiversation..., not only on the part of those to whom the revealed truth is new but also, and much more significantly, on the part of those to whom the truth is old, believers and non-believers, the credulous and the incredulous (it being important to note that neither belief nor unbelief as such is found in the extra-biblical world). Not pagan ignorance but idolatrous belief or unbelief—what today we call rationalization, false consciousness, reductionism, bad faith, repression...—is the issue to be faced. The issue is the conflation of truth with the cultural certainties of the day. Especially potent, historically, in their subversion of truth have been two cultural ideologies, one dominant in the ancient and medieval world but still very much with us today, the second coming into existence and gaining overweening domination in modernity. The first is Platonism. The second is the science of nature (including technology, that is, what critical theorists call technological rationality).

By Platonism I mean to gather together the whole of Greek thought centering on Socrates, including the major pre-Socratic thinkers, Parmenides and Heraclitus; his major opponents, the Sophists; and his disciple, Plato, Plato's disciple, Aristotle, and the major Hellenistic schools of philosophy stemming from Socrates through them: Stoicism, Skepticism, and Neoplatonism, plus Epicureanism (including the most eclectic admixtures of philosophical sophistication and vulgar traditions involving theurgy, astrology, nature religions, popular cults... such as Hermeticism, and the like). Not only is the world not to be divided between Platonists and Aristotelians, but the Socratic tradition is not to be divided against the atomists, Democritus and the Epicureans, for, as we have already seen, all Greek thinkers, in following the law of contradictory opposites, are fatally blind to, ignorant of, and other than the truth of themselves. Aristotelian teleology is but a specific version of Platonism. The finite end of humanity—the unmoved mover, fate always other than itself—is precisely that which is immovably opposed to those who, living, seek it in their blindness and ignorance and which is always identical with those who are dead to life. The extra-biblical world, generally, including that of the Greeks, is dominated by finite opposites, which, like the impenetrable atoms of Democritus, metamorphose infinitely. But the differences which are infinitely generated by finite atoms ineluctably other than themselves—

in the world of extra-biblical paganism—are blind to and ignorant of what constitutes their difference.

Platonism, as I shall call the amalgam of paganism stemming from the Greeks which is so very seductive in its attraction, above all, to intellectuals, both literary and philosophical, is displaced in the seventeenth century from the scientific study of nature by the elimination of teleology. But it is here that the old paganism, Platonism, and the brave new world of scientific knowledge come together in a convenient marriage of opposites which defies rational self-understanding by producing the chasm between science and art, truth and feeling, objectivity and subjectivity, between, in the terms of this essay in thinking, truth and interpretation, so characteristic of modernity with its eclipse of God and the revolt of the masses. It is precisely because of the domination of science and technology in our lives, including the way in which positivism, with its pseudo imitation of scientific methodology, comes to dominate the social scientific study of human beings, that Platonism becomes the refuge of the humanities, the world of both art (literary, visual, and musical) and humanistic thought and scholarship. Science, having eliminated the question why? from the study of nature, leaves the other disciplines in a dilemma, the humanities, above all, for the humanities do remain inalterably opposed to the reduction of human thought and existence to the objective realm of scientific knowledge. But science is so powerful, gaining enormously in prestige as its anti-teleological and often blatantly utilitarian and technological ideology is wedded to the ideology of, first, the democratic (bourgeois) revolutions in the early modern period and, then, the socialistic revolutions in our own century in their opposition to the authoritarianism of church and throne, that the humanities either retreat into the subjective realm of art for art's sake, increasingly formalistic and devoid of human content, or, from the viewpoint of Marxist humanists, adumbrate a vague future whose aesthetic utopia is to be liberated from dirty bourgeois hands. The humanities—and I am especially concerned here with philosophy—have enormous difficulty in replacing the teleology of Aristotle with a meaningful end. Indeed, since science is so central a part of the whole process of modernism which we call secularization, and since secularization, both intellectual and political, comes into thought and existence in opposition to both political and ecclesiastical authoritarianism, the humanities find that human values, those associated with traditional morality and religion, have been not only discredited by the political revolutions liberating men and women from the tyranny of ecclesiastical and political elites but also displaced by the scientific study of nature, which is accessible to all.

The bitter irony for the humanities, including religious studies as an academic discipline (or what today is often politely called comparative religion), is that they are caught between Scylla and Charybdis. To be anti-scientific or even anti-technological is merely foolish, romantic, antiquarian, and, not infrequently, reactionary, reflecting a desire to return to a past order based on traditional hierarchies, both social and spiritual. To oppose science is also simply wrong—epistemologically and politically—for the elimination of teleology from the study of nature *qua* nature is a gain for all time. There is no going back to the blindness and ignorance of extrabiblical paganism. Science is not to be blamed for the dehumanization of the modern world, whatever its role in it. Even when the humanities, in their concern for articulating human values, recognize that they have no right to oppose science or technology, as such—and this recognition is, at best, fitful and inconclusive—they typically accept science's elimination of teleological questions as definitive. But, since the elimination of teleology involves the elimination of the morality and religion traditionally associated with it, humanists, assuming that they do not simply reject science and technology through irrational sentimentality or the rage of impotence, have no choice outside of either becoming spokespersons for science and its technological triumphs (whence socialist realism, philosophy of science, science fiction...) or retreating into the subjective realm of feeling or of art for art's sake. In surrendering truth to science they are left embracing a shadowy version of interpretation without an objective correlative. In allowing truth to be reduced to the scientific knowledge of natural objects, without interpretation, the interpretation which humanists retain as their own is indistinguishable from the relativity of subjective opinion, without reference to a conception of truth which is universal for all.

The bitter irony for the humanities is to be found in the fact that, while they recognize the legitimacy of science and yet oppose the reduction of human beings to natural objects subject to scientific measurement and technological manipulation, they abandon, nevertheless, the question why? as either meaningless or unanswerable. Although they oppose dehumanization, the humanities ground their opposition, not in morality and religion, which have been discredited and displaced by the elimination of teleology, but in subjective opinion, in feeling, in art for art's sake, in form, in what I am here calling Platonism, although it is a Platonism utterly foreign to Plato and Aristotle and to their pagan predecessors and successors. I call it Platonism, not merely because humanists are eternally seduced by Socratic blandishments, but, more significantly, because humanists, despairing over the elimination of teleology from the world of appearances, claim to seek it in a world of subjective forms, while at the same time saying that it is unattainable and certainly not open to objective scrutiny or verification. The ironies of modern Platonism thus burst into view for those who, following Kant, say, are prepared to acknowledge the reliably certain knowledge of nature which science attains but who recognize that the scientific elimination of finite teleology is grounded in the infinite *telos* of the thing-in-itself. The subjective Platonism of modern humanism (including that of Whitehead's version of the natural sciences) is thus opposed to the objective knowledge of nature, something inconceivable to Plato and Aristotle. Modern Platonism accepts the elimination of natural teleology (I am assuming an "enlightened" Platonism in my discussion, not antediluvian opposition to science and technology, however common it remains among humanists), something equally inconceivable to the Greeks (including Democritus, for whom the finite atom is its own blind and ignorant *telos*). The irony of modern Platonism is that, in both accepting and opposing science, it is but the mirror reflection of the inability on the part of science either to pose or to answer the question why? Modern Platonism is thus itself but another version of the triumph of science and technology in eliminating the question why? from legitimate human concern.

The bitter irony of modern Platonism is that, in claiming to possess a subjective certainty without an objective base, a position unthinkable to Plato and Aristotle, it is but the mirror reflection of science, which, along with technology, claims to possess an objective certainty without acknowledging its base in the human subject. To divorce human subjectivity from objectivity, that is, from a ground in truth, only lends support to the view that the human subject is but one more object of nature accessible to scientific and technological manipulation. The bitterest irony of all for humanist Platonism is, however, that, unlike science, it is utterly bogus and fraudulent. Science, it is true, does become an uncontrolled and uncontrollable sorcerer's apprentice when its elimination of the teleological question why? is not understood to be grounded in the human subject. But Platonism, having no legitimacy in the world of nature, surrenders all claims to truth in the name of feeling and subjectivity, of cultural relativism and the beauty of form lacking all content.

It is particularly instructive to compare modern Platonism, which natural science strips bare of both its teleological logic and its moral and religious content, with its counterpart in the Middle Ages. Great Muslim, Jewish, and Christian thinkers like Averroes, Maimonides, and Aquinas are typically concerned to show how their religious teachings comport with the world of Aristotelian teleology. They claim, using various distinctions and such varied strategies as Maimonides' argument that the truth which he teaches is contradictory, that the biblical doctrines of creation and salvation are consonant with Aristotle's conception of nature, *telos*, and the immortality of the soul (*nous*). But these medieval thinkers neither intend nor undertake to repudiate, in formal terms, the dogmatic truths of their religious tradition. In the eyes of their opponents, however, the claim to teach not only the divine truth of the Bible but also the natural or human truth of Aristotle involves a double, or contradictory (opposed), truth. The riposte of those accused of teaching the double truth of God and Aristotle is that, since the two truths belong to different realms (heaven and earth), they do not ultimately contradict—they are not opposed to or irreconcilable with—each other.

The Platonism of medieval Muslim, Jewish, and Christian thinkers—and I repeat that I understand Platonism here as the general structure of pagan thought coming from the Greeks, based, in whatever sophisticated or vulgar version, on the doctrine of opposites, a teleological conception of nature, and the law of contradiction—is, however, a contradictory admixture of biblical values and pagan notions. It is precisely the claim that the truth of the biblical God (faith) and the truth of Aristotle's conception of nature (reason) can both be truthfully taught which fourteenth and fifteenth century thinkers like William of Occam, Marsilius of Padua, and Nicholas of Cusa challenge so pertinaciously. They show, in substance, that veracious discussion of two (or any number of) truths presupposes a universal framework of truth common to all. Against the Aristotelian notion of teleological nature William of Occam appeals to the *potentia absoluta Dei*, the absolute power of God, for whom, he shows, everything natural is possible insofar as it is actual or existent. Even God's absolute power is restricted to (or limited by) existence, for the power and the existence of God are identical. God does not have the power (the possibility) not to be, for the power of God is the power to be, the power to exist, the power to act, the power to create.... William replaces the Aristotelian notion of potentiality or possibility, according to which everything actual is always ignorant of and blind to, always opposed to, its potential, with the biblical revelation to all of the *potentia*, the potency, the power of existence. The pure *actus* of the unmoved mover, whose "act" is always other than and opposed to the potentiality, the possibility, of its apparent actions, is replaced by the action of God (the God of action), whose revelation of the priority of existence is philosophically formulated as the ontological argument of existence (the existence of divine and human being). The only true argument—demonstration or proof—is that which begins with existence, the existence of God, that which argues *de potentia absoluta Dei*. Existence is the beginning, the priority, which replaces the double truth (the double-mindedness) of all teleological arguments which ineluctably oppose end and beginning, essence and existence, potentiality (possibility) and actuality.... Marsilius of Padua understands the existence of God, the *potentia absoluta Dei*, to be represented in, by, and through the people of God who, in arguing from their existence to the democratic constitution of church and state, constitute their community on the basis of their democratic existence. Just as William of Occam uses the absolute power of divine existence to destroy the hierarchical view of nature held by the Aristotelians, so Marsilius is able to overcome the hierarchical view of politics, as found in Aristotle and his medieval followers, according to which one, some, or many rule over others in their natural opposition to them, by conceiving of the people as representing the absolute power of God. That the double truth of opposites is to be understood, not on the basis of the law of contradiction whose *telos* is ineluctably opposed to and other than itself, but on the basis of the law of existence, according to which all humans are equal and free as the children of God, is formulated by Nicholas of Cusa as the *coincidentia oppositorum*. It is in God, understood, not as the unmoved mover, in which all are opposed, but as the one whose existence is revealed as the absolute truth for all, in whom all opposites coincide as one.

The bitter irony which a comprehensive understanding of the intellectual history of medieval, early modern, and modern thought reveals is that the post-scientific Platonism of modernity is stripped naked of all conceptual content. Whereas Muslim, Jewish, and Christian thinkers in the Middle Ages remain largely oblivious to the utter incompatibility of biblical values with the teleological notions of Platonism, the founders of the scientific revolution in the sixteenth and seventeenth centuries show that nature can be objectively studied only if it is stripped of any notion of *telos*. Not only have modern Platonists been deprived of the teleological conception of nature central to Plato and Aristotle, but they fail to understand that the conception of nature central to scientific study is not merely compatible with but has its ground in, and only in, the conception of existence which is biblical in origin. Modern Platonists—that is, most philosophers and other humanists concerned with values—not only have lost, irretrievably, the Greek notion of *telos*, but they have failed to develop a conception of existence which would give reality to their thought. They fail to see that science and its technological might can be limited by, and only by, a conception of existence which is not reducible to the objects of nature; and the reason that they fail to embrace such a conception of existence is that they remain blind to and ignorant of the theological principle in which it is grounded. They would have to recognize that the only conception of reason, or thinking, which is true to human beings is one which grounds nature in existence and that the only conception of existence worthy of human beings is the one whose origin is biblical.

Medieval Platonists had been right to engage the issue of double truth, the issue of the relationship of the truth of divine existence and the truth of Aristotelian nature, the truths of spirit and flesh, of salvation and the world, of the people of the Book and extra-biblical peoples. To comprehend the relationship of God and nature, that relationship which Rousseau calls human nature, is an intellectual task, a spiritual undertaking, of truly formidable proportions, than which there is none greater. To conceive, in comprehensive terms, of how divine creation encompasses both the chosen people—those to whom choice is revealed—and all peoples—those ignorant of and blind to choice—is a task which remains no less formidable today, for it is the task which every generation, every people, every individual must face. It is the very task—the task of comprehending the dialectic of truth and interpretation—in which both the author and the reader of this book are mutually engaged.

But medieval thinkers, once they had begun to absorb the endlessly seductive corpus of Aristotelian writings, find it enormously difficult to realize that the Bible possesses a conception of nature utterly different from that found in Aristotle. In simple terms, the task which they face is to distinguish between existence—divine and human—and nature; and, in order to effect this distinction, they must recognize that neither existence nor nature, neither spirit nor letter, has its principle in Greek teleology, in paganism, generally. Existence is not Platonic appearance always opposed to, contradicted by, and other than what it is in reality (nature). Nature is not the Aristotelian end to which all things blindly move and of which we, in existence, are eternally ignorant. *Creatio ex nihilo*, the creation of existence from nothing, from nothing natural, from nothing which is not creative of human existence, is its own standard, the standard of both existence and nature. The double truth of existence and nature is not a contradictory admixture of biblical truth and teleological truths but the singularly paradoxical truth that nature has its *telos* in (divine and human) existence. That humankind is its own nature is the truth of nature, a truth which can be scientifically known solely through the appearances of natural space and time but which can be thought as the thing-in-itself only in its freedom to will the existence of the kingdom of ends true for all human beings. This truth had been comprehended by a few late medieval thinkers of the stature of William of Occam, Marsilius of Padua, and Nicholas of Cusa. But, with the subsequent triumph of the scientific study of nature over natural teleology, the rejection of Aristotelian philosophy means that theology, which, in the scholastic thought of the Middle Ages, had been profoundly compromised by its union with Aristotle, is equally rejected. Scientific objectivity, freed from Aristotelian teleology, becomes the universal truth eclipsing the existence of the subject, both divine and human.

It is important to note that thinkers like William of Occam, Marsilius of Padua, and Nicholas of Cusa, in using the absolute power of God to deconstruct the hierarchical conception of teleological nature held by the followers of Aristotle, are not simply opposing (divine) faith to (human) reason in the manner of those who denounce the worldly concerns of (Aristotelian) reason as seducing the faithful from their heavenly vocation. Rather, they oppose the teleological conception of nature not simply because it is faithless but equally because it is utterly devoid of a concept of reason. In their critique of natural teleology they show that abiding faith in the absolute power of divine existence involves a conception of reason, of rational inquiry, of ratiocination which is altogether incompatible with

Aristotle's conception of mind (*nous*). They show that to hold that the truths of God and Aristotle are both true, each in its own sphere, is to hold, falsely, a conception of double, or contradictory, truth. They show that—to adopt the language of dialectic whose conceptual content they are in the process of creating—the double truth to be embraced is the dialectic of faith and reason, both of which are to be identified with existence, whether divine or human, and neither of which is to be identified with nature. They show that the notions of nature and mind found in Aristotle, in Greek or extra-biblical thought, generally, have nothing to do with either the nature which is accessible to human study or the reason which studies nature. They show that, where faith is absent, neither reason nor nature is present and that, where faith is present, there is equally present the responsibility of developing properly human conceptions of both reason and nature. Thus, they are opposed, not to Aristotle, as such, for it would have been inconceivable to Aristotle to attempt to adapt his natural teleology, of which humans are ignorant and by which they are blinded, to existence understood as human creation and salvation (liberation). They are opposed, rather, both to those who would reduce biblical faith to Aristotle and to those who, pretending to defend biblical faith, censure the study of paganism and thus inhibit the emergence of faithful thinking. They show that, whereas the Aristotelian notions of mind and nature are interchangeable, for each is fatally blind to and ignorant of its *telos*, the biblical conceptions of reason and nature are not interchangeable. Precisely because thinking belongs to existence, as Descartes shows us, the claim "I think, therefore, I am" reveals the truth of nature.

Modern Platonism, blindly and ignorantly—idolatrously—striving to defend the autonomy of human subjects, the subjectivity of truth (the truth of subjectivity), retreats into relativity. Not only has it lost its anchor in teleology, but it is unable to recognize that the true ground of objectivity, of the scientific knowledge of the objects of possible experience, is the existence of the subject (subjective existence). To understand that the question why?—*cur deus homo*?—encompasses Descartes' claim—I think, therefore, I am—is to understand the importance of recognizing that we can develop a comprehensive and proper conception of truth only if we come to terms with its biblical (theological) origins. For it is only the Bible which allows us both to recognize the legitimacy of the science of nature, with its elimination of pagan teleology, and to place science and technology within the more encompassing framework of thought and existence for which the question why? remains critical. It is uniquely the dialectic of biblical critique which, on the one hand, reveals the ignorance and blindness of finite teleology and, on the other, shows that science, along with its shadow Platonism, can be protected from becoming the most hideous idolatry of all time only if truth is shown to inhere in the existing subject, not in the natural object. But the enemy to be exposed is not only scientific fundamentalism (science misconceived as knowledge of the thing-in-itself) and pseudo Platonism (pagan contradiction falsely embraced as the truth). It is equally important to expose the idolatry of religious fundamentalism, the reduction of the biblical conception of truth to immediate, direct, and literal knowledge of the thing-in-itself. The concept of truth must be defended not only against scientific objectivism and humanistic subjectivism but also against religious dogmatism which reduces the truths of dogma to idols, as if they can be known in themselves as natural objects. If we are to overcome the dualism, the double truth, of modern Platonism and modern science, the first of which is false and the second of which is not true in itself, and to embrace the concept of truth without falling into religious dogmatism, we must develop a conception of truth such that something is true only in and through its interpretation and a conception of interpretation such that something can be interpreted only in and through its truth. Once we show, in the next chapter, the significance of recognizing that the dialectic of truth and interpretation is grounded in the Bible, we shall then be in a position, in the subsequent two chapters, to develop a comprehensive conception, first, of the relationship between faith and reason, such that for either to be true the other must be its interpretation, and, second, of the secular, such that it embodies the dialectic of truth and interpretation. The paradox—one version of the paradox—is that the Bible is revealed simultaneously as the truth of interpretation and as the interpretation of truth only in the secular world.

4

The Bible

I. INTRODUCTION: THINKING THE BIBLE AS OUR EXISTENCE

I want to think about the Bible. I want us—author and reader—to think about the Bible. I want to show that there is no thinking outside the Bible; but to show that, I want to show, is equally to show that the Bible does not exist outside our thinking about it, our thought about it, our thoughtful response to it, our interpreting, living, criticizing, abiding by... the Bible. I want to show that to think about the Bible is to say, with Descartes, *ergo*, I exist. I want to show that, just as to exist is to think about the Bible, to think is to exist in and through the Bible. This demonstration—and it is a demonstration, the most exacting demonstration there is, the only demonstration of which we humans are capable, the only demonstration of which we humans desire, or will, to be capable—involves our pondering the critical elements which constitute the structure of thought and existence fundamental to the Bible, elements which not only believers but also non-believers have pondered from their creation and in whose tradition of ponderation all thinking and existence are to be located.

Believers surely ask, at least once in their life, how it is possible that from so obscure a people as the ancient Israelites or from something so small as a mustard seed (not to mention a babe in a manger) an indomitable tradition of law and faith grows to world-historical proportions. Non-believers frequently ask what justice there is in the fact that God chose one people to bear witness to his revelation of thought and existence, to the exclusion of other peoples. Christians must be particularly careful, then, not to claim that they rectify the covenant which God made with the ancient Jews, excluding all others, by making it universally inclusive of all peoples. If Christians view their covenant as inclusive of all the world, then they stand condemned by Kierkegaard's devastating attack on Christendom which represents, as distinguished from Christianity's militant critique of the world, the triumph of the world, paganism rationalized in the name of the Bible—idolatry—something inconceivable to Socrates, who, at least, did not pretend to be a Christian.

It is naturally possible that non-believers, those who are not (or no longer) Jews or Christians (or Muslims), will claim that the very issue of inclusivity and exclusivity, of universality and uniqueness (particularity or individuality) is, at most, an intramural problem facing Jews and Christians without larger significance. Still, the issue lurking below the surface is whether the Bible (Hebrew and/or Christian) is unique and/or universal. Is it conceivable that God would (could) reveal his truth—that truth would be revealed—to one, and only one (and an admittedly obscure), people? In contemplating Anselm's question, *cur deus homo?*, is it conceivable that God (the principle of thought and existence, of truth and interpretation) would be incarnated in one human being to the exclusion of others? What is the nature of the claim of Christianity to universal truth when it locates its beginnings, its principle, in Judaism, and when, today, although it is a triumphant, if sectarian, success, counting perhaps a billion adherents—while there are fewer than fifteen million Jews in the world—the majority of the world's people do not say, with the Bible: I think, therefore, I am? What if nonbelievers, but also believers, doubt that the revelation of truth and interpretation—of thinking and existence—can, in principle, begin in only one place at one time? What if they refer to the great eastern ways of life— Hinduism, Buddhism, Confucianism, Taoism, and their numerous branchings—not to mention the religions of aboriginal peoples, theosophical systems, and the like? Is it not imperialistic of the biblical religions to claim priority over other religions with regard to uniqueness, exclusiveness and/or inclusiveness, originality, and universality? Are not all criteria involving priority, because they are relative to those making prior claims, contaminated by their own interest, bias, or point of view?

I am not competent to respond to these questions which naturally, and properly, arise for any thoughtful person, insofar as answers to them would presuppose extensive knowledge of eastern and traditional ways of life, etc. I am confident, however, that thoughtful existence and the existence of thought cannot, and must not, be based merely on personal experience and scholarly information, on simply gathering ever more data, although they cannot be found outside of, and are constantly found to be inadequate in the light of, ever richer experience and information. I am confident that, once the dialectic of thought and existence is comprehended (lived), then the distinctions which this work both presupposes and demonstrates will be recognized as the *sine qua non* of thinking and existence.

The reason that I place so much emphasis on comprehending the Greeks as incomprehensible, as possessing neither thought nor existence, is to provide a concrete contrast with the presuppositions of thought and existence which are necessarily the subject of demonstration and to show that demonstrations are never better (other) than their presuppositions. I am not an anthropologist or a student of eastern ways of life. My interest in truth and interpretation emerges, professionally, from problems which work (including teaching) in history, literature, philosophy, social and political thought, and religious studies raises. But I am confident that, once the structure of thought and existence is comprehended—and it can be comprehended only when distinguished systematically both from that which is uncomprehending of thought and existence (for example, the Greeks) and from that which undertakes to render incomprehensible, to distort, pervert, or annihilate, thought and existence (idolatry)—then it will be seen that the doctrine of opposites, whose *logos* is the law of contradiction, shapes all extra-biblical ways of life, notwithstanding their infinite variety. What we need at this point is not more experience and information but deeper, more systematic thinking which risks facing, boldly and imaginatively, but also in awe and humility, the enormous paradox which is our human thought and existence.

What is both unique and universal about the Bible is that it is the paradox. It gives readers (believers, interested parties...) no choice but to choose the paradox, the paradox of thought and existence. It is imperious, indeed, tyrannical, in claiming that the reader has no choice but to choose to think and to exist. It recognizes, throughout its amplitude, that those who do not choose are innumerable, but it never relents in its insistence that to be numbered among the living you must choose the paradox, the dialectic of thought and existence. Because of the absolute commitment to thought and existence the Bible holds that not to choose, to refuse choice or to remain ignorant of thought and existence, is, indeed, a choice, albeit one that is idolatrous and subversive of meaningful human community. The fool says in his heart, the Bible recognizes, that the Bible is only a tissue of human lies, that it is but one more book of mythology, that it is full of inconsistencies and incongruities, that, for all its pretense to fob off its claims on an almighty God, it is an all-too-human work. But what is so maddening about the Bible is that it recognizes the justice of these criticisms; it embraces them; it acknowledges responsibility in creating them; it shows that it cannot be thought to exist outside them (this it says, in particular, to those dogmatic literalists who attempt to make the letter of the Bible perfect, which is naturally only one more species of idolatry, of which the Bible is the severest critic and most perfect master). The Bible, in claiming to create the presuppositions of thought and existence, and thus all demonstrations involving thought and expressing existence, claims both that nothing precedes it and that nothing succeeds it. It claims that the very dialectic of thought and existence which is required to appropriate it it brings into existence, from nothing, from nothing natural, from nothing fatally other than or contradictory of itself. Not only does the Bible show that whatever claims to precede it it creates from nothing, but it also shows that nothing succeeds it except that which it has created from nothing, that whatever does not show the marks of thought and existence cannot be creative. The Bible holds, in other words, that there is nothing which is thoughtful or exists outside its authority and that whatever possesses thought or existence belongs to it.

The demonstration of these presuppositions—the demonstration that demonstration is properly the articulation of the thought and existence which the Bible presupposes—has two broad movements, it seems to me. The first I would call speculative or ontological, the second exegetical or hermeneutical. The distinction between speculation and exegesis, however artificial, is useful, not primarily because of the constitution of thought and existence itself but because of the way in which the Bible is conventionally treated. Since, among the great philosophers, only Spinoza risks taking the Bible seriously, although it is true that Kant, Hegel, and Kierkegaard acknowledge the profound debt which their thinking and existence owe to the Bible, philosophical speculation—sustained, probing, systematic, imaginative ratiocination—remains shallow in its failure to recognize its foundations in the Bible, when it is not simply altogether thoughtless in its pretense that Athens has nothing to do with Jerusalem. Theologians— Bultmann, Van Leeuwen, Lonergan, Rahner, Fackenheim come to mind— are profound, but, in attempting either to help their own particular biblical communities understand themselves in the world or to help the world understand their own particular biblical communities, their speculation overlooks (understandably) the problems facing us all. Right from the beginning we face the dilemma that, while theologians are limited in addressing the Bible on the basis of the thought and existence of a particular biblical tradition, philosophers fail to recognize their limitation in not recognizing their relation to the Bible. In addition to philosophers and theologians there are individual philosophers of religion and religious thinkers whose speculations are deeply moving—one thinks of Eliade and Buber—but even they fail to combine ontology and hermeneutics, to link speculative thinking with imaginative exegesis. (Buber was an imaginative translator of Scripture and commented extensively upon the Bible; but his speculative work is conceived separately.)

Biblical exegetes, scholars, and critics—when they are not either dogmatic apologists for their own religious tradition or skeptics who join the legion of fools in saying in their heart that the Bible does not create their thought and existence from nothing—typically undertake to compensate for their own particular biblical bias either by aping the tradition of positivist scholarship (both Jews and Christians) or by claiming without argument that the principles appropriate to exegesis of Hebrew Scripture are other than those appropriate to Christian Scripture, as if the God of Abraham, Isaac, and Jacob is not the God of Jesus (especially Jews). However illuminating are the data which such scholarship generates, they do little to enhance our appropriation of thought and existence. I do not believe, with the positivistic skeptics, that there is a universal (neutral) perspective separate from its unique embodiment in history. But I do believe—and this will doubtless prove to be of cold comfort to the dogmatists—that biblical thinking, the dialectic of biblical critique, combining speculation and exegesis, is our salvation precisely because it demonstrates, unlike normal philosophy, theology, and biblical scholarship, that the Bible expresses the structure of our thought and existence and that thought and existence involve the structure of the Bible.

The Bible represents—embodies—the structure of thinking and existence. It claims that the world into which it comes is its own creation, its creation from nothing in the natural appearances of space and time existing prior to its own thinking. The Bible shows that it can be read (followed) only by those who represent—embody—its principle (its beginning and end). It shows that its readers are, must be, created in its own likeness, in the image of metaphor, beyond all comparison, not in the finite images of natural space and time. Only those readers who say—in good faith—I think, therefore, I am—are faithful readers of the Bible. The only faithful readers of the Bible are those who say, in good faith, I think, therefore, I am. But, the discerning reader asks, is this to say that those who do not or choose not to read, or have never read, or, finally, have not even heard of or made contact with the Bible do not think or do not exist? The answer to such questions is yes, so long as it is equally recognized that claims about reading, believing in, or accepting the authority of the Bible do not in themselves guarantee or give proof of thoughtful existence (of existing in one's thought). Just as the Bible creates the very conditions of thought and existence, of originality, of priority, so the revelation of these conditions is once and for all. Revelation is both one and universal, at once unique and absolute. Revelation, for example, cannot originally occur in two different places at two different times, for then we should have but the conditions of extra-biblical paganism in which opposites generate, *ad infinitum*, their opposition to each other. Revelation of the truth (of interpretation and of the interpretation of truth) is the condition of conditions, the condition which allows us to understand, which confronts us with the obligation of understanding, the truth of each condition, the worth of every difference. But to recognize the worth or truth of every condition and difference is to see them grounded in the truth (or worth), in the unconditioned, in that which is not the product of any one condition or any number of conditions in blind and ignorant opposition to others.

That our meditation on the Bible needs to be both speculative and exegetical captures the dialectic of thought and existence, truth and interpretation, spirit and letter. I want to show that thinking about the Bible, as such, commits us to recognizing the very paradox of thought and existence, the paradox of the Cartesian "I think, therefore, I am." The paradox of the Bible, precisely like thinking and existence, is that it is its own standard, the standard of both thinking and existence and what is neither thinking nor existence. If the Bible has always been in the world (of nature), then it has never been in the world (of nature). The Bible comes into thought and existence, from nothing, from nothing which is not thoughtful existence (the existence of thought). The Bible bears the marks of its conscious existence, of its existing in its own consciousness, for its authority, its sovereignty, is precisely its own recognition that its authoritative claims to thought and existence cannot have begun outside (independently) of itself. Just as there is only one Bible, one God, one creation, one revelation, one humankind (one man and one woman), one human story, one covenant, one thought (consciousness), one existence, so all these claims to oneness, to unity, are claims equally to being first and last. Nothing can either precede or succeed what is first, except that which understands itself to exist as first; and, in the precedence and succession of firsts, history is born as the story that nothing precedes or succeeds what is first. The Bible claims that there is nothing in conscious existence prior to its own coming thoughtfully into existence—notwithstanding the fact that it does not exist before, say, 2000 B.C.E. and that it emerges in a world of richly diverse civilizations, whose thought and existence it claims to create from the beginning, insofar as they do think and exist. Speculatively formulated, the Bible holds that there cannot have originally been two beginnings, two histories, two priorities, two ones, two firsts, for that is precisely the life of paganism, based on the law of contradiction, which ineluctably divides the historical unity of humanity—its thought and existence—into those who are first and those who are last, ruler and ruled, one and many.... The Bible reveals the fact that the thought and existence of the human self, both individual and communal, involves concepts of completeness, wholeness, integrity, honesty.... Individuals (and communities) must recognize that, in order to be unified in their thought and existence, they come into existence from nothing which is divided against itself, that they owe their life to that which cannot be thought except insofar as it exists and which cannot exist except insofar as it is thought. Thought and existence involve human beings in expressing the ontological argument, the demonstration that I think, therefore, I am.

It is not literally necessary for those who appropriate the dialectic of thought and existence in their lives to have read or to have heard of the Bible (although it is very unlikely, I think, that they will not have). At the least, however, they will have had to experience its revelation indirectly,

the revelation whose history, both individual and communal (psychological and social), connecting them with the Bible they must (be able to)
reconstruct in order for them to appropriate its (their) thought and existence. Once one really works through what it means to read the Bible, however, one recognizes the impossibility, the inconceivability and the
unimaginability, of experiencing the revelation of thought and existence
except through the mediation of the Bible, than which there is none other.
This mediation may or appear to be unintended, indirect, untraditional,
disguised, underground, surreptitious, repressed.... Psychoanalysis and
Marxism, for example, are two of the most powerful vehicles of biblical
thought and existence in the modern world, and, like all powerful expressions of the liberation inherent within biblical revelation, like Judaism and
Christianity themselves, their exponents frequently misunderstand and/or
enslave the very principles of integrity and freedom central to the biblical
self (individual and communal). All coming into the thought and existence
of truth, freedom, justice, love... involves history, the relatedness of beginnings and ends, the world as one action. History is finally unitary, the
single story of all human beings. There is only one human history, however divergent and even divided are our stories and our story tellers. It is
true, however, that, once the Bible shows that the doctrinal opposites endlessly dividing extra-biblical peoples against themselves presuppose the
dialectic of thought and existence, then the struggle for control over the
thought and existence of others is initiated, the struggle to build the unity
of humankind in the image of the Tower of Babel. The Exodus story of the
liberation of the Hebrew slaves from their pagan master Pharaoh is noble
and enduring, and it remains central today not merely to Jewish and Christian meditation but also to liberation movements throughout the world.
When the narrator in Exodus reiterates that God hardens Pharaoh's heart—
indicating that, as a pagan king, he knows not what he does—sensitive
biblical readers, those who identify the unity of their thought and existence
with that of the text which they are reading, know in their hearts that it is
the hardened hearts of idolaters—that is, themselves—which confront
them with an infinitely more difficult problem than paganism itself. Once
thought and existence are revealed to the world as the unity of self, both
individual and communal, freely accessible to all, then every age has to
confront the idolatry of embracing pagan opposites as dualistic nihilism

destructive of that unity, something inconceivable and unimaginable to Pharaoh.

It is critically important that we recognize that the Bible, in providing the story—simultaneously, always, individual and communal—of human beginning, priority, originality, and unity, in contrast with the reign of contradictory opposites which fatally divide extra-biblical life against itself, is also the story of idolatry. Because extra-biblical peoples begin their life without the consciousness of beginning—they think without their existence, and they exist without their thought—not only do they begin without unity (the unity of their life is always opposed to and other than itself), but they also end unconscious of their dualistic beginning in opposition to themselves (for death is but a return to the undifferentiated unity of nature separate from its generation of contradictory opposites). Once the Bible, however, erupts into the world, transforming the doctrine of opposites into the dialectic of thought and existence, it renders not only unity (priority, sovereignty, originality, creativity...) but also duality (of thought and existence) the shibboleths of humanity. Precisely because the unity of God, the unity of humankind, the unity of the Bible, the unity of truth and interpretation—the unity of thought and existence—is not given in the contradictory nature of things but is created from nothing, this unity can also be lost, given up, perverted, corrupted, annihilated, that is, reduced to nothing. In revealing that thought and existence are created from nothing, from nothing which unconsciously reflects the extra-biblical doctrine of opposites, the Bible no less reveals idolatry to be the conscious dualism of reducing thought and existence to the pagan doctrine of opposites. In the idolatry of dualism one side denies, dogmatically or skeptically, the thought and existence of the opposite side which it sees as opposed to itself, something inconceivable and unimaginable in paganism. Just as creation—the creation of thought and existence from nothing—is inconceivable as existing in the extra-biblical world, so its reduction to nothing—nihilism—also cannot be thought to exist in the world of extra-biblical paganism. The extra-biblical world of paganism knows neither the unity of creation nor the dualism of nihilism.

We see, therefore, that it is the Bible, which, in coming into thought and existence from nothing other than its own creativity, creates the very possibility that creativity, freedom, justice, love...—the unity of human thought and existence—will be perverted, falsified, enslaved, denied, annihilated.... It is precisely because the Bible creates our human freedom to think and to exist—and the freedom to think and to exist involves and expresses the unity of humanity—that there emerges the possibility of denying to others the freedom of thinking and existing in unity with others. Insanity also emerges as the possible loss of the unity and freedom of mind (to think and to exist) presupposed by the Bible. When persons find their thought and existence dualistically opposed, their unity shattered, and their freedom lost, they experience themselves to be nothing at all. The loss of self as the unity of freely thinking one's existence and of existing freely in one's thought is inconceivable as existing in the extra-biblical world, for insanity, in describing a self which, in its disintegration, becomes alien to its own thought and existence, presupposes an integrated self which exists freely in its own thought. In the extra-biblical doctrine of opposites there is no freely thinking, existing self which can lose its integrity and unity, for, from the beginning and unto the end, the self is always other than—ignorant of and blind to—itself. Precisely because the extra-biblical self (both individual and communal) is modeled on the contradictions of nature (the nature of contradiction), its dualisms remain the opposites of which it is ignorant and by which it is blinded (it is unconscious of them). But when the self is created from nothing natural, when it is revealed as the origin and unity of thought and existence, as the cause of itself, then it can lose itself. Once the self is exiled from the natural garden of paradise, not to mention from the life of ruler-ruled opposition under the Pharaohs, it becomes subject to the temptations of idolatrous dualism. The unity of thought and existence which the Bible brings as the redemption of the pagan world also bears its dualistic opposition, the hideous diremption of idolatry—both individual and social. The pagan doctrine of opposites bursts into the dualism of nihilism which, by the twentieth century, becomes totalitarian psychosis. The unity of thought and existence—the freedom to think and to exist—is consciously reduced to their dualistic opposition, such that persons who are thought to be unworthy of existence are reduced to nothing (the death camps) and persons who view themselves as contradicted by the opposition between their thought and existence experience themselves as nothing (insanity).

Having reflected on some of the general implications of the biblical explication of thought and existence, especially as they arise from consideration of the distinction between extra-biblical paganism and idolatry, I want to pursue this distinction further in Section II, especially as it applies to the relationship between letter and spirit and between sin (error) and truth. We shall then be in a position to adumbrate our understanding of the dialectic of truth and interpretation, before taking up, in Sections III and IV, the fundamental biblical concepts which cannot be thought outside of our existing in them, those of golden rule, creation, fall, covenant, and eternal life.

II. THE BIBLICAL CRITIQUE OF IDOLATRY

Although the Bible celebrates, as we know, the liberation of the Israelite slaves from their pagan master, Pharaoh, what it opposes, from beginning to end, both explicitly and implicitly, is idolatry, whether in the guise of pagan gods, false prophets, or Antichrists. To understand, to grasp in thought and existence, the critical and absolute, but yet so subtle, distinction between pagan image and idolatrous image is to understand the structure of the Bible, what I call the dialectic of biblical critique. The distinction between pagan and idolatrous images involves the distinction which I have already introduced between simile and metaphor. The pagan image is simile, while the idolatrous image, the idol, is the reduction of metaphor to, the reification of metaphor as, simile. When, at the very beginning of Genesis, as part of the story of creation and in preparation for the story of the first man and the first woman and their expulsion from the garden of natural paradise into the world of thought and existence, it is said that the human being is created in the image of God, there is enunciated the very distinction between simile as pagan image and metaphor as befitting the self-conscious existence of human being.

We shall recur later to the story of human creation, which is central to understanding the two principal figures of the biblical drama, God and human being (both individual and communal). Here it is sufficient to note that, from the beginning, the Bible distinguishes between the image—metaphor—which is relative to all, which involves and expresses the relationship of all, and the pagan image of nature which, in order to be thought and to exist, must appear, yet, when it does appear, it contradicts both thought and existence, showing the individual, in his appearance (image), to be both ignorant of and blind to that which he is in himself, which is that he is always other than and opposed to his appearance. The appearance of pagan images is, as we have seen, the contradictory secret of the extra-biblical world of which it is fatally ignorant and by which it is endlessly blinded. But this secret is revealed for the contradiction which it is by the Bible, by the revelation that what constitutes human being is not the appearances of natural space and time but the principle, the beginning, God, that which cannot be thought without (our) existing and that which cannot exist without (our) thinking. To be compared with nature, in the tradition of extra-biblical paganism, is ineluctably to be compared with that which, because it cannot be known in itself, always reflects you back into appearances whose metamorphoses are endlessly contradictory. To seek your end or *telos* in nature, to view your *telos* as natural (in extra-biblical reality nature and *telos* are inseparable), is always to locate your end in opposition to yourself; for to seek your end in nature is to discover that nature is endlessly other than and opposed to your end.

The Bible is the first, and the last, text to reveal the pagan tradition of teleology to be the contradiction of thought and existence (both human and divine). The Bible recognizes that the one thing which the law of contradiction cannot recognize is that it is contradictory. The law of contradiction, precisely because both its thought and its existence are endlessly other than itself, is blind to and ignorant of its own contradiction. In order for the law of contradiction to be thought, it must exist; and in order for the law of contradiction to exist, it must be contained in thought (self-consciousness). It must both be thought by someone existing and have existence (the existence of someone) as its object (subject). But the contradiction to which the law of contradiction is blind and of which it is ignorant, as it blinds us by that of which we are ignorant, is that it cannot both be thought and exist. The pagan doctrine of opposites is the subject of the law of contradiction for the precise reason that thought and existence are endlessly opposed to each other. In order for us to think, there must be both someone existing who thinks and something (someone) existing which is thought; but, since existence is simply that which appears contradictory, to have existence as the object (subject) of your thought is simply to discover that what you think is contradictory, that your thought is contradictory. In order for something to exist, it must appear; but appearance is precisely that which is opposed to and contradicts thinking. It is little wonder, then, that Aristotle defines *theos*, the unmoved mover, as that which, logically consistent with itself as the law of contradiction, thinks only itself: thinking thinking thinking. If thinking is to escape the existence of contradiction (the con-

tradiction of existence), it cannot be thought either to exist or to have existence as its subject (object): it cannot be the subject of existence. We see,
then, that Aristotle's thought of thought thinking itself (but not of existing
Aristotle—that is, Aristotle does not exist within his own thought) is, typically, both a more sophisticated and a more mythically laden version of
Plato's doctrine of Forms. Plato's Form is that which, when it is thought (or
when it thinks itself), contradicts existence as appearance and yet whose
appearance in existence (in Plato's works, for example) contradicts
thought.

The Bible represents the paradox that, in contrast with the tradition
of paganism in which every claim to be first is reversed by the *logos* of contradiction, there has to be a first text if human beings are, first of all, to become conscious of their existence (and to exist in their consciousness).
But—and this paradox recurs constantly in our work—there is, and can be,
only one first, although, in order for there to be one first for the first time,
there must also be a history of firsts, a universal history in which every individual (and community) is, in principle, first, not first insofar as individuals are compared with each other according to their finite
appearances in natural space and time, but first when each and every individual is infinitely compared to God. Whereas finite or natural comparison is simile, infinite comparison, the comparison demanding that we
think through our existence and that we exist in our thought, is metaphor.
That the first text is also the last text shows that the first will be last and the
last will be first, contradicting, explicitly, the finitely blind, teleological
order of natural implication wherein the first, the ruling heroes for whom
the unexamined life is not worth living, are, in their ignorance, reversed at
(by) the last, and the last, the unheroic ruled who are excessive in nothing,
are blindly reversed from (by) the first.

The distinction between being made blindly in the image of nature,
of whose reality one remains endlessly ignorant, and being revealed in the
light of God's image—knowing good and evil, as we shall see—is, to
repeat, the distinction between simile and metaphor, between nature and
existence, between contradiction and paradox. All comparisons with nature, all images based on the finite appearances of space and time, force individuals into blind opposition to themselves, both individually and
socially: they are always other than and opposed to themselves. All comparisons with God, the infinite principle of nature, the one whose begin-

ning and end cannot be directly identified with, reduced to, or reified as
this or that finite image of nature, reveal human beings to be free and equal
in the solidarity of their beginning and end. The principle of God is
precisely that which reveals to human beings that their beginning—in
thought and existence—is liberation from the blindness and ignorance of
the law of contradiction and its natural teleology. Thought and existence,
as Descartes shows, begin not with nature as their end but with a swerve,
an alienation, from nature. If all human beings are, in principle, to be
revealed as worthy of saying with Descartes—I think, therefore, I am—
they must understand themselves as aliens who, having been expelled
from the natural paradise of opposition blind to and ignorant of their contradictions, seek their home in the promised land where the very unnatural
(metaphorical) lion lies down with the very unnatural (metaphorical) lamb.
The only way in which nature can be known, the only way in which the
contradictions, to which nature in its ignorance of self is blindly subject,
can be comprehended, is through the revelation of its principle of thoughtful existence, that which the Bible calls God. The awesome paradox of nature is that it can be known—its contradictions comprehended—only from
a perspective which is other than itself: what Descartes calls self-conscious
existence (the existence of the self in its consciousness). This is the principle
captured by the theological formulation that God creates thought and existence (divine and human) from nothing, from nothing which is natural,
from nothing which is directly subject to the law of contradictory nature.

But the paradox of nature (the nature of paradox) becomes even
more awful when we realize that, precisely because nature is comprehended from the perspective of thoughtful existence which is nothing,
no thing appearing in finite space and time, the possibility of idolatry
emerges. So long as nature remains the contradictory secret hidden within
the doctrine of opposites, the natural image, as simile, always appears to be
other than what it is in itself. The moment, however, that the nature of contradiction is revealed to the world as the contradiction of nature, contradiction enters the world as the idolatrous practice of viewing God—the
principle of beginning: thought and existence both divine and human—in
the images of nature. The idol is inconceivable and unimaginable in extra-
biblical paganism, for the image, in appearing natural, always shows itself
to be other than and opposed to the nature of things (to fate). Within the
biblical world, on the other hand, idolatry emerges as the eternal seduction

for human beings precisely because nature can now be known, but known only as contradictory, that is, not in itself, to recall the Kantian formulation. Because the nature of contradiction—the contradiction of nature—is now revealed to the world, the possibility emerges for contradicting nature, for appropriating the nature of contradiction for one's own contradictory end, something inconceivable and unimaginable in extra-biblical paganism. The extreme of idolatry, as I have already indicated, is nihilism (annihilation), the finite repetition of the infinite act of *creatio ex nihilo*: the reduction of thought and existence to the nothing whence they are created. The Bible views idolatry as the direct identification of God and natural image, such that what is not natural but creative becomes natural or such that what is natural, that is, created, becomes its creator, something impossible outside the Bible. In paganism, because the immortal gods are identified, from the beginning and in the end, with nature, with their *telos*, their contradictions remain hidden within the opposition of fate no less than do the contradictions of mortal humans. In extra-biblical paganism gods and humans, because they are natural and thus contradictory, cannot become natural and thus reveal contradiction for what it is, which is nothing.

The paradox revealing humankind to be created in the image of God—in contrast with extra-biblical paganism—is that thought and existence are liberated from the blind contradictions of nature of which human beings are endlessly ignorant. Because the divine command to human beings—their responsibility—is for them to live the dialectic of thought and existence, to think their existence freely, to exist freely in their thought, idolatry becomes the sin against the spirit which, as Jesus says, cannot be forgiven. The idolatry of sinning against the spirit cannot be forgiven insofar as we fail (refuse) to recognize idolatry as the constant seduction of those who view themselves as the natural image of God (who view God as their natural image). Because thought and existence—both divine and human—are revealed as the truth which had lain hidden within the ignorance and blindness of pagan fate, idolatry now emerges as the possibility of sinning, of abusing the responsibility of thoughtful existence (the existence of thought). The eternal problematic which human beings now face is that, since all thought and existence are found only in their images, the images of nature, it takes constant effort, struggle, determination, perseverance—Spinoza calls it *conatus*—on their part to follow the divine law, to maintain their faith in God, to recognize that all images of which they are worthy and all images in which they find their worth are divinely inspired. The paradox constantly to be faced by human beings, once thought and existence are revealed to the world, is that images bear the truth but never in themselves but only in and through their interpretation. Equally, the paradox to be faced is that interpretation always involves images but only insofar as the images are true.

In extra-biblical paganism, because images, as appearances, are always other than and opposed to their truth and interpretation, the responsibility ever to show that truth involves interpretation and that interpretation expresses truth is absent. Once, however, the image of thought and existence is revealed to the world as the truth, not in itself but as its interpretation, there emerges the constant danger that truth and its interpretation, that nature and its image, will become immediately identified. Since God and the human being are to be thought as existing in the world and to exist in the world as thoughtful, their revelation is always within the flesh, within nature, within the immediate appearances of images. The ban of the second commandment against depicting God in images embodies the very paradox of metaphor, the paradox of truth and interpretation. Were images literally banned, then the image which is the image of images, human thought and existence, would itself vanish into the blind contradictions of paganism ignorant of its own appearances. The image *sans pareil* is the image of God, human thought and existence. Were images literally banned, then the ban against images would impugn not only the statement itself but equally the context in which the statement is made, the Bible itself. The ban against images is not against images in themselves but against images which pretend to be the thing-in-itself, not only God but equally humankind, both divine and human thought and existence. It is only because images are incomparable metaphors that the very danger of comparison, which enslaves one comparison to another, bursts into thought and existence. Precisely because the image is the sole bearer of divinity (and humanity), its status, its thought and existence, becomes the constant subject of human struggle (both personal and social, both psychological and sociological). There is no truth or interpretation outside the image. Yet the image is not in itself the truth or its interpretation. The human being is not true and cannot be interpreted outside of God. But the human being is not God, not the thing-in-itself which can be known in itself. Human being is the *imago Dei*.

The paradoxical status which the image assumes in biblical thought and existence emerges as the dialectical contrast between paganism and idolatry. The revelation of the contradiction of natural images means that the images of nature can become contradictory, something inconceivable and unimaginable within extra-biblical paganism. The image which has been revealed as the truth, whose interpretation is our task, can become untruthful, its interpretation falsified. The one thing which the pagan image, in being directly identified with nature and thus being indistinguishable from the contradictory appearances of nature in their endless metamorphoses, cannot be (or become) is truthful (and equally it cannot be interpreted or become interpretable), for it is always other than and opposed to itself. The pagan image is its own self-contradiction by which it is blinded and of which it is ignorant. But the one thing which the biblical image, which is not found outside its natural appearances and yet which is always other than its natural appearances, can become is false to its truth and interpretation. The explicit contradiction of the biblical idol, in contrast with the implicit contradiction of the pagan image, is that it becomes pagan, something inconceivable to extra-biblical peoples who are pagan (and thus, in their implicit or blind contradiction, do not become pagan). The paradox of biblical thought and existence is that they can become what they are not, which is pagan, natural, explicitly (openly) contradictory, what, in theological terms, has traditionally been called rebellious, blasphemous, heretical... sinful. The enormous seduction eternally present to those committed to thought and existence is that they can become pagans, something outside the possibility of pagan thought and existence, given that extra-biblical peoples do not (yet) exist in their own thought or think of themselves as existing. The contradiction of pagan thought and existence is that, precisely because they are, they equally are not. The paradox of biblical thought and existence is that, precisely because they are, they must constantly either become (through choice, as we shall see) what they (not yet) are or become (through the failure of choice) what they are not, which is nothing. The second position, which represents idolatry, is the position of sin which is no position: the contradiction of thought and existence.

The law of contradiction is endlessly blind to and ignorant of its contradictions. Not only do its thought and existence blindly contradict each other, but each, in reflecting its own ignorance, is no less ignorant of itself. The law of paradox, in contrast, is the revelation of contradiction as the dialectic of truth and interpretation. Either become what you are (you are what you become), or become what you are not (you are not what you become). No pagan can become contradictory—the pagan cannot recognize or account for (his) contradiction—for he is contradictory; and the unique end of contradiction, its *telos*, is death (the only happy man is a dead man; the only non-contradictory individual is the one who is dead to the contradictory appearances of life). It is only the individual of the Bible, the one to whom the revelation of thought and existence is made in all their paradoxical relations, who can become contradictory, for he is not contradictory in himself but paradoxical. The contradiction of the law of contradiction is that it is contradictory and thus blind to and ignorant of its very contradictions. The paradox of paradox is that it can become contradictory. In extra-biblical paganism, nature, and thus all there is, including human nature, is (blindly) contradictory. It knows not whereof it speaks. It speaks not whereof it knows. Within the Bible nature, and thus all there is, including human nature, is explicitly, knowingly, contradictory, that is, paradoxical. This is why the either/or structure of paradox is central to biblical thought and existence. Either believe or be offended. Either believe—in the paradox—or be offended—by your contradiction of the paradox, by the paradox of your contradiction. Either recognize that the only subject worthy of thought is existence and that only existence can be thought, or be offended by the inadequacy of your thought to your existence and/or the inadequacy of your existence to your thought. Offence captures the paradoxical quality of repression and oppression (and their infinitely psychological and social variations), whereby the secret hidden from (by, in, as...) self and others cannot be a secret unless it has been revealed and made known in the world, yet that it is revealed and known is precisely the secret which is repressed in personal and oppressed in social relationships. It is only within the structure of revelation—the revelation of thought and existence to all—that censorship, propaganda, partisan ideology, etc., become the big lie, for the notion of false (falsified) truth and interpretation as the offence against the spirit of thought and existence is inconceivable and unimaginable in extra-biblical paganism.

Idolatry, including the specter of false prophets and Antichrists, is so relentlessly opposed in and by the Bible because it reverses—it oppresses and represses—the structure of revelation, of thought and existence, of truth and interpretation. Whereas the Bible is—involves and expresses—

the liberation of paganism from its blind and ignorant contradiction, idolatry represents the subversion of this revelation. While the Bible realizes the truthful interpretation and the interpretation of the truth of paganism, idolatry realizes, as the shadow ever accompanying the biblical light of revelation, the contradictory nature of paganism. Contradiction brought to light—by the paradox of truth and interpretation—can be lost, through repression and oppression, in the very shadows of that light. It is precisely because of the separation from paganism, on the part of biblical peoples, that paganism becomes that which it is not in itself (it is not in itself that which it becomes). Through biblical creation paganism is made, or created, the relationship (the covenant) of thought and existence. Paganism thus becomes the great fear, the temptation, the seduction, the anxiety of biblical thought and existence, not in itself but through idolatry, as that which it is not and thus what it can become. For what paganism becomes in being rendered idolatrous is the pretension to the truth of interpretation and to the interpretation of truth. It becomes lying, falsehood, oppression, repression... sin, something altogether inconceivable and unimaginable in paganism as such.

The idolater—it cannot be repeated too often—is thus the individual to whom the truth and interpretation of the Bible have been revealed, not the extra-biblical individual whose natural contradictions have not been revealed. Not having originally been in the world as part of nature (as lying hidden in the nature of the law of contradiction), thought and existence are now revealed as present in the world. Error—sin—becomes the responsibility of the believer (and the nonbeliever). Error or sin cannot either be thought to exist or exist within our thought outside the revelation of truth and interpretation. In their constant seduction by paganism the people of the Bible are to blame, not others, not those who are fatally other than and opposed to themselves, but solely those who are constantly tempted to become other than themselves. For something to become other than (alien to) what it is in itself embodies that contradictory movement which is inconceivable and unimaginable within paganism. Paganism, because it both is and is not what it is in itself, because it is that which is other than and opposed to (and thus ignorantly and blindly identical with) what it is in itself, can never become other than what it is in itself.

The implications which the idolatrization of thought and existence creates for us moderns, the heirs of the Bible, are enormous. One need but think of the totalitarianism in our own century as represented, on the one hand, by psychological repression and, on the other, by social, economic, and political oppression. In later chapters some of the larger implications of idolatry as the reduction of the biblical law of paradox to the natural law of contradiction will be explored. Here, however, I want to remain within the speculative ambit of the Bible. It is especially important to recognize the paradoxical structure of error or sin (although we shall continue to defer our discussion of the story of the fall, of Adam and Eve's transgression, to Section IV of this chapter). With the divine revelation of thought and existence to humankind, error or sin as idolatry, as transgression against thought and existence, enters the world. Sin, in the extra-biblical world of Socrates, is ignorance, to adopt a familiar but paradoxical formulation of pagan contradiction. Since everything done or thought in the pagan world is fatally other than or opposed to—both ignorant of and blind to—what it is in itself, there is no consciousness of sin or error, no thought of sin as existence and no sinful existence as thought. But the biblical conception of sin is that it exists, and the existence of sin for the Bible is that it is thought (conscious). Sin, as idolatry, represents both the liberation of human beings from paganism and their enslavement to paganism. One sins only because one has been liberated from sin. One overcomes sin only because one recognizes—lives—the dialectic of thought and existence. Sin-consciousness—the existence of sin—involves and expresses the paradox of thought and existence, the position that, precisely because they are not the givens of nature but the gifts of creative spirit, they can also be annihilated.

The Bible reveals the hard teaching that human thought and existence are sinful, not from their birth, their birth in nature, but from their beginning, their liberation from the contradictory appearances of natural space and time. Sin is both human glory and human curse: the glory of fulfilling thoughtfully one's existence and existing fully in one's thought, and the curse of idolatrously contradicting human thought and existence by reducing them to the appearances of nature. Both the glory and the curse of thought and existence are unknown and unlived within the natural law of pagan contradiction. The paradox of the Bible's revelation of sin is that there is no choice but to sin. Sin is the choice. Either sin, or be offended by your sin. Either sin or be offensive in your sin. Not to sin, not to conceive of the dialectic of thought and existence as sinful is to commit the one sin

which will never be forgiven, the sin of not embracing, of not acknowledging, one's sin as one's own thought and existence.

Once again, the paradoxical implications of sin, or idolatry, as the explication of the pagan law of natural contradiction are enormous. But what
I want to point out here is that, if the Bible reveals sin as the nature of
human beings created in the image of God, then the Bible itself cannot be
less sinful than its content, than its story of erring men and women who are
committed, in their sin, to the law of God. Jesus formulates the biblical conception of sin as human thought and existence in radical terms when he
says that God comes to save, not the righteous but the sinful, those who are
thoughtful in their existence and those who exist in their thought. The radical hermeneutic which the Bible entails is that the Bible is to be saved, not
from sinners, not from those who are committed to making truth the interpretation of the Bible and to interpreting the Bible truthfully, but from the
righteous, from those who impute to the Bible a literal inerrancy, a dogmatic literalism which contradicts both the concept and the content, both
the thought and the existence, of the Bible. (I am here more concerned with
dogmatic believers than with skeptical nonbelievers, just as, when the context is philosophical rather than theological, my polemic tends to be
directed more against skeptics than against dogmatists, although it is important to keep in mind Kant's insurpassable demonstration that the only
defense which dogmatism ultimately has against skepticism is skeptical
blindness, which skeptics are skilled in pointing out, while the only
defense which skepticism ultimately has against dogmatism is dogmatic
ignorance, which dogmatists are no less skilled in pointing out. Dogmatism and skepticism are but the mirror image of each other, each blind
to its own contradiction in contradicting the other.)

That the Bible is the revelation of truth and interpretation as their
own standard, the standard both of truth and interpretation and of their
falsifications, means that the Bible is itself subject to its own standard of
truth and interpretation and cannot be directly identified with or assimilated to it. This hard truth (it is hard because it always demands interpretation) is the paradox that the truth, any value commitment, is
simultaneously itself and subject to its own critique (interpretation). It is
both self and other, the dialectic of thought and existence such that either
can be true only insofar as both are true. That this dialectic involves and expresses the golden rule, the ontological demonstration which cannot be

thought except as existing (and which cannot exist except as thought), will be taken up later in this chapter. Here I want to show that the notion of truth and interpretation as their own revealed standard, the standard of sin as both true and false, expresses the relationship of spirit and letter.

The paradoxical structure of spirit and letter is precisely that of creation and nature, of the law of biblical paradox and the law of extra-biblical or pagan contradiction. The spirit or meaning of the text is found only in and through the letter of the text, yet it cannot be directly identified with or assimilated to the letter of the text. It is critically important—and very hard to accept, especially on the part of, it is my experience, classical philologists and cultural anthropologists—to recognize that the text, understood as its own standard, the standard both of what constitutes a text and of what does not constitute (or falsifies) a text, is not found outside the Bible. Just as there is no thought or existence in the Greek, or extra-biblical, world, so also the Greek text, like any pagan text, precisely because it possesses neither thought nor existence—it does not conceive of itself as existing, and its existence is not that of its own thought—is not a text, when the term "text" is understood, like all terms of value, as involving and expressing our commitment to, simultaneously, thought and existence. In the beginning is the text, the text as its own principle and end, the text as its own *telos*. The Greek text is always other than and opposed to, always ignorant of and blind to, what it is in itself. The sole text in the extra-biblical world of paganism is fate, the text which, reflecting the doctrine of opposites, cannot be thought as existing and cannot exist as thought. Just as thought and existence are always opposed to each other as appearance, whose metamorphoses are endless, and as nature, whose end is always other than its appearances, so thought and existence are each equally opposed to or other than themselves. The text of paganism cannot be known as written and cannot be written as known—and the fact that I here paraphrase famous statements of Plato in the *Phaedrus* and his Seventh Epistle that that which is known can be known only within the soul (dead to the appearances of life) and cannot be written (and so is not subject to contradictory metamorphosis) is not fortuitous. The immortality of the soul, conceived of as the *telos* of nature (the nature of *telos*), is eternally opposed to and is the contradiction of any text in which it appears. To write (or to speak) about the immortality of the soul (the immortality of nature) is to remain fatally other than and opposed to (and by) the very subject, the *telos*, of your discourse.

The hard thing to accept—as I keep repeating in my work—is that Plato, as any extra-biblical writer, means what he says and says what he means. But when saying and meaning, letter and spirit, are directly identified—as nature is directly identified with its own *telos* in the extra-biblical world of paganism—then they are equally opposed to and other than themselves, *ad infinitum*. When Plato and Aristotle declare that the law of contradiction (along with its sister laws of identity and the excluded middle) is the unprincipled principle with which they begin, that the beginning of demonstration is that which is without demonstration, they demonstrate that their own demonstration, in blindly following the fatal logic of contradiction, is ignorant of its own beginning. The text of fate, the text as fate endlessly other than and opposed to itself, always appears in the *logos*, whether oral or written, of contradiction. To write or to speak the *logos* of contradiction is always to demonstrate, ineluctably, that what you say and what you mean, the thinking of your existence and the existence of what you think, are endlessly other than and opposed to, fatally ignorant of and blind to, what they are in themselves.

Fate as the text of extra-biblical paganism possesses no truth which can be interpreted and no interpretation whose truth is discernible. There is neither surface nor depth in extra-biblical discourse, neither a letter to be truthfully interpreted nor the spirit of true interpretation. Just as we saw in an earlier chapter that, although communication (written or oral, verbal or nonverbal) presupposes language, the generation of language does not presuppose the creation of communication, so meaning or spirit presupposes the letter, but the letter, in whatever appearance, does not in itself presuppose meaning or spirit. The problematic position of the letter of the text is precisely that of image or nature (flesh). There is no meaning or spirit outside the letter of the text, but the spirit of the text cannot be directly located in or reduced to its letter. The devotion to and piety for the letter of the text which biblical religion has inspired in its adherents, both believers and nonbelievers, is unique in the world. Its glory is a joyful seriousness conscious that the more lovingly the letter of the text is cultivated (the more carefully the letter of the text is preserved), the more deeply the spirit of the text is meditated (the more profoundly do we engage our thought and existence). The curse of the piety generated by the intense cultivation of the letter in the biblical tradition (and this applies not only to the Bible but also to extra-biblical texts, to, above all, those of the Greeks) is that it becomes the literalism of idolatry, the reduction of the text to itself, of its meaning to its letter, this idolatry being found in both its dogmatic or pious and its skeptical or scholarly modes.

As the revelation of idolatry in the world the Bible is itself the unique, and the universal, source of idolatry. Without the Bible idolatry is the secret fatally hidden in the natural law of pagan contradiction. Within the Bible idolatry is revealed as the contradiction of thought and existence, whether divine or human. Just as the Bible is the text which brings textuality into the world, so it is the text which brings the idol, the anti-text, into the world. The idol, as anti-text, is the shadow ever accompanying the light of textuality. The Bible, as textuality, is the glory and the curse of humanity. As the glory, it is the principle, the beginning and end, of all thought and existence. As the curse, it is the reduction of the text to an idol, the subversion of the dialectic of spirit and letter. There is no text in the world without its idols, just as idols do not exist without the text as its own standard, the standard of both itself and its idols. The task which the Bible constitutes from the beginning is that it must account for its own idols. In the end the Bible must account for itself as its own idol.

Central to the Bible as the text which constitutes the text as the account of its own idols is the dialectic of truth and interpretation. In revealing truth to the world, the truth of thought and existence, the Bible is itself the first (and last) text to realize that a text must be subject to its own standard, its own criterion, its own judgment, its own interpretation. The Bible is the truth insofar as this claim of identity is understood to embrace the task of interpretation and not to contradict the spirit of interpretation by reducing truth to direct identity with the letter of the text. Indeed, the human image of God can be preserved from either dogmatic or skeptical idolatry, whether that of believers or that of nonbelievers, only by the account which holds that truth is to be found solely in (its) interpretation and interpretation is to be found solely in (its) truth.

Truth is not to be found in extra-biblical discourse in which whatever is said (or done) is fatally subject to the law of contradiction which shows all discourse about truth to be other than and opposed to what is said about truth. The very truth about the law of contradiction itself is that it is blind to and ignorant of what it says, for, in order for the law of contradiction to be spoken (or lived), it must appear in the images of natural space and time, and, according to the truth of contradictory *logos*, everything which appears contradicts the truth. The truth is, but, in order to be, it must appear, and appearance is other than and opposed to being truth (the truth of being). Truth both is and is not, and thus, once again, violates the law of contradiction. The law of contradiction itself both is and appears to be and thus both is and is not and is thus contradictory; or, rather, the law of contradiction itself both is and is not contradictory and thus is (unbeknownst to itself) contradictory. Contradiction opposed to and contradictory of itself is formulated in the hauntingly contradictory image of the Cretan liar who, as we have noted before, says simultaneously truthfully and falsely that he always lies. Inconceivable to the Cretan liar would have been the claim that one always tells the truth, that is, that one always wills to tell the truth, or, as Montaigne observes about himself, that he contradicts himself from time to time but the truth he never contradicts. The Cretan liar both contradicts himself—it is true that he lies (his truth is his lie)—and does not contradict himself—it is a lie that he speaks the truth (his lie is his truth). His truth and his lie, his non-contradiction and his contradiction are opposites which, multiplying without end, cannot be distinguished from each other, yet they are fatally opposed to each other. They are both identical with and other than each other. Each, in being directly identified with its opposite, is fatally opposed to it. The Cretan liar is unable either to think of himself as thinking falsely, as lying (as existing in his lie), or to exist in his false thought, as existing falsely (as lying in his existence). Whatever the Cretan liar thinks he is he is not, and whatever he is he is not what he thinks. In light of the fact that the contradictory life of extra-biblical paganism is always blind to and ignorant of its own contradiction, it is interesting to recall that the law of contradiction is also known as the law of non-contradiction! Such contradictory opposites, like Democritus' finite atoms, ramify infinitely in the finite rituals and myths of extra-biblical paganism. Only death appears to bring contradiction to its end, but death is itself only one more contradictory appearance of nature; for the generation and destruction of nature are an endlessly cosmic process of opposition which knows neither beginning nor end. The beginning and end of nature, in their infinite opposition and contradiction, are fate itself, and fate is but the natural reflection of opposition in which every image, in seeking its natural end, always finds itself blindly and ignorantly reversed from the beginning.

Just as truth is not found in the extra-biblical world, so interpretation is equally absent from it. Interpretation, like truth, does not abide by the law of contradictory ignorance and blindness. Where fate is the text whose discourse is always other than and opposed to what it means, the existence of interpretation is neither conceivable nor imaginable. Interpretation is not mere opinion which, following the doctrine of opposites, must either rule over others or be ruled by others. Precisely because, in the extra-biblical world, the self is always the other in opposition to itself and the other is always the self in its otherness, interpretation as the relationship which is the truth of self and other is utterly absent. In order to interpret something, that is, something existing, a text (whether a piece of discourse, an action, a person...), we must hold both self and other—and this can be both the self in its own self-relationship which we call person and the relationship of selves which we call community—in and to, as, a common framework. But there is no common framework, point of view, or perspective by which extra-biblical discourse (or action) can be interpreted. In the extra-biblical world every point of view or perspective is always other than and opposed to itself. The only universal perspective in extra-biblical paganism is fate, that which, when it is thought, cannot exist, and, when it exists, cannot be thought. We might say that fate is the interpretation of extra-biblical paganism, but this is a self-consciously contradictory, that is, paradoxical, way of bespeaking the incomprehensibility of that which is blind to and ignorant of interpretation.

In contrast with extra-biblical paganism the Bible reveals the truth of interpretation and the interpretation of truth. Neither truth nor interpretation can be attained in itself, for each is found only in and through the other. The Bible reveals itself as the text which, as the standard of both truth and interpretation, cannot be directly identified with either truth or interpretation. The Bible demands that the very criterion or standard by which it is interpreted be truthful, but it equally demands that its criterion or standard of truth be interpreted. Indeed, it is precisely within the context of truth and interpretation that idolatry emerges. Idolatry is absent from the extra-biblical world of paganism, for idolatry presupposes truth and interpretation in its very subversion of them. Idolatry is the shadow which ever accompanies the revealed light of truth and interpretation. Because truth and interpretation come into thought and existence from nothing—for, if they have always been naturally in the world, then they have never been naturally in the world—their reduction to nothing remains an eternal seduction for the people of the Bible.

It is a hard lesson to learn and ever to relearn: that it is the Bible itself which, in distinguishing itself from the pagan law of natural contradiction, in bringing to light the contradictions of the pagan world, creates paganism as the very condition of idolatry. When truth and interpretation are absent from the world, there is no possibility, in conception or existence, of transforming an image of nature into an idol such that it claims to represent the truth of interpretation and the interpretation of truth. But once truth and interpretation enter the world as the creation of thought and existence from nothing, from nothing which is found in the images of natural space and time, there is constantly the interest, on the part of human beings, to reduce truth to their own particular interpretation and to reduce interpretation to their own particular truth. Normally, the idolatrous tendency among dogmatists is to minimize the significance of interpretation for comprehending what they consider to be the truth, while the idolatrous tendency among skeptics is to minimize the importance of truth for comprehending what they consider to be interpretation. But what the Bible shows to those who have eyes to see and ears to hear is that truth involves commitment to interpretation and that interpretation expresses commitment to the truth. The Bible shows that the limit to truth and interpretation is uncreative paganism which, insofar as it remains fatally subject to the contradictions of natural law, is blind to and ignorant of truth and interpretation. The Bible equally shows that, in creating thought and existence, not only divine but also human, from nothing, from nothing subject to the natural law of contradiction, paganism is made creative, not in itself but in spirit. But it is precisely because the spirit of creation brings the letter (nature, flesh...) into thought and existence that the spirit of truth and interpretation can be subverted by the letter (by nature or flesh). The contradictory nature of the idol is seen in the fact that, while claiming to be true interpretation and the interpretation of truth, it subverts both, a position inconceivable and unimaginable within extra-biblical paganism. The paradox of the Bible is that, in creating thought and existence from nothing, in showing to the world of paganism that it is based not on the contradictions of nature but on its own creative thought and existence, it introduces the specter of idolatry into the world. Idolatry is the reduction of truth and interpretation to the contradictory images of pagan nature. Idolatry is the explicit embracing of paganism as nihilism, a position made possible only by the creation of thought and existence from nothing, from nothing which is pagan.

To probe, speculatively, the biblical dialectic of thought and existence reveals the importance of seeing how the Bible sharply distinguishes its structure of truth and interpretation from both paganism (which it creates from nothing) and idolatry (which, as paganism rendered creative, reduces creation to pagan nothingness). But speculative thought is also content, the content of our lives, the content of our thought and existence. In the next sections of this chapter I want to show how truth and interpretation are embodied in the structure of the Bible, in its fundamental drama involving God and human beings in that relationship of self and other which is expressed through the fundamental commitments to creation, fall, covenant, and eternal life, all centered on the golden rule.

III. THE GOLDEN RULE OF ONTOLOGY

The fundamental doctrine—teaching—of the Bible is the golden rule: do unto others as you would have them do unto you; love God above all others and your neighbor as yourself. I do not mean that the golden rule is more fundamental than other central biblical doctrines such as creation, fall, covenant, or eternal life or that it is any more their ground than they are the ground of the golden rule. Indeed, the golden rule involves creation, fall, covenant, and eternal life just as they express the golden rule. But what is so precious about the golden rule is that its very formulations, involving self and other as God and neighbor, express the dialectic which I make central to my work and which I argue (undertake to demonstrate) must be central to all work, insofar as it is meaningful work: for one position to be true, the position opposite it, that with which it works or communicates, must be equally true. Even truth is subject to its own standard of dialectic: there is nothing true in itself. Truth is its own standard in the exacting sense that it is subject to both your and my interpretation. Something (someone) is true only insofar as the position opposite it is equally true. Something is true only insofar as it expressly involves the golden rule. I can interpret—will—something to be true only insofar as I will to interpret the truth for you as you will to interpret the truth for me.

The golden rule is not a talisman; indeed, it is the shibboleth of humanity, the password which, degenerating into an idol, reifies one side of the golden rule—self or other, God or person—at the expense of, to the sacrifice of, the other. But the beauty of the golden rule is that, from the beginning, it demands that we encompass the paradox of thought and existence in our lives. We cannot say—in good faith—I think, therefore, I am, without acknowledging the relationship of thought and existence, without recognizing that the sole object of thought is existence and the sole subject of existence is thought. There are no thinkers outside their existence, and there are no existing individuals outside their thought. That my formulation is but an explication of the ontological argument for existence, for the existence of God—that which cannot be thought except existing (and which cannot exist except as thought)—only shows that the ontological argument is itself but an explication of the fundamental, biblical teaching of the golden rule.

I bring together the golden rule, relationship, the Cartesian *cogito, ergo sum* and the ontological argument for God's existence—which, so far as I am aware, has never been done before—to pursue my demonstration that the Bible is the very ground of speculation (of thinking, whose only subject is existence) and that it is precisely speculation on the Bible which is needed in an age like ours, an age split between post-modern deconstruction of truth and interpretation and pre-modern belief in the constructions of truth and interpretation. In deconstructing truth and interpretation, post-modern authors, the advanced skeptics of our age, are blind to the fact that deconstruction presupposes the very thought and existence of that which it deconstructs. The devastating critique of the deconstructionists presupposes the ontological argument of thought and existence, the golden rule of communication. Skeptical deconstructionism is thus but the mirror image of pre-modern dogmatism which is ignorant that its constructions are subject to the dialectic of truth and interpretation. Both the skepticism of *outré* deconstructionism and the dogmatism of reactionary constructionism reflect the idolatry of identifying contemporary ideologies with truth and interpretation, the post-modern deconstructionists through their despair at being unwilling to locate their thought in existence and the pre-modern constructionists through their arrogance at being unwilling to locate their existence in thought.

Hegel's brilliant analysis of the contradiction riving the Enlightenment may be fittingly applied to our contemporary situation. Unlike the
critical theorists, whose heirs the deconstructionist thinkers, in part, are
and who cannot account for the eclipse of Enlightenment reason in the
work of either their predecessors or themselves, Hegel shows that, in the
eighteenth century, dogma and critique, truth and interpretation are split
up and opposed to each other as defensive (regressive) theology and as
critical (progressive) philosophy. When, on the one hand, theological
reflection defends religion against philosophical critique, it conserves the
great dogmatic truths of the Bible, while being unable to articulate the
principles of its defense in rational, critical, or thoughtful terms. When, on
the other hand, philosophical criticism attacks theology as dogmatic, it is
unable to distinguish between dogmatism (in method) and the truths of
dogma, with the result that it is unable to articulate the rational, critical,
and thoughtful principles which underlie its attack on dogmatic theology.
Whereas theological truth finds itself opposed to (and by) interpretative
critique, philosophical interpretation finds itself opposed to (and by)
theological truth. The content of truth (faith) fails to recognize that its content involves the concept of reason. The concept of critical reason fails to
recognize that its concept expresses the content of truth (faith). The opposition in the eighteenth century Enlightenment between philosophy and
religion (reason and faith) or between thought and existence (interpretation
and truth) is precisely that today between post-modern deconstructionism
and pre-modern construction. Our most advanced philosophy lacks a
heart, while the traditional faith of common humanity lacks a critical spirit.
Critique is faithless, and faith is uncritical. Thought, separated from its
ground in existence, becomes esoteric cult, while existence, separated from
its ground in thought, becomes vulgar tradition. Post-modern skepticism
and pre-modern dogmatism—each equally skeptical and dogmatic—exist
in every age, in every age which accounts for the anxiety of evading the
consequences of biblical history as the idolatrous claim either to succeed or
to precede them. The only choice worthy of truth and interpretation, however, is to take one's stand, as a modern, with the Bible, embracing its consequences. The consequences of the Bible are always modern, always
original, always critical, always historical, always creative of thought and
existence, so long as we view them as demanding, yet again, and eternally,

that we abide by the commitment to the golden rule of truth and interpretation.

The golden rule is the structure of relationship—of God and person,
on the one hand, and of person and person, on the other. But who is God—
the God of creation, the God of the fall, the God of the covenant, the God of
the Incarnation, the God of eternal life, the God whom one is commanded
to love above all others? The God that is common to the so-called Judeo-
Christian tradition is one God (above all others), yet Jews and Christians
repeatedly remind each other that their God is not to be conflated with the
God of the other. There have been many thoughtful responses to the question who is God?: that which cannot be thought by us except existing (that
which cannot exist without our thinking), the ultimate concern of our lives,
the I-thou relationship, that for which all things are possible, totality, infinity... (not to mention countless other responses which are idolatrous).
There are also many who are indifferent to the question whether God exists. There are also those who, calling themselves agnostics, claim not to
know whether or not God exists. There are also atheists who deny that God
exists. The fool says in his heart that there is no God. What agnostics and
atheists fail to see, however, is that the existence of God, their thinking
about the existence of God, is grounded in their own thought and existence
(that their own thought and existence are grounded in the thought and existence of God). To claim not to know whether or not God exists or to claim
that one knows that God does not exist reflects directly upon the thought
and existence of those who make these claims. The ontological argument
applies no less to human than to divine thought and existence. If either is
true, both are true. If either is false, both are false.

Agnostics are those who deny that God can be known to exist. The
existence of God, they argue, is a hypothesis for which the evidence is
never sufficient. It has often enough been pointed out in response to agnostics, however, that agnosticism (*a-gnosis*) ultimately begs the very question
of existence (divine or human). For either something is known (to exist), or
it is not known (to exist). If something is not known (to exist), then the existence of the agnostic as something known disappears along with his critique (and this is the common fate of agnostics who think that existence,
whether divine or human, is to be understood in empiricist terms). If, on
the other hand, something is known, then something is known to exist. If
something is known to exist, whether the subject or the object of the think-

ing agnostic, then—once it is understood that human existence either vanishes into extra-biblical ignorance of existence as natural or is identical with divine existence which is created from nothing, from nothing natural—the existence of God follows directly upon the agnostic's thinking about his own existence.

What the agnostic evades acknowledging is that the option of Socratic ignorance—Socrates knows that he is ignorant, but he does not know what he is ignorant of—has been closed to him forever by the biblical revelation of thought and existence as never having been an option in the first place. In order to think, in order, that is, to know what he does not know, the agnostic must know something, he must recognize what it is that he does not know. Socrates is no agnostic. Indeed, the idea that he might know what he does not know, that he might oppose what he knows, is inconceivable and unimaginable to Socrates. The agnostic finds himself inexplicably between falsely embracing Socratic ignorance and falsely rejecting the Cartesian circle of thought and existence. The agnostic cannot choose Socratic ignorance. But what he fails to comprehend is that he also cannot choose agnosticism. In order to avoid Socratic ignorance he must know what he does not know: he must know his thought and existence. He must engage the paradox of Cartesian doubt. From the beginning, the paradox of Cartesian doubt deconstructs agnosticism before the agnostics, in the context of the debate between Darwinian science and religion in later nineteenth century Britain, introduce their contradictory, that is, idolatrous, claim not to know what it is that exists. What Descartes points out, following the Bible, is that the one thing which we cannot doubt, so long as we doubt in good faith, so long as our doubt involves us in our thinking, is that which we doubt: our thought and existence (which are both divine and human). The very notion of doubt presupposes and is grounded in, that is, it demonstrates, the justice of the claim: I think, therefore, I am. The issue is thought and existence, Descartes shows. If we doubt in good faith, then the one thing which we cannot doubt is the existence of the thinking self (the thinking of the existing self), and the thought and the existence of the human self entail the thought and existence of God.

What I am pointing out here is the double paradox that the unique (and universal) subject of thinking (knowledge) is existence and that human thought and existence stand and fall with the thought and existence of God. The thought and existence of human beings are no less

demonstrable—and no more demonstrable—than the thought and existence of God (and vice versa). If the agnostic is to be skeptical of divine
thought and existence—always a fruitful exercise—this skepticism will escape dogmatic blindness if, and only if, it recognizes that it involves three
moments, all fundamental to the ontological argument: (1) to be skeptical
about—to question, to probe, to attack—the thought and existence of God
is equally to be skeptical about the thought and existence of human beings;
(2) thought and existence are a dialectical unity (the unity of dialectic): for
either to be true both must be true; (3) thought and existence are no less
divine than human (or otherwise thought and existence are reduced to the
contradictory idols of natural space and time). The paradox of thought and
existence is that to embrace one is to embrace both and that to deny either
is to deny both. To embrace (human) thought and existence is to embrace
God, and to reject God is to reject (human) thought and existence.

The self-contradictory position of agnosticism is but one more representation of Hume's pseudo argument against necessary existence (against
the ontological argument necessarily linking thought and existence, the
concept and the content): whatever *is* may *not be*. Hume, together with the
later agnostics, shows that there is nothing contradictory in the non-existence of an empirical fact. Something in space and time can just as well not
exist as exist. Necessity belongs not to objects existing in space and time
but to relations of ideas outside the realm of experience. But it is Hume, as
we have seen, who then finds himself existing inexplicably betwixt a false
thought and no thought at all. The agnostic, in opposing existence and
necessity (thought) to each other, in relegating existence to the empirical
facts of nature devoid of thought, on the one hand, and necessity to
abstract ideas devoid of existence, on the other, is unable to account for
himself except on the basis of not knowing who he is (that is, he does not
acknowledge that it is he who says: I think, therefore, I am). To conclude
that existence cannot be known, that is, that it is either a false thought or no
thought at all, is a claim totally incomprehensible to extra-biblical
paganism as oxymoronic and totally comprehensible within the framework
of the Bible as a contradictory idol whose account as paradoxical
oxymoron has been repressed.

Atheism is but muscular agnosticism. Indeed, the atheist is the dogmatic opposite of the skeptical agnostic. The atheist assumes that which he
opposes—*theos* (God)—and then denies it, just as Hume denies the very

reason (his own existence as a thinking being) whose necessary existence his very critique presupposes. When we realize that extra-biblical paganism has no conception of divine thought or existence but possesses only myths of immortal nature whose mortal appearances are endlessly contradictory, then we see that atheism is no less inconceivable and unimaginable in extra-biblical paganism than is theism. Atheism, like agnosticism, is a uniquely biblical stance, reflecting either profound devotion to truth and interpretation, in deconstructing the idols of God which multiply without end, or profound despair in multiplying without end the idols of God, while continuing to abide, unaccountably, in the realm of truth and interpretation. It goes without saying that it is not the presence or absence of God, as such, in our discourse, or action, which reveals our commitment, or lack of commitment, to truth and interpretation. What counts is the quality and depth of the commitment, whatever the terms of the discourse. Agnosticism and atheism can provide much needed criticism of pseudo piety and overweening dogmatism. Frequently, the most profoundly religious position is that which appears to be irreligious or even antireligious, at least to the superficially faithful (not to mention to the superficially faithless). Because of the sovereign presence of God in the Bible, agnosticism and atheism often provide a critical antidote to the idolatrization of God. God is clearly our most fearful idol, above all others.

What is typically not appreciated, however, by agnostics or atheists, not to mention theists or, more generally, philosophers, whatever their view of the Bible, is that the death of God is no less the death of human beings (just as the death of human beings is also the death of God). I do not mean to espouse, uncritically or without fear and trembling, the traditional claim of pre-modern theists that atheism leads to or entails immorality, the idea that, if one does not believe in God, then all things are possible. But I do mean to note that, just as there is neither thought nor existence without the Bible, there is also no morality without the Bible. If morality—like God, faith, human beings themselves—has always been in the world, then it has never been in the world. What is important to observe here is that, within the golden rule, morality is complete and, without the golden rule, it neither can be thought nor exists (outside the golden rule morality is without either concept or content). The golden rule is that which cannot be thought without existing, and it cannot exist except insofar as it is thought (except insofar as we are conscious of our existence in and through the

golden rule, of what it means to exist in the golden rule). When the golden
rule is formulated in terms of the ontological argument for existence (there
is one concept which cannot be thought without existing), we may note
that it applies equally to God and to the human individual, to both divine
and human being, and that divine and human being involves and expresses what in this essay in thinking I call the dialectic of thought and existence, Descartes' I think, therefore, I am. We must see not only that the
ontological argument for God's existence is equally the epistemological argument for thought—for ontology and epistemology are ultimately indistinguishable, except to benighted Platonists—but also that it applies no less
to human than to divine thought and existence.

When we repeat the traditional formulation of the ontological argument (which, by the way, Anselm is the first to have articulated in the
terms which establish the tradition of theistic speculation in which we continue to have our thought and existence), it is important to realize that its
terms can and must be interchanged. Dialectical thinking is fruitful precisely because, in recognizing that its dialectic thinks—lives—the golden rule,
it constantly strives to see itself in and from the point of view of the other.
To hold that there is one concept which cannot be thought without existing—in contrast to Hume's irrational position that whatever *is* may *not
be*—is to hold, simultaneously, to two double positions, those which form
the warp and weft of my essay in thinking (existence). The recognition that
to think envelops or encompasses the thinker in his existence, that the only
subject (or object) worthy of thought is existence, shows, first, that thought
and existence are mutually entwined or interrelated. This recognition
shows, second, that the consciousness of existence and the existence of consciousness, which the ontological argument entails, applies no less to the
subject than to its object, no less to the human being (for example, Anselm)
thinking his existence than to the subject of his thinking (existence), who
(for Anselm) is God. To think the existence of the other—God—is to recognize (to think) the existence of yourself. To exist in your own thought is to
exist in the thought of the other. Thought and existence, when distinguished from the images of nature which, as we have shown time and
again, neither can be thought nor exist in themselves, apply no less to the
individual than to the other (the neighbor), no less to the individual than to
God. To do unto others as you would have them do unto you, to love God
above all others and your neighbor as yourself, is to think such that there is

one concept which cannot be thought without existing—God—and to exist such that there is one being which cannot exist without being thought—God. But just as thought and existence are mutually entwined by the Cartesian *ergo*, so the ontological argument (together with its biblical ground the golden rule) involves human no less than divine thought and existence.

The death of God thus involves the death of human beings (thoughtfully existing/existing thoughtfully). But the death of human beings is no less the death of God. It follows, therefore, that, when a profound critic of Christianity like Nietzsche, a thinker who recognizes that the very possibility of his critique of Christianity is grounded in the actual thought and existence of Christianity, announces the death of God, we must recognize the (double) paradox that he presupposes. To announce the death of God in your age is to announce that all meaningful thought and existence have vanished, that God has become the idol than which none is greater, and that a reevaluation of all values—of thought and existence—can take place only if all the dead thought and existence bound up with the God who has died in human thought and existence are negated. Let the dead bury the dead. To announce the death of God is thus to announce your own death, that your own thought and existence, the thought and existence of your age, are dead or, in the terms of this work, idolatrous. But Nietzsche, whose work is so consciously, even painfully, redolent of biblical imagery, announces not only the twilight of the idols but equally the dawn of the new age, the age of the *Übermensch*, the age in which human beings are to overcome their *ressentiment*, their resentment at being but an idol in the shadow in God, and to appropriate the thought and existence which are their own.

If Nietzsche is to escape the inconsequentiality of Hume's argument that existence is unnecessary, he—and we—must recognize that, in announcing that God and thus human being is dead, it is only the living (the thoughtfully existing) who can make and hear, who can bear, this announcement. Thought and existence, when distinguished from both their implicit contradiction in extra-biblical paganism and their explicit contradiction in the biblical idolatry of paganism, invest both divine and human being equally. A particular thinker may choose, for his own polemical purposes, to emphasize divine or human thought and existence at the expense of the other, although it is always possible that he may be blinded, in part or in whole, by the object (subject) of his polemic. As Kant demonstrates in his magisterial deconstruction of the ontological argument for the existence of God in *The Critique of Pure Reason*, thought (concept) and existence are categories not of nature but of practice, of willing the good, of the golden rule. (Kant also shows that the two other traditional arguments for God's existence, the teleological and the cosmological, those claiming to argue from nature to the concept of divine existence, depend on the ontological argument.) The concept of necessary (that is, thoughtful) existence—the necessity of thinking existence—is neither inductive (immediately empirical) nor deductive (abstractly rational). To think is to recognize that one's existence as the thing-in-itself, although it cánnot be known outside its possible appearances in natural space and time, is necessarily its own concept, that which Spinoza calls the cause of itself. Necessity—the *ergo* binding thought and existence in Descartes' I think, therefore, I am—is not the blind fate of nature, which, in its self-ignorance, is always other than and opposed to itself. The necessity binding thought and existence to one another is precisely the bond of the golden rule uniting God and persons, neighbors in relation, in love.

IV. CREATION, FALL, COVENANT, AND ETERNAL LIFE: THE PARADOX OF BEGINNING WITH THE BIBLE

Just as Nietzsche, in claiming that God is dead, reveals the vital thought and existence of both the one who makes the proclamation and those who attend to it—if they have ears to hear and eyes to see—so the Bible, in claiming that God lives, that the living God is the creator and savior of life, reveals the thought and existence of both the one who makes the proclamation and those who attend to it—if they have ears to hear and eyes to see. The structure of biblical narrative is puzzling and often appears contradictory, until we learn to comprehend the character of paradox (until we realize that the Bible reveals paradox to the world, that revelation is paradox). In the Bible God is always viewed as, or proclaimed to be, the author of creation, the author of human life, indeed, the author, it would follow, of the Bible itself. In the beginning God creates the heavens and the earth, the Bible begins. Attentive readers of the Bible have recognized from the beginning, however, how peculiar or paradoxical this beginning, *ergo*, every beginning, is (including beginning to read at the beginning). God is proclaimed at the beginning as the beginning, as the creator, of life. Yet, at the beginning there must already be present the very beginning of life which cannot be directly identified with that of God. God cannot be his own immediate revelation, for then God would be indistinguishable from an idol. The revelation of God, in the beginning, presupposes that in the beginning is relationship. At the beginning there must already be someone attending, or bearing witness to, the beginning, the creation, of God. In the beginning there is already beginning. The beginning, we see from the beginning, is the creation of the beginning. The beginning cannot be any literal beginning in natural space and time.

The hermeneutical implication of beginning, or creation, is that authorship, if it is to be creative of or responsible for its beginning, involves both thought and existence. The ontological implication of beginning, or creation, is that it cannot be natural, whether pagan or idolatrous. Authorship, the creation of beginning, is from nothing, from nothing which is found in the nature of space and time (extra-biblical paganism) and from nothing which is reducible to the nature of space and time (the biblical idolatry of paganism). The question whether God creates humankind (and is the author of the Bible) or whether human beings create God (and author the Bible) is not a question—it is a question in natural form but not in either concept or content—if an answer to it is sought in either empirical data or innate ideas, in what Kant would call either *a posteriori* or *a priori* arguments. Authorship—creation—is neither posterior nor prior to itself. Creative authorship is the cause of itself; its content is its own concept: its concept is its own content. All creation, authorship, or beginning expresses what Kant calls *a priori* synthetic judgments, judgments whose prior concept expresses the synthesis of its posterior content and the existential content of whose synthesis involves its own conceptual priority.

Biblical authors hide their creative or authorial light under a bushel, saying, time and again, in the beginning, God created..., while eternally revealing to the attentive reader that neither author nor reader is posterior to God in nature, just as God is not naturally prior to human beings. It is precisely the revelation of God that, in the beginning, he creates the heavens and the earth which reveals to human beings that all natural beings, mortals and immortals, the entire cosmos of paganism, are nothing in themselves and obtain their being—their thought and existence—in the beginning from the creation of God. To begin, at least once in your life, is to begin, creatively, saying with Descartes: I think, therefore, I am. To begin is to begin, not in nature, but with God as the author of creation.

God, we may remark, is the master of metaphor and paradox. He is the creator of nature. It is God whose revelation makes nature creative. But God does not create the space and time of nature (the nature of space and time), all that is finite, that which is subject to the blindness and ignorance of the contradictory law of fate. Creation—the creation of thought and existence—is utterly unlike the generation of nature from similes which metamorphose without end. The God of the Bible, unlike the poetic *demiourgos* celebrated by Plato as the generator of the cosmos (and who is no less subject to natural destruction than is the cosmos itself), is not a poet whose makings are similar to and thus ignorantly and blindly dependent on the finite images of space and time. God, in the beginning, creates the heavens and the earth from nothing, from nothing which is natural. But, whereas the Bible comes into human thought and existence as their creation sometime after 2000 B.C.E but well before 1000 B.C.E., creating at the same time the very framework in terms of which all space and time are rendered creative as history, nature, as the cosmos, scientists now estimate, is some eighteen billion years old. God creates nature, in the beginning. God creates the beginning of nature. But God has nothing, as such, to do with the cosmic cycle of natural generation and destruction, as we read it, for instance, in the fossil record which is fundamental to the theory of evolution. God is no scientist. Scientists study not creation but the natural cycle of generation and destruction. We properly say that God is creative of science and that scientists do creative science, insofar as we do not idolatrously conflate the thought and existence which God creates, in the beginning, with the nature of space and time which, in themselves, are without beginning or end.

The heavens and the earth created by God are not natural but metaphorical. In their creation God reveals the context for thought and existence, for history. In beginning the story of creation God makes use, like any good poet (or philosopher) working in (creating) the biblical tradition, of the materials at hand, in this case, mythological fragments from the Babylonian sagas of generation and destruction. To begin—to begin by overcoming or freeing oneself from the infinite regress (and progress) of pagan mythology—is to accept the fact that you have to begin, naturally, in nature (in the space and time of your birth), while at the same time locating your beginning (or creativity) in your own originality or authorship. To be a person is to be born of woman, but to become a person is to recognize that neither you nor anyone else can account for your originality, authority, or creativity in the terms of your natural inheritance. The God of the ancient Israelites has no choice, clearly, but to begin with the fragments of pagan civilization at hand. He is going to begin, naturally enough, with stories of the ancient Near East, the home of the ancient Israelites, not with stories found in the ancient civilizations of, for instance, the Far East or the New World. But, wherever the God of the Bible begins his human story (or wherever the human authors of the Bible begin their story of God), what he (they) will show, from beginning to end, is that the story of thought and existence cannot be comprehended on analogy with the cosmic process of natural generation and destruction. Indeed, as we have already indicated, all attempts to reduce the story of creation to creationism, to direct knowledge of what nature is in itself, are, from beginning to end, branded by the Bible as idolatry. God has no choice but to make use of the natural chronology of time in accounting for the creation of life. His creation is said to unfold from one day to the next, until, in the sixth and seemingly last day of creation, behold, what he creates is very good: man and woman. Then God rests—the seventh day. But the Sabbath is not just the seventh day in chronology; for the Sabbath is the day of the Lord, the hallowed day, the day in which all the preceding days of labor are hallowed. It is the day which renders the entire week creative. Indeed, the Sabbath is the creation of the week, the week's creativity, transforming the passage of time into the time of fulfillment, thanksgiving, and renewal.

But it is precisely the intense devotion inspired by the creation of time as the Sabbath which generates the possibility that time itself can become an idol. The Sabbath is created for human beings, not human beings for the Sabbath, Jesus says. Jesus does not attack the Sabbath or any other practice whose observance serves to make human beings mindful of the existence of God. Rather, Jesus attacks as idolatrous, in the tradition of the prophets, any practice in which thought (mindfulness) and existence are not united in a heartfelt way. There is nothing good in the Sabbath itself; indeed, the Sabbath, like God himself, becomes an idol the instant it is made an excuse for evading the demands of thoughtful existence (of existing thoughtfully). The Sabbath is both the rest of the seventh day and the rest, the peace, the graciousness of all days. Once God creates the Sabbath, once God makes the seventh day and thus all days creative, the awesome demand of Sabbath holiness enters the world of space and time. But how or under what conditions holiness is to be attained—in observance of the Sabbath, in ascetic practice, in temple worship, in service to others, in artistic or intellectual endeavor, in marriage, in raising a family, in Bible study, in scientific study of nature...—can never be told ahead of time. What can be told ahead of time, however—and this is the burden of prophecy—is that, whatever the practice, it will be holy (*Übermenschlich*) and overcome the idolatry of both the all-too-human and the all-too-divine insofar as it supports one's saying in good faith: I think, therefore, I am.

Just as the story of divine creation shows that human thought and existence are mysteriously present, from the beginning, in the story of God's beginning—man and woman are the subject of divine creation in the beginning—so the story of creation involves a second beginning in which man and woman fall from their beginning in God whose presence in the story of their second beginning is mysterious. We read that Adam and Eve are forbidden by God to eat of the fruit of the tree of the knowledge of good and evil; that they are seduced by a serpent and do eat of the forbidden fruit; and that, having become like the gods, God says, repeating the serpent's seductive speech, knowing good and evil, he expels them, having clothed them by his own hand, from the garden, lest they should eat of the fruit of the tree of life, to suffer a life of conception, labor, and death. It is instructive to think about this famous story, which shapes the entire structure of modern thought and existence, both ontologically and hermeneutically. Ontologically, we ponder what it is about creation—human and divine—which involves man and woman, and God, too, in the story of a fall: transgression, sin, mortality, ultimately, death. Hermeneutically, the story of Adam and Eve, like the story of creation, like all significant biblical stories, confronts its readers with a literal surface whose immediate, natural, or finite images are contradictory. Readers of the story of Adam and Eve find that they are confronted with two choices. On the one hand, they can take the contradictory images of the story on their own terms, as if they were true in themselves, and then sacrifice either their thought (with the dogmatists) or their existence (with the skeptics), with both of these opposed positions being occupied by believers and nonbelievers alike. On the other hand, they can recognize that these contradictory images can be true only if they are interpreted—as paradox—consistent with both thought and existence.

The obvious problem which the story of the garden of paradise presents to the reader is that either God's prohibition not to eat of the fruit of the tree of the knowledge of good and evil is comprehensible to Adam and Eve—and thus they must already have eaten the forbidden fruit—or it is not comprehensible to them—and thus God's prohibition is arbitrary and meaningless to them. Either God's existence is thoughtful, demanding comprehension (the knowledge of good and evil) on the part of Adam and Eve, from the beginning; or God's existence is thoughtless (irrational) and hence not worthy of human thought and existence, in the beginning. Either we make the contradictions of the story subject—as paradox—to human thought and existence (the thought and existence of not only Adam and Eve but, indeed, all readers of their story); or human thought and existence are made subject to the law of idolatrous contradiction. But, clearly, it is sheer idolatry to hold, according to the conventional piety of believers, that Adam and Eve transgress God's command not to eat of the forbidden fruit before they comprehend (in both their thought and existence) the concept and content not merely of divine command, prohibition, and transgression but also of God and themselves as human beings. Adam and Eve cannot fall before they have fallen, that is, before they fall. They cannot sin before they sin. They cannot sin before they are sinners. There is no first sin in the space and time of nature, which is without beginning or end. The first sin in thought and existence is the very creation of thought and existence, in the beginning. There is no beginning before the beginning of sin, before sin begins. There is only the beginning of sin, that is, the history of sinning. In the beginning, clearly, is sin. Sin is not pagan ignorance; sin is not the contradictory pagan position that one cannot knowingly do evil (which is the equivalent of never knowingly doing good), that anything evil which is done is always done in ignorance of the good. It is equally sheer idolatry to hold, according to the conventional rationality of nonbelievers, that the story of Adam and Eve is but a primitive myth which, like the myths of all primitive peoples, reflects the naïve lack of (modern) rationality on the part of its progenitors. A variant of the position of nonbelief (which is also not infrequently embraced by believers) holds that biblical myths, because they are poetic, are not true, for poetry, it is said, has nothing to do with truth and the rational claims of philosophy.

The story of Adam and Eve, like all significant biblical stories, has as its aim the deconstruction of mythology, not in itself but as the idolatrous reduction of either thought or existence to the contradictions of nature. Indeed, one could say, consistent with Kant and Hegel who explicitly and systematically identify the fundamental elements of their philosophy—freedom, reason, dialectic, spirit, morality, absolute knowledge (what Kant calls will, practical reason, and thought)—with the story of Adam and Eve, that the myth of the fall is the very archetype for deconstructing mythical presence. As always, the Bible is not opposed as such to the myths of nature which all peoples outside the story of creation tell, the contradictory stories of generation and destruction following the natural cycle of nature. What the Bible is fiercely and unrelentingly opposed to, however, is the idolatrization of pagan mythology within the story of creation, the ignorant reduction of creative thought and existence to blind fate. Extra-biblical myth is the story whose images are similes reflecting the *telos* of nature which is always other than and opposed to itself. The *logos* of extra-biblical mythology is the law of contradiction for which all appearances are myths whose beginnings and ends are ineluctably reversed. The myth fatally underlying all myth in the extra-biblical world is nature itself, nature whose appearances, or similes, are endlessly blind to and ignorant of what nature, as fate, is in itself. The myth of nature—fate, the law of contradiction, the doctrine of opposites—is, in its opposition to itself, always blind to and ignorant of itself as myth. Natural, pagan, or extra-biblical myth, in endlessly opposing thought and existence to each other, possesses neither. Myth can neither be thought nor exist, for something can be thought or exist only when it can be thought and exist simultaneously.

The Bible exposes the natural myth of paganism as contradictory of thought and existence. It shows that all myths which locate the origins of gods and humans in nature are ignorant of what they say and blind to what they mean, for what they say and mean is hidden in the fatal secret of nature whose beginnings and ends are inexorably opposed to each other. The story of Adam and Eve shows that the first man and the first woman have their beginning and end, their principle, not in the paradise of contradictory nature but in thought and existence, not blind to and ignorant of but knowing (thinking: willing) good and evil. The garden of paradise is conjured up by biblical authors (divine and human) to serve as the natural limit to human thought and existence. It is nature, they show us, whose contradictions must be exposed as the paradise of appearances which are unworthy of thought and existence. The garden is the natural paradise of (extra-biblical) paganism which the Bible now exposes as the structure of idolatry which will eternally haunt biblical men and women as they seek to relieve themselves of the burdens of being responsible to the thought and existence of good and evil. The contrast between the innocence of natural paradise and the sin (guilt) of life in the world, the second involving conception, labor, and death, often leads biblical men and women to envisage eternal life, not as the freedom to live the contradictions of thought and existence embraced as paradox and metaphor but as the return to the innocence of paradisiacal nature. Biblical authors place the story of natural paradise immediately after the story of creation to emphasize that creation is from nothing, from nothing natural, and that those whose covenant with God obligates them to choose thought and existence as their human task must recognize that the way of natural paganism has been eternally closed to them. Human beings are expelled forever from the contradictory innocence of nature blind to and ignorant of its own thought and existence. They have fallen from natural innocence to embrace true innocence, which is not ignorance of sin but the overcoming of evil on behalf of the good. To be innocent is not to be without knowledge of good and evil (for innocence, rooted in *nocere*, to do harm to, means to be harmless, that is, to negate or to overcome harm). To possess true innocence, the truth of innocence, is to act not from the ignorance of good and evil but from the power of willing the good, notwithstanding the seductive power of idols. (Kant would call idols individual maxims or opinions which are not disciplined by making them universally subject to the thought and existence of all.)

The paradox of the Bible, its authors want us to see, is that the Bible exists within the garden, within the paradise of nature, just as the tree of the knowledge of good and evil is located within the garden. The Bible reflects self-critically upon its own expulsion from the mythology of pagan naturalism in its presentation of the story of the expulsion of Adam and Eve from paradisiacal nature. It is not that pagan mythology, the myth of nature as always other than and opposed to itself, is literally exorcised or left behind. Rather, it is that we—biblical readers—we who are made in the image of God, must acknowledge the revelation that we do not think and exist within nature. We must acknowledge that it is we who create nature from nothing, not literally, of course (for that would be the grossest idolatry), but figuratively, as metaphor and paradox. It is we whose finite beginnings and ends are in nature but whose infinite (divine and human) beginnings and ends are the creation of nature, just as Copernicus discovered, as we have seen, that, in Kant's formulation, in order to liberate the appearances of nature from contradiction, we have to open our eyes to the *a priori* synthetic fact that it is we whose thought and existence move (determine) nature, not nature which blindly moves us with the unmoved necessity of fate. The tree of the knowledge of good and evil grows in nature, but it can be identified only by those whose eyes have been opened to metaphor, to knowing that good and evil involve not natural contradiction but the paradox of human thought and existence. To be forbidden to eat of the fruit of the tree of knowledge of good and evil is either a contradiction or a paradox. As a contradiction, it makes either God or human beings and thus both, equally, unworthy of thought and existence. As a paradox, it shows that even what appears to be divine command must be interpreted—thought through in one's existence—with all the divine love and serpent-like finesse of which one is possessed. One is forced to confront the contradiction of nature in the very command of God: how to understand the command not to know when that command presupposes that that which is not to be known must be known in order for the command not to know to be known.

The story of Adam and Eve is exemplary of biblical story, of the Bible, from beginning to end, for the Bible, in part and in whole, constantly confronts its readers with the choice of either/or: either choose to interpret truthfully, not being satisfied with facile contradiction (idolatry); or be offended by your choice whose contradictions involve you in idolatrous interpretations. The Bible commands its readers to choose life, not death, to recall the final words which Moses addresses to the chosen people before they pass over into the promised land. The paradox of the story of Adam and Eve is that the tree of knowledge, whose fruit, the thought and existence of good and evil, bears the seeds of human nature, is the tree of eternal life. In addition to the tree of knowledge, however, another tree, which is called the tree of life, is said to grow naturally in the garden. It is further said that those who eat of the fruit of the tree of life will obtain immortal life. But, just as the fruit of the tree of knowledge of good and evil is the truly human choice, so human beings must learn, and ever relearn, that the fruit of the tree of life generating natural immortality represents the falsification of human choice. The tree of life is the tree of death whose image of natural immortality fatally contradicts human being, showing that immortal happiness is always dead to life, that it is always other than and opposed to the thought and existence of the living. It is little wonder, then, that human beings are expelled from the garden of natural paganism in which there grows a tree of immortal life whose fatal fruit promises illusory happiness to those who die to the contradictions of natural metamorphosis.

As always, the teaching of a biblical story is simultaneously ontological and hermeneutical, involving both being (thought and existence) and reading. Ontologically we learn that the contradictions of natural immortality—which fatally thrust us back into the endlessly mortal cycle of natural metamorphosis—must be forsworn. To eat of the living tree of the knowledge of good and evil is to die, to die to the mythological life of nature, the life of the endless cycle of natural mortality and immortality, for which death fatally holds the contradictory secret of life. Exemplary masters of the pagan secret of death are the Egyptian pharaohs, well known to the ancient Israelites. As representatives (similes) of the immortal gods of nature, the pharaohs hide their lives in burial chambers deep within pyramidal labyrinths out of the light of human revelation. Yet their secret treasures are shamelessly robbed, often immediately after the burial of the ruler-god within the tomb of death and often by a subsequent ruler-god, who then proceeds to devote his life to burying his secret deep within nature whose labyrinthine artifice contradicts, like the shattered visage of Ozymandias, all those who look upon it. Let the dead bury the dead.

From beginning to end the Bible is resolutely opposed to immortality of the soul, to life after death, to any pagan notion that death bears the hidden (contradictory) secret of life. Life is to be conceived and lived in accordance, not with the contradictory similes of nature, but with the law of the living God: the golden rule of love, justice, freedom.... God is the God of the living, not of the dead. But immortality of the soul is one of the most seductive images of natural paganism for biblical men and women, especially in its gnostic versions (that a knowing elite, in opposition to the ignorant many, can, through giving up the sinful burden of created flesh, of thought and existence, of knowing good and evil, regain their immortal soul, which has unaccountably fallen in creation, and enjoy immediate identity with God, the ultimate idolatry of paradise). The authors of the story of Adam and Eve rigorously eschew the natural immortality of paradise, which, they know, fatally reduces life to the contradictions of death, and resolutely embrace death, not in itself, but as part of life, as the natural consequence of life, with life now understood as created, not in the contradictory images of nature but in the paradoxical metaphors of thought and existence. Man and woman are expelled from the deadly garden of natural paradise into life—conception and labor—with the knowledge that they will die. Death is not a natural secret to be hidden away from itself, from life, in the labyrinthine depths of artifice whose natural similes are blind to and ignorant of their artful mythology. Death is to be embraced by life as the revelation of thought and existence. Humans die. Indeed, if humans did not die, they would be subject to the contradictions of immortal nature which, because it never dies, never lives. The paradox of life is that life is its own standard, the standard of both the living and the dead.

The hermeneutical implications of the story of Adam and Eve are consonant with its ontology. The story teaches us how to read; it shows us that reading involves our becoming sensitive to conflict, contradiction, tension, ambiguity, paradox, irony, dissonance, metaphor, disparity, parody... not, ultimately, as barriers to, but as the very structure of, truthful interpretation. It is the very truth of our thought and existence which reading as interpretation must engage. How we are to distinguish between natural mythology (the doctrine of contradictory opposites) and biblical truth (the doctrine of dialectical opposites whose structure is the golden rule of mutual self-recognition) is never easy, and it is given not in itself but in our conception and labor, in our thought and existence. But it is this distinction which is presupposed by the distinction which the Bible makes fundamental to its own thought and existence, the distinction between truth and interpretation, on the one hand, and idolatry, on the other. In the story of Adam and Eve biblical authors appropriate pagan mythology of nature as the paradisiacal seduction which the chosen people, those who choose the God of life, must eternally confront and overcome. From the very beginning, in the story of beginning, in the story of the creation of man and woman and their beginning, readers must confront the paradox of beginning by beginning, themselves, not in the natural paradise of contradiction but in the paradoxical world of thought and existence, both divine and human. All great biblical stories—from the stories of creation and fall through the stories of Abraham, Moses, exodus and settlement, the prophets, the psalmist, Job, and the Preacher to the New Testament stories of beginnings—reveal to readers, who attend to the Word of God, that truth eternally involves the paradox of beginning with the interpretation of the golden rule of thought and existence. There is no beginning in nature, for the only beginning is creation from nothing, expulsion from nature into the self-conscious existence of beginning, ever again.

The story of Adam and Eve is the eternal reminder that, precisely because all beginnings appear arbitrary (and thus ambiguous, ironic, perplexing, paradoxical...), the task of the reader is to interpret them faithfully—rationally—consistent with human thought and existence. When the golden rule of thought and existence, such that each is the interpretation of the truth of the other, is relinquished, then the reader falls into the idolatrous contradictions of natural mythology, from which Adam and Eve are once and for all expelled. The teaching, finally, of the story of Adam of Eve, as of all biblical story, is the paradox that thought and existence are simultaneously divine and human. Any attempt to give up thought and existence as both or simultaneously divine and human results, ineluctably, in the idolatrous reduction of either thought or existence, alike divine and human, and thus both, to natural contradiction, something unthinkable to pagans but the seduction eternally present to us moderns, the heirs of our first parents.

Having now reflected upon the central biblical concepts of golden rule, creation, and fall, I want to conclude my speculative consideration of the Bible with reflection upon the notion of covenant and its attendant idea of eternal life. The concept of covenant, like all concepts (as distinct from mere terms), cannot be thought except existing (without our existing in and through it). The covenant is the primary notion, both metaphoric and paradoxical, through which biblical authors narrate the story of the relationship of God and the chosen people. No less than the golden rule and creation, with their closely related notion of the expulsion from nature, that is, liberation from nature or eternal life, the covenant is unique to the Bible, yet universal for all humanity. It lies at the origin of democratic theory, for it is the biblical covenant which shapes the contract theory of Hobbes, Spinoza, Locke, and Rousseau and then enters more generally into the democratic principle that the people, as the cause of themselves, are not subject to some unknown power or force either (politically) outside or (psychologically) inside them. The covenant underlies the revolutionary practice of liberty, equality, and solidarity and has recently inspired the prefatory words introducing the new Canadian Charter of Rights and Freedoms, according to which it is said: "Canada is founded upon principles that recognize the supremacy of God and the rule of law."

The very notion that God makes a covenant, his covenant, with a people in history, that he is bound to the covenant which he makes with his people no less than the people are bound to the covenant which they make with their God is a revolutionary idea, revolutionary for the exacting reason that it is based on notions of mutuality, reciprocity, relationship, and responsibility...—the golden rule—which have no analogy in the natural (or contradictory) revolutions of the heavenly spheres. The notion of the covenant is revolutionary because it involves not only the supremacy of God but also the rule of law. God is the one God to be loved above all other gods, the gods of paganism, because he is not a ruler who rules only insofar as he rules over others. He is the one God who is subject to the rule of law, not any law, but the one law which is to be obeyed above all other laws, the law which is universally valid for all. The covenant between God and his people is equally the covenant which the people make with themselves, both individually and collectively. To love God supremely above all others and your neighbor as the rule of law for yourself is to do unto others as you would have them do unto you. That the very thought and existence of God and humankind presuppose the covenant is evident, from the beginning, in the story of Adam and Eve. Either God's command forbidding Adam and Eve to eat of the fruit of the knowledge of good and evil is arbitrary and unlawful, not binding on those who adhere to the covenant, or it shows that knowledge of good and evil cannot be thought to exist (cannot exist in thought) outside the covenant binding on both God and human beings. The story of Adam and Eve could have been authored (both written and comprehended) only by and for those who belong to the covenant. It is inconceivable and unimaginable to anyone living in the natural paradise of mythical contradiction, including Adam and Eve.

That the covenant between God and his chosen people is shown to begin a number of times as the covenant (the Bible) is fitting and proper, for the very notion of the covenant ever beginning again is history, the fulfillment and renewal of time as the Sabbath, eternally, from the beginning. The covenant begins with creation, with the first man and the first woman, with Noah, with Abraham, with Moses, with the prophets (the new covenant of Jeremiah), with Jesus, with Paul, with the Gospel writers.... It begins with each new person, with each new reader. The covenant is the relationship of thought and existence such that for either to be true (and interpretable) both must be interpreted as true. But the covenant is, therefore, always both inclusive—of those choosing knowledge of good and evil— and exclusive—of those who exclude themselves in not recognizing that exclusion from the covenant between God and humankind is the choice which fails to recognize itself as choice or inclusion. That God, according to biblical narrative, makes his covenant with a particular people (the ancient Israelites) and with a particular Israelite (Jesus) shows, again, how arbitrary are the appearances of biblical beginning. If we ask—*cur deus populus*? or *cur deus homo*? Why did (does/will) God become [this particular] people or [this particular] human being? (Why did/does/will [this particular] people or individual become God?)—we must see, as we indicated earlier, that this question can be asked only if we understand ourselves to be grounded, from the beginning (in principle), in its thought and existence. That God chooses—or is represented as choosing—one people or one individual, as opposed to another, is arbitrary and unjust, the problematic of beginning being here no different from that expressed in the stories of creation and fall. How is God (or how are we) to begin, in the midst of nature, which is without beginning or end? God (the principle, the principal of beginning) begins; and the beginning is like the grain of mustard seed, something so small and humble that it seems unworthy of divine omnipotence and omniscience.

Why, we ask, can't God begin more, well, God-like? But who, indeed, is God? we keep asking. God, it is clear, is the principle of covenant. God is freedom, choice, the demand that individuals exclude themselves from the contradictory nature of fate and include themselves within the story of creative life, choosing the life of thought and existence, not death. Whatever the content of the original choice, what counts is that the content be the concept, that it be thought only as existing. We, the heirs of the content chosen as necessary (thoughtful), have no choice but to choose, to recognize that, if the arbitrary beginning—the inclusion of some, the exclusion of many—is to be rendered faithful as the beginning of faith, we must continue to bear witness to the revelation that only those are excluded from the covenant who fail to see that inclusion within the covenant involves an exclusiveness, a choice, which then makes possible an authentic inclusiveness which excludes no one. But it is precisely because the covenant bears the marks of the dialectic of inclusiveness and exclusiveness that it also bears the seeds of idolatry, whereby the practice of making choices, distinctions, and discriminations can become arbitrary and unjust. When barriers of discrimination are erected upon the idolatry of nature, others are unjustly excluded (or included) on the basis of race, gender, and class.

The beginning of the covenant is fraught with risks—to one's thought and existence—for, once beginning becomes a free choice involving equality, freedom, and solidarity, one can also begin falsely. The risk that one will tire of beginning ever anew is the risk of identifying one's beginnings with the immediate content of natural space and time, the risk of idolatry. Just as the covenant is unimaginable and inconceivable as existing within extra-biblical paganism, so it is only within the biblical covenant that humans sin. To sin—against God and neighbor, against the relationship of thought and existence—is to fail to recognize that the covenant begins anew with every generation, with every people, with every individual. The glories of the past will, without exception, become idols generating *ressentiment*, the anxiety of consequence, until and unless they are renewed as the future of thought and existence.

The covenant is consonant not only with creation—they both express the responsibility for beginning in thought and existence—but also with eternal life. Just as there is no sin outside the covenant, so there is also no salvation outside the covenant, outside of choosing to abide, eternally, with the covenantal demands of the supremacy of God and the rule of law. But once salvation—liberation: choice—is understood to express eternal life in the covenant, the eternal choice of the covenant, then all similitudes to natural immortality, to life after death, to some heavenly space and time beyond this natural world, are radically deconstructed as blatantly idolatrous. The heaven and earth of creation are the covenant, the proper home of those who choose the life of thought and existence. The heaven and earth of creation are not the space and time of nature, whose contradictions appear to end in death but which unaccountably begin all over again. There is no life—no thought or existence—outside the covenant. All life within the covenant is eternal life, eternity understood as the fulfillment of time as history. Eternal life is the golden rule, the recognition that natural death does not encompass the life of covenantal spirit. Eternal life expresses the fullness of living the covenant of thought and existence. To begin life in the covenant is the recognition that beginning always involves death, the recognition that death is neither the end nor the beginning, that the principle of death is life whose end is not natural death but the creation of eternal life.

V. CONCLUSION: THE BIBLICAL PRINCIPLE OF THOUGHT AND EXISTENCE

Eternal life, in contrast with the idolatrous reduction of thought and existence to the contradictions of immortal nature, describes how we live the golden rule of the covenant. However different are the Hebrew covenant and the Christian covenant, the Hebrew Bible and the Christian Bible—and they are vastly different, for they reflect different situations, exigencies, concerns, problems, demands—their differences can be understood as genuinely different only within the shared context of God, human being, creation, fall, covenant, the golden rule, salvation, eternal life, the unrelenting attack on idolatry, the shared context of what I am calling in this work the dialectic of thought and existence. The jejune distinctions which are characteristically made between the Hebrew Bible and the Christian Bible (especially by pre-modern Christians)—between collective life and individual life, between law and faith, between the messiah who is yet to come and the messiah who has come, between a jealous god and a loving god, between a god of vengeance and a god of forgiveness—impugn the integrity of both Judaism and Christianity. Judaism and Christianity are each true or complete in itself; yet each is true or complete only insofar as the other is true or complete, just as one Jew, one Christian, one person is completely true in him(her)self yet is true only insofar as his (her) truth is completed through the truth of the other (Jew, Christian, person). It is absolutely characteristic of the Bible, which constantly presents us with the challenge of beginning eternally in the covenant created from nothing, from nothing appearing in the natural space and time of contradiction, to make two beginnings: a first beginning (the first or what Christians call the Old Testament), and a second beginning (the second or the New Testament). But the comprehensive teaching of the entire Bible, both Jewish and Christian, from beginning to end, is that every authentic beginning is originally first and that every original beginning is consequent upon a prior beginning. In the beginning was (is) the beginning. The covenant is both original and ever to be renewed, remade, and recreated as first.

It is uniquely the challenge to Jews and Christians (to all readers of the Bible, including so-called secular or even atheistical readers of the Bible) to comprehend why God makes two covenants which are simultaneously identical and different. To ask whether there might have been, is, or perhaps yet will be a third testament, etc., may be useful, insofar as hypothetical or counter-conceptual questions may serve to liberate the mind from rigidly held views (idols). But the real question, paraphrasing Kant and keeping in mind Anselm's question, is categorical. How is the Bible as the *a priori* synthetic judgment possible? How is the Bible, whose judgment expresses the priority synthesizing thought and existence, possible? This question, like any question, in order to be meaningfully asked, must encompass, as we have already seen, the questioner within the prior synthesis of thought and existence. To ask how the Bible is possible is to ask: given that the Bible is actual, that it exists in our thought and is the concept which cannot be thought without our existing, how do we read it, how do we practice it, how do we think it, how do we exist within it? The revelation of the question is biblical, both Jewish and Christian. That the question, *qua* question, is biblical, equally Jewish and Christian, bears witness to the fact that questions legitimately have different answers, different interpretations, or different conceptions of the truth so long as that which constitutes meaningful difference among our different answers, interpretations, and truths is the golden rule of truth and interpretation, the *a priori* synthetic judgment, the dialectic of thought and existence. Answers, interpretations, or truths are infinite; but that we recognize the infinity of truthful difference only serves to emphasize that there are also false and falsifying, that is, idolatrous, answers, interpretations, and truths—and they are legion—those which reduce infinity as its own standard, the standard of both the infinite and the finite, to finite objects of nature.

It is the Bible—the Jewish Bible and the Christian Bible, which are the same Bible, yet they are different Bibles—which both introduces the concept of difference into the world, the difference of the chosen people from those who are enslaved to the fatally blind mythology of contradictory nature, the difference which the choice of difference makes in the world of nature, and shows the world that difference can be liberated from indifference only if it is chosen, only if it is thought and exists as meaningful difference. The category of meaning is both ontological and hermeneutical. It encompasses, and is encompassed by, the ontological argument, the recognition, the practice, that the concept is the content which cannot be thought without existing and that the content is the concept which does not exist outside of our consciousness of it. Meaningful difference—distinction or discrimination—enters the world, as we have seen, as the revelation that it is utterly different from the differences of natural paganism, where all differences are fatally indifferent both to themselves and to others, following the contradictory *logos* of the doctrine of opposites. Blindness to and ignorance of the difference which difference makes in the world reflects the fate of identity which is always other than and opposed to the contradictory appearances of its differences. The moment, however, that identity is revealed in the world as the meaningful structure of thought and existence, saving the different appearances of nature from the fate of indifferent contradiction, idolatry enters the world in the shadow of the revelation of meaningful difference as the discrimination against others in terms of identifying them according to their natural differences, something inconceivable and unimaginable in extra-biblical paganism.

In revealing its utter difference from the contradictory differences of natural paganism and in opposing in the most resolute terms the idolatry of reducing identity to the contradictions of natural differences, the Bible shows that the difference between divine being and human being, between God and person, is grounded in the identity of their thought and existence. The ontological argument applies no less to thought than to existence, for the truth of each is the interpretation of the other. The ontological argument for thought and existence applies no less to human than to divine being. The hermeneutic of reading the Bible—of reading any text—embodies the ontology (and epistemology) of thought and existence. The very structure of beginning "in the beginning" shows that the creation of God is the creation of human beings. God can be conceived as that whose concept expresses his existence only as this thinking is the human practice which involves the thinker in the existence of his thought. The ontological, that is, the hermeneutical argument for both the thought of existence and the existence of thought—equally divine and human—is expressed in the Bible as the covenant, that which binds God and person no less than it binds person and person in relation, in the beginning. The relation of God and person is the relation of person and person, just as the relation of person and person is the relation of person and God. Neither relation is conceivable without the existence of both.

Not only the first human beings but God himself as first must fall from the contradictory otherness of nature as the first secret whose end is never known if the revelation of thought and existence is to be made accessible to all as the first choice. The notion that some human beings take natural precedence, in the beginning, over others is eschewed in the same radical sense that the notion that God, in the beginning, takes natural precedence over human beings is radically eschewed. Both God and human beings are sovereign (as Spinoza argues so eloquently). Each, as we have indicated, is the author, the creator, of the Bible. The Bible itself is sovereign, ruling, not over its readers, as if they were but slaves who had yet to learn the lesson of the story of Exodus, but together with its readers, whose task, as always, is to embody the sovereignty of God in their lives, to be responsible to God in their relationship with others (including themselves) as they are responsible to others (including themselves) in their relationship to God. Once again, the philosophic reader, the secular reader, the atheistical reader, the skeptical reader, the impatient reader may say: if God and human beings are equally sovereign, if God is but the representation (the creation) of human beings, surely this but repeats the cheap psychologism which was already exposed as human projection in the emerging biblical criticism of nineteenth century thinkers like Feuerbach and Strauss, not to mention in the trenchant criticism of Nietzsche. Are human beings not sufficient unto themselves? Are we not finally to be freed from the future of a divine illusion? (We silently note that dogmatic readers will question the identity of divine and human sovereignty from the opposite, that is, from the same, point of view.)

Our patient answer is always the same. There is no magic as such in using the language of God (just as there is no magic as such in using the language of the human). We may properly choose to avoid or to eschew the language of God, and it may be important to attack the idol of God with the single-minded devotion of Kierkegaard (in his withering attack on Christendom) or of Nietzsche (in his scathing attack identified as Antichrist). It is worth recalling, however, that the truly great critics of God are no less searching critics of humanity, unlike Strauss and Feuerbach, whose critiques of God and the Bible as human representation remain unconsciously and uncritically theological (that is, Platonic), as Marx has no difficulty in pointing out. We may not properly choose, however, to avoid or to eschew communication, and communication always involves the dialectic of thought and existence, whatever the linguistic terms of its expression. The Bible is the supreme, the unique, the complete demonstration that human sovereignty, the authority of human thought and existence, can be properly differentiated from the pagan mythology of natural contradiction and can be truly protected from the idolatry of being reduced to the contradictions of nature if, and only if, it is not either falsely opposed to God or falsely identified with God. God is indeed the representation (creation) of human being such that it is sovereign, both independent of and irreducible to nature. To forget that God is the communication of human being is to risk forgetting that human thought and existence—I think, therefore, I am—are no less subject to idolatry than God himself. Indeed, along with God, man is the idol par excellence. The idolatry of both God and man—one thinks today of, for example, the powerful feministic critique of patriarchal authority, alike divine and human—can be overcome only if it is understood that thought and existence are sovereign and that, as sovereign, they simultaneously embody divine and human being, both the supremacy of God and the rule of law.

It is only when we develop a comprehensive and systematic view of the relationship of thought and existence that we can develop a proper conception (and practice) of truth and interpretation. But, as we have now seen, we can develop a proper conception of thought and existence only if we comprehend them, in the beginning, as the revelation of the Bible. It is not (only) that the Bible is the first text to reveal the ontological argument—the golden rule of thought and existence—to the world, even though that statement is true. Rather, what we must see—at least once in our life: it demands our conversion to biblical thought and existence—is that the Bible and the dialectic of thought and existence bear precisely the same structure, the *a priori* synthetic judgment of reality. For something to be first—first in truth and interpretation—it must reveal itself as first, first not in the natural and thus contradictory geography and chronology of space and time but rather in all space and time, in history, for all eternity. The Bible is first not because it is first in space and time—for in that sense it is not first but altogether parochial and very late, indeed, as it emerges in the midst of richly diverse and complex civilizations which it is the first, however, to reveal as fatally hidden in the secret contradictions of nature.

The Bible is first because it is the first—and the last—text to reveal the consequences of being first, the consequences of priority. It is the first to reveal the consequences of viewing thought and existence as both absolutely separate from the contradictory *telos* of nature and resolutely opposed to the idolatry of reducing the thought and existence of either God or human being to the nature of contradiction. It is only in comprehending the priority of biblical thought and existence that we shall be in a position to develop a comprehensive conception of truth and interpretation which is not only separate from the contradictions of pagan naturalism but irreducible to the idolatry of either skepticism or dogmatism. As we shall see in the subsequent two chapters, it is only in developing a conception of truth as involving interpretation and of interpretation as expressing truth that we shall be in a position not only to overcome the false and falsifying dualism between faith and reason so pervasive in our pre- and post-modernist worlds but also to comprehend the secular world as the proper home of human beings who embrace the modernity of beginning, ever again, with the God of the Bible.

5

Faith and Reason and the
Problem of Dualism

I. INTRODUCTION: MODERNITY AND THE PARADOX OF BEGINNING AS BEING AND BECOMING

When Spinoza observes in the *Ethics* (which was published posthumously in 1677) that it is obvious to all that human beings are born conscious of their desire but ignorant of the causes of things, he captures the structure of modernity, of that which Montaigne had a little under a century earlier called the *condition humaine*. Not quite a century later, at the beginning of the *Social Contract*, Rousseau formulates the paradox of modern desire conscious of its ignorance in the provocative terms that man is born free and everywhere is in chains. Rousseau proceeds immediately to pose two questions about the condition of human beings whose free birth involves their bondage. How did this change come about? What can render this change legitimate? Rousseau answers the first question with the blunt statement that he does not know. The second question, he believes, he can answer. It is the answer to this second question which constitutes the *Social Contract*. Like Spinoza before him, Rousseau recognizes that the paradox confronting us moderns is to comprehend how our human desire, consciousness, and freedom involve us in ignorance and slavery. Spinoza, like Rousseau after him, proceeds to point out that, because human beings are born conscious of their desire but ignorant of the ends (causes) of their desire, they constantly project the ends they desire into the certain or objective things of nature, thus enchaining themselves to final causes which, although they are originally the product of their own desires, become the chains (both psychological, internally, and social, externally) by which they consciously, yet ignorantly, freely, yet compulsively, enslave themselves.

Why does Spinoza not argue for but merely presuppose his conception of the human condition as consciousness ignorant of what constitutes its desire? What is the ontological status of such a presupposition? Why does Spinoza state, apparently so casually (or confidently), that this is the situation which all (readers) will, without question, recognize as their own? Why is Rousseau so peremptory in his refusal to answer the question why human beings fall from freedom into slavery, as if it is obvious to all that it is not a legitimate question for either himself or his readers to ask? What does he mean when he writes that he will devote the *Social Contract,* not to discussing the fall of human beings, that is, why slavery exists, but to justifying the chains by which human beings have enslaved themselves?

We ourselves, in the beginning, do not know whether or how either Spinoza or Rousseau is justified in beginning with his initial presupposition or question, for the very paradox of reading a text, of beginning a work, or, indeed, of living one's life is that the end is presupposed in the beginning, but, in the beginning, we are conscious of beginning ignorant of our end. We are born free, but we must enslave ourselves to a text if we are to learn from it, although we constantly run the risk of emerging from the text having either enslaved the text to our blind ends or enslaved ourselves to the ends of the text of which we are ignorant. But therefore we do know that Spinoza and Rousseau are justified in beginning where they do, in beginning with their presuppositions and questions, for they articulate precisely the position of their readers who are both conscious of their desire and ignorant of what will constitute or fulfill their desire. The modern condition of humanity is constituted by those who are conscious of their freedom, yet conscious that it is precisely their having been born free which shows them how much teaching and learning are required, how great is the education (revolution) which must be effected, if they are to legitimize the chains of ignorance and slavery to which they are presently subject.

We do not, in the beginning, know whether Spinoza or Rousseau is justified in his beginning presupposition, in the question with which he begins, in beginning not with this but with that assertion or question.

Given the enormous authority which Spinoza and Rousseau enjoy, readers are apt to respect their beginning, to see where it takes them. The typical response of readers to an authoritative text, however, is to read it because it is said (by others) to be authoritative and thus to evade confronting or being confronted by its authority. Authority is something which readers have difficulty taking on, for either to accept or to reject the authority of a text (its authorship) is never an easy choice, when acceptance or rejection of authority implicates readers directly in their own authorship. In either case, whether they reject or accept the authority of the text, readers are responsible for constituting the ends of their desire, of becoming conscious of their desirable end, of justifying the bonds in which their freedom implicates them. The issue of how we begin to legitimize the ends of our desire becomes particularly interesting when we learn that the authority of texts like those of Spinoza and Rousseau is directly grounded in the sophistication and profundity with which they articulate the paradox of consciousness and ignorance, of freedom and slavery, this paradox both reflecting the dualism by which human beings consciously enslave themselves to their own ignorance and constituting the dialectic by which they are empowered to liberate themselves from their own self-imposed slavery.

How we humans consciously enchain our desire to ignorance, how we humans freely enslave ourselves: these are the issues that define modernity. Humans are conscious of their desire but ignorant of their ends. Humans are free in the beginning, but everywhere they are in chains. Spinoza and Rousseau alike deny, both explicitly and implicitly through the structure of their works, that we can legitimately ask how this change came about. Indeed, their work presupposes that it is only if readers accept these very presuppositions that they will be able to begin, to begin the task of reading, of thinking, of living. (It is worth noting, by the way, that the texts with which we here begin and which are among the handful of great texts in the early modern world which comprehensively articulate our human beginnings are called *Ethics* and *Social Contract*). But how are we to begin such that we can become conscious of the ends of our desire, such that we can constitute consciously the ends of our desire of which, in the beginning, we are ignorant? How are we to transform the chains by which we are presently enslaved into the bonds of our original freedom?

Both Spinoza and Rousseau know, or perhaps it is more fitting to say that their texts reveal to us the knowledge, that such questions, like

Anselm's question, already presuppose our conscious desire or freedom. If we do not know what we are ignorant of, if we do not know what the nature of our enslavement is, if, in other words, we are not conscious of our freedom, then our condition will be indistinguishable from that of Socratic ignorance, of extra-biblical paganism, which knows that it is opposed to and other than itself but does not know what this opposition or otherness, in fact, is. But the contradiction which is endlessly ignorant of and blind to itself in the extra-biblical world is revealed in the modern world of the Bible as the very condition of ignorance and slavery from which human beings consciously desire to be liberated. Ignorance and slavery—in their infinitely idolatrous versions—are the product not of nature but of human consciousness (desire) and freedom, of what I am calling in this essay in thinking the dialectic of thought and existence. We are not born slaves to our ignorance, but, because our ends are not given in the blind contradictions of nature but in the consciousness of our desire for freedom, we are constantly seduced by the idols of our own creation which reduce our creativity to ignorance and slavery. Unlike extra-biblical peoples, who are born into nature and thus are subject to the vicissitudes of natural metamorphosis, biblical men and women and their modern heirs are born free and thus can and do lose (pervert, oppress, repress, annihilate...) their conscious desire for freedom.

Whereas extra-biblical peoples, because they are natural, cannot lose, in the beginning, what they do not possess, which is the consciousness of being liberated from the fatal otherness of nature, biblical men and women, because they are grounded in the conscious desire of being free, can become, in the beginning, other than what they are, which is unfree. Because extra-biblical peoples are, in the beginning, other than what they are—in the beginning they are opposed to and the reverse of what they are in the beginning—they can never become what they are not; for, from the beginning, they are what they are not; they are and they are not, as they fatally obey the law of contradictory opposites of which they are endlessly ignorant and by which they are eternally blinded. But biblical men and women, because, in the beginning, they are born, not in the image of nature but in the image of God—conscious of their free desire—have the obligation—they are commanded!—to become what they are (not). Because extra-biblical peoples are not what they are (they are what they are not), they can never become what they are (not). The terrible price of conscious desire and freedom for biblical men and women and their modern heirs, the heirs of Adam and Eve, however, is that they must become what they are (not), which is conscious and free human beings desiring the ends of human consciousness and freedom (thought and existence). But, precisely because what they are—human beings conscious that they are commanded to love God above all others and their neighbors as themselves—is what they must constantly become, since consciousness and freedom are not innate or natural givens but gifts of the spirit always to be shared, communicated, and created, the burden of ever becoming what one is—of being what one is ever becoming—is enormous. It is little wonder that biblical men and women and their modern heirs compulsively forsake the covenant, whose being is its free and conscious becoming, for the fleshpots of the world, for foreign gods or ideologies which promise an easy, an immediate, direct, or certain, equation between our desire and things as they are.

The relation of being and becoming is what we identify in this essay in thinking as dialectic, paradox, and metaphor. It is founded in desire (Spinoza's actual Latin term is *appetitus*), that which Kant calls will. Spinoza sets as the task of desire that it become conscious that it is its own end as the cause of itself, independent of natural compulsions, whether internal or external. For Rousseau, our task is to become that which we naturally are, which is independent of the *status quo*, the degrading and dehumanizing conventions, artificialities, and superfluities of our society whose ideology holds, in reflecting the impotence of Hume's argument against the slavery of custom, that whatever is, is. If one holds that there is no necessity in matters of empirical fact (which cannot be thought) but only in relations of ideas (which do not exist), then the existential necessity by which some actually rule over others (in whatever sphere of life) is *de facto* legitimated. Although the social facts could be other than what they are, for they lack necessity (this is the power of the empirical argument), there is no necessity that they be other than what they are (this is the impotence of the empirical argument). In dualistic opposition to (and thus in complete agreement with) the empiricist like Hume, the rationalist like Leibniz holds that, since social facts lack necessity, they could not be other than they are, for they reflect the best of all possible worlds whose necessary ideas (monads) could not be other than what they are. Since necessity has been relegated, by both empiricist and rationalist, to the impotence of non-existent ideas, the only necessity dominating the personal and social relations of thought and existence is force, the force of traditional and customary power relations.

When Rousseau holds, rejecting the dualism between empiricism and rationalism, that to be human is to argue from the necessity of right (the right of necessity) to the constitution of fact, and not from fact (whether construed empirically or rationally) to right, he is articulating anew his initial insight that human beings constantly sell their birthright of freedom for enslavement to immediate satisfaction. That facts are created *ex nihilo* from right, that what we are (born with), our conscious desire and freedom, is created from nothing, from nothing which is found in the contradictory opposites of natural space and time, means that there is the constant danger of compulsively confusing our ends with natural idols which reflect our contradictory ignorance and blindness. We are... nothing, and we must become... nothing, nothing natural in space and time. We are... everything, and we must become... everything, everything not found in natural space and time. It is properly biblical to say that we are... God and that we become... God, so long as God retains for us the dialectical tension between being and becoming, each of which is true and subject to interpretation only so long as both are interpreted as (being and becoming) the truth. It is also properly biblical to say that we are... human and that we become... human, insofar as humanity bears the wisdom of the oxymoron identifying the difference between being and becoming. To be or not to be is clearly not the question which is worthy of humanity, as Hamlet is so profoundly aware. To be and (therefore) to become what one is: that is the quest to which the human condition is the eternal response. Only those who are prepared to live the dialectic of thought and existence, knowing that every question is its becoming response, can say betimes: the readiness is all.

I begin this chapter on the problem of dualism—and I am particularly concerned with how our thinking is profoundly distorted by the dualism between faith and reason—with reflections on the presuppositions made in great texts such as those by Spinoza and Rousseau in order to suggest that the very presuppositions which are central to all thinking whose subject is existence involve conscious desire or freedom, the identity of the difference between being and becoming. I begin with texts which do not appear to be heavily loaded towards the discourse of either faith or reason, of either theology or philosophy, although they would normally be called philosophical (notwithstanding the fact that the *Ethics* begins with the ontological argument for God's existence and ends with the intellectual love of God and that the last substantial chapter of the *Social Contract* is concerned with civil religion). What I want to show, however, is that these texts, like all great modern texts (whether theological or philosophical, whether philosophical or artistic—verbal, visual, or musical), are biblical in their structure and thus no more or less faithful than they are rational, whatever the immediate language of their discourse. Indeed, the concept of modernity, or modernism, to the degree it communicates meaning, is biblical, for modernism can mean nothing other than our becoming that which we are already, in the beginning, in contrast with paradisiacal idols of future utopias or past golden ages. (Christianity, we may note, is particularly prone to adopt either of these dualistic opposites, willy-nilly.) To begin—to begin with the dialectic of thought and existence—is to begin conscious of our desire that we can overcome the dualisms of the idols which enslave us to that which we are not in the beginning only if we freely become that which we are in the beginning.

II. THE DUALISM OF POST-MODERNISM AND PRE-MODERNISM: THE ANXIETY OF CONSEQUENCE

If we are to become the modern heirs of Adam and Eve, we shall have to learn to overcome the dualism between post-modernism and pre-modernism, each of which evades becoming what it is in the beginning. Either the future is viewed as post-modern, without beginning (the future has no beginning in the past). Or the past is viewed as pre-modern, without beginning (the past has no beginning in the future). The skepticism of post-modernism and the dogmatism of pre-modernism represent the anxiety of consequence, the anxiety of evading the consequences of living within the modern tradition of beginning ever anew with the Bible. Post-modernists and pre-modernists, of whatever ilk, undertake to evade the consequences of living within the biblical tradition by claiming, respectively, either to succeed or to precede the Bible. Post-modernists, who are but another species of skeptics, suffer the consequences of coming posterior to the truth of interpretation. They may well be willing to embrace hermeneutics (the theory of interpretation), but they are loath to acknowledge that, in the beginning, interpretation is revealed in the world as the practice of truth.

Post-modernists are extremely unhappy with the prospect that originality, creativity, or authority preceded them. Pre-modernists, who are but another species of dogmatists, suffer the consequences of coming prior to the interpretation of truth. Without exception they claim to embrace the truth (in the guise of certainty), but they are loath to acknowledge that, in the beginning, truth is revealed in the world as interpretative practice. Post-modernists claim to come into the world after the Bible. The Bible, they contend (often in guilty silence), can be forgotten; they can go further than faith as its successors. Whatever the (past) consequences of the Bible, they no longer count. Pre-modernists equally claim to come into the world after the Bible. The Bible, they contend (often in guilty volubility), can be forgotten; they can go no further than what precedes them. Pre-modernists claim that, because the Bible comes into the world before they do, the beginning is in the past. No new beginning is to be made. Whatever the (future) consequences of the Bible, they no longer count.

What is characteristic of both post-modernists and pre-modernists, the skeptics and the dogmatists who vie blindly for authority in every era so long as the Bible's consequences are modern, is that both suffer the anxiety of consequence. Both deny the consequences of the Bible. Both deny that, in beginning, the Bible must become what it is in every era which is modern. Both deny that the Bible, in beginning, is both future and past, both coming after itself and preceding itself, both its own successor and its own predecessor. Whereas post-modernists deny that they are the consequence of the Bible, pre-modernists deny that the Bible is their consequence. Post-modernists lack the faith to believe that they follow in consequence of the Bible. Pre-modernists lack the reason to think that the Bible follows in their consequence. Post-modernists see nothing of consequence coming after the Bible. Pre-modernists see nothing of the Bible coming as their consequence. For both, the Bible is complete, for the post-modernists, before their time, for the pre-modernists, after their time. For both, the Bible is past, leaving the post-modernists with a future which has no historical past and the pre-modernists with a past which has no historical future. For both, the Bible is future (over), leaving the post-modernists with a past which has no historical future and the pre-modernists with a future which has no historical past. For both post-modernists and pre-modernists the notions of originality, authority, and creativity have neither past nor future. Post-modernists view originality, authority, and creativity (including their own) as without any consequences, whereas pre-modernists view their own consequences as lacking any originality, authority, or creativity.

The only way in which the dualism between post-modern skepticism and pre-modern dogmatism, each suffering what I am calling here the anxiety of consequence, the anxiety that one is a consequence of the Bible and that the Bible is one's own consequence, can be overcome is by embracing the modern consequence of beginning with the Bible. Modernity is the recognition of the paradox both that no beginning is original (the anxiety of consequence suffered by post-modernists) and that every beginning is original (the anxiety of consequence suffered by pre-modernists). Modernity is the recognition that it is the Bible which brings the conception of beginning, of originality and creativity, into thought and existence, in the beginning, from nothing, from nothing which is unoriginal or uncreative. This beginning is thus always historical (we shall develop our concept of history in the next chapter in the context of showing that the Bible is the creation of space and time as the secular world of humanity). Not only is modernity, in appropriating the Bible as that which reveals the world to be the true space and time for human beginning, the recognition that we begin with the Bible (thus post-modernism as post-biblicism is shown to be unauthentic), but modernity is also the revelation that the Bible begins with us (thus pre-modernism or pre-biblicism is shown to be no less unauthentic). We do not come either after or before the Bible, except in the chronology of time whose quantities are spatial. We do not come either posterior to or prior to the Bible in the sense that our consequences are not its consequences or that its consequences are not our consequences. We are the creation of the Bible's consequences, in the double or paradoxical sense that, just as we belong to its creation (God creates human beings), its creation belongs to us (human beings create God). We are neither the success of the Bible nor its precedence, in the sense that post- and pre-modernists refuse to acknowledge that their success or precedence in evading the consequence of the Bible can be understood only in light of their own inconsequentiality. Whereas post-modernists refuse to acknowledge that they are the consequence of the Bible, that they owe their success to the Bible, pre-modernists refuse to acknowledge that the Bible is their consequence, that their precedence is a completely biblical notion. To recognize the consequences of the Bible, to embrace them, to appropriate them is to recognize that the very notion of post- and pre-, of success and precedence, of consequences is uniquely (and universally) modern, because biblical.

It is important to note how common sense (the habit of repressed idolatry) equally supports post-modern skepticism and pre-modern dogmatism and thus how dependent (parasitic) each is on its opposite. It is obvious to post-modern skeptics that, because they come after the Bible, the consequences of the Bible are in the past. The future is separated, that is, different, from past consequences. But it is equally obvious to pre-modern dogmatists that, because they come after the Bible, the consequences of the Bible are in the past. The future is inseparable from, that is, identical with, the consequences of the past. Post-modernists emphasize the certainty, that is, the isolation (the solipsism), of the subject. This emphasis is particularly evident in the near-hysteria with which post-modernists insist upon the autonomy of objects. Pre-modernists emphasize the certainty, that is, the isolation (the objectivity), of the object. This emphasis is particularly evident in the enormous fear which the autonomy of subjects inspires in pre-modernists.

The Bible is itself the text of all texts precisely because it, above all texts, suffers, from beginning to end, the anxiety of its own consequence. It comes into existence belatedly, with both the world of nature preceding it by billions of years and the richly diverse civilizations of the world preceding it by thousands of years. Not only, however, does the Bible find that there is a vast world which precedes it, but it equally finds that there is a vast world which succeeds it. Still, the Bible enters the world with the revelation that all success is owed to it and that it takes precedence over everything else. Nothing succeeds or precedes the Bible except as a consequence of beginning (and ending) with the Bible. Success is properly measured by the quality of suffering the consequences of your beginning with the Bible, while precedence is properly measured by the quality of your suffering the consequences of the Bible's beginning with you.

The Bible itself suffers, above all others, the most massive anxiety of consequence when it enters the world with the announcement that the world exists conscious of its own freedom insofar as, and only insofar as, it recognizes itself to be revealed in and through the creation of the Bible. The Bible shows that everything which succeeds or precedes it exists consciously (or thinks its existence) only through having been created from nothing, from nothing which precedes or succeeds the Bible. The God of the Bible is a jealous God, brooking no opposition from either his successors or his predecessors. In the decalogue the chosen people are commanded, first, to choose no other gods before the original Lord of the covenant, while Jesus, when importuned by fellow members of the covenant to give his view of the original choice of the law, tells them to choose God above all others (in choosing their neighbor as themselves). Not only does the Bible, as we have seen, represent a series of beginnings, beginnings in which success avoids the idolatrous dualism of post-modernism solely by appropriating, yet again, the Bible as the precedent of modernity. But the Bible also reflects its own massive anxiety of consequence in its (Christian) end with the revelation of the apocalypse, the unveiling of the seventh seal. Having begun its story as creation from nothing, from nothing uncreative, how is the Bible going to conclude its story of creation? Does the story of creation end in nothing? Having begun with a big bang, does the Bible end apocalyptically with a whimper?

Just as stories of creation have a tendency of becoming post-modern idols in which authors evade the consequences of beginning with the Bible, so stories of apocalypse have a tendency of becoming pre-modern idols in which authors evade the consequences of viewing the Bible as beginning with them. Whereas post-modernists suffer the anxiety of consequence in claiming to bring textuality into existence on their own and thus in claiming that textuality has no end after the beginning, so pre-modernists, in claiming that textuality has no beginning after the end and thus in claiming that textuality brings them into existence on its own, equally suffer the anxiety of consequence. If, however, the Bible terminates with or perfects its *telos* in its end, if the seventh and last seal is not the Sabbath sanctifying all time, the time equally posterior and prior, the time of both success and precedence, then the Bible will become an idol reducing revelation to the nothingness whence it is created. The Bible suffers the anxiety of consequence as both end and beginning, as both omega and alpha.

The Bible is the original or first judgment of humankind, revealing that it is only in its own light that judgments overcome the contradictions of blindly locating their beginnings in the mythical *logos* of nature. The Bible is also the last judgment of humankind, revealing that the first (in natural precedence) will be last (in the succession of the spirit) and that the last (those who enter the world belatedly, suffering the anxiety of consequence) will be first as the people of choice. The Bible is last, the Bible is the final judgment on the world in the exact sense that no judgment succeeds it, that every judgment must be made in the light of its revelation. Just as every judgment which we—we who choose the golden rule of thought and existence—make is the first choice, the choice of the first, so every choice that we make is also the last judgment, the choice of the last, the choice by which we are willing to be judged without evading its consequences. Every choice, every judgment is thus always the paradox of being simultaneously first and last, the creation and the fulfillment of time. The seventh seal of the apocalypse is the Sabbath, the seventh day of creation, the last judgment of creation, the fulfillment of creation, the day of rest in which the holiness of the Lord is made manifest. The Sabbath day of rest involves unbending, relaxing the bonds of routine, letting the morrow take care of itself, and enjoying, with the lilies of the field and the birds of the air, the day of the Lord as it unfolds (eternally) in its own time. The Sabbath is also the day of study, prayer, and concentration, the day of rededication, remembering, and recalling the Lord of creation, and thus of beginning again, renewed and refreshed, willing to suffer, evermore, the anxiety of the consequence of seeing one's end revealed in the beginning and of seeing one's beginning revealed in the end. But when the revelation of the seventh seal is understood to be the termination of the Bible's consequences, then the Bible is reduced to the nothing from which it is created. The last judgment becomes, then, a pre-modern idol repressing the anxiety of its consequence, not having sufficient faith in the morrow to let it take care of itself.

The Bible no more ends with the revelation of the apocalypse than it begins with the story of creation. The Bible no more begins in the postmodernism of creation than it ends in the pre-modernism of the apocalypse. The Bible begins and ends with modernity. It brings modernity into creation from nothing, eliminating, for all time, the skepticism of postmodernism. It reveals modernity to be the last judgment, eliminating, for all time, the dogmatism of pre-modernism. The story of creation shows us that we must begin, like Adam and Eve, with the consequences of creation revealing to us the choice of good and evil. To claim that we have gone further than Adam and Eve, that we no longer face the choice of good and evil, is to fall, with post-modernist skeptics, into the idolatry of equating the natural surfaces of the linguistic world (the letter) with reality, as if there were no past consequences to our choices involving character, plot, future, history, point of view, truth, insight, self-consciousness, and closure. The revelation of the last judgment shows us that we must end, like Adam and Eve, with the consequences of creation revealing to us the choice of good and evil. To claim that our end is complete in and that we can go no further than Adam and Eve, that the choice of good and evil is no longer to be faced, that our end is to return to the beginning of original paradise, or that Christ as the new Adam (and Eve) has delivered us from any further consequences of revelation is to fall, with pre-modernist dogmatists, into the idolatry of equating reality with the natural surfaces of the biblical text (the letter), as if there were no future consequences to our choices, involving character, plot, past, history, point of view, interpretation, insight, self-consciousness, and openness. The revelation of the seventh seal of the apocalypse is that we must suffer, yet again, the anxiety of consequence, the consequence that, precisely because the Bible begins with us, we must have faith that those who come after us will keep the faith, whatever the consequences of our choices.

Whereas post-modernist skeptics lack faith in the past, repressing history as the choice of good and evil, pre-modernist dogmatists lack faith in the future, equally repressing history as the choice of good and evil. Post-modernists claim to begin—they claim that deconstruction begins with them, they claim that all beginning is (now) deconstruction—yet they repress all conception of beginning (creation from nothing) as historical consequence. Pre-modernists claim to end—they claim that the construction of the Bible ends with them, they claim that the beginning has (now) been constructed—yet they repress all conception of ending (the last judgment of the apocalypse) as historical consequence. Creation from nothing is the last judgment, the final judgment on the contradictory *logos* of the pagan doctrine of opposites whose myth of natural beginnings and ends ineluctably reflects the fate of always being (and thinking) other than itself. Every judgment is always the last judgment. The last judgment is not the last in some finite sequence of judgments, for that which is last, in any finite or natural order, is always reversed, showing that in the end it is blind to and ignorant of its beginning. If every judgment, if every choice involving the knowledge (the thought and existence) of good and evil, is not our last choice, our best choice, the choice by which we are willing to be judged, then we shall fall, once again, into the idolatrous dogmatism of the pre-modernists who evade the anxiety of consequence, the consequence that others follow them, their children and heirs, those who will themselves have to be responsible for their own choices, their own final judgments, notwithstanding the last judgment of their forebears, their predecessors. If the last judgment which we make is not to reduce to nothing, to the idolatry of nihilism, the creation from nothing with which we begin, then every judgment will have to be understood as the last judgment revealing the seventh seal of the apocalypse. The revelation of the seventh seal is precisely that moment in which Adam and Eve begin from nothing, from nothing which does not express their thought and existence, choosing good and evil as their final judgment. The last judgment is the revelation of the seventh seal as creation from nothing.

The ultimate realization, the ultimate recognition of the anxiety of consequence is choice: to choose God above all others and your neighbor as yourself. The freedom of thought and existence to choose expresses the recognition that choice is consequential, that it involves consequences. In the beginning is the choice. The first thing to be chosen is choice, for to choose something already presupposes the freedom to choose. There is no first choice, for choice is always first, the creation from nothing, from nothing which is not first. There is equally no last or final choice, for choice is always last, the last judgment. To choose is to recognize that, already, there are consequences to one's choice, that, in the very act of choosing, one recognizes that choices of others (including oneself) both succeed and precede one's choice. One cannot choose unless (successive) others choose. One cannot choose unless (preceding) others choose. But it is equally the case that others (successors and predecessors) will not choose and have not chosen unless one chooses. It is precisely choice—the freedom to think and to exist—which neither post-modernist skeptics nor pre-modernist dogmatists freely choose. Post-modernists repress the choice which they make by claiming that everything is (now) different, not that their deconstruction makes any difference but that it shows that whatever there is is different (from whatever there is). Difference which is always yet different from itself, never choosing itself as that which makes a difference, is unidentifiably different. Pre-modernists repress the choices they make by claiming that nothing (now) makes any difference, for the construction of the Bible whose identity they claim to possess has made all the difference there is. Difference which is always identical with itself, never choosing itself as that which identifies difference, is indifferently unidentifiable. Whereas post-modernist skeptics sacrifice identity to difference, pre-modernist dogmatists sacrifice difference to identity.

Because choice is always the choice involving the anxiety of consequence, the fear and trembling of loving God above all others and your neighbor as yourself, it is important to realize that choice, the freedom to think and to exist, is never a choice between two things, options, possibilities, situations, etc., whatever the appearances. Choice is the recognition eternally—the revelation or last judgment—that there is no choice but to choose (choice). There is no choice between post-modernism and pre-modernism, between skepticism and dogmatism. There is no choice, as we shall see, between faith and reason. The only choice is modernism, that which embraces the anxiety of consequence which is both faithful and rational. There is no choice between choosing and not choosing, for choice is its own standard, the standard of both choosing and not choosing, the standard of what both constitutes and does not constitute choice. Not to choose is a choice. Not to choose is idolatry, the sin against the spirit which is never forgiven, unless and until, insofar as, individuals recognize their idolatry as their own false choice which they undertake to overcome by never forgetting that the choice not to choose (there was no choice, the choice was made by others...) is a choice for whose consequences they bear eternal responsibility.

What we learn through the paradoxical story of Adam and Eve is that they (we) have no choice but to choose to eat of the fruit of the tree of the knowledge of good and evil. They are condemned to the freedom of choosing, of bearing, in the world of the flesh, mortality, and death, the anxiety of consequence. They must be shown—they must show us—that, in order to begin, they must already have chosen to die, that, in order to die freely, they must already have chosen to begin life, eternally. But the story of Adam and Eve, like all stories, is equally about us: it is our story. If we are to go beyond (the dualism of) good and evil, in the famous words of Nietzsche, if we are to go beyond the idolatry of choosing between good and evil, we must understand that what we choose is good and evil. Nietzsche, in the tradition of the biblical prophets, so strongly attacks the conventional notions of good and evil, of choosing between them, for the very reason that the claim that one chooses between good and evil represses the awesome fact that it is only in choosing the good that the evil is revealed for what it is, which is the subversion (in multifarious fashion) of the good.

Nobody chooses the evil without presupposing the good, without claiming that what one does is the good, without decking it out in the appearances of the good—from Satan (in Milton's version), whose hatred of God is founded on the revelation of Christ as the priority whose consequences cannot be evaded; through the robber band, whose very subversion of justice, Augustine recognizes, presupposes the bonds of justice; to Hitler and his demonic lieutenants whose final solution to racial difference is grounded on the eternal difference which difference makes. When Satan undertakes to extend his rule from hell to earth through the seduction of Adam and Eve in order take revenge on God for the priority shown Christ in heaven, what he reveals is the legitimacy of God's rule on earth, while showing that there is no legitimacy to his own unequal rule in hell. Augustine shows that the members of a robber band can successfully operate in the city of earth only if they presuppose the just rule of the city of God. Indeed, it is the constitution of the actual robber band, within the dialectic of the two cities, idolatrous and biblical, which reveals the structure of justice, not the pagan city of Cicero's *De republica*, which, because it is based on the contradictory law of rulers ruling naturally over the ruled, has no conception of just existence. The Satanic Nazis do not will evil—notwithstanding the nihilistic horror of their extermination camps without parallel in history. Neither they nor others would have swallowed the big lie, no matter how convenient and soothing it was to many who accepted it, had it not been presented as the big truth, as the truth which once and for all embodies the apocalyptic end of history. This is doubtless cold comfort to those who do not choose to face the horror of the holocaust. But what it shows us is that it is precisely in willing the good that evil is revealed for the horror it is.

The relationship between good and evil is infinitely fine. To grasp the fact that evil is revealed only in willing the good does not mean that it is good to do evil or that those who will that which is (inclusively) good for some as opposed to (excluding) others do not will the evil for which they are to be held accountable and considered responsible. In his Letter to the Romans Paul has to contend with what he calls the slander that, because he teaches that God's truthfulness is revealed in human falsehood, evil is to be done so that good may come of it. One can recall the Jewish, messianic figure of the seventeenth century, Sabbatai Zevi, who, in the apostasy of his conversion to Islam, claims that the faith which is ultimately required for belief in (him as) the Messiah is the very opposite of the messianic conception of existence. How easy it is for the requirement that we must become that which we are (not) to be perverted into the immediate, certain, and thus flagrantly contradictory identity of opposites. The Messiah demands immediate belief in his opposite! It is little wonder that the Bible, from beginning to end, suffers the anxiety of seeing its dialectical demands uniting being and becoming, existence and thought, bring into conscious existence dualistic idols, false prophets, and Antichrists. The blatant contradiction—denial or annihilation—of human thought and existence as the truth represents a Satanic heroism utterly inconceivable and unimaginable in extra-biblical paganism.

The story of the fall, the story that, in Augustine's or Milton's terms, God brings good out of evil, out of idolatrous or Satanic dualism, is loaded. Nothing is good in itself, not even the covenant or God himself, for just as creation is from nothing, from nothing which is not creative, so God—the thought and existence of God—is from nothing, from nothing which is not thought existing and whose existence is not its concept. Because nothing creative—whether creator or creature—is made in the image of contradictory nature, it can appear in whatever contradictory image of nature. It can appear to be its very opposite, for what it is in itself is never something given in nature but only in the truth of its interpretation and in the interpretation of its truth. The distinction between truthful interpretation (and the interpretation of truth) and its idol, although absolute, is never certain; it is also never uncertain. The dialectic of truth and interpretation involves paradox and metaphor, whose absolutes can be and are falsified—reified as idols—but they can be neither certain nor uncertain, for certainty and uncertainty belong to the realm of natural appearances, systematic knowledge of which constitutes the natural (or so-called exact) sciences and unsystematic knowledge of which reflects uncritical common sense or idolatry.

To choose knowledge of good and evil is to suffer the anxiety of consequence. It is to recognize that choice is always modern, at once beginning, yet at its end. To claim with post-modernists that there are no consequences to our choices is always to be beginning, without end, while to claim with pre-modernists that our choices have no consequences is always to be at our end, without beginning. Both post-modernist skeptics and pre-modernist dogmatists repress the knowledge of choosing good and evil. It is precisely the chosen people—those who are chosen by and choose God as their beginning and end—who are always modern, constantly choosing God above all others and their neighbors as themselves, while acknowledging that it is the very choice of God and neighbor which reveals the choice of paganism as the idolatrous contradiction of natural opposition. The dialectic of exclusion and inclusion shaping the choice of the chosen people is identical with that of post- and pre-modernism. It is only because the chosen people exclude themselves from the contradictory doctrine of opposites shaping the mythical *logos* of nature that all peoples can be included with the covenant of the golden rule respecting the absolute difference of otherness. But when the principles of exclusion and inclusion are dualistically opposed to each, then we have but another version of skeptical post-modernism and dogmatic pre-modernism. Post-modernists, evading the consequences of the chosen people, exclude themselves from the choice; they make the choice exclusive of all, including themselves. Pre-modernists, in contrast, evade the consequences of the chosen people by including themselves within the choice; they make the choice inclusive only of themselves. But the choice of the chosen people, as of their heirs, is both exclusive and inclusive, both post-modern and pre-modern, both skeptical and dogmatic. Precisely because choice—the freedom to think and to exist—is necessarily both inclusive and exclusive, it is modern and will eternally suffer the anxiety of consequence.

III. FAITH AND REASON AND THE DUALISM BETWEEN CERTAINTY AND UNCERTAINTY

I have dwelt at length upon the fruitless dualism between what I am here calling post-modernism (skepticism) and pre-modernism (dogmatism) in the hope that readers, whether religious or secular, will begin to recognize that it is precisely structures of dualism which compromise thinking. But thinking itself, as it is the aim of this essay to demonstrate, will overcome dualism only insofar as we say, with Descartes: I think, therefore, I am. Thinking is that activity which does not take place outside its existence, just as existence is that activity which does not take place outside its thought. Especially hard to break down, in our culture, are the dualisms not only between thinking and existence but also between faith and reason (theology and philosophy), between emotion and reason, between practice and theory, between philosophy and art, between, in the terms of this essay, truth and interpretation. It is precisely because of the dualisms that riven our life—our thought and existence—that we constantly fall into the false and falsifying polarity between relativism (uncertainty or skepticism) and absolutism (certainty or dogmatism). The exposure of the falsities and falsifications of dualism is complicated by the fact that, following common usage, there are two different species of dualism. There are, first, dualisms such as that between relativism and absolutism, where each of the one-sided oppositions must be negated, overcome, and appropriated (to adopt the language of Hegel) such that we understand that the absolute is the relationship (the golden rule) and that the relationship is the absolute (the love of God, say). There are, second, dualisms such as that between faith and reason, whose terms we shall want to retain—for there are no better—while undertaking to eliminate the opposition between the two opposed terms by showing that one can be true only insofar as both are true. Neither, in other words, can be true in itself but only insofar as it involves and expresses the other.

The example of the dualism between post-modernism and pre-modernism allows us to indicate, with some indirectness, to begin with, that dualism, without exception, reflects the incapacity to comprehend the dialectical structure of the Bible. The whole aim of this essay in thinking is to show, to invoke the simple terms of its conceptual framework, that dualism can be identified and overcome only when it is comprehended, by dialectic, as the contradictory claim that pagan opposites can be known in themselves as true (certain), something inconceivable and unimaginable to extra-biblical paganism. But, however useful terms are in helping us articulate, in a systematic and comprehensive way, the basic concepts of thinking (existence), what is essential to this demonstration is the recognition that concepts are true only if they exist, to give a simplified version of the ontological argument. In other words, what has been not merely enormously difficult but altogether insuperable for most secular thinkers—not only philosophic but also artistic—to see is that, as I have been indicating throughout my essay in thinking, the dialectic of thinking is created by the Bible from nothing. It has also been no less difficult for religious authors to recognize that the Bible is dialectical, that it contains a complete structure of reason. Religious thinkers have found the secular (post-modernist) attack on theological structures so rebarbative that, in their revulsion against any kind of rationalism which cannot account for faith, they have wholly rejected the adequacy of reason, thus reflecting their own blindness to and ignorance of the structure of dialectic central to the golden rule.

I have already appealed to Hegel's exposure of the dualism between philosophy and religion in the Enlightenment, of which the dualism between post-modernism and pre-modernism is but the contemporary avatar. That Hegel himself, however, then proceeds, in blatant contradiction of his own dialectical principles, to make philosophy superior to religion (and also religion superior to art) only suggests how rightfully suspicious religious thinkers are of philosophers when even the strongest among them do not ultimately sustain or comprehend the anxiety of consequence but fall back into hierarchical distinctions reflecting, in Hegel's case, a false dualism between philosophy and religion and thus also between religion and art and between art and philosophy. I hardly need add that, with the persecution, repression, censorship, bigotry, racism, intolerance, and authoritarianism associated with organized religion, not to mention the inquisitions, pogroms, and witch-burnings of previous centuries, secular authors have every reason to be profoundly skeptical of overtures of good faith on the part of ecclesiastical establishments. But this is an essay in the dialectic of biblical critique, not in the history, let alone the sociology, of ideas, however closely entwined they, indeed, are.

When Milton writes that to reason is but to choose, he embraces the modernism of the Bible. The task before us is to show that the dualism between faith and reason is both false and falsifying and that, in order to overcome it, we must demonstrate how both faith and reason involve and express the dialectic of the golden rule such that, for either to be interpreted as true, each must be true in the interpretation of the other. Another way of putting this to say that both faith and reason embody the dialectic of truth and interpretation, that either can overcome the dualism between relativism and absolutism only if each is understood to embrace relationship, the golden rule, as the absolute of modernism. I have introduced the relatively "neutral" language of truth and interpretation, of thought and existence, of choice and "human being" in order to prepare the way for comprehending the common ground of faith and reason (and their common variants such as theology and philosophy, the religious and the secular). Clearly, we shall want to eschew a conception of either faith (faithfulness) or reason (thoughtfulness) which does not embrace truth, interpretation, thinking, existence, choice, and the human being. I have already indicated, however, that the death of God reflects, announces, and results in the death of human being if, in killing God, we relinquish all commitment to the truth of interpretation and the interpretation of truth and fall into the idolatry of relativism (skepticism) which, in its very opposition to absolutism (dogmatism), merely replicates its self-contradiction dualistically.

I have also already shown that extra-biblical paganism possesses no conception of thought such that, in order to think, one must exist (or no conception of existence such that, in order to exist, one must exist consciously in one's thought). I have shown that the *logos* of contradiction, in reflecting the doctrine of opposites as the fate that whatever is thought or exists is always other than—both ignorant of and blind to—its appearance, is incapable of containing in a common framework (point of view) both thought and existence (thinking individuals and their existence). What I call the doctrine of opposites is the law, the *logos* and the myth, of extra-biblical paganism universally, without exception, notwithstanding, indeed, precisely because of, the infinite variety of the metamorphosing opposites, each always blind to and ignorant of both itself and its other (both thought and existence), which it generates. What is to be distinguished, absolutely, from the pagan doctrine of opposites is the structure of biblical dialectic, whose idolatrous perversion is dualism, of which the most extreme form is nihilism, the reduction to nothing of the thought and existence which are created from nothing, from nothing other than that whose concept can only be thought existing and whose existence is solely its concept. Why it is so critically important to distinguish among the pagan doctrine of opposites, biblical dialectic, and the dualism of idolatry is that it is only this double distinction—the distinction between the Bible and extra-biblical paganism, on the one hand, and between the Bible's commitment to thought and existence and their idolatrous perversions, on the other—which allows us to overcome, once and for all, the dualism between faith and reason (along with all other dualisms). In other terms, we can take account of, become responsible for, and appropriate our dualisms only if we recognize that they cannot exist or be thought separate from the structure of biblical reality.

But the dialectical rub becomes particularly acute here because dualism, when generated philosophically, typically hides its biblical ground by claiming that philosophy and the structure of reason have their beginning in the Greeks. What we have to learn, therefore, and what my work undertakes to demonstrate is that all Greek texts, without exception, like the texts of all extra-biblical peoples—texts whether oral or written, whether verbal or non-verbal, whether sophisticated or popular—have no conception of either faith or reason, of either letter or spirit, of either truth or interpretation. Greek texts neither exist in their own thought nor conceive of their own existence, given that thought and existence fatally obey the doctrine of opposites such that what thinks is ignorant of its existence and what exists is blind to its thought. It is only when modern (that is, biblical) readers recognize, finally, that the very limit to their thought and existence is the extra-biblical world, that no Greek or extra-biblical text can be thought to exist or can exist in its thought, that they can truly begin to appropriate the dialectic of biblical critique and its eternal task, which is the constant overcoming of idolatry, of dualism, for which it is uniquely responsible.

Our polemic is not against Athens, for to ask what Jerusalem has to do with Athens is to lay the responsibility for the question, and its answer, squarely on the side of biblical dialectic, not on the side of the doctrine of opposites which is endlessly blind to and ignorant of the very notion of responsibility. Our polemic, rather, is against those who (being ourselves) suffer the anxiety of consequence—the paradox that the Bible, in creating thought and existence from nothing, brings the consequences of truth and interpretation into the world—and, being unable to sustain them, fall into the dualism of pitting Athens against Jerusalem. (As always, we also recognize that the dogmatists will, in their opposition to Athens, fail to recognize that reason, in the beginning, belongs not to Athens but to the Bible and thus fall no less abjectly into the opposite dogmatism of opposing faith to reason. Dogmatists are no more faithful to the Bible than are skeptics.)

This is not the place and, in any case, I am not competent, to tell the complex and wonderfully ironic story of how the modern language of reason, language which is not found in the letter of Scripture, comes into thought and existence from nothing, from nothing which does not belong to spirit. It begins to emerge in the Common Era as Christian thinkers not only polemicize against their heretical (idolatrous) and also Jewish opponents but also undertake to come to terms with pagan (above all, Greek) experience. From the Middle Ages on (beginning, broadly, with Anselm), the task of thinking—which is to show that we can conceive of that only which exists, divine and human being, notwithstanding the fact that the philosophical terms central to this task have their origin in classical paganism—becomes our common heritage. What is important to note, however, in the context of the history and usage of terms, is the fundamental biblical teaching whose truth, although profoundly simple, is rarely grasped systematically, comprehensively, or imaginatively. This is the methodological rule that concepts are not to be confused with their terms, which we have already invoked in an earlier chapter. This rule, although it could be construed in the terms of Occam's razor—entities are not to be multiplied beyond necessity—is fundamental in the sense that Occam's razor, which begs the question of what constitutes the necessity, that is, the truth, of entities, is not. If the fundamental entity is the being, whether divine or human, whose existence cannot be thought except as necessary (and whose concept cannot be thought except as necessarily existing), then what Occam's razor fails to tell us is what it is that allows us to distinguish between what is necessary and what is contingent or, in Rousseau's language, between right and fact. The rule that concepts are not to be confused with (or reduced to) the terms in which they are expressed articulates the ontological argument as the method than which there is none more perfect.

The claim that the Bible is the principle—the origin, the beginning, the ground, the end—of method, of methodological sophistication, is doubtless very hard for sophisticated post-modernists, not to mention benighted pre-modernists, to countenance. When Hegel demonstrates, however, that, because the method (the method of dialectic) is the concept, the method is the content, he provides, once and for all, the modernist critique of the dualism, no less characteristic of our world than of his, between post-modernist method, which cannot ground its critique in commitment to (in choosing) existence, and pre-modernist content, which cannot ground its commitment to (its choice of) existence in critical thinking. That the best scholarship, the finest thinking—what the Germans call *Wissenschaft*—of our era in the humanities and social sciences is characteristically jejune is due to one thing and to one thing only, the dualism between sophisticated method lacking embodiment in rich data and rich data collected, organized, and presented without a sophisticated grasp of methodology. But this typically formulated lament, which is no less characteristic of our era, simply itself reflects but does not appropriate the profound anxiety of consequence insofar as it fails to acknowledge both that method is not neutral, applying indifferently to data, and that data themselves are not neutral, indifferent to the method applied to them. Precisely because the method is the content—and the content itself expresses and involves the dialectic of thought and existence—the sole content which supports methodological sophistication is that which the Bible creates *ex nihilo*. The only content which supports a method embodying the dialectic of truth and interpretation is precisely that which is itself grounded in the ontological argument, that which cannot be thought except existing and which cannot exist except as thought.

When Spinoza formulates his conception of biblical interpretation, and thus of interpretation, generally, as the principle that the Bible (any text) must be interpreted from itself alone, what he means is that we can interpret only that which possesses its own (or is grounded in the) principle of interpretation. Spinoza then goes on to show that the principle according to which the Bible is to be interpreted from itself alone is love (*caritas*), the golden rule, what in this essay in thinking I am (also) calling truth. We can interpret a text only when that text possesses the principle of interpretation, only when that text interprets us as it would have us interpret it. We can interpret human beings only insofar as they interpret us as they would have us interpret them. If the principle of interpretation is not shared between reader and text (between persons in relation), then the dualism of relativism and absolutism (totalitarianism) bursts into play. But interpretation, as it is the burden of this essay in thinking to demonstrate, is itself not neutral. Interpretation is not something which is given in nature; it is not natural or innate. Interpretation comes into thought and existence, with the creation of the Bible, from nothing, from nothing which does not involve and express the choice of the chosen people to love God above all others and their neighbors as themselves. There is no interpretation outside of our commitment to loving—to bearing witness to—the truth, truth as its own standard, and there is no love, or truth, outside of our commitment to interpretation. Interpretation, as method, involves the content in which ontology, epistemology, and ethics are united. Once we understand that interpretation, as the methodological sophistication of the golden rule, reveals the dialectic of biblical critique, then we understand that extra-biblical texts, for example, those of the Greeks, cannot be interpreted, for they have no conception of interpretation or truth, no conception of existence (they do not exist in their concept). That which has no conception of the truth of interpretation has no conception of interpretation as involving and expressing truth. To speak baldly (but with deadly accuracy): Greek texts cannot be interpreted; Greek texts have no conception of interpretation (either of being interpreted by or interpreting their reader); Greek texts have no conception of truth, of truth which they share with the reader, of truth both by which the text judges (reads) the reader and by which the reader judges (reads) the text. The *logos* of contradiction, which shapes the life (the texts) of all extra-biblical peoples, is neither faithful (loving) nor rational. It is neither faithful nor faithless, neither rational nor irrational. The law of contradictory opposites shows that thought and existence are each fatally other than and opposed to the other and thus equally itself.

The simple methodological teaching of the Bible is that we must distinguish between concept and term (between communication and language, meaning and saying, spirit and nature, figure and letter, metaphor and simile, paradox and contradiction). It is simple like the grain of mustard seed, yet it requires, paradoxically, enormous commentary if the anxiety of consequence which it creates is to be contained by sophisticated readers. We can say anything (anything can be said), within the natural resources of language, whether the terms we use are oral or written, whether verbal or nonverbal, just as we can make any physical motion (I could hit you), within our physical limits (within the limits of the laws of nature). But we cannot mean (just) anything, we cannot do (just) anything, for simply because I say or do something does not, in itself, make what I say or do meaningful. Physical (or natural) capacity and moral capacity, although profoundly related, cannot be directly identified (for their identity is idolatry, when it does not reflect extra-biblical paganism). I have the power to say anything (within the physical limits of nature), but that does not mean that I have the right (the rightful or legitimate power) to say anything. Just because I say something does not make it right (or meaningful). I have the power to hit you, but that does not mean that I have the right to hit you (my hitting you does not in itself make it right or meaningful, although this is not to deny that there could be contexts in which my hitting you would be right and meaningful, etc.). I do not have the right to exercise my natural power, whether linguistic or behavioral, outside a moral context, outside the context of communication, of community, of the golden rule of truth and interpretation. Rousseau appropriates the profoundly simple methodology of biblical dialectic, whereby the concept distinguishes itself from its terms, when he shows that all demonstration of the truth of human thought and existence argues from right to (the interpretation of) fact, not from fact to right. The first, and last, choice—the irreversible direction—of demonstration is from the constitution of right (the dialectic of truth and interpretation) to the determination of the meaningfulness of the facts. Just as we do not choose between right and facts but choose right as that which constitutes the facts, so we do not choose between concepts and terms, as if choice were neutral and not itself the concept which cannot be thought except existing and which does not exist except as (in and through) our conscious (responsible) choice. Our choice is the concept of existence.

The distinction between concept and term, because it is profoundly simple, is also exceedingly complex, involving both identity and difference. Every concept is a term, but not every term is a concept, although there is no term (or word) which cannot become a concept, just as there is no concept which cannot be reduced to (or reified as)—consciously or unconsciously—a term. Concepts are perplexing because they exist (as terms), because they can be thought only as existing, because existence is the concept than which there is none more perfect or other. The existence of concepts (the concept of existence) is perplexing because existence is not to be understood (conceptualized) in the terms of natural space and time (what Hegel and Kierkegaard call the terms of immediate sensation: seeing is direct knowing or believing). Existence involves and expresses moral power, not physical or natural power. We cannot exist without (a minimum of) physical being; but our existence, that which empowers us as moral beings, cannot be reduced to or understood in the terms of physical capacity. The concept of existence (the existence of the concept)—thinking—is perplexing, because the concept is not to be understood (lived, practiced) in the terms of abstract reason (what Hegel and Kierkegaard call immediate cognition: knowing or believing is direct seeing). The concept (thinking) involves and expresses moral power, not physical or natural power. We cannot use the concept, we cannot think, without (a minimum of) physical being (brain power); but the concept, our thinking, that which empowers us as moral beings, cannot be reduced to or understood in the terms of knowing as direct or unmediated seeing.

The distinction between concept and term is both so obvious and yet so difficult, for it embodies itself the ontological argument for (God's) existence. There is one term which cannot be thought without existing as the concept. There is one term which is the concept. We cannot recognize terms for what they are in themselves—which is nothing—without recognizing that the very term is itself a concept. We possess the concept of term (we possess the term concept). The concept of term (which cannot be conceived without existing: God) comes into thought and existence distinguishing itself from terms, from the terms of nature, distinguishing the terms as the very nothing from which all thought and existence are created. The concept does not create terms in the sense that natural entities (both physical things and mental abstractions: what Plato calls appearances and Forms) endlessly undergo the metamorphosis of generation and destruction. The extra-biblical terms of natural paganism do not recognize or acknowledge (conceive of) themselves as terms for the precise reason that, reflecting the doctrine of opposites, they are always other than, blind to, and ignorant of what they are in themselves. The concept, however, does create terms in the sense that, in coming into thought and existence from nothing, from nothing which is blind to and ignorant of terminological opposition, it makes terms creative. The concept reveals to terms that, precisely because they are created from nothing, they are grounded in the concept which cannot be thought without existing (which does not exist outside its thought). The concept is the creation, the creativity, of the term. When terms fail to recognize their conceptual and existential creativity, they become idols (similes) whose dualisms reify our thinking and existence by reducing them to natural contradiction.

To comprehend the distinction between concept and term—that the concept creates (identifies) the term in its very distinction from it—is to acknowledge the truth of the ontological argument for the existence of God (which does not mean that we embrace its idolatrous formulations; it is equally the case, however, that we do not succumb to the innumerably false formulations of it). But precisely because our life, both academic and practical, is so deeply riven by dualisms, the dualisms between, for example, linguistics and ontology, between the philosophy of language and theology (whose *logos* is the Word: the covenant of communication and community), our thought is left impotent to comprehend our existence (as our existence is left without the power of thought). We can overcome the impotence of idolatrous dualism only by acknowledging that the distinction between concept and term is not merely the distinction between one thing and another, as if the distinction we make does not confront us with the choice of distinguishing ourselves from the nature of things (or objects), that is, from the terms (language) of our discourse (communication). To show that the simple distinction between concept and term involves us in fundamental ontology, in the ontological argument revealing the necessary connection between what we think and who we are, between our concepts (thought, consciousness) and our existence (practice), is to demonstrate the fundamental dialectic of our speech acts. But it is also to show (to philosophers of language) that, because the distinction between concept and term is not linguistic but communicative, because it involves the ontological argument for the existence of God, it is equally theological. Without philosophers—without those who adhere, consistent with Anselm, to the tradition of *fides quaerens intellectum*—we would still be in the dark ages of philosophy. The ontological argument brings the Bible into the world, showing that it must involve and express our understanding (*intellectus*) in the world, in the *saeculum*, the age in which time is redeemed (bought back) from the contradictory doctrine of pagan opposition. But today the situation has changed, as Hegel and Kierkegaard testify so powerfully. Although it is originally the philosophers who save us from religious obscurantism, it is the philosophers from whom we must presently be saved. Having attained *intellectus*, they now forsake their beginning in faith (*fides*). Theologians, however, may take little comfort in the fact that our beginning is faithful when it is pointed out to them that our beginning is no less rational: *intellectus quaerens fidem*. The ontological argument for the existence of God applies to all existence, divine and human, as distinct from the contradictory nature of space and time which is subject to the endless metamorphoses of generation and destruction. Precisely because the concept of existence—the existence of the concept—is biblical, it is equally divine and human, equally faithful and rational, equally theological and philosophical, equally religious and secular.

The terms of discourse (existence) are naturally opposed to each other. In the extra-biblical world of paganism they are embodied in what I call the doctrine of opposites: appearance and reality, matter and form, many and one, ruled and ruler, mortal and immortal, moved and mover, body and soul (Aristotle's *nous* or reason).... As the world becomes self-consciously aware, in the seventeenth century, that it is modern, the opposed terms of natural discourse form the contradictory paradise from which humans must be expelled if they are to conceptualize the covenantal community as capable of containing opposition. Descartes shows that the one thing which we cannot doubt is, not nature, whose contradictory opposites fatally hide the secret power of human thought and existence, but thought and existence itself. To say, with Descartes, I think, therefore, I am, is to recognize with Hobbes that human life within the state of nature is nasty, brutish, and short. The only way in which my thought and existence can be liberated (redeemed) from contradicting not merely your own but equally my own thought and existence is by my constituting my life, along with yours, on the basis of a contract whose rule is not the *logos* of contradiction but that of the life of the spirit, the golden rule. Pascal, at exactly the same time, makes the hard observation that human beings naturally hate each other, as we noted in an earlier chapter. What Pascal means is that, if human beings base their nature on the immediacies of their sensation and cognition, on those natural faculties which are given to all human beings at birth, then all that they do and think—involving and expressing the emotions which Spinoza, in his *Ethics*, shows to be inadequate—reflect the opposition of nature, that is, hatred. Pascal, like his great fellow seventeenth century thinkers, Descartes, Hobbes, and Spinoza, shows that only if we give up comparing ourselves with nature shall we be able to live at peace with our fellow human beings. So long as we compare ourselves with nature, we shall hate both our fellow human beings and ourselves, for that which is natural is always opposed both to itself and to us. Nature, understood as the congeries of finite objects found in space and time (what Descartes calls extended matter), is precisely that which, when sought, can never be possessed; for, when it is possessed, it contradicts us by showing that it is not yet what we are seeking. All comparisons with the finite, with finite nature, are painful, Pascal observes. When we compare ourselves with the finite, when what we desire is only comparative (relative), then we discover that, in attempting to possess the thing-in-itself, to adopt Kant's terms, we are always either outside or inside ourselves but never in possession of our actual selves. The only comparison worthy of human beings, Pascal shows, is God, in whose infinite love all human beings can equally participate to the fullness of their capacity, without finite (or natural) comparison with their fellow human beings, which inevitably reduces them to hatred (hostility, anger, frustration, *ressentiment*, desire for domination...).

It is only when we learn to comprehend—in our covenantal existence, in good faith, in full consciousness—the distinction between concept and term, the fact that terms owe their thought and existence to the concept, that we shall be able to overcome the dualisms reflecting the anxiety of consequence and to embrace the modernity of the Bible as simultaneously faithful and rational. The distinction between concept and term presupposes a category of humanity—I call it thought and existence in this essay in thinking—which is absent, utterly absent, from human nature as we find it represented in extra-biblical paganism. If we call upon the triadic structure of mind which Kant and Hegel articulate (and the equivalent of which Kierkegaard also expresses), then we shall possess the distinctions which will allow us to show that the terms describing mind (or reason) in the Greek world, as in the extra-biblical world, generally, are without any concept of reason (rationality), not to mention faith (faithfulness).

What Kant and Hegel call sensibility and understanding and Kierkegaard immediate sensation and immediate cognition (and also the aesthetic and the ethical spheres of human life) are naturally present in all human beings. They are innate and develop naturally, assuming that nature does not make a leap. But what all three thinkers demonstrate, in their varied and richly diverse ways, is that the natural opposition between sensibility and understanding has become today, in the modern world, the contradictory dualisms between materialism and idealism (empiricism and rationalism), resulting in the cul-de-sac of blind relativism (skepticism) and ignorant absolutism (dogmatism). Then they proceed to show that the only way in which the natural oppositions dualistically dividing human beings against each other can be contained, appropriated, and overcome is by demonstrating that sensibility (empiricism) and understanding (rationalism) can each be true only if both are true, which is precisely what each denies to the other and thus equally to itself. The only way in which both our natural faculties of sensibility and understanding can be appropriated as true is on grounds which cannot be directly or immediately identified with either but only with both, that is, with a third position which is the truth or appropriation of the two, equally, what Kant and Hegel call reason (but also spirit, practice, will, and thinking) and Kierkegaard calls the paradox, the leap of faith (the religious sphere of existence as the appropriation of aesthetic immediacy and ethical abstraction).

No one of our three thinkers, however, is perciently comprehensive in recognizing that this third category of mind or spirit, that which they call reason or the paradoxical leap of faith, is absent from the Greek world or from the extra-biblical world, generally (although all three, directly and indirectly, recognize that their thinking is but an articulation of the ontological argument of existence, so long as the demonstration of the necessary link, that is, the leap, between thought and existence, is not confused with arguments based on the contradictory elements of natural space and time). But, taken together, our three thinkers provide the most profound diagnoses we possess—along with those of Nietzsche, Marx, and Freud—of the dualisms (epistemological, moral, existential, psychological, aesthetic) which riven our modern thought and existence. Their grasp of these dualisms is profound for the simple reason that they contain them within their conceptions of reason and faith and do not blindly reflect them back by replicating them once again in their ignorance. (This is not the place in which to examine the complex interrelationship of Kant, Hegel, and Kierkegaard, but it is important to note that each of them characteristically uses dualistic terms to advance the polemic of his dialectical conception of existence.) The distinction between adequate thinkers (writers and artists of whatever medium) and inadequate thinkers is precisely whether they diagnose the malaise of dualism and overcome it with the strength of their dialectic (whatever the terms they use to express their concepts or metaphors) or whether they simply replicate the dualism of their era in the terms of (say) post-modernist skepticism and pre-modernist dogmatism.

What Kant, Hegel, and Kierkegaard recognize in articulating their dialectic of thought and existence—and it is interesting to note that these three thinkers, along with Marx, are our explicit masters of dialectic—is that nature does indeed make a leap, a conceptual leap, a leap in existence which cannot be comprehended in the terms of extra-biblical discourse, although it can be expressed in the terms of any natural discourse (no matter how apparently vulgar, low, or humble). This leap is reason (in Kant and Hegel) and faith (in Kierkegaard). It is the leap, the paradox, whereby and wherein spirit recognizes itself as the concept of nature, as that which is both the exclusiveness from and the inclusiveness of nature. The leap of spirit is creation from nothing, choice, the recognition that the one thing which cannot be doubted is not nature itself but the nature of thought thinking itself as existing and the nature of existence which cannot exist outside its thinking.

It is worth noting that Darwin also participates in the dialectical articulation of modernity as the leap which allows us to account for the contradictions of nature. Darwin recognizes that, if there is to be a comprehensive and systematic science of evolution explaining the origins of species, if we are to be able to understand how all life, both organic and ultimately inorganic, belongs to a common natural history, then, as Kant had already recognized, the transitions between species cannot be *per saltum*, by a leap, jump, or gap. (Kant is not only a radical philosopher of science but equally a radical theologian who points out that God creates not nature but thought and existence *ex nihilo*, the leap out of nature which allows us to live the paradox of nature but not according to the contradictions of nature.) The paradox of thought and existence—which is not fully comprehended by Darwin and rarely comprehended at all by those who defend the science of evolution against its creationist detractors—is that our very capacity to observe the facts of nature as involving evolutionary transitions which are not radical (creative) leaps depends on a point of view which is itself grounded in the leap, in the creation of thought and existence, including Darwin's, from nothing, from nothing which is subject to natural evolution. Because the theory of evolution accounts for the non-saltatory extension of nature, it cannot itself directly belong (extend) to or reflect that which it explains or describes, as I indicated in an earlier chapter. The theory of evolution is the leap, both faithful and rational, which a great scientist takes to account for that which does not operate *per saltum*, the nature of evolution, nature whose vast extent is to be conceived of according to the non-saltatory conception of evolution. One has to fall, one has to separate oneself, from nature—call it a leap of reason or a leap of faith—in order to account not only for nature, scientifically, but also for our scientific account of nature, faithfully and rationally. This second account, which is actually the first in priority, if not in nature, is not to be reduced to, identified with, or opposed to science. When this second-order accounting, which is the primary story of our thought and existence, is not understood to be both faithful and rational, to involve both religion and philosophy, then our accounting falls into the dualisms which I identify as idolatry.

Once we learn to distinguish between the extra-biblical doctrine of opposites and biblical dialectic and thus between dialectic and dualism—each of these distinctions involves the other—not only are we able to deal accurately with both non-modern (that is, extra-biblical) and modern (that is, biblical) texts, to speak methodologically, but we are also able to address the content which is central to this method, to understand the fundamental importance of learning that the critical separation between theology and philosophy, as Spinoza conceives of it, involves their common ground. When we oppose faith and reason dualistically to each other, instead of understanding their relationship as dialectical, we gravely impair each of them, no matter which side we claim to be defending or supporting. Since each can be true only insofar as it is the interpretation of the other, when either is placed in dualistic opposition to its other, then it reflects back into itself, uncritically (unfaithfully), the very contradiction which it claims to find in the other. So Hume, as we have seen, finds himself betwixt a false reason and no reason at all.

When reason dualistically opposes itself to faith, it typically reduces itself to a conception of cognitive certainty, describing itself in such terms as objective, scientific, technological, secular, public, utilitarian, and pragmatic (while its opponents view it in terms of the reification and reductionism of skeptical positivism). It is also the case that when reason dualistically opposes itself to faith, it reduces faith to the uncertainty of subjectivity. When faith dualistically opposes itself to reason, it typically reduces itself to a conception of intuitive certainty, describing itself in such terms as subjective, mystical, otherworldly, religious, personal, real, and meaningful (while its opponents view it in terms of the superstition and mystification of dogmatic authoritarianism). It is also the case that when faith dualistically opposes itself to reason, it reduces reason to the uncertainty of objectivity. Each, then, in claiming to be certain, accuses the other of being uncertain, although we must recognize that, because of the prestige of science and technology in our world, especially in the pragmatic North America of empiricist individualism, the dualistic language of science tends to dominate public discourse while the dualistic language of faith tends to predominate in personal discourse. It is also true that, because we—individualistic North Americans—ultimately expect less from science than from our more profound commitments (to love, tenderness, generosity, decency, justice, freedom, fairness, equality, peace, toleration...), we tend to be less harshly critical of public discourse—that of technological, political, rationalistic, and, yes, male domination—than of discourse which is more personal, loving, tender, and trusting (dare we call it feminine?).

We see, therefore, that, when faith and reason, like any pair of opposites, are dualistically opposed to each other, each, in claiming to rule over its opposite, claims to appropriate certainty to itself while reducing its opponent to uncertainty. The result is that each becomes an idol which, in claiming identity with nature or denying that the one opposite it is natural, falsifies the truth of both. Then, when either faith or reason attempts to defend itself against the claim of uncertainty to which its certain opponent tries to reduce it, what typically occurs is that it will take up the stance, not of truth, in recognizing the falsity of the positions of certainty and uncertainty, but that of certainty in opposition to the uncertainty of the other. Reason points out to faith that its ground in subjective certainty (the certainty of the subject) is indistinguishable from relativism or uncertainty, but faith has equal facility in pointing out to reason that its ground in objective certainty (the certainty of the object) is no less relativistic or uncertain. Whether one adopts the coherence model or the correspondence model of knowledge, there is no way of explaining either the relationship (of coherence) between the subject and itself (subjective certainty) or the relationship (of correspondence) between the subject and its object (objective certainty). The dualism between faith and reason only replicates the dualism between subject and object and that between certainty and uncertainty, with faith and reason each accusing its opponent of uncertainty, while being unable itself to defend its own position (subjective or objective) against the same criticism. The outcome, inevitably, is the perpetuation of the dualism of idolatry. Thus we see that the dualism between faith and reason, objectivity and subjectivity, and certainty and uncertainty is that between skepticism and dogmatism, where the skeptic is no more or less certain or uncertain than is the dogmatist. It is only when we learn, once and for all, and finally, that truth (along with interpretation) is neither certain nor uncertain, although it can certainly be falsified, that we shall be able to overcome the dualisms falsely opposing the realms of faith and reason. It is equally the case, I believe, that we shall learn that truth and interpretation belong, not to the realm of certainty and uncertainty, but to that of relationship, the relationship of thought and existence, the relationship which the Bible articulates as the golden rule of the covenant, only when we finally grasp the fact that the Bible's story of God and humankind is both faithful and rational.

When Pilate asks Jesus, what is truth?, he means, clearly: you are not so foolhardy as to oppose imperial certainty. Pilate is right, superficially, and thus wrong, profoundly. Jesus, like anyone conscious of existing within the biblical tradition of truth and interpretation, is not going to answer on any other than their grounds, although the style or mode of his answer may be infinitely serpentine (ironic, parodic, oxymoronic, paradoxical, hyperbolic... silent). Pilate is correct that Jesus will not undertake to contradict the force of imperial certainty by opposing it from (what Pilate would see to be as inevitably) a position of uncertainty. What is deliciously contradictory about Pilate's question, however, is that, if Jesus were subject to the imperial law of certain contradiction, he would certainly answer in the tradition of Socrates by opposing Pilate (or Caesar) as uncertain, by showing that the one opposite him is ignorant of and blind to—uncertain of—the very imperial law he proclaims, the law of contradictory opposition. If you oppose imperial power from within the extra-biblical world of paganism, you will undertake to show that the one opposite you is uncertain, that he knows not whereof he speaks. But what Pilate does not know—it is utterly inconceivable to him—is that Jesus, in the paradoxical tradition of the law and the prophets, a tradition equally faithful and rational, takes his stand on truth (along with interpretation), on that which is not and never will be either certain or uncertain, except in the idolatrous guise of dualism. In the extra-biblical world of Pilate, the world in which the doctrine of opposites naturally reigns according to the law of contradiction, one rules over another (the Roman emperor rules over an obscure Jew whom some, Pilate has fearfully heard, proclaim to be the king of the Jews) as heroic certainty rules over slavish uncertainty. Socrates brilliantly inverts the heroic model, in a manner completely consistent with the doctrine of contradictory opposites, by showing that it is the uncertain one—he who knows that he knows nothing, he who holds that it is better to suffer evil from others than to do evil to others, for all evil is done in ignorance of the good—who rules over those who claim to be certain (but know not whereof they speak). When certainty, as one of the members of the pair of blind opposites, rules over the other as uncertain, it is fatally dependent, as I have shown in a previous chapter, on that uncertainty of which it is ignorant, precisely as all otherness, difference, or distinction is dependent on the uncertainty of which it is the opposite, that is, on fate, whose certainty necessarily appears and is experienced as the uncertainty of chance.

Jesus has no difficulty in avoiding Pilate's Socratic *aporia* (the blind way) of ignorance because he knows that the creation of truth *ex nihilo* has been revealed to the world. The contradictory opposition between certainty and uncertainty ruling the pagan world as fatal otherness is now revealed as the finite dualism of idolatry (however infinite are its guises). Idolatry is precisely the reduction of truth (and interpretation) to certainty, to the immediacy of natural objects. Because the truth is neither certain nor uncertain, Jesus knows that it can be falsified in the idolatrous terms of dualism and that this is what happens when the truth is represented as certain, with the inexorable consequence that the position opposite it is reified as uncertain. In our contemporary world the idolatrous dualism between certainty and uncertainty is represented by the dualism between post-modernist skepticism, for which everything is always uncertain (or different), and pre-modernist dogmatism, for which everything is always certain (or identical). But the truth of human beings is neither certain nor uncertain, although it can be falsified (and ultimately reduced to nothing certain or uncertain). It is the realm of nature, organized as scientific knowledge of objects, which is either objectively certain or objectively uncertain, but nature is never true or false in itself.

Kant's critique of the thing-in-itself shows us that we can possess objectively certain knowledge not of the thing-in-itself but only of its appearances as the possible experience of nature, while it is precisely the thing-in-itself, that is, human persons living by the golden rule, who are true or false in their relationships with others (including God). Indeed, as Kant demonstrates, with a perspicacity unique in the history of philosophy, if science claims to possess knowledge of things-in-themselves as objectively certain, not only science as objective knowledge of nature vanishes into illusion but also human relations are falsified. If human beings are treated as things which can be known as finite objects of nature, as means, and are not viewed as ends which can be thought (willed) solely as things-in-themselves, then the idolatrous dualism opposing faith and reason takes its Satanic toll. (It is equally the case, as always, that, if theology claims to know human beings on analogy with the objective certainty of nature, not only the freedom of human beings to think and to exist but also the objective science of nature vanish.) The very confusion of truth with, or its reduction to, certainty—so widespread and pervasive in our era—embodies the structure of dualism. We shall be able to overcome the reduction of truth to certainty and thus to uncertainty only when we recognize that it reflects the dualism between faith and reason. We shall be able to overcome the dualism between faith and reason only when we recognize that faith and reason inhere equally in the subject of thought and existence, not in the objects of nature.

It is important to note here, given our Cartesian beginning—I think, therefore, I am—that what Descartes means by truth he often calls certainty. Descartes is particularly acute about his meaning, however, when he shows that, notwithstanding how clear and distinct our ideas are, that is, how certain they are, we can never protect them from becoming uncertain if we do not show them to be true. The clarity and distinction of our ideas are, in themselves, no more certain than uncertain. Indeed, when Descartes undertakes his monumental search for a criterion constituting the validity of ideas, he recognizes that the entrenched dualism between dogmatism and skepticism, between absolutism and relativism, between certainty and uncertainty cannot be overcome so long as the dualism between faith and reason prevails. What Descartes discovers, in his undivided search for truth, is that dogmatists and skeptics equally claim that their ideas are clear and distinct and that each camp, in claiming that its clear and distinct ideas are certain, merely succeeds in showing that the clear and distinct ideas of the enemy camp are uncertain. (Once again, we recall that dogmatists and skeptics are indifferently philosophers and theologians.)

If he is to transcend the fruitless dualism between certainty and uncertainty, Descartes realizes, he will have to elaborate a conception of thinking consistent with the existence of God, a conception of thinking that provides a radical critique of both faith and reason. For some fifteen hundred years not only theologians but also philosophers had, with few exceptions (as we have noted), based their ideas of thought and existence on the Greeks, thus generating the very dualism between faith and reason which is inconceivable and unimaginable to extra-biblical paganism and which the Bible brands as idolatry. Descartes demonstrates (1) that we can transcend the dualism between certainty and uncertainty only if clear and distinct ideas are shown to be true and (2) that clear and distinct ideas can be shown to be true only if God exists. The terms in which Descartes formulates the ontological argument for the existence of God are crude (at least in the eyes of the skeptic, not to mention the dogmatist). But what he shows beyond the shadow of a doubt is that truth expresses commitment to existence, while existence involves the conception of truth. Ideas or concepts are true (although they may not by any means be clear and distinct, at least to skeptics and dogmatists) insofar as their very thought involves their existence. Concepts are neither immediate perceptions nor immediate cognitions, for it is concepts which overcome the dualism between the terms of sensation (empiricism) and cognition (rationalism) by revealing their commitment to existence whose necessary thought is the golden rule of relationship. The perplexing thing about the truth, as Descartes so keenly recognizes, is that its very concept involves its existence, yet it is precisely because truth exists that it can be falsified or rendered idolatrous by the claim that it is either certain or uncertain (merely clear and distinct). The blind opposition between certainty and uncertainty in the extra-biblical world of paganism becomes revealed in the light of biblical truth as the dualism of idolatry.

I conceive of this essay in thinking as the dialectic of truth and interpretation for the precise reason that truth will be distinguished, once and for all, from certainty, and thus from uncertainty, only when we understand that interpretation equally has nothing to do with either certainty or uncertainty and that it simultaneously involves faith and reason. To interpret something, to engage in the act of interpretation, is to show, to recall Spinoza's formulation, that you interpret it from itself alone. But this notion of interpreting a text (any human communication, verbal or nonverbal) from itself alone is to be understood in terms of truth (the concept) and not in terms of certainty (the term). To interpret something—a person, a text, oneself—from itself alone does not mean that whatever the individual text says about itself, for example, is true, for it could indeed be false (evasive, hypocritical, deceptive...). But it does mean that you cannot interpret another (including yourself) any more effectively than the other undertakes to interpret you. The text, if it is a strong text, will hold you (the reader, a strong reader) responsible to the same structure of interpretation to which you hold it responsible, and the structure of interpretation is truth, precisely as the structure of truth is interpretation, for together truth and interpretation embody the dialectic such that neither can be thought as existing unless both exist as thought.

The only way in which truth can be redeemed from the idolatry of absolutist certainty is if it is comprehended as interpretation which always involves the golden rule. The only way in which interpretation can be redeemed from the idolatry of relativist uncertainty is if it is always understood to involve the relationship of truth. Interpretation, like truth, does not involve neutrality, and it does not express relativism. Interpretation is infinite. Interpretations are infinite. But this does not mean that interpretation cannot be falsified or that interpretations are not false. Interpretation is falsified and interpretations are false when they either claim to be certain or claim grounds that can be reduced to uncertainty. Interpretation, like truth, embodies the golden rule. In the beginning is interpretation. Interpretation is created from nothing, from nothing which cannot be interpreted as true and from nothing which cannot be falsified by reduction to an idol either certain or uncertain (either natural or unnatural). Truth cannot exist outside its thinking, which is interpretation, and interpretation cannot think outside its existence, which is truth. Neither truth nor interpretation is either relative or absolutist, although both are absolute as the relationship of dialectic, that covenantal relationship in which God is loved above all others and one's neighbor as oneself. The absolute—truth or interpretation—is neither certain nor uncertain, although the relationship which it is is constantly falsified by its reduction to (or reification as) the idols of certainty and uncertainty (dogmatism and skepticism).

It is enormously difficult, above all, for those who are unable to comprehend the modes of truth and interpretation as simultaneously faithful and rational, to liberate themselves from the idolatry of conceiving of absolute truth in the terms of absolute certainty and of the relationship of interpretation in the terms of relative uncertainty, both of which are idolatrous dualisms which can be overcome solely by showing that not only the absolute but also relationship are true but neither certain nor uncertain. Interpretation is the absolute in the precise sense that we—we who say with Descartes, I think, therefore, I am—have no choice but to choose interpretation. We have no choice but to interpret. Indeed, not only is to reason but to choose, to recall Milton, but also to interpret is but to choose, for interpretation always involves us in choosing, in making discriminations and distinctions, such that we are responsible to and for their truth.

Interpretation embodies the very structure of reason, as it does of faith. To reason is to practice the golden rule, the golden rule of interpretation, according to which I will interpret you as I would have you interpret me. If you choose not to engage in or to practice interpretation, my interpretation of your refusal to engage in interpretative practice is that your very refusal is an interpretation (an acceptance, perchance, of the *status quo*, which you are ashamed to acknowledge). Just as we are not free not to be free, just as we have no choice but to choose, so also we are not free not to interpret others as we would have them interpret us. Not to acknowledge our will to interpretation (what Nietzsche calls the will to power) is to accept, uncritically and unfreely, both unfaithfully and irrationally, the interpretations of others (as certain). Interpretation is the will to truth in precisely the same sense that truth is the will to interpretation. Neither can be conceived as existing (neither can exist as the concept) except insofar as both express the absolute relationship of the golden rule whose demonstration is Descartes' articulation of the dialectic of truth and interpretation: I interpret, therefore, I am the truth.

IV. CONCLUSION: THINKING AS THE DIALECTIC OF FAITH AND REASON

When Spinoza and Rousseau begin thinking, as we have seen, with the presupposition (the beginning) that we humans begin our existence conscious of our desire to be free, yet everywhere we are in chains, ignorant of the causes of things, they articulate the paradox of the *condition humaine*. It is the very characteristic of modernity, of the dialectic of thought and existence whose structure is biblical in origin, that we are conscious of our desire yet ignorant (unconscious) of what constitutes the cause of our desire, that we are free, yet in chains. Our early modern thinkers thus articulate the biblical story of sin and salvation in the (reversed, secular) terms of consciousness and ignorance, of freedom and slavery. Human beings are created free members of the covenant in their relationship with God—they are liberated (in the New Testament version) through the sacrifice of Jesus—but now they sin, blind to the cause of their salvation (liberation). The biblical story shows that truth has been revealed to the world, that human beings are born free. The chosen people are created from nothing, from nothing which chains them to the contradictory ignorance and blindness of nature. Their will or desire has been liberated from the doctrine of opposites which locates will in fate such that those who are fatally subject to the contradictions of nature are eternally blind to and ignorant of their desire. It would have been inconceivable and unimaginable (undesirable) to the extra-biblical world that the opposites of knowledge and ignorance, of end (cause) and desire, or of freedom and slavery are now united in one people, in one person, in one God, in one covenant, in one book, in one story, in the human condition itself. Through the biblical story of one creation, thought and existence are now united as one (both individually and collectively). There is one concept which cannot be thought except existing (as one)—both divine and human—and there is that which can exist as one only as it is thought (one)—both divine and human.

But it is precisely the concept of one existence, the existence of the one concept, which generates dualism. When the opposites endlessly divided against each other in the pagan world of natural contradiction are shown to be united as one in the story of their creation from nothing—the story of the covenant—a wholly new world, the world of modernity, emerges, one that is inconceivable and unimaginable to the world whose thought and existence are endlessly opposed to each other (just as the biblical, that is, the modern, world of creation finds that the world fatally other than one is equally inconceivable and unimaginable, the very limit to its dialectic of truth and interpretation). When the natural opposites of knowledge and ignorance and of freedom and slavery are dialectically united as the one creation from nothing, they emerge in a wholly new framework, that of modernity which recognizes nothing either pre-modern or post-modern, except as the idolatrous dualism of being unable to maintain the dialectic of modernity as the one thought of existence, as the one existing as thought. The one, natural limit to modernity is the non-modern, the world of extra-biblical paganism, whose mythology of opposites without beginning or end is the natural *logos* of contradiction (just as history, equally characteristic of modernity, as we shall see in the next chapter, recognizes nothing as either pre-historical or post-historical independent of history, for nothing historical can come before or after history. History recognizes as its limit only the non-historical, the world of extra-biblical paganism whose mythology is based on the contradictory images of natural opposites, not on the dialectical metaphors of one history.)

That we are conscious (desirous) of knowing our ends but are ignorant of them means that we belong, not to the Socratic mode of ignorance, but to the biblical mode of sin. In contrast with Socrates, who knows that he is ignorant (Socrates knows that he does not know) but does not know what he is ignorant of, we know, as members of the covenant, not only that we are ignorant but what we are ignorant of (we know what we do not know). We desire (know) what we do not know (desire). That we are born free but are everywhere in chains means not that we are ignorant of our freedom but rather that we are free to know (desire) our chains, to render them legitimate, as Rousseau puts it. The paradox of the human condition is that, because we are conscious and free, we must become consciously free (freely conscious). But it is precisely because we are free to be free and must, therefore, become free (or liberated) in order to be free—it is because we are conscious of our desire to know our cause and must, therefore, become conscious (liberated) in order to be consciously free—that we can lose the consciousness and freedom of being our own cause through the repression and oppression which we associate, as I indicated in an earlier chapter, with insanity and slavery, with nihilism, whether individual or collective.

Dualism thus bursts into the modern (biblical) world with Satanic fury as the evasion of the anxiety of consequence, the consequences of consciously and freely ever willing to become freely conscious of our existence, notwithstanding the adversities. The burden of maintaining the dialectic between being and becoming conscious, between being and becoming free, is enormous. Consciousness and freedom—thought and existence—are given in the beginning, in the creation of the *condition humaine* from nothing, from nothing which is not worthy of human consciousness and freedom. But the beginning is not the future which has no beginning (as it is for post-modernist skeptics). The beginning is not the past which is now over (as it is for pre-modernist dogmatists). As Spinoza and Rousseau know so well, the certainties of nature and custom become the great idols for modern men and women as they labor under the burden of knowing what they do not know—the one concept which cannot be thought except existing. The seduction to which modern heirs of the Bible are constantly subject is to translate the dialectic of consciousness and ignorance, the dialectic of knowing what we do not know, into the idolatry of reducing both our thought and existence to certainty, in dualistic opposition to that which we reduce to uncertainty. The dualism between faith and reason, along with all the other dualisms, emerges, then, with faith reduced to the subjective certainty of either sensibility or understanding—subjects believe in the certainty of whatever they immediately see or know—while reason takes refuge in the objective certainty of either sensation or cognition—whatever object is immediately seen or known is certain. Each of the dualistic opposites characteristically accuses its opponent of reducing the human condition to means, both objective and subjective, which violate the ends of humanity—their thought and existence; and, while this criticism is accurate, the irony is that it fails to recognize that it applies no less to the subject than to the object of the criticism.

The only way in which we can overcome the infinitely multifarious dualisms between thought and existence, and, in particular, the dualism between faith and reason, is to articulate a notion of thinking (which is indistinguishable, fundamentally, from desire or will) which involves and expresses the dialectic of truth and interpretation. Central to this project, as my work elaborates, is to learn to distinguish comprehensively and systematically between extra-biblical ignorance of fate, which is always other than and opposed to its contradictory appearances, and biblical revelation, the choice which both excludes all from the contradictory opposites of nature and includes all within the dialectic of truth and interpretation. But the distinction between extra-biblical fate and biblical revelation brings to light the critical distinction between dialectic and dualism, between the golden rule of thought and existence and its idolatrous subversion such that thought and existence are made explicitly contradictory, something inconceivable to extra-biblical paganism. We can become responsible for the idolatry of our dualism only insofar as we comprehend the biblical dialectic of thought and existence as both faithful and rational. Then we are able to develop a conception of thinking such that to think the truth as our subject (the subject of truth) involves the subject in interpretation and to interpret the subject of truth (the truth as our subject) involves the subject in the truth.

6

The World of the Secular

I. INTRODUCTION: THE COMMON ERA OF THE BIBLE

When Jesus tells Pilate that he comes to bear witness to the truth—of interpretation and to the interpretation of truth—he stands in the tradition of
the law and the prophets. He comes, he says, not to change but to fulfill the
Scripture which he shares with his fellow Jews as the golden rule: to love
God above all others and your neighbor as yourself. In this confrontation
between Pilate, the representative of extra-biblical imperialism, and Jesus,
the representative of biblical law, we are present at the critical moment in
world history, at the moment in which the story of human thought and existence becomes the common story for the entire world. The Common Era
of humanity is born, for we are present at the transition not between the
old world and the new but between the non-modern or non-historical
world and the modern, historical world. The transition from what is not
modern or historical to what is historically modern is the fulfillment of the
old, modern, historical world in the new, modern, historical world. From
this moment on, the Common Era of humanity becomes the eternal fulfillment of what is first, original, and old, in the beginning, in terms of what is
first, original, and new, in the beginning.

The crux of the situation—the cross on which Jesus dies to the
doomed paganism of the extra-biblical world of contradictory nature to be
reborn to the secular world revealed in the truth and interpretation of
paradoxical spirit—is that the Roman Empire crucifies as a common
criminal a Jew whose forebears had been liberated from the imperial might

of the Pharaohs, the forerunners of the Roman emperors. Never before had a significant Jewish figure been publicly put to death by a foreign (extra-biblical) power. Never before had a significant Jewish figure confronted the official representative of paganism, saying, here I stand, before God and neighbor: I can go no further. It is true that, when Moses bears witness to the truth of God in the burning bush, which he must interpret like no bush ever before seen in the contradictory realm of nature, he is commanded by God, who tells him that I am (who/what I am/was/shall be), to carry the ontological argument of thought and existence back to his people enslaved to the Pharaoh. In demonstrating to his people that there is one concept only which can be thought existing—the concept of God and people as chosen above all others—and that there is one existence only which can be thought—the chosen existence of God and people—Moses has to confront their master, the Pharaoh, whose exalted official he himself is. But Moses and his fellow Jews, repeating the experience of Joseph, the last in the line of the patriarchs who had himself become a high official of the Pharaoh, inaugurate history by renouncing slavery to paganism and beginning (again) the trek to the promised land where the desert blooms with the eternal flame of those who choose the freedom to think and to exist.

The Bible begins and ends with the confrontation on the part of Moses and Jesus with the imperial powers of paganism. Moses lives to lead his people to the promised land (although he himself dies with only a vision of it across the Jordan River from the height of Pisgah), while Jesus dies in the promised land on the cross of the power which, scarcely more than a generation later, razes Jerusalem, destroys the Temple, and disperses the Jews from the city of David (the city which, by the way, David does not found but captures from its pagan inhabitants). This time, the Diaspora, repeating that of the Babylonian Captivity, becomes definitive (although, as I remarked in an earlier chapter, major Jewish communities had already for years been living in Babylon and Alexandria, seats of ancient imperial power).

Today, the Diaspora (following the Holocaust) is over. The ingathering of Jews into the state of Israel is definitive. Yet there are nearly as many Jews living in New York City as in the whole of Israel, and by far the majority of Jews continues to live in the Diaspora. The Holy City of Jerusalem is once again in the hands of Jews, but how the times have changed since the time of David! Jerusalem is the holiest site of Christianity, scene of the passion of Jesus leading to his crucifixion and resurrection (while the biggest of the Christian sects, the Roman Catholic Church, theocratically occupies less than half a square kilometer of imperial Rome). Jerusalem is the second holiest site of Islam (for the prophet Muhammad, the descendant of the patriarchs, ascended to heaven from the temple mount, the place where, it is held, God tested Abraham by ordering him to sacrifice his son Isaac). East Jerusalem is controlled *de facto* by Israel, having been captured from Jordan which joined the Arab forces in their 1967 assault upon Israel, but Jerusalem has not been recognized as the *de jure* capital of Israel by the world community. (To keep the position of Jerusalem in perspective, given the Arab opposition to the existence of Israel, it is useful to recall that not all Arabs are Muslims—some are Christians, and some even are Jews, etc.—while most Muslims are not Arabs, for the vast majority of Muslims, besides those who are Persian and Afghan, lives in the Soviet Union, Pakistan, India, Bangladesh, China, and Indonesia.) The Temple has not been rebuilt. Indeed, although the Wailing Wall, the most sacred site for Jews in Jerusalem, is looked upon by the orthodox as part of the original Temple, secular archaeologists point out that there is no historical evidence reliably connecting it with Solomon's Temple.

The Bible begins and ends enclosed within paganism. Jews come into thought and existence as the chosen people who, in loving God above all others and their neighbors as themselves, both exclude all (pagans) who are enslaved to the contradictions of natural fate and include all (among the chosen people) who recognize that they are created from nothing, from nothing which does not exist as thought and is not thought to exist. Christians come into thought and existence as the chosen people who, in loving God above all others and their neighbors as themselves, include all (gentiles) who are enslaved to the contradictions of natural fate but who exclude all (gentiles and Jews) who do not make the choice—the leap of reason no less than the leap of faith—to live and to think in the freedom provided universally, yet uniquely, by the dialectic of truth and interpretation. The revelation of truth and interpretation excludes no one through prior choice, through fate which, as the contradictory secret of beginnings and ends, is always other than its thought and existence—whether Jew or gentile, free person or slave, male or female. But the revelation of truth and interpretation also includes no one who does not choose that which is prior: God and neighbor. (We hardly need point out that many Christians, not to mention Jews, are not included, while not excluded are many who, while adhering to the golden rule, may either refuse to associate themselves directly with what they view to be biblical idolatry or indeed deny any relationship to the Bible.)

The Bible, having excluded itself from paganism, from all that is extra-biblical, in the story of Exodus, is now poised on the brink of discovery, in the story of Jesus, that there is nothing exclusive about paganism, that there is nothing which the Bible excludes, that there is nothing extra-biblical. The writers of the New Testament—Paul and the authors of the Gospels, the other epistles, and the Apocalypse—make haste to tell their story, not knowing, any more than their Jewish forebears had originally known, that they are writing the Bible. Then both Jews and Christians—in the radically new context of the Common Era—hasten to define what is canonically or authoritatively Scripture, to provide a definitive determination of their biblical canon, of the writings to be included within or excluded from the Bible. What is remarkable is that the Bible— now two Bibles, Jewish and Christian, which operate according to the same principles of inclusion and exclusion, each of which is both unique and universal: the principle of creation from nothing as the last judgment and the principle of doing unto others as you would have them do unto you as the golden rule of life—both includes and excludes what the other includes and excludes. For Jews, the Bible is all-inclusive, excluding the New Testament. For Christians, the Bible includes what they call the Old Testament, yet they exclude the Jews (those who do not recognize Jesus as the Messiah) from the biblical story of salvation.

The canon of the Bible is closed in the first centuries of the Common Era. Enclosed within the stories of its great heroes—Moses, who liberates his people from enslavement to the natural contradictions of paganism; and Jesus, who dies on the cross of pagan ignorance and blindness promising eternal salvation to all who adhere to the law and the prophets—the Bible is made self-inclusive, excluding everything nonbiblical from its midst. It is during the very time when the biblical canon is closed, however, that the Bible is creating from nothing the thought and existence of the Common Era. Just as the biblical canon is something new in the history of the world, so the Common Era is new. Indeed, the newness of the Common Era as a concept which can only be thought existing (the Common Era exists solely as its concept) is such that it pervades human consciousness and existence very slowly and unsteadily, and, even today, it remains still very much the dawn of the new era, the era, as Nietzsche would say, of the *Übermensch*. The Common Era presupposes that there is a point in time, a point zero, a moment of transition such that all peoples, whatever their natural origins in particular spaces and times, commonly pass through it. This point zero is the transition which owes its beginning to nothing prior to creation from nothing; it marks the original and eternal transition from fate to freedom, from the natural law of contradictory opposition to the golden rule of common recognition of difference. The Common Era presupposes that there is a universal perspective—the concept of existence, the existence of the concept: I think, therefore, I am—which is true for all and can and must be interpreted as the truth for all: truth as its own standard, the standard both of true interpretation and of false interpretation as idolatry. The Common Era presupposes the critical distinction between dialectic and dualism, between dialectic and idolatry, showing that, from the perspective of the Common Era, the extra-biblical world cannot be thought to exist and does not exist in thought, being blind to and ignorant of the choice of opposition as knowledge of good and evil. In making the choice of thought and existence universal to all, the Common Era shows that the lack or absence of choice, the contradictory position of paganism naturally ignorant of and blind to the fact that it is a position, now becomes revealed as the contradictory position of sin characterized by the idolatrous denial of choice: open rebellion against loving God above all others and your neighbor as yourself.

The Common Era is new for Jews who find themselves in a radically changed situation. They are now confronted with a new religion which not only is not pagan but which includes their Bible within its own, while excluding them from it. Jews face a religion which is so tremendous a threat to them, as it is to no others, precisely because it is biblical and thus, from their own perspective, idolatrous, a threat unlike anything which had confronted them in imperial paganism from the Pharaoh to the Roman Emperor. This is the case notwithstanding the Roman destruction of Jerusalem which makes the Diaspora permanent, for not only do Jews now have to live in the world, separated from Jerusalem, but the world in which they live is the Common Era whose universality expresses the ontology, the thought and existence, of the Bible, the Bible which they share with ever-expanding Christianity and which, a few centuries later, also gives rise to Islam, the third and last of the great biblical religions.

For Christians, the Common Era is the permanently new situation, as they face Jews (fellow biblicists) and later Muslims (whose origins are also biblical), heretics (the heterodox), and pagans (those whose thought and existence remain extra-biblical, hidden within the fatal otherness of nature). Each of these groups confronts Christianity with a unique challenge, for no one of these groups can be thought by us to exist, or to exist in our thought, outside the Bible, outside the Common Era. Jews eternally remind Christians that to include God within the human condition, the world within the covenant, the texts of humanity within the Bible, and the spaces and times of all peoples within the Common Era is to risk losing the love of God and neighbor as the exclusive choice, the priority than which no other can be thought to exist (than which no other can exist as thought). Muslims remind Christians (and Jews) that the principles of exclusion and inclusion can be used such that truth as inclusive excludes (all) interpretation and interpretation as exclusive includes (only) one truth. Heretics remind Christians that orthodox determination of truth and interpretation risks falling into idolatry, into the dualism between exclusion from the world (rationalism) and inclusion within the world (empiricism), with both the exclusionist and inclusionist tendencies finding expression alike in skepticism and dogmatism by reducing either human to divine being or divine to human being. The eternally seductive Christological heresies—concerned with probing the dialectic of the Incarnation, the relationship which is the God-man—reflect the enormous difficulties which, first, Christians and, later, their heirs, modern secular thinkers, have in articulating (living) the ontological argument, the relationship between thought and existence, both divine and human, beyond the canonical formulae from behind whose barriers the orthodox are wont to hurl their anathemas. Extra-biblical pagans remind Christians that their biblical principle of choice, in the name of which they wield the sword of exclusivity and inclusivity with enormous and often savage power, cuts in both directions. Indeed, it is precisely Christians (along with Jews) who bear the responsibility of remembering but who compulsively forget that it is they—members of the covenant—and no others who are to be judged by the choice which they make to live by the double-edged sword of the golden rule. In distinguishing choice as the principle which cuts through all human differences, it is the people of the book and their heirs, and they alone, who are to be judged by their use of the sword of discrimination. The archangel Michael holds aloft his flaming sword, forbidding any return on the part of the chosen people to the paradisiacal garden of innocence, while Jesus, bringing not peace but the sword at the last judgment, comes to judge sinners, not the righteous, as he represents the ultimate discrimination between those who are first and those who are last.

It is fitting that the Bible is closed and that its dialectic of exclusion and inclusion is articulated in the early years of the Common Era, at the very time when its creators, Jewish and Christian, are taking their Bible into the world, not only making the world open to the Bible but also making the Bible open to the world. The history of the Common Era, that of the ancient, medieval, and modern periods, is the history of the conquest of the world by the Bible, but it is also the history of the conquest of the Bible by the world. I am not concerned here, and I am not competent, to relate this history. I am concerned, rather, with how this history informs our thinking and how our thinking informs this history. I want to reflect in this chapter on two critical features of the Common Era which are biblical in inspiration, from the beginning, and which, in emerging from the early modern period on, become central to modernism: history and secularism, including democracy. Meditation on the Bible shows us that, as I indicated in a previous chapter, the Bible is concerned fundamentally not with paganism—the natural law of fate whose contradictions condemn its followers to ignorance and blindness—but with idolatry—the fateful reduction of the freedom to think and to exist to natural contradiction, to nothing. It is becoming, therefore, that, notwithstanding the confrontations of Moses and Jesus with the contradictory power of pagan imperialism, the Bible is concerned, above all, with articulating how it is that the chosen people, precisely because they are the heirs of Adam and Eve choosing knowledge of good and evil, are to live in the world of the Common Era. The Common Era brings the era of extra-biblical paganism to an end by revealing that it has no beginning or principle in itself, that it is the nothing from which the thought and existence of all human beings are created. The Common Era is henceforth to be characterized by the eternal struggle to make the world a suitable place for human thought and existence and to account for and to overcome the constant temptations to lay down the burden of freely thinking and existing for the idols of paganism, something inconceivable and unimaginable to extra-biblical peoples.

Idolatry, the reduction of free thought and existence, both divine and human, to pagan idols, is the eternal seduction for biblical men and women. Idolatry would not exist were it not for paganism—the realm of contradictory nature subject to the fatal doctrine of opposites. But paganism would not exist were it not for the Bible; for the Bible, in creating thought and existence, both human and divine, from nothing, from nothing which is not worthy of thought and existence, shows that paganism is precisely the choice that is not a choice for either divine or human being and thus the choice which humans falsely make as they foist their choice upon the idol they call God. As I have already shown in my discussion of idolatry, the choice to become pagans, the choice of paganism, is a choice inconceivable and unimaginable to extra-biblical peoples. Pagans are and are not—following and thus contradicting the law of contradiction, for which something cannot both be and not be in the same space and time, yet whose appearances at once both are and are not what they are (not). Extra-biblical peoples cannot choose either to become what they are (not) or (not) to be what they are to become. They simply are and are not. It is precisely the gap between being and becoming, the fall from paradise, the leap of spirit on the part of faith and reason beyond the contradictions of nature which constitutes the freedom of spirit for biblical men and women and thus the possibility of abusing or losing that freedom.

That Moses originally liberates the chosen people from enslavement to the imperial might of the Pharaoh and that Jesus ultimately dies to the imperial might of the Roman Emperor as the savior of the world is not the principal issue with which the Bible confronts the world and with which it is then equally confronted. The issue, above all others, is the nature of the world once nature, the world of nature, all that there is, is revealed to have been created from nothing, from nothing which is subject to the contradictions of natural space and time, to the contradictions of finite objects or things, what Descartes call extended (measurable) matter and Darwin organic matter blindly living by the mechanism of natural selection according to which the fittest survive. Once again, however, I repeat that the biblical doctrine of creation from nothing is not to be understood in the idolatrous terms that "nothing" is some mystifying thing from which space and time are mysteriously generated. Rather, the nothing from which human thought and existence are created is the gap, the leap, the difference between freedom and nature, between spirit and matter, between consciousness and fate, between the golden rule and the law of contradiction such that the natural oppositions between human beings—those of race, gender, and class, those whose origins are natural or factual (and the difference between nature and fact is without significance)—can be reconciled, made right or legitimate, in Rousseau's terms. The nothing from which human life—the life of thought and existence—is created is not something surreptitiously introduced on analogy with space and time (this is what the Bible calls idolatry and Kant the subreption of the hypostatized consciousness). The nothing from which creation comes is properly "no thing," nothing found in the thought and existence of natural space and time.

The doctrine of *creatio ex nihilo* is thus the theological formulation for what philosophers call the ontological argument for (thought and) existence. There is nothing prior to existence conscious of itself (there is nothing prior to the concept of existence). Creation—divine and human being—is its own ground, its own standard, its own beginning, its own priority, the cause of itself, not subject to finite or natural causes understood as either extrinsic or intrinsic to itself. Freedom is not the result of a prior state; freedom is the revolutionary (radical) break with the pagan mythology of nature such that there has to be a beginning, a beginning which is its own beginning, if there is to be an end to the blindness and ignorance of the contradictory doctrine of opposites always other than and opposed to themselves. The biblical doctrine of creation from nothing is bluntly articulated by that astute democrat, Harry Truman: the buck stops here—in the human right to think and to exist freely, in human responsibility. Men and women will eternally disagree about who is passing the buck, about who is making a fast buck, about where the buck stops: such is the story of the free choice made in the beginning by biblical men and women. But, with the common creation of thought and existence from nothing, from nothing which is not creative of thought and existence, men and women are not free to pass the buck.

The biblical doctrine of creation from nothing exposes the natural differences between human beings to be insignificant—in themselves. Indeed, the doctrine of creation from nothing shows that we can truly desire, enjoy, and appropriate our natural differences—both our own and those of others—only if we do not oppose them in our blindness and ignorance. The opportunity—and the danger!—is that it is only in light of the doctrine of creation from nothing that difference does not vanish into the indifference of the law of contradiction. What counts is how human beings make use of their natural differences in their relations with others (including themselves), how they make their differences becoming, such that they become what they are (not) and are (not) what they become. But what is so perplexing about the Bible is that it is precisely because natural differences are shown to be nothing in themselves that they can become something in themselves—idols, a possibility completely inconceivable and unimaginable to extra-biblical paganism. Because, in the pagan world, the end or nature of things is never directly identified with human beings or even with the gods but is always that principle, whether extrinsic or intrinsic, which moves things, mortal and immortal, ultimately, the cosmos, but which remains unmoved by things, it is always other than and opposed to whatever appears, in either thought or existence, to be the end or nature of things. The end or nature of things always both is and is not—the end or nature of things. To live—in thought and existence—within the extra-biblical world is to seek the end, the end of the law of contradiction. But it is the very law of contradiction which is without an end, for it shows that every end is always contradictory, always other than and opposed to living individuals who seek their end in ignorance of the end of contradiction.

To seek the end of the law of contradiction is ineluctably to live blind to and ignorant of the end. To possess the end, to be identical with or to know your end—for to know the good is to be the good—is to be at your end, to be dead, to be dead to the contradictory appearances of life, to be at the end of your contradictory life. If you seek the end—and you are fated to seek the end (of life), for the unexamined life is not worth living—you will discover that life is contradictory, completely opposed to and other than its end, of which it is ignorant and by which it is blinded. If you attain or possess your end—and you are fated to attain the end (of life), for recall the fate of Socrates—you show that death is the end of contradiction, completely opposed to and other than its beginning, of which it is ignorant and by which it is blinded. To begin in the extra-biblical world is always to begin in contradiction, for the very notion of contradiction contradicts the possibility of beginning, of being (becoming) what one is not, of becoming (being) what one is. To end in the extra-biblical world is equally to end in contradiction (that is, to end contradiction, to contradict the end); for the very notion of contradiction contradicts the notion of ending, of not being what one is, of becoming what one is (not).

Once the secret fate of contradictory beginnings and ends, however, has been revealed for what it is—which is nothing—then the idolatrous possibility—the horrendous reality—emerges of contradicting nature, of contradicting one's end, something inconceivable and unimaginable to extra-biblical paganism. The claim to know nature as the thing-in-itself and thus the claim that somebody's nature (involving race, gender, or class) is contradictory and thus should be contradicted (that is, annihilated) is the idolatry of nihilism completely alien to and unthinkable within extra-biblical paganism. Nature takes on so ambiguous and explosive a position within the biblical story of creation from nothing for the very reason that, because human beings are created from nothing, from nothing natural, not only is there is nothing which cannot become or be made natural, but there is also nothing which cannot become or be made unnatural. The things of nature are not what they are in themselves but what they become, not in the sense that we literally create things in space and time from nothing— for that is the idolatry of dualism—but in the sense that we are responsible for our creation of them, for our relationship to them. The preeminent thing of nature is thought and existence—divine and human being. The priority of nature is spirit—the spirit of God and the spirit of being human—that which recognizes that it comes first, in the beginning, from nothing. Once it is we, however, who are responsible for the beginnings and ends of nature—something inconceivable in the extra-biblical world, for it is the finite (perfect, complete, finished) beginnings and ends of nature which are always the secret fatally hidden from thought and existence, both divine and human—we can abuse these beginnings and ends of nature by claiming to know them, not as our fellow human beings, but as things-in-themselves. Instead of making our judgments subject to the golden rule, we call unnatural that which contradicts our view of nature, that which we deem unfit to survive. (So we say that Jews are not racially pure by nature, that homosexuality is unnatural, that women are inferior in nature, that blacks are a naturally inferior race....)

The realm of natural science, as I indicated in a previous chapter, is particularly prone to idolatrous misconception. It is solely because of the biblical creation from nothing, not of nature, but of human nature, that nature, the extended space and time of nature, is liberated from the ignorance and blindness of contradictory logic and can be known by human researchers as objects of possible experience, to use the language of Kant, which has never been improved upon (and rarely equalled). It is because of the triadic distinction between reality, appearance and illusion that knowledge of natural objects, not as things real in themselves but altogether to be distinguished from mere illusion, is attainable. (I continue here to follow Kant's usage, as I did in the tripartite division of the faculties of sensibility, understanding, and reason which the present triad mirrors and which I invoked in an earlier chapter.) By reality Kant means that which can be thought only existing and which can exist only as thought: the thing-in-itself, what Kant calls rational beings, those who think or will, both divine and human. By appearance Kant means that which is known certainly (and uncertainly) as the objects of nature subject to the causal laws of nature (and which today are formulated in statistical terms). By illusion Kant does not mean primarily the perceptual, cognitive, or logical illusions which naturally result from the distortions of sensibility and understanding and with which we are all familiar. (The oar in the water appears bent; I judge the sun, which appears to be no bigger than a disk, to be only a short distance away; I misunderstand the meaning of a term and fail to follow an argument.) Once we have discerned such commonplace illusions, we easily account for them and normally are not further misled by them. The illusion which Kant has in mind and whose very account is itself implicated in illusion is what he calls transcendental illusion, the confusion between reality (the actual thing-in-itself) and appearance (the objects of possible, that is, natural, experience), between what I call, in this essay in thinking, truth and interpretation, on the one hand, and idolatry, on the other, between dialectic and dualism.

The transcendental illusion of idolatry is not something which we can merely learn to correct and which, once corrected, we can dismiss as insignificant. It is something for which we must eternally account. It is precisely because extra-biblical paganism does not make a triadic distinction between reality (creation from nothing natural), appearance (as the objects of nature), and illusion (the idolatrous confusion between reality and appearance) that it does not possess any faithful or rational conception of persons (who cannot be thought except existing) or any knowledge of nature. Again, what is so perplexing about the thought and existence which the Bible creates from nothing is that their creation from nothing involves a critical distinction between reality and appearance, between spirit and nature, between thought (will, action, faith, practice...) and knowledge, between person and thing, between ethics and science. Still more perplexing, however, is that the distinction between spirit and nature involves yet a third distinction, that which Kant calls transcendental illusion, the Bible idolatry, and I in this essay in thinking dualism. It is only if we distinguish between (in Kant's language) reality as the thing-in-itself—which cannot be known in itself but only thought or willed (according to the law of the golden rule)—and nature—as the congeries of objects which can be known not in themselves but only as objects of possible experience—that we can possess both. But it is precisely this distinction between the freedom to think and to exist and nature as the objects of possible experience which creates the very possibility—unthinkable outside the biblical tradition— that they will be confused, conflated, reified, or reduced one to the other, with transcendental illusion, the idolatry of dualism, as the fateful result.

Because the natural world is the creation of the Bible, but not as creative but only as apparent or uncreative in itself, we are constantly seduced into taking the finite terms of nature as the concepts of our thought and existence, into seeking to know nature as the thing-in-itself, with the result that not only human thought and existence but equally knowledge of nature vanish into sheer illusion, into nothing, something inconceivable and unimaginable in the extra-biblical world. Neither the freedom to think and to exist nor knowledge of nature, neither the ethics of the golden rule nor natural science, is found in the extra-biblical world, but then neither is illusion (idolatry or dualism). The enormous challenge to biblical men and women and their modernist heirs is to appropriate both the freedom to think and to exist and scientific knowledge such that the critical distinction between them is preserved. For, the moment we undertake either to know our thought and existence in the terms of natural objects or to view our appearances in nature as things-in-themselves which can be thought (willed) to exist (which exist as thought or willed), we fall into the transcendental dualism of idolatrous illusion. It is thought and existence, alike divine and human, on the one hand, and natural science, on the other, which constitute the Common Era of the Bible. It is in this context that it becomes essential to comprehend thought and existence, whether divine or human, as both historical and secular. If it is believed that either history or the secular world can be understood on analogy with nature, if it is believed that either history or the secular world can be known scientifically, or if it is believed that the concept of reason appropriate for the historical and secular realms can be understood in terms of science and not of faith, then the transcendental illusion of dualistic idolatry as both anti-human and un-scientific will be insurmountable.

II. HISTORY AS OUR BEGINNING

All peoples have a past, and they also have a future. All peoples possess a memory of past events, and it is this memory which allows them to an-ticipate future events. Indeed, memory is no more of past events than it is of future events, for clearly we remember no more about the past, about past events, than we anticipate as being relevant, essential, or important to the future. It is precisely in terms of our anticipation of the future that we select and remember, that we memorialize, events of the past. People do not live in the past any more than they live in the future, or how people live in the past reflects how they live in the future; for, indeed, they live in the present, in the intersection of past and future, Janus-faced, anticipating the future in light of the past and recalling past events in terms of future possibilities. That which shapes or defines a past event—whether small or large, whether we remember the toe which we stubbed yesterday, doubt-less because we are presently walking, rather painfully, into the future, or we remember the confrontation between Moses and Pharaoh, between Socrates and the citizen body of Athens, or between Jesus and Pilate—is precisely because of its future possibilities. Once the future goes out of the past, the past is forgotten as part of, as the anticipation of, the future.

Stories are told—by a parent to a child, by elders to youths, by peers to themselves, by experts (professionals) to their communities—not merely as entertainment or, rather, precisely for entertainment, for then the lis-teners imbibe their basic values, themes, and examples as the story of their life, and their life is not merely or primarily past but rather future. How life was lived in the past they learn in the present to anticipate as their future. Indeed, the stories themselves will involve their own past perfect and their own future perfect, shaping the very structure of past and future for their listeners. Listeners, however, are by no means merely passive in listening to the stories of their life (whatever the appearances). They bring already—however implicitly or unconsciously—a strong notion of the future to their

listening, and, indeed, if the story to which they listen is too discordant
with their view of the future, they will have to be reshaped to conform to
the dominant views of the future or perhaps be actually rejected (sup-
pressed) or simply forgotten (repressed) as irrelevant to the future lives of
their listeners.

That memory, although we tend to associate it with the past, involves the future no less than the past prepares us for the fact that history, although it appears to be associated with the past—both past events and our
knowledge of those past events—no less involves the future than it does
the past. It is true that historians study the past and not the future (at least
in appearance); that the materials of their history—texts, archival deposits,
archaeological remains...—are produced by our forebears, not our heirs;
that the librarian whose advise is solicited by a reader looking for books on
the history of, say, Canada will ask, among other things, about the particular period in the past in which the reader is interested; and that, when
people meet and begin to learn about each other, they start telling their history (where they were born and have lived; their schooling; their travels;
their work; their accomplishments; major events in their lives; their personal lives... their children... their concerns...). But, when we think about
this last example—people sharing their stories—it is clear that not only
what individuals narrate about their own history but also how they narrate
this history (including, often, their view of their own national history, not
to mention the history of the world, or at least that portion of it which interests them) involve them deeply in the future. How they view the future—as a conspiracy or a bowl of roses, as closed or open (a reflection
more extrinsic to themselves), in a manner cynical or romantic, jaundiced
or jovial (a reflection more intrinsic to themselves), and I provide only the
most hackneyed of alternatives from an infinity of possibilities—will deeply influence the history which they view themselves as possessing and the
future possibilities (or dead ends) which they see in it. It is equally the case
that the stories told by professional historians for sophisticated readers are
deeply laden with values, attitudes, and concerns which both consider essential to their future. Why else would they write and read these histories?
Even history scorned (properly) as antiquarian reflects a particular conception of the future, in this case as uninteresting, insignificant, irrelevant.... A
trivial view of the past reflects a trivial view of the future. A rich, dynamic
view of the past embodies a rich and dynamic view of the future.

I do not contend that the future is more important than the past, for not only is that not the case, but it is no less a dualistic falsehood than its opposite, that memory and history deal with the past and not equally with the future. But to recognize, from the beginning, that memory and history deal with not only the past but also and equally the future, that they are deeply implicated in both, will help us to comprehend thought and existence as historical, to show that the Cartesian project—I think historically, therefore, I am history—is the historical ground of truth and interpretation.

All peoples have a past which they recall in light of their future. But not all peoples view their past and their future historically. Indeed, it is only the people of the Bible who choose the past and the future in (as) the historical image of God, relinquishing forever a notion of past and future based on the images of natural space and time whose contradictory beginnings and ends constantly reverse past and future. The natural images of space and time by which extra-biblical peoples view their beginnings and ends, the past and future, are the line and circle. Notwithstanding the fact that it remains extremely hard for us moderns not to view history—both our thought and existence—as either linear or circular, history is neither linear nor circular, although it is both, their simultaneous appropriation (creation). History belongs neither to immediate (linear) perception nor to immediate (circular) cognition, although, as always, it cannot either be thought to exist or exist as our thought without both. History is neither linear nor circular, neither empiricist nor rationalist, neither external (extrinsic) nor innate (intrinsic or internal) to us. We certainly cannot understand our history—as our thought and existence—with either our eyes or our minds closed. But when we open our eyes and our minds, whether how we see (our thought) and what we see (our existence) is historical depends completely on the adequacy of our conception of not only reason but equally faith.

The appeal to the triumphs of scientific knowledge, to the certainties of science—forgetting that science is no less uncertain than certain until and unless we ground it in our thought and existence, in the conception of our past and our future—is the idolatrous seduction which not only academic but also popular historians and their readers, including politicians and policy planners, are nearly incapable of resisting. That the structure of history is not only rational—as Hegel demonstrates with the profound grandeur of which he alone is capable—but equally faithful—as

Kierkegaard shows with a depth of insight the rigorous articulation of which is unique—is impossible to comprehend for those who view history as an empirical science with a methodology involving the logical canons of scientific verification. Philosophers who view history on analogy with science have never been able to explain, however, how the subject matter of history, the thought and existence of human beings, no matter how quantified or subjected to statistical or aggregate analysis, can be understood on the model of natural cause and effect (where every cause is the effect of yet another cause). Human beings do not give "causes" for their actions, although they have causes, explicit and implicit, conscious and unconscious, just and unjust, in terms of which they shape their past and future. Human beings give reasons for what they think and do, reasons which are both explicit and implicit, both written and oral, both verbal and non-verbal, reasons which may be inadequately understood, half-understood, or hardly if at all understood by the actors of the time, reasons which inevitably involve various kinds and degrees of miscalculation, rationalization, self-interest, class bias, projection, repression.... It is precisely these reasons (which are evident no less in data which must be evaluated statistically than in documents which have been consciously elaborated) about which historians write, which they and their readers debate, and which lead to further research.

Not only do philosophers of history who try to reduce history to science confuse the certainty of scientific explanation with the truth of historical interpretation, but also they have never come up with a single covering law—theories connecting cause and effect—which explains historical phenomena, that is, human action, such that scientific laws (for example, the theory of evolution) cover natural phenomena and provide an adequate (certain) explanation of them. The public yawns and sound, practicing historians are aghast when the logician of history suggests, as covering laws, such common sense and jejune generalizations as human beings pursue their own self-interest, capitalism undertakes to replace the risk of competition with the security of monopoly, or centralization results in alienation while decentralization produces inefficiency.

I should add that the empiricist blindness of British and North American philosophers of history is matched only by the rationalist blindness of continental and mainly Marxist philosophers of history. Whereas a shallow notion of the past leads empiricist philosophers of history to envisage a shallow notion of the future, rationalist philosophers of history impose a shallow notion of the future on the past. It is important to note, however, that historical practice—the actual writing (and reading) of history—has generally been of much higher quality than philosophical reflection on history, a point which unhappily intensifies the alienation between the practice and theory of history. It is also worth noting that Marx is himself a great historian (as he is also a great theorist). His analysis of the conflicts—social, political, economic, ideological—in the France of his time (the Revolution of 1848 and the accession to power of Emperor Louis Napoleon Bonaparte) is profoundly acute. But the explanations which Marx provides for these conflicts are not causes, on the scientific model of cause and effect, but reasons, reasons which take us to the heart of what constitutes human thought and existence, reasons which involve us—both historian and his readers—in the passionate debate of what it is that constitutes our human history. Marx is a great historian not because of, but in spite of, his (and Engels') benighted efforts to reify the story of human liberation in the terms of (a very mechanistic conception of) scientific laws (the celestial mechanics of prediction, which is not very distinct from the machinations of astrological prediction, although both are equally to be distinguished from the prophecy of history).

Marx is a great historian because of the dialectical sophistication with which he understands human relations (on the model of political economy). He resists the standard empiricist and rationalist dualisms between action and thought, data and explanation, past and future, materialism and idealism, production and consciousness (although his followers, except for those who rediscover him by way of Hegel, turn his dialectical materialism into the matter of pseudo science lacking the conscious spirit of dialectic). The great strength of Marxist philosophy of history is its conception of human data as dialectical, of the data as themselves bearing the conflict of human interest and thus involving a deep sense of both past and future. But the strength of Marxism is also its appalling weakness: the anxiety of consequence on the part of Marxists, the fear that their dialectical conception of human thought and existence is no less religious than rational, no less biblical than secular, a fear so overwhelming for orthodox Marxists that it produces (in them) the dogmatism with which they relentlessly insist that their explanations are scientific and (in us, their astounded critics) the (historical) explanation that this pseudo-scientific dogmatism, in repressing all that is profound in Marx, must be viewed as deep-seated anxiety resisting the consequences of history. The deep repression of history in Marxism is matched only by the trivial conception of history held by empiricists. Empiricist history and Marxist (rationalist) history, when understood as scientific, is neither scientific nor historical, neither employing the methods of science nor providing us with a comprehension of human history.

In order to understand history we must comprehend it as both faithful and rational. We must comprehend the fact that, unless we view history as involving both faith and reason, we shall constantly find ourselves, to recall and to reverse Hume, betwixt no reason at all, the shoals in whose shallows empiricists shipwreck, and a false reason, the depths in whose profundities Marxists (and other rationalists) founder. In order to comprehend history we must go back to the beginning, to the historical beginning, to the beginning of history and to history as the beginning. But the next step to be taken in understanding that our quintessentially historical task involves our going back to our beginnings, to our origins and our principles, is delicate, critical, and dialectical, involving a leap of consciousness, a leap not only of faith but also of reason, on our part, as our essay in thinking will, by this point, already have led us (author and reader) to anticipate, I believe. To go back to the beginning of history, to the history of beginning, to the history of our beginnings, is to go back to—ourselves, to our thought and existence; and, since thought and existence, as it is the burden of my essay in thinking to demonstrate, are no less divine than human, to go back to our beginning, to go back to the beginning of our history, is to go back to God. The reason that thinkers like Rousseau, in demonstrating that the constitution of human thought and existence is founded on right and not on fact, appeal to nature, to natural right, and not to history, is that they find that history had been reduced to and reified as the custom supporting the *status quo* of the immediate perception and cognition of those in power. Eighteenth century thinkers are also deeply—and rightly—skeptical of claims locating human beginnings in God; for God is the ultimate *telos* to which dogmatists appeal in their defense of monarchy, whether secular or religious, although their idolatrous arguments ultimately reflect Aristotle (paganism rationalized as history), not the faith or reason of the Bible (Christianity). The ambiguities obscuring the conceptual understanding of what we mean by such terms as God, human being, history, fact, and nature are legion. They can be clarified, not eliminated but fruitfully realigned, only when we become clear about what it is that constitutes our human beginning.

Rousseau recognizes that, in order to reflect on the origins of inequality, we must go back to our beginnings and that to go back to our beginnings is to discover that our beginning is the social contract, that we have already begun. We cannot begin to think about our existence, we cannot begin to exist consciously without already having begun, without adhering to the social contract. The question of how we begin (began), as if we can (could) leap outside of our beginning and begin again, forgetting or repressing the fact that we have (had) already begun, cannot be answered because it is not a question. The only question demanding a true—faithful and reasoned—response is how we can render our beginning legitimate, how we can take the leap—of faith and reason—which is our beginning and thus translate (transform) the chains of slavery and ignorance into the bonds of our human thought and existence. No beginning can take place outside of our beginning again (our already having begun), outside of our returning to ourselves, outside of our reconstituting our thought and existence, from the beginning, once again, and eternally. To go back to the beginning—the beginning which is history and the history which is the beginning—is to recognize that we are in the beginning and that the beginning is in us. It is to eschew all images of space and time which suggest that to go back to the beginning of history is to go back in chronological time to some temporal point which is spatially identifiable, which is certain. What is so perplexing about history is that, although it is deeply concerned with chronology—the *logos* of *chronos* (time)—we all know that history is a matter of relationships which cannot be directly identified with or reduced to mere chronology (events coming before or after other events as causes precede effects and effects succeed causes). But nor is the diachronic (sequential) to be flattened out to mirror the merely synchronic (simultaneous), for time does count, but the issue is how it counts, how we are to account for the time of our lives. The dualism between synchronic and diachronic notions of time, so current today, with skeptical post-modernists opting for the synchronic as opposed to the dogmatism of the diachronic, as we would expect, simply replicates, at a more sophisticated but ultimately no more comprehensible level, the dualism between circular and linear notions of time, each notion alike generating its skeptical and dogmatic versions.

To account for the time of our lives, to make our time count, is to realize that, in the beginning, we—God and human beings, persons in relation, author and reader...—are created from nothing, from nothing either generated or destroyed by the contradictory images of nature whose linear beginning and circular end are always other than and opposed to their thought and existence. The God of the Bible is the God of history, and the chosen people whose choice of God creates the Bible are the people of history. In the beginning is history. History is in the beginning. History is the beginning. The beginning is history. History—whether conceived in materialist or idealist terms—is the recognition that the dialectic of thought and existence, both divine and human, is not located in the contradictory nature of space and time but is constituted as the paradoxical relationship of the golden rule. The paradox is the recognition that all beginning is dialectical, both individual and communal. I cannot begin—without relationship, the relationship of both self and other. You equally cannot begin, without relationship, the relationship of both self and other. There is no first beginning except in the *a priori* synthetic sense that those conscious of existing in the beginning know that they are first. They know that their history is the story of their constitution of the priority of right over immediate fact, but they also know that their history is equally the history of their back-sliding, of their appalling slide into the idolatry of identifying their priorities with the immediacies of fact and nature (with custom, hierarchy, the oppression of others, the repression of self...).

History is inconceivable and unimaginable—it does not exist—in the extra-biblical world. Herodotus is no more the father of history than Thucydides is the first scientific historian (to remain with the Greek exemplification of extra-biblical paganism). The memory found in extra-biblical peoples reflects the doctrine of contradictory opposites whereby it is always other than and opposed to itself. The memory of extra-biblical peoples is, ultimately, fate. What extra-biblical peoples remember is that they are ignorant of and blind to their beginning and fated to be reversed in the end. They remember that there have always been and always will be rulers and ruled (so the famous Melian dialogue reported by Thucydides): presently you have conquered, presently you will be conquered; one day I rule (over you), one day you rule (over me). All that memory recalls is that there is an eternal metamorphosis of rulers and ruled. The combinations of those who rule and of those who are ruled (in their chance appearances) endlessly change, but the ruler-ruled pattern remains the unchanging fate whose end is the unending reversal of its beginning. All that extra-biblical memory recalls is myth whose beginnings and ends are always other than and opposed to, both ignorant of and blind to, what they are in themselves.

Just as the world divides between extra-biblical paganism and the chosen people of the Bible, so it also divides between memory and history. History comes into thought and existence from nothing, from nothing whose memory of beginnings and ends reflects the natural contradictions of space and time. History is the product, not of the natural faculties of sensibility and understanding, which form the memory innate in all peoples, but of faith and reason, which constitute the thought and existence of the biblical peoples and their heirs. History involves the dialectic of truth and interpretation. History can never be either certain or uncertain, for it is not subject to the methods of verification central to the natural sciences. But, precisely because history involves truth and interpretation—historical truth is always subject to interpretation, the interpretation of history always involves its truth—it can be falsified. Historical truth and interpretation are rendered dualistic or idolatrous when history is reduced to the idols of certainty and thus is rendered uncertain either through pseudo-scientific methodology or through ideological distortion (propaganda).

Historical truth—along with its interpretation—is identical with the canons by which we evaluate thought and existence, whether we view those canons as philosophical or theological, secular or religious, rational or faithful, or, to invoke different categories, moral or aesthetic. All truth—along with its interpretation—is historical, and history involves the dialectic of truth and interpretation. History is one with metaphor, paradox, and dialectic. It embodies the golden rule, just as the golden rule involves and expresses history, history as both the content and the method of our lives: both our existence and our thought. Because history embodies the golden rule of human relations, it is alike one and universal. There is only one history—the history of humanity (and, to put this theologically: the history of one people in its rich and complex relations with its one God). But history is one only insofar as it is one for all, insofar as it is as true to you who are one as it is true to me who am one. It is only because history is one—in the beginning—that it transcends and appropriates the natural contradictions dividing humankind. The natural differences which divide human beings by race, gender, and class and as individuals (in terms of their naturally unequal endowments, talents, strengths, limitations...) can all be seen as belonging to a common history which is universal and one only when that history is based, not on natural differences, but on the thought and existence of humanity which express the *coincidentia oppositorum*. The story of humanity has one plot, the transformation of what Spinoza and Rousseau call the ignorance and chains of bondage, by which human beings consciously enslave their existence, into the freedom to think and to exist. All history is revolution—although it does not revolve in a circle (except when it is reduced to the idols of natural immediacy). All history is radical—rooted in the biblical story of sin and redemption. History is the story of liberty, to recall the fashion in which Croce epitomizes Hegel's conception of historical existence.

To indicate—briefly—that history is one, that it has one plot and involves one people and one God, is not to be construed to mean that history is not infinite, that it is not open to the widest and deepest possible variety of human thought and existence. Rather, it is to indicate that it is only in light of the creation of history from nothing, from nothing natural dividing peoples blindly against each other, that all their individualities, particularities, varieties, and differences can be not only preserved but also enhanced and cultivated as all justly belonging to the one story of humanity. But history, as the story of truth, freedom, love, and justice does know one limit, one sin which will never be forgiven, the sin of limiting history to one side of any dualistic opposition at the expense of the other side. Any history which supports the dignity of some in opposition to the dignity of others is not history but the sin against the truth of interpretation and against the interpretation of truth which is unforgivable. The only reason that truth is accessible to all is precisely because it can and must be interpreted by all as their truth. The only reason that interpretation is accessible to all is precisely because the only thing which can be interpreted is the truth, that which is true for all. The interpretation of historical truth is infinite, and the truth of historical interpretation is infinite, insofar as it is understood that truth and interpretation are falsified the moment they are reduced to some finite, partial, or one-sided representation of what it is which constitutes the historical thought and existence of human beings. It is the historical content—and method!—of human thought and existence whose truth demands interpretation by all and whose interpretation is the truth for all.

In contrast with extra-biblical memory, the secrets of whose past and future are blindly reflected as fate always other than and opposed to its contradictory appearances in natural space and time, historical memory binds past and future to the present as eternal presence. Indeed, according to the doctrine of opposites, whose law of contradiction rules over the world of extra-biblical peoples, the present, as that which exists only as thought and which is thought only as existing, cannot be thought to exist or exist as thought. In extra-biblical paganism the present always divides between beginnings of which we are ignorant and ends to (by) which we are blinded. If one begins, logically, there is no way in which to account for reaching one's end. (Zeno's arguments against the reality of motion are definitive, notwithstanding Aristotle's heroic attempts to refute them, attempts which are fated to fail, so long as one remains wedded to beginning with the law of contradiction as the beginning which cannot be demonstrated as the beginning, that beginning of whose beginning we are endlessly ignorant.) For to begin is always to find that one has begun ignorant of one's end, for to begin to exist (and to think) is to find that one's beginning is only in appearance, but appearance is that which violates the law of contradiction from beginning to end, for appearance is precisely that which both is and is not at the same time. To begin is to begin seeking one's end, and to seek, to desire, to will, to think, that is, to live—to recall Socrates' representation of the logical contradiction, the *aporia* (that which has no openings: it is not porous, it lacks pores) to which all life is fatally subject—is ineluctably to discover that one begins one's search in ignorance of and blindness to the end. To end, to bring one's beginning to an end, is—with Socrates, Oedipus, and Pentheus, not to mention Herodotus' Persians defeated by the Greeks and Thucydides' Athenians defeated by the Syracusans—to be dead to the contradictions of appearances, to be ruled by fate whose nemesis brings all human effort, all hubris in seeking one's end, to its shatteringly contradictory end. Beginnings and ends are inexorably opposed to each other in the extra-biblical world, as are ruler and ruled, one and many, reality and appearance.

To strive to be present to oneself, to strive to be in the presence of others is ineluctably to bring into play the deadly nemesis of the law of contradiction whose doctrine of opposites divides the present—of the self, of society, of, ultimately, the cosmos—between ruler and ruled, between beginning and end. The only winner of the race of life is the one who does not begin, who is not born, whose otherness remained buried in the nature of contradiction (the contradictions of nature). Once one is born, however, the nemesis of the law of generation and destruction wreaks its vengeance, for to be born is to be subject to destruction, without exception. To begin the race of life in apparent victory—with Agamemnon, Achilles, and the other Greek heroes at Troy; with the various Greek heroes in tragedy; with the victorious athletes at the Olympic and other Greek games; with the Greek victors at Marathon; with the Athenians in the golden age of Pericles at the beginning of the Peloponnesian War—only makes the fatal end more spectacular, more worthy of catharsis on the part of those celebrating the victory, wiping away, once again, the memory that the higher you rise on the wheel of fortune the more spectacularly you are dashed down, as both Thucydides in his history and Aristotle in his poetics brilliantly demonstrate and the tragedians, Euripides, above all, vividly exhibit in their plays.

The notion of immortality, which is central to the life of all extra-biblical peoples, without exception, reflects the line dividing past and future, beginning and end, leaving the present as the contradictory space and time of nature whose appearances are always opposed to and other than what they are in themselves. Whether immortality is imputed to the gods, to the soul, to that part of the soul called reason (*nous*), to the unmoved mover (to the ungenerated generator, the nonbeginning beginner, the undestroyed destroyer, the unending ender), to the celestial spheres, to the cosmos (either its fiery element or its quintessence whose perfect motion is circular)—these are all standard Greek notions—what immortality designates is that which is other than and opposed to its living or mortal self whose appearances ineluctably violate the law of contradiction. Immortality represents the lack, the absence, the ignorance, the void, the blindness which constitute life without presence, without capacity to bring together its beginnings and ends as historical presence, without the presence of history. Immortality is the very contradiction of historical life, showing that all life in the present as beginning, as seeking, as appearance is ignorant of and blind to the immortal end which it seeks to possess.

Immortality is the secret of extra-biblical life, the secret to which all blindly aspire. It is the secret of which all are ignorant during life and the secret which all possess, at death, in their return to mother nature, the immortal principle par excellence, by which all are both generated (in their blind beginning) and destroyed (in the end of which they are ignorant). Immortality, in extra-biblical life, is the secret of contradiction, the secret which is endlessly contradictory. Indeed, the immortal secret of extra-biblical life is the law of contradiction itself. The secret of immortality cannot even be thought to exist by (it cannot even exist in the thought of) the law of contradiction itself (we might say), for both thought and existence alike violate the law of contradiction which is itself without thought or existence (it cannot either be thought, that is willed, or exist). The secret of immortality underlying the life of all extra-biblical peoples is the doctrine of opposites according to which, in order to be immortal, human beings cannot be or begin as mortal—for, by the law of contradiction, something cannot both be mortal and immortal in the same space and time—but then, if they are or begin as immortals, they cannot be mortal. The line of mortality and the circle of immortality never intersect as metaphor (paradox or dialectic) in the extra-biblical world but remain endlessly opposed to each other as natural images or similes. The beginning on the mortal line of life reflects human ignorance of and blindness to the beginning and end of life's line, for the apparent line is infinite, imperfect, multiple, partial, and endless. In opposition to the infinite line of mortality is the finite, perfect, one, complete, final, and dead circle of immortality which is oblivious to its spatial and temporal beginnings and ends, for they are identical with it. Thanks to the doctrine of recollection, according to which all memory of the life of contradictory appearance is wiped out, mortal beginnings and the ends of life are forgotten in the immortal circle which has no beginning or end. The circle of immortality is the death of contradictory beginnings and ends.

Plato and Aristotle seek heroically—daring nemesis!—to connect the line of earthly human life, the mortal beginning never present to its end and the mortal end always other than and opposed to its present beginning, with the immortal (celestial) circle in which beginning and end are obliterated as dead appearances. But they no more than any Greek or anybody living within the extra-biblical world can naturally square the circle and live to tell it. Natural similes are mutually repellent, each seeking to rule over the other. Within the contradictory world of natural space and time, the line is and cannot be (or become) the circle, and the circle is and cannot be (or become) the line. There is no movement from the mortal line (life), which is without beginning or end, to the immortal circle (death), which is equally without beginning or end, just as there is no movement from the immortal sphere to the mortal sphere. For, by the law of contradiction, each, in being what it is, is opposed to and contradicted by the other. But, by the same law of contradiction, each is naturally reversed or metamorphosed without surcease into the appearances of the other, these chance appearances reflecting the contingency of fate, just as slaves and masters, as we noted in an earlier chapter, are constantly reversed into their opposite (due, above all, to the conquest of one *polis* by another or the revolt of one *polis* against another). Slaves, whom Aristotle defines as tools lacking reason whose end is their master, are frequently manumitted, and they also revolt, while free individuals possessing reason are frequently enslaved. The passage of free men from freedom to slavery and of slaves from slavery to freedom, each becoming other than and opposed to itself, is inexplicable as contrary to nature, although it happens constantly. Aristotle possess acute powers of observation, as is typical among extra-biblical peoples. Given the endemic warfare among the Greek *poloi*, he had ample opportunity to observe the revolution (*stasis*) of rulers and ruled, masters and slaves, each attempting to make its particular line in life the circle absorbing and thus obliterating the linear beginnings and ends of others. But what is incomprehensible to Aristotle, as to anyone living within the extra-biblical world, is how the passage from slavery to freedom or from freedom to slavery begins (or ends). The fatal *aporia* is impenetrable. There is no single story relating the common beginning of slaves and masters, no universal history in which slaves and masters are related in their common humanity. There is no historical present in which both slaves and masters can meet in mutual recognition or acknowledgement, doing unto the other as they would have the other do unto them. The two parties, the two selves—the very self in its own self-relation—are always divided against themselves by the contradictory doctrine of opposites, which shows human beings that, in their ignorance of and blindness to their beginnings and ends, they are endlessly opposed to and other than themselves. Rulers and ruled, masters and slaves are incomprehensible without their opposite, just as they are equally incomprehensible with their opposite.

What, readers may ask, does all this talk about immortality and the law of contradiction in Greek (extra-biblical) life have to do with history, with viewing human thought and existence as historical? Surely, nothing, they answer. I agree—so long as this nothing is understood to be the nothing from which the Bible comes into historical thought and existence. I spin out what I understand to be the contradictory nature of extra-biblical life in the belief that it is only when we comprehend, once and for all, the limit to historical thought and existence, that which is utterly without history, that history—the history of human thought and existence and the thought and existence of human history—will be liberated from the (idolatrous) dualisms by which it is so typically riven. It is only when we distinguish between extra-biblical life and the historical life of human thought and existence that we shall be in a position to comprehend that history, both historical method and content, both the thought and the existence of history, precisely because they are secular, are not scientific but biblical in structure.

History is not simply a neutral method which can be applied, willy-nilly, to whatever past content. History is not just some neutral content of the past to which, willy-nilly, any method can be applied. History is both method and content, both thought and existence. History embodies (articulates) the ontological argument for thought and existence, both divine and human. The concept which cannot be thought except existing is history, while that which can exist only as it is thought is no less history. The history (existence) of the concept is the concept of history (historical existence). That Anselm can see in the ontology of the Bible an argument—relating thought and existence—which biblical authors do not yet see, that Hegel can see in the ontological argument the structure of history which Anselm does not yet see, that we—I dare hope—can see in Hegel's grasp of thought and existence as historical a conception of truth as interpretation which Hegel does not yet see: such are the implications which the explication of history as creation from nothing, from nothing which does not bear the historical implications of thought and existence, has for the future.

We shall remain faithful to the implications of historical creation only insofar as we recognize that, precisely because history is neither neutral method nor neutral content but the history of the thought and existence of the chosen people, there is a limit to history. History is the paradox that it is universal and one but only as the universal is chosen as one and as the one is chosen as universal. History involves and expresses all human content, not, however, in itself but only as it embodies and articulates the ontological argument for thought and existence, both divine and human. Just as I indicated in a previous chapter that interpretation, although universal and one, cannot be applied to texts which lack the thought and existence of interpretation, so history cannot be applied to that which is ignorant of and blind to history, to history as the ontological argument, as the dialectic of thought and existence. In the same way as that which is blind to and ignorant of interpretation cannot be interpreted from itself alone, so that which is non-historical cannot be understood or studied historically. History is no more to be imposed on that which is other than history than a democratic constitution, the concept of freedom, or the notion of love central to the golden rule is to be imposed on those who are ignorant of and blind to the dialectic of thought and existence. The deep paradox to be descried here, as I indicate throughout my essay in thinking, is that, precisely because history is at once unique (individual) and universal, it is accessible to all peoples, understood both individually and collectively. But history to be history must be chosen—chosen consciously as that which exists for one and all. History is thus a double-edged sword which cuts in two directions.

The notion of the history of, say, ancient Greece, pre-Columbian America, or the traditional civilizations of East Asia is an oxymoron few practitioners of history are willing to recognize, let alone their theorists or their readers. Ancient Greece, pre-Columbian America, or the traditional civilizations of East Asia have no history—in the strong, rigorous, comprehensive sense of the ontological argument which I present here. The categories of history brought to the study of these extra-biblical peoples are utterly without foundation in their lives. These people naturally have a past and a future, often constructed out of enormously impressive monuments—cultural, social, bureaucratic—which are worthy of the most sustained study and contemplation. But the past and the future generated by these vast civilizations, and by an infinite number of lesser ones, are not, I repeat, historical. Still, these civilizations are historical in the critical sense that they belong to the Common Era, to our common human history, to modernity, to the story of the creation from nothing of the thought and existence of human (and divine) history.

There is tremendous irony in the fact that non-historical peoples are brought into the ambit of history by—as part of the extraordinary process of modernization—professional historians who fail to realize that they are secular missionaries for the thought and existence whose universality is uniquely biblical. History is perhaps the most subversive presence of biblical religion in the world, if only because its practitioners, as I indicated earlier, profoundly suffer the anxiety of consequence of (their own) history. Historians are loathe, indeed, normally appalled, to recognize that they are missionaries in the tradition of the biblical prophets, showing that the Messiah is found neither in the future nor in the past but now, in the fullness of time, in the eternal present, what Hegel calls the rose in the cross. History is subversive of all traditional values on the basis of which right—inevitably, the hierarchical right of some to dominate others—is derived from natural fact. Indeed, history is particularly revolutionary because, with its commitment to the freedom of thought and existence, it views the reign of the extra-biblical doctrine of opposites to be terminated by the creation of thought and existence from nothing, from nothing based on the idolatry of the Tower of Babel. The unity of humankind is given not in nature but in the golden rule of liberty, equality, and solidarity.

Not only does the story of the Tower of Babel provide a profound critique of paganism, but the fact that it comes at the beginning of the very chapter of Genesis at whose end the family of Abraham, the father of faith, emerges is striking (chapter 11). When the story of biblical—world-historical—thought and existence then begins, in the opening verses of chapter 12, with the call of Abraham from paganism, we marvel at the extraordinary juxtaposition of the natural unity of languages smashed by God in the image of the Tower of Babel and the unity of communication, of community, which is represented in the story of Abraham and in which we, reader and author, continue to participate. Like Abraham we all begin in paganism, in possession of the natural faculties of sensibility and understanding which are common to all human beings. But what the story of Abraham shows us, especially when juxtaposed with the story of the Tower of Babel, is that, if we are to establish a historical unity which all peoples can share, we must fall from the paradisiacal unity of speaking in natural tongues. The paradox—which is the paradox of history—is that the babel of contradictory tongues is the natural condition which inevitably results from attempting to derive the right of unity from natural facts, for right based on nature ineluctably erects a hierarchy of rulers and ruled. The unity of history begins not in nature but with the creation of history from nothing, from nothing subject to the contradictions of natural space and time, with the call of humanity from nothing, from nothing subject to the contradictions of natural paganism. Abraham is called from the paganism of nature, and thus the story of his call, his vocation, is paradoxical precisely as the stories of creation and of the garden of paradise are paradoxical. There is nothing in the paganism of natural contradiction with which Abraham, or the history of human thought and existence, can begin. Abraham begins as one who is extra-biblical, but his story is, fittingly, enclosed within the Bible. His beginning or creation is from nothing, in the sense not that he is not pagan, in the beginning, but that there is nothing pagan which can explain his beginning, for extra-biblical paganism is precisely that which is without beginning, until and unless it is revealed to be the nothing from which the Bible creates thought and existence.

My point in elaborating the biblical stories of the Tower of Babel and the call of Abraham is not to argue that, from a historical point of view, extra-biblical peoples can be other than what they are—which is ignorant of and blind to history as the revelation of the freedom of all peoples to think and to exist. My claim, rather, is that, today, we—historians and readers of history, human beings who have no choice but to choose the anxiety of consequence, the consequence that our thinking and existence are historical—must recognize that, with the creation of the Common Era of history from nothing, from nothing beginning in extra-biblical paganism, extra-biblical paganism is not an option for human beings. It is not an option for two reasons (which ultimately are the same reason). From the point of view of extra-biblical paganism—which is no point of view but only that point of view which is ignorant of itself as a point of view—the natural law of contradiction is not an option but a given whose fate is always to be other than and opposed to itself. From the point of view of history, extra-biblical paganism, which is not an option in itself, becomes, for the chosen people, the option of idolatry, dualism, or transcendental illusion, that which reduces the thought and existence of others (including oneself) to nothing. Within the Common Era history is radically subversive, for, in revealing all thought and existence to begin with the golden rule of life, it shows all hierarchies of domination given in nature to be the options of idolatrous and illusory domination. History is the revelation that it is only that which becomes nothing—nothing based on the contradictory law of natural space and time—which can become somethir' something for which history as the book of life, as the story of hu· ın beings who freely think and exist, can account. History thus supports, as the very story of, all values whose account is the golden rule of life.

Unlike extra-biblical memory, which opposes beginnings and ends such that they reflect the contradictory images of natural space and time, historical memory binds together our beginning and ends, our past and our future. Whereas natural memory, based on the innate dispositions of sensibility and understanding, is never present to itself but is always other than and opposed to its thought and existence, historical memory, based on the critical faculties of faith and reason, those which constantly throw it into crisis, overcomes natural differences by uniting all peoples into the common story eternally present to all. Eternal life, in critical distinction from extra-biblical notions of immortality, describes the thought and existence of history. Eternal life is not located in a natural space and time whose immortal beginning or end is always other than or opposed to present life. Eternal life is the present, not the divided line of extra-biblical paganism whose adherence to the law of contradiction ineluctably forces people into a past or a future, a beginning or an end, both ignorant of and blind to the present. Rather, eternal life is the present as the presence of all those who choose to love God above all others and their neighbors as themselves. Eternal life, the presence of past and future as the fulfillment of time (and space) in the present, is the concentration of our thought and existence such that we remember the past as our future story and we remember the future as the eternal unveiling of the seventh seal of the past. Our thought and existence, precisely as historical, as created from nothing subject to the contradictions of nature, are eternal. We are eternally committed—faithfully and rationally—to living the golden rule of life. The commitment is for all time (and space); it is eternal; it is historical. History is its own eternal or absolute standard, the standard both of what is eternal and of what is merely natural (idolatrous).

The paradox of history as eternal—thought and existence—is that it is inconceivable and unimaginable outside the context of natural space and time. God is no more or less conceivable and imaginable outside his creation, his creation of human life from nothing natural, than is human being. The creation of thought and existence from "nothing natural" provides the very respect which we owe to nature. It has been revealed to us forever that nature is our limit: a limit to be respected, the limit of which we are the eternal stewards. The idolatry than which there is none more hideous is to think that we can achieve the immortality of nature without dying, by living immortally on analogy with the contradictory images of space and time, something eternally inconceivable and unimaginable to extra-biblical pagans. The notion that one can become immortal is a contradiction which generates biblical, that is, modern dualism. Either one is immortal—with extra-biblical pagans, and thus alike mortal, with all the contradictions of which one is ignorant. Or one both is and becomes eternal, eternally, that is, historically—with biblical men and women and their heirs. But to become immortal: that is the contradictory impossibility which generates the actual idols, false prophets and Antichrists which the Bible attacks with relentless fury from beginning to end and which Kierkegaard and Nietzsche, in their savage condemnation of Christendom, identify with the idolatry of Antichrist.

The critical distinction which the Bible introduces into the world is that between history (historical memory), as the eternal recollection (return) of natural opposites, and natural memory, as oblivion, the distinction between eternal life and natural death. The creation of eternal life, of historical thought and existence, from the contradictions of natural memory does not eliminate, on the level of nature, the natural cycle of generation and destruction, that which we moderns understand as the science of evolution. Rather, it is precisely because we become eternally present to ourselves in our historical thought and existence that we come to respect nature as our difference, indeed, as the mirror in which we ultimately see, not nature but ourselves. But the mirror remains, seducing us with its idolatrous images as it never seduces Narcissus. Because the relation between creation and nothingness, between spirit and nature, between life and death, between eternity and immortality, between metaphor and simile, between paradox and contradiction is so delicate, it constantly throws us into crisis—a crisis of faith, a crisis of reason—forcing us, ever again, to address the idols with which we identify our present. It takes enormous effort to sustain the anxiety of consequence, the consequence that we must give up, once and for all, both our lust to become immortal like nature and our outrage against nature that we are unable to lay down our historical burden of eternity for the immortality of the natural soul.

The historical life of eternal spirit, the recognition that eternity can only be lived historically, is never certain—for it eschews identification with the similes of nature—but it is also never uncertain. Historical life as the eternal story of humankind is true; it demands that its thought and existence be lived with the fullest commitment to truth (integrity, probity, conscientiousness, fairness, respect for others...). But it is also the recognition that truth is falsified as an idol the moment it is understood on terms analogous with natural certainty. Truth is not certain, nor is it uncertain, precisely because it is historical, because it is eternally subject to interpretation by others, as their interpretation is subject to interpretation by me. What is truth, the truth of history? Pilate asks. It is the presence of our lives, that which makes our lives present to ourselves, present to each other. Truth is the history of our lives, demanding from us the most intense, the most informed, the most passionate, both the most reasoned and the most faithful interpretation. Truth is historical and eternally subject to interpretation (as the truth) precisely because it is accessible to all, because all persons and peoples have the responsibility of making history—thought and existence—their history. There is only one history—of truth and interpretation. There is only one truth and interpretation—of history. The one history is eternally true and eternally subject to our historical interpretation. Either/or. Either choose history, eternally; or be eternally offended by your historical choice (by your choice of history, by the history of your choice). Either history is your choice; or you relinquish your historical choice to others. History is the eternal story that there is no choice but history, that there is no history but historical choice.

History, however, is not to be understood as the particular choices of a given period; for those whose choices dominate a particular period, as Rousseau so acutely observes, constantly strive to have their choices accepted as natural, certain, and immortal. The truths and their interpretations of any given period inevitably become the idols that must be deconstructed—faithfully and rationally. It is precisely because our choices reveal our thought and existence to abide not by the law of contradiction but by the golden rule of life that they constantly threaten to become idols, something inconceivable and unimaginable in the extra-biblical or non-modern world. But, because history is constantly open to our choice, we moderns have the eternal responsibility of undertaking to interpret history—to make history—according to the most exalted canon of truth, the thought and existence worthy of human beings, than which there is none more perfect.

III. THE SECULAR AS THE SELF OF DEMOCRACY

The only space and time in which we can make history—our own history, both personal and collective—is the secular city of democracy. When, in the early years of the fifth century of the Common Era, St. Augustine, in *The City of God*, produces the definitive critique of pagan antiquity, as embodied in the democracy of Hellenistic and, above all, the republic of Roman imperialism, he grounds his critique in the dialectic of the *civitas Dei* and the *civitas terrena*, the city of God and the earthly city. What Augustine shows us is that the thought and existence of humanity, unlike the contradictory life of extra-biblical peoples, are constituted as the secular world by the dialectic of the two cities, divine and human. The world in which human beings are to live in full possession of their thought and existence is not the world of extra-biblical paganism, whether that of mortal humans or that of immortal gods, who, because they are actually indistinguishable from each other, both are and are not themselves, in their blind opposition not only to each other but also to themselves, as we have seen. The world in which human beings are to live together, liberated from the natural law of contradiction, is the *saeculum*, the democratic age of the golden rule of loving God above all others and your neighbor as yourself. The secular age is to be understood, not according to the natural images of space and time, whose linear and circular similes are endlessly contradictory, but according to the historical metaphors of fulfillment, redemption, salvation, liberation, justification....

The secular world is that in which, as Augustine shows, fully anticipating Descartes, the knowledge possessed by human beings that they are deceived (that they are sinners) leads not to the contradictory opposition of the Cretan liar but to the ontological demonstration of the paradox of thought and existence. Because I am deceived—because I sin, because I live in the secular world—I know not merely that I am deceived but also and primarily what I am deceived about: my life, my thought and existence. The recognition of deception—Adam and Eve's sinful knowledge of good and evil; Descartes' doubt: I think, therefore, I am; Spinoza's desire consciously ignorant of its ends; Rousseau's chains—does not lead to the elimination of life through the law of contradictory fate whose presence is always other than its beginning and end. The recognition of the deception of sin leads, rather, to the confirmation, the affirmation, the demonstration, the confession of life as the thought and existence of men and women uniting their beginnings and ends in and through the presence of God. God comes to save not the wise, not those who are ineluctably contradicted by their vain attempt to seek to know the immortal otherness of fate endlessly opposed to their selves, but the foolish, the oxymoronic, those whose recognition of deception engages them in doing unto others as they would have them do unto them.

In presenting his story of the pilgrim city of God sojourning on earth, Augustine does not stray very far from the immediate structure of biblical narrative: Old Testament prophecy, New Testament fulfillment, the ultimate sanctification of the saved living in eternal joy with God. Still, when, in the final chapter of *The City of God*, Augustine describes the life of blessed redemption with God which the saints enjoy, he is careful to point out that the saints remember—they do not forget—that they were (are!) sinners, that they owe their salvation to God, that their identity with God is also the recognition of their (historical) difference from God. Salvation in heaven, in other words, does not wipe out the memory of sin, the history of humanity, the ontological proof which comes into thought and existence only through deception, in stark contrast to the conclusion of the *Odyssey*, where Zeus, in his immortal attempt to stop the cycle of mortal revenge from blindly beginning again—as the families of the suitors seek to wreak vengeance upon Odysseus and his son Telemachus for massacring their sons and brothers—wipes out the memory of the contradictory events celebrated in the poem. Unlike the *Odyssey*, which participates in the contradictory forgetting of its own narration—it celebrates the spectacular contradiction of ending with the forgetting of its beginning—*The City of God* ends by importing memory, history, sin, deception..., the secular city, directly into the heavenly city of our divine beginning. The end of the city of God remains united with the historical recollection of its beginning in the earthly city of sin. Indeed, we are forced to recognize that the end of the city of God is the beginning, the history, of the earthly city. The end is the beginning.

It is true that Augustine remains quite tentative about the implications of the dialectic of the two cities for present life. Not only are the structures of paganism still deeply entrenched in his world—Augustine is himself a pagan convert to Christianity—but the Germanic tribes are on their way to destroying the Roman Empire in the Latin West. The ensuing period of the Dark Ages—the age which is dark from the point of view of the nonhistorical enlightenment of Gibbon and his fellow classicists, not from the point of view of the city of God—is, however, the matrix of modern history, thanks to the convergence of two unique elements. The Germanic (barbaric!) tribes, which conquer the Latin West while converting with fervor to Christianity, and the Christian ascetics, who withdraw from the world to combine prayer and contemplation with copying classical texts, together preserve ancient civilization—the memory, the history, of pagan antiquity—while owing nothing of substance to it, unlike the Byzantine Empire of the Greeks, the direct successor of the Roman Empire. (The period of the Dark Ages also sees a critical development of Judaism and the rise and spread of Islam.)

Although Augustine remains, for the most part, oblivious to the implications of the dialectic of the city of God and the earthly city for a pagan world still largely resistant to spiritual, intellectual, and social and political transformation, he explicates this dialectic, which is, in fact, the principle of secular history, in clear, systematic, and comprehensive terms. Augustine shows that the life of human beings in the *saeculum* is constituted by the two cities in their relationship. The two cities represent neither the blind opposition between mortality and immortality, as found in extra-biblical paganism, nor the dualism between earth and heaven, as found in the idolatrous heresies of, for example, gnosticism (and repeated, as we have seen, in the modern dualism between post-modernism and pre-modernism). Rather, the two cities represent the creation of human thought and existence from nothing, from nothing which is subject to the contradictions of natural space and time. Because creation from nothing brings into our conscious existence the nature of contradiction and thus the contradictions which rule nature—but not human beings made in the image of God—we have the responsibility of grasping, faithfully and rationally, the natural oppositions between our innate faculties of sensibility and understanding and the natural oppositions between peoples which are based on these innate differences. The two cities represent our human task, the perseverance with which we must strive to embody the city of God—the golden rule of loving God above all others and our neighbor as ourselves—in the city of natural differences, distinctions, inequalities, oppositions, hatreds, oppressions, repressions.... The fact that these two cities remain entangled together unto the end of time, as Augustine insists, is but another indication that he recognizes (in principle, at least) that the end of time represents not some ultimate (finite) separation, on the model of either pagan opposition or idolatrous dualism, between the two cities, but the eternal fulfillment of earthly space and time through the heavenly promise of human freedom, equality, and solidarity.

The city of God is the eternal consummation of the city of earth, our very nature; it is not some idolatrously immortal space and time located, in dualistic opposition to the original garden of naturally immortal paradise, beyond our mortal space and time and thus only replicating their contradictions. As Augustine himself recognizes with a staggering sense of bemusement, wonderment, enthrallment, excitement, and joy: there is no time when there is no time. There is no creation when there is no creation. There is no God when there is no God. There are no human beings when there are no human beings. Nothing can come before or after God, for God himself is the very concept (existence) of before and after. There is no first or last time, for the very notion of first and last involves time as history, as the time of the *saeculum*. Nothing can come before or after time, creation, human beings, or history, for our very discourse, our very communication, is embedded in time for all time. Our task is not to eliminate time—through either the blind opposition of pagan contradiction or the willful dualism of idolatrous contradiction—but to render time creative, that is, historical, to make time secular, embodying the time of the two cities. Capturing the magnitude of Augustine's insight, we can say that there is no history when there is no history. History is its own creative standard, the standard of both what is historical and what is not historical (nothing is historical except what is historical).

Given the sophistication of Augustine's understanding of the dialectic of the two cities as simultaneously secular yet theological, we should not be surprised to see this dialectic subsequently split apart into the dualism of its two opposing sides. In the Middle Ages, Christian theologians characteristically identify the city of God with the Church (and especially with the hierarchy of ascetics and ecclesiastics, as distinct from the mass of lay people), in opposition to the earthly city, which they identify with the world of (female) flesh, nature, reason, politics, the people, paganism, an identification which Augustine had vigorously rejected and which his dialectic of the two cities eliminates for all time. In the early modern period, writers (followed, especially, by historians in the last century) characteristically identify the city of earth with the rise of secular values and institutions—science, democracy, freedom, reason—in opposition to the city of God—the Church, faith, religion, the Bible—an identification which Augustine had equally rejected and which his dialectic of the two cities eliminates for all time. I have omitted art—especially the visual arts and music—from either side of the dualistic opposition between the secular and the religious, because the very fact that art remains profoundly concerned with the expression of religious values, yet is clearly something new in the history of the church, vividly reminds us that we shall never be able to comprehend our history if we continue to oppose the two cities in the dualistic manner of the enlightened reason of a Gibbon. We must overcome the dualism of viewing the city of God as religious and the earthly city as secular by grasping that it is the dialectic, the relationship, between the two cities which is simultaneously religious and secular. It is only the dialectic of the two cities which will allow us to begin to comprehend how it is that Bach's *St. Matthew Passion* and Mozart's *Requiem* are the two greatest works of Enlightenment music. Gibbon's nonhistorical lament over the destruction of pagan wisdom by Christian obscurantism and superstition, in the decline and fall of the Roman Empire, will not take us far in appreciating—indeed, it will prevent our understanding—these works (not to mention the fact that their composers are also among the great creators of secular music).

The secular is the recognition that we live in the world of natural opposition but by the covenant of the golden rule which exposes to us the fact that nature itself can be redeemed from its fatal doctrine of contradictory opposites only from the point of view of spirit, of history. (Kant, in his transcendental deduction of the categories of possible experience, the categories of science whereby we comprehend the contradictions of nature without being blindly contradicted by them, shows that the categories by which we comprehend nature as the contradictory appearances of space and time transcend nature, that is, they belong to the thing-in-itself, to spirit, which cannot be thought to exist as natural objects are known to appear.) The secular, like history, begins and ends with the Bible; it expresses the dialectic of creation from nothing no more or less than does the religious. If one asks why it is—or what it is that we learn from contemplating the fact—that our world divides into the opposites of secular and religious, flesh and spirit, reason and faith..., the only answer which appears to me to be both simple and comprehensive—that is, true and consistently interpretable—is that these dialectical opposites represent the natural oppositions of the world: male and female, self and other, sensibility and understanding, those which are opposed to and other than themselves in the extra-biblical traditions of paganism and which, with the creation of the Bible from nothing as the thing-in-itself, become either the creative matrix (matter) of our salvation (liberation) or the charnel house of idolatrous dualism unable to embrace, to appropriate, the anxiety of historical consequence. It is only when we realize, profoundly, that we must constantly attempt to embody both sides of our nature in our lives, our lives individual and collective, that we shall be able to overcome the dualisms that divide us, both as individuals and as communities.

There is no importance as such to be attached to the term secular, but what the concept secular reminds us of, eternally, is that we must not allow the term religious to become the self-justifying (rationalizing) thing-in-itself. I have chosen, therefore, for the supreme representative of the relationship between the secular and the religious in my essay in thinking the dialectic of thought and existence and, ultimately, the dialectic of truth and interpretation: the ontological argument for thought and existence, alike divine and human. Neither side of the dualism, neither the secular nor the religious, is true in itself but only as it is interpreted in and through the truth of its dialectical opposite. Equally, neither the secular nor the religious—and each side of whatever pair of opposites—is to be interpreted except as each is the truth of and for the other. There is no magic as such in the notion of the secular; but, since the language of the secular has become so dominant in the terminology of our age, we should be especially critical of any self-justifying (rationalizing) tendencies on the part of those who identify themselves as secular in dualistic opposition to the religious. Indeed, it is by no means obvious that our age, notwithstanding the standard chorus of the pundits, is (any) less religious than the ages of Moses, Jesus, Augustine, or Anselm, not to mention the ages of Pascal, Bach, or Kierkegaard. In fact, a very good case can be made, as has been made by the apologists of the secular city, that our secular age is more profoundly and properly religious than any of the so-called religious ages of the past. It is precisely the secular which reveals the religious for what it is: the salvation of humankind. But it is equally the secular which reveals to us the fact that there is no more diabolical idolatry than that of religious sensibility when it opposes itself dualistically to what is truly secular. The so-called

Ages of Faith Reason, the thirteenth and eighteenth centuries, are both largely ages of superstition, like every age, each typically characterized (by historians!) according to the particular side of the dualism to which it is blindly wedded, religious or secular, in ignorant opposition to what properly characterizes the dialectic of history.

Contemplation of the dialectical relationship between the secular and the religious shows us that the concept of progress can be understood to be truly secular only when it is also interpreted as fundamentally religious. There is no progress outside creation from nothing, for there is no progress conceivable or imaginable within the extra-biblical doctrine of opposites according to which human beings are always other than and opposed to what they are in themselves. When progress enters the world, however, as the priority of the golden rule, the priority that we cannot progress further than treating God and neighbor as first, as the beginning or the priority of our lives, then we learn that progress is indeed a paradoxical or dialectical concept. Progress exists as the eternal deepening and widening of our human thought and existence—personal and collective—but it is also constantly endangered by the ever deeper and wider dualisms whose opposition the idolatry of *ressentiment* generates, the reduction of progress to either material (secular) or spiritual (religious) success, the dualistic varieties of which are endless.

The secular can be preserved from reduction to the contradictions of nature only when it is understood that it neither exists nor can be thought outside the biblical world. The secular embodies the ontological argument for the thought and existence of God no less than the ontological argument expresses the thought and existence of human beings. Not only is the secular not found in the Greek or any other extra-biblical people—for whom it is simply inconceivable and unimaginable—but also it is not found in the modern world in opposition to the religious, for then it but falls into the dualism of idolatry, being indistinguishable from a denatured conception of reason. The arguments of Descartes and Rousseau which I make central to my essay in thinking are properly viewed as secular, so long as secular is understood to be the concept whose truth can be interpreted only as the appropriation of, not the opposition to, the concept which cannot be thought except as religious existence (the existence of religion). The secular is not to be found in the extra-biblical doctrine of opposites, and it must not be surrendered to the biblical dualism of idolatry.

The secular is so important to the religious, as we have seen in our exposition of Augustine's *City of God*, for the precise reason that it shows us that the religious is expressed only in and through, but not by, the world of natural opposition. Whereas the language of religion reminds us that what is first for men and women is not to be found in the natural oppositions which divide them, the language of the secular equally reminds us that what is first, God, is to be found, not in the opposition of God to the world but in the relationship of God to the world, in our human relations, where each individual embodies God for the other as the other embodies God for each individual. The secular comprehends the dialectic of faith and reason, as the religious comprehends the dialectic of reason and faith. Individuals are completely free to choose one or the other bodies of expression, religious or secular, as appropriate for themselves and others; but they are not free to oppose either body of terminology dualistically to the other, for then they alienate their freedom to think and exist, and individuals are not free, as Rousseau reminds us, to alienate their own selfhood, their very thought and existence. It is the inalienable right of human beings to constitute their fundamental relationships, both personal and collective, as alike religious and secular. To oppose one dualistically to the other is to alienate one's right to both.

Central to a comprehensive notion of the secular is the thought and existence of democracy, our democratic thought and existence. Democracy will be understood as our inalienable right to judge the facts of human life only when, once again, we do not confuse concepts with terms. Notwithstanding the Greek origin of democracy, linguistically, democracy as that which can be conceived only as existing and whose existence is the sole concept of our thought is created by the Bible from nothing, from nothing subject to the natural oppositions between human beings. Democracy for the Greeks, as for all extra-biblical peoples, is only one of three basic versions of the ruler-ruled opposition: the rule of one over others (monarchy or autocracy), the rule of some over others (aristocracy), and the rule of many over others (democracy). As Hegel astutely points out, however, the modern (that is, biblical) notion of democracy as the rule of all over all—embodying the golden rule of law—is inconceivable and unimaginable to all extra-biblical peoples, including the Greeks. There is nothing in natural space and time which provides the image of all, equally and freely, subject to and ruling all, although there are natural images of one, some, or many ruling over others. The only image which reveals to both you and me that I am subject to you as you are subject to me—in the equality, freedom, and solidarity of our relationships—is the paradox represented both by God, to speak theologically, and by the people, what Rousseau calls the General Will, to speak in the secular terms of political theory. The moment human beings undertake to establish their relationships on what is immediately or naturally between them—their roles, possessions, power, race, gender, class, age, position...—they divide into hierarchical relations of domination as distinct from relations based on equality, freedom, and solidarity.

In comprehending democracy as that which cannot be thought except existing and which cannot exist except as thought, it is critically important to realize that democracy applies no less to the individual than to the community, no less to the person than to the collective. It is the self, both individual and communal, which is democratic, not simply the state over against the individual. The self, whose thought and existence are democratic, alike individual and communal, is absent from the extra-biblical world of opposition, where the self, whether individual or collective, is ineluctably divided against itself. The doctrine of opposites divides individuals against themselves (so Socrates and Oedipus), just as it divides individuals (and communities) against communities (so Socrates and Oedipus, on the one hand, and the cities of Athens and Thebes, on the other). The self of whose thought (concept) and existence Socrates is ignorant applies alike to himself and to the *polis*.

In the earlier dialogues of Plato (the term dialogue having nothing to do in principle with the concept dialogue which cannot be thought except existing), Socrates shows that both the soul of the individual within the *polis* and the collectivity of individuals which constitutes the *polis* are subject to the law of contradiction which demonstrates that the appearances of the self, both individual and collective, are always other than and opposed to what the self is in itself. The self is utterly contradictory. The good (justice, virtue, piety, wisdom...), whether individual or collective, cannot be taught either by or to the self, whether individual or collective. To teach is to subject both teacher and learner to the same contradictory law of opposites which all human seeking or activity (life) generates. To teach is to seek, and to seek is to show that you (both teacher and disciple) do not possess, that you do not know, that you are ignorant of that which you are seeking (teaching or learning). Either you teach (learn) what you do not know, or you know what you do not teach (learn). The law of contradiction inexorably divides the self between teaching (learning) that of which it is ignorant (the law of contradiction) and knowing that which cannot be taught (or learned: the law of contradiction). The moment one begins teaching (learning) the law of contradiction one inevitably begins to generate opposition between the subject teaching (the teacher) and the subject taught (the good), within the individual self, and between the subject teaching (the teacher) and the subject taught (the pupil), within the collective self. Teaching, like all extra-biblical activity, because it reflects the doctrine of opposites, ineluctably presupposes the ruler-ruled relation of the self, both individual and collective. The self, both individual and collective, is political, and, as political, it is utterly ignorant of the good of the *polis*, which is both individual and collective; for the good, the good (of the) law of contradiction, can never be taught (learned), and it can be known (but never taught or learned) only by those who are dead to the contradictory appearance of the *polis*, that is, to the law of contradiction itself, to fate.

In contrast to his earlier dialogues, in which Plato has Socrates represent aristocratic opposition to rule by democratic ignorance, in the *Republic* Plato reverses (and thus does not alter) his point of view. He now has Socrates present the opposite side of the argument, that of aristocratic rule over others, and, consistent with the Greek tradition of rhetoric and sophistry, Socrates argues that those who rule over others rule over them for their own good, of which they are ignorant. In showing that both the soul and the *polis* are composed of parts, each of which has a ruling (wise) part ruling over a ruled (ignorant) part, Socrates only indicates (to us) how systematically (blindly) Plato adheres to the law of contradiction as that which rules in its wisdom over his own contradictory ignorance and appearance. We may recall that Socrates is careful to indicate, completely consistent with the Greek tradition of *sophia*, that the rule of the philosopher-kings, who unite might and right, force and justice, in their rule over those ignorant of the good, has its origin in the contradictory myth of the four metals. According to this noble myth, the souls of the philosopher-kings spring from the earth, that is, from nature, from that which is secret, without demonstration, without beginning or end. Thus we see that the philosopher-kings, who claim to rule over others for their own good (of which they are ignorant), locate the beginning, the demonstration, of their rule in the myth of nature, in that which is without beginning or demonstration, in that of which they are totally ignorant. Those naturally born with golden souls are superior to those who are born with silver, iron, or bronze souls. It then follows logically that those who cannot demonstrate the beginning (or principle) of their natural rule blindly contradict the law of contradiction by claiming to rule over the actual *logos* of the ruled by uniting the contradictory opposites of right and might, of philosophy and politics, into the possibility of their *logos*, that is, into the logical discourse of contradiction whose appearances—in the other!—endlessly contradict it. In the world of extra-biblical paganism the contradiction of others' (actual) ignorance always blindly reflects your own (possible) ignorance. The myth of rulers ruling naturally over the ruled has no beginning or end, no principle, no demonstration. It begins and ends in the ignorance and blindness of nature whose mortal appearances are immortally contradictory.

It is useful to recall that Aristotle, consistent, as always, with Socrates and Plato—for, however much he opposes them, he, like them, adheres, blindly and ignorantly, to the law of contradiction—also shows that both soul and *polis* are equally divided against each other. Following strictly the inexorable demands of the *logos* of contradiction, Aristotle divides the soul between its psychic characteristics, involving sensibility and understanding (the organic soul), and its noumenal characteristics (the logical soul or *nous*). The opposition which Aristotle establishes between soul and *nous* provides a veritable catalogue of the heroic opposites whose natural, that is, mythical, battles shape the life and death of all extra-biblical peoples. Aristotle shows that the soul, whose infinitely many, imperfect, mortal, metamorphosing, contradictory, and changing appearances in life are always other than what it is in itself (*nous*), is opposed to the *nous*, whose one, finite, perfect, immortal, permanent, separated, and unchanging thought is without any memory of its appearance in life (as soul). The memory of *nous* is the catharsis or purgation of all its contradictory appearances as soul. The memory of *nous* is a total blank (like Plato's Forms). It is the catharsis of thinking thinking (itself) thinking, thinking utterly purged and devoid of—dead to—the appearance of the contradictory otherness of the soul.

That the self of the individual is the *nous* whose contradictory memory of having, in the beginning, been a soul in appearance has been wiped out or purged, in the end, Aristotle duplicates in his presentation of the collective self of the *polis*. As always, Aristotle is brilliantly logical (that is, he is blinded by the ignorance imposed by the law of contradiction whose fate is always other than and opposed to its appearances, including the appearances of *nous* called Aristotle). In his discussion of politics, Aristotle recognizes from the outset that the politician (the good citizen) and the good politician (the good man) are forever divided against each other and also themselves—the politician being the one whose nature (or *telos*) is political, that is, he is a member of the *polis*. The politician lives within the *polis* as he lives within his soul. He is subject to contradiction by appearance; his memory is utterly contradictory. The good politician lives separated in the separated *polis* of the separated *nous*. He is purged of all contradictory appearance. He is utterly devoid of contradictory memory. The politician is the one whose good changes relative to the changing good of the changing rule of the actual *polis*, as political rule endlessly revolves through the cycle of one, some, and many rulers ruling over others (autocracy, aristocracy, and democracy). Political good is thus subject to endless metamorphosis. But the good whose metamorphosing appearances contradict the good as that which is one and unchanging in itself is precisely the good of which all human beings as politicians, members of the *polis*, are ignorant, as Socrates demonstrates. The good politician, in contrast to the politician whose good is always changing relative to the changing rule of the *polis*, is the one whose end is the perfect, unchanging good, total identity with the good. The good politician is the one whose *nous* is dead in thought to the vital existence of the *polis* whose appearances endlessly contradict the thought (form) of the good. The good politician can live only in the good *polis*, the *polis* identical with the good. But, since the good *polis* is to the *polis* what the *nous* is to the soul, the good *polis* must be that which is one, finite, perfect, immortal, permanent, separate, unchanging, without any memory of appearance—that is, its memory has been purged of all contradictory appearances—unlike the *polis* which constantly turns through the three orders of rulers ruling over the ruled. Whereas the politician lives in the actual *polis*, ignorant of and contradicting the good, the good politician lives (completely dead) in the good *polis*, whose logical possibility is purged of all life and memory. The law of contradiction is the fate ruling indifferently over each, showing that the actual life of appearances—in soul and *polis*—blindly contradicts its logical possibilities and that the possible death of logic—in *nous* and the good *polis*—is oblivious to the actual appearance of contradiction.

As the wheel of fortune fatally revolves, endlessly reversing actuality and possibility, soul and *nous*, the politician and his three orders of rule over others and the good politician and his rule in the good *polis*, the one thing stationary is the *stasis* of the contradictory opposition between rulers and ruled, within both individual and *polis*. (Aristotle's term for the revolutionary metamorphosis through which the *polis* passes in endless appearance but during which its ruler-ruled opposition remains unchanged in reality is *stasis*.) Mortal appearances change; the reality of the fatal domination of life, individual and political, by the immortal law of contradiction is unchanging. The natural division between appearance and reality, between sensibility and understanding, is irreconcilable on the basis of the logic of contradiction. Both individual and collective are equally subject to the fatal doctrine of opposites. This helps us to understand that the (aristocratic) opposition on the part of Socrates, Plato, and Aristotle to Athenian democracy is a variation within the static logic of contradiction, the natural generation of whose oppositions ineluctably leads to the nemesis of natural destruction. Athenian democracy, together with its opposition, has nothing at all to do with the beginning or principle of democracy, with the democratic leap out of the law of contradiction into the ontological argument which demonstrates that there is one concept which cannot begin to be thought except as it exists democratically and that there is one existence which cannot begin to exist except as the concept of democracy.

We now see clearly the fundamental difference between the blinding either-or opposition which extra-biblical paganism generates (and by which it is also destroyed) and the binding either-or choice which the Bible creates from nothing as the secular dialectic overcoming and appropriating the nature of pagan opposition which otherwise is rationalized in the terms of idolatrous dualism whose effects are ultimately nihilistic. For extra-biblical peoples, there is no choice of either/or, no choice of doing unto others as you would have them do unto you, no choice of the other as yourself, no choice, in short, no conception of choice, will, or freedom as that which can exist only as you think (will) it and as that which can be thought (willed) only as you exist in it. To choose one, in the extra-biblical world, is always to find oneself opposed by one other than (what) one (is). It is inconceivable and unimaginable by the law of contradiction that—in the same space and time—one can be both one and other than one, the one other or the other one. For biblical or modern peoples, however, the *condition humaine* has been transformed by the reduction of natural oppositions to the nothing from which the thought and existence of all peoples are created as one, the infinite (indivisible) one which is true only as we are all related in the democratic mutuality of equality, freedom, and solidarity, not the finite one of paganism which ineluctably divides into contradictory ones blindly opposed to and ignorant of each other.

That all are one and one is all is the democratic choice of either-or. To be confronted with the choice of either/or is to recognize that to choose—faithfully and rationally—is to choose such that one does not discriminate against others (including oneself) by falling into the idolatrous dualisms of life-denying nihilism. We never choose between two options, as I indicated in an earlier chapter. What we choose, always, in choosing is choice itself, the choice of self, the democratic self both individual and communal, both self and other, both God and the human person. We have no choice but to choose to love God above all others and our neighbor as ourselves. The choice, however, is hard, demanding, perplexing, ambiguous, oxymoronic, paradoxical.... We are constantly seduced into reducing our either-or choice of democracy, in which one is all and all are one, to the choice of some over others, with the result that we deny to others the dignity of choice, a choice inconceivable and unimaginable in extra-biblical paganism.

The impasse of extra-biblical paganism cannot be overcome by going further than Socrates, for there is no place at all to go in the extra-biblical world—one cannot even begin in the contradictory nature of space and time, as Socrates so brilliantly demonstrates. The only solution to the contradictory *aporia*, which shows that the way in space and time is blocked by the logic of contradiction, is to begin, to begin anew, to begin such that every beginning is always to begin with the beginning, to begin for the first time with the self, as one and all, as democratic, both individual and social, both divine and human, both religious and secular. There is no beginning (or end) in nature. The only beginning is in the free choice of beginning, in the thought and existence of the democratic self which is simultaneously individual and communal, just as God is both covenant and person. The self understood as the thought and existence of the individual (in the community) is no less democratic than the self understood as the thought and existence of the community (of individuals). The self is relationship. The relationship of self is its otherness, again, both individual and collective. The self is to be understood democratically in the terms of the golden rule, for it is only the golden rule (with its infinite expressions) which provides that relationship which throws the self—again, both individual and collective—into crisis, into the recognition of its doubt, deception, or sin. The self is always becoming historically what it is (not), until and unless it gives up its dialectical burden and falls into the idolatry of dualism (the false images of progress, immortality, success, etc.). The dialectic of being and becoming—in thought and existence, equally—expresses the *condition humaine*, whether viewed individually or collectively.

The democratic self, both individual and collective, alike religious and secular, is omnipotent, absolute, unerring, and autonomous. God is traditionally said to be omnipotent (although skeptics properly scoff at dogmatic representations of omnipotence when they are naively if not dualistically conceived), and Kierkegaard calls the relationship of the personal and the divine selves the absolute relation to the absolute. Rousseau says that the general will cannot err. Kant views the self as autonomous: a law unto itself. I have already presented the dialectic of truth and interpretation as absolute, the absolute standard of itself, the standard of both what is absolute and what is not absolute but relative (certain or uncertain, that is, immediate). But what is omnipotent, absolute, unerring, and autonomous is the self as relationship, the fact that we (individuals and communities) do unto others as we would have them do unto us, that we love God above all others and our neighbors as ourselves. God, self, and community—all terms for the same concept which cannot be thought except existing and which cannot exist except as thought—are the thing-in-itself which cannot be known (through our innate dispositions of sensibility and understanding) except in their natural appearances but which can—must!—be thought, willed, loved, practiced, lived... as our highest, our supreme, our universal, our unique priority.

It is important to realize that the absolute terms of the spirit—of truth and interpretation—fall back into the idolatry of dualism, ultimately, nihilism (annihilation), if the nothing from which they are created is not understood as the limit which their very omnipotence recognizes and embraces. Omnipotence does not mean that God can do anything he wants, anything which is arbitrary. Omnipotence is the free or obligatory recognition of limits on God's part. God is not free to violate either nature, which he reveals to be nothing in itself, or thought and existence, whether divine or human, which he creates from nothing, from nothing arbitrary or contradictory. If biblical miracles are viewed as God's intervention in the natural order of things, if God is held to contradict nature, then God will be reduced to the very contradictions of nature which it is the task of the doctrine of *creatio ex nihilo* to overcome. Thought and existence, both divine and human, are liberated from natural contradiction (the nature of contradiction) only because the contradictions of nature are revealed for what they are in themselves—nothing. The doctrine of creation from nothing thus reveals that knowledge of nature—natural science—is grounded in the concept of spirit—in the ontological argument of thought and existence—and not thought and existence in nature. Thus Rousseau teaches that fact is created (from nothing) by right, not right by (contradictory) fact. The first is the miracle (that we argue from right to fact), not the second (the idolatrous reduction of right to fact). The divine miracles central to biblical narrative are not the violation of nature or the contradiction of natural law on the part of God. The notion that natural appearances are contradictory is paganism rationalized in the idolatry of dualism and falsely called theology, as we saw in our discussion of the idolatry of creationism.

God cannot violate himself. God cannot contradict himself. God is omnipotent, absolute, unerring, and autonomous. God cannot be other than God. God—as freedom, will, choice—cannot choose, cannot will, is not free not to be God. God cannot be other than his thought and existence, except as the other which can be thought only as the existing one (one existence) and can exist only as the one concept (the concept of one). God cannot violate his thought and existence. God cannot contradict the covenant of thought and existence, whether the covenant be viewed as divine or human (which does not mean that God's actions, when we use that style of narration, do not often appear arbitrary or contradictory to human beings who have lost themselves in the common sense dualisms of idolatry, or that God is not often manipulated by dogmatists for their own arbitrary and contradictory ends). In creating thought and existence from nothing, from nothing which is subject to the contradictory nature of space and time, God is creator, but he is not a scientist, and he is no creationist. God does not create nature, as such, from nothing. He shows, rather, that nature is nothing, nothing in itself. Nature is not the thing-in-itself but the appearances of the thing-in-itself in natural space and time. In creating thought and existence from nothing, from nothing subject to the contradiction of nature, human beings are liberated from the fate of natural ignorance and blindness. It is the very creation of their humanity from nothing which reveals to men and women the paradoxical nature of natural contradiction, which reveals to them, as subjects of nature, that they die naturally (no more immortal than mortal) and that their thought and existence are eternal (neither mortal nor immortal). The omnipotence of God is thus subject to the critical limitation that his thought and existence preserve their separation from nature, with the result that his thought and existence cannot become immortal, according to the extra-biblical doctrine of opposites, and they cannot become mortal, according to the idolatrous doctrine of dualism. It is only through the concept of omnipotence, divine or human, that the notion of power, what Nietzsche calls the will to power, can be understood as relationship and liberated from the hierarchy of natural domination.

Human beings are omnipotent in precisely the same sense that God is omnipotent. Human power—the power of human thought and existence—is infinite. Human power is democratic. (Nietzsche's vitriolic attacks on democratic equality as leveling are launched against, not democracy as the preservation and enhancement of true difference, but mass society as composed of indifferent manipulators and consumers.) Human power is thought or willed not on analogy with finite nature but according to the leap of infinite spirit outside nature—and thus it must be (it has the obligation of being) profoundly conscious (thoughtful) of the limits of existence. Our conscious existence is limited to the other, to God and neighbor, to the self of democracy, both individual and social. We must not confuse natural power, whose limit is the laws of nature, and moral power, whose limit is our neighbor, as I indicated in an earlier chapter. Our will to power is also limited in the sense that we must radically eschew all idolatry of claiming to know our self as the natural thing immortal in itself. Nature is the very limit to our omnipotence, for how we know nature reveals the paradox of human thought and existence. I, a subject, know nature, as a finite object in space and time, altogether differently from how I know human subjects, other selves (including my own self), which are infinite and which I know only in that relationship of self which is the golden rule. The self as the general will, both individual and collective, thus never errs, as Rousseau says, because it always wills the truth. It always wills that its truth be subject to the interpretation of all, as all will that their truth be subject to my interpretation. In the dialectic of constantly willing the truth of interpretation the self brings to light, uncovers, probes, examines, questions, criticizes... the chains of its enslavement to deceptions, inhibitions, dualisms, idolatries, oppressions, repressions.... The notion that the self— God, individual, and community—is unerring does not mean that deception, error, or sin is absent from the world. On the contrary, what it means is that the golden rule, in the infinity of its expressions, is present such that we can comprehend our deception only within the structure of faith and reason, within our commitment to the absolute creation of truth and interpretation from nothing, from nothing which is deceptive. It is solely because creation is from nothing deceptive that we constantly confuse truth and interpretation with deceptive idols, with that which is given immediately (naturally!) in our customary thought and existence, this custom being represented, as always, in terms both religious and secular. The self—God, individual, community—is equally absolute or autonomous. The absolute is the absolute of relationship, the relationship of absolute selves, just as autonomy (self-law) means a law unto itself for all selves in their relationships.

Such concepts as omnipotence, the absolute, inerrancy, and autonomy are dangerous—as are the concepts of truth and interpretation!—for they are constantly subject to conflation and confusion with and reduction to the idolatrous terms of certainty (dogmatism) which, in their turn generate, as we have seen, the idolatrous terms of their dualistic opposite, uncertainty (skepticism). But it is precisely the democratic self as omnipotent, absolute, unerring, and autonomous which, because it is neither certain nor uncertain but true and accessible to the interpretation of all, is historical. For history is itself omnipotent, absolute, unerring, and autonomous, but not in the sense that every historical claim is true or completely true, for historical claims are constantly one-sided, distorted, ideological, partisan, etc. Rather, history is omnipotent or absolute in the sense that we have no choice but to view human (and divine) thought and existence within the framework of history. It is only because the historical framework includes all selves, individual and communal, that we can discern the inequalities, distortions, and injustices of past history and undertake to overcome them in our future relations. History is unerring, not in the sense that the past or the future is perfect but in the sense that the dialectic of past and future means that the past of all is subject to the future interpretation of all. The thought and existence of all selves, individual and collective, grow, develop, and enrich their capacity for comprehending their errors solely within the dialectic of truth and interpretation. History is autonomous, a law unto itself, not in some pseudo-Hegelian sense that it takes place over our heads without our choice, but in the sense that we have no choice but to choose to be historical. The question is what we shall do with our history, not whether or not we shall be historical. Indeed, if we do not make history our question, to which our answer is, always, to make our thought and existence autonomous, then history will be autonomous in the idolatrous sense that it is the history of some for some and not the history of all for all.

That the self—individual and collective—lives in the world of natural opposition but of the secular world of democracy captures the dialectic of Augustine's city of God and city of earth. The city of God—heaven or salvation—is not the religious city in opposition to the secular city of earthly life. The city of God is the secular fulfillment of our earthly life, the liberation of our natural opposition from blind contradiction such that we can become responsible for our human relations, both personal and collective. If human error, deception, or sin (including our abuse of the language of God) is identified directly with our earthly life, in opposition to our religious values, then we shall fall into the idolatrous dualisms dividing the life of reason from the life of faith. We shall be unable to comprehend how it is that it is precisely our secular life which is the democratic life of the golden rule according to which the natural differences dividing individuals and communities can be overcome in the name of the universal values of equality, freedom, and solidarity.

The unique value of secular discourse is that it reminds us, eternally, that the heavenly promise of earthly fulfillment is to be found solely in our human relations, in the secular self insofar as it is simultaneously personal and communal. From the point of view of the secular we recognize that there is no city of God located in some immortal space and time outside this present world after death. For, as Augustine ecstatically recognizes, there is no space where there is no space; there is no time when there is no time. The claim that there is an immortal space after death which is no space and an immortal time after death which is no time only replicates the spatial and temporal contradictions of nature such that we see that immortality is the projection of dualisms, which have not been freely, lovingly, truthfully—democratically!—dealt with within this world in a fittingly secular fashion, into another world of spatial and temporal opposition. The only way in which these dualisms can be truly identified and interpreted is in recognizing that the secular self is itself the realization, the fulfillment, the consummation of the city of God.

But not only is secular discourse uniquely valuable in appropriating theological rhetoric, it is also uniquely dangerous. So easily does the secular becomes associated with what is immediately rational, natural, empirical, or earthly that Rousseau's argument that we deduce fact from right is lost and we fall into the truly anti-democratic, anti-human idolatry of deducing the right of human beings—their thought and existence—from immediate fact, from the contemporary structures of hierarchical domination. The only way in which we can preserve the secular from replicating the dualism between faith and reason is to recognize that the secular, precisely like the religious, expresses the paradox—the miracle—of the creation of human thought and existence from nothing, from nothing which is subject to the contradictions of natural space and time. If we fail to recognize that our secular life is the fulfillment of divine creation, then we shall fall into the fatal dualism whereby we either elevate the religious to natural (immortal) opposition in the next world or reduce the secular to natural (mortal) opposition in this world. The secular is no more to be associated directly with the oppositions to which all peoples are naturally subject than is the religious. The secular, like the religious, expresses the democratic solidarity in which all differences—the infinite variety of human thought and existence—are to be respected so long as they involve the equality and the freedom of all for all. The secular is the recognition that God is the first—and last—democrat; for it is only because God creates human thought and existence from nothing, from nothing which does not involve and express democracy, that the world as the *saeculum* is the proper home of all men and women. That God is the first and last democrat—whether the city of God is conceived as republican, socialist, conservative, or liberal, as rightist, leftist, or centrist, it is first and last democratic—shows that the sole subject of divine creation is the secular self, individual and communal, and that the sole subject of human creation is the divine self, individual and communal. Democracy is omnipotent, absolute, unerring, and autonomous as the relation of selves who recognize the creation of God to be secular life.

IV. CONCLUSION: THE WORLD OF THE SECULAR AS CREATION FROM NOTHING

The world of the secular the Bible creates from nothing. In redeeming space and time from the contradictions of nature to which the beginnings and ends of extra-biblical peoples are forever subject, the Bible narrates the history of the people whose creative choice is the secular covenant of democracy. The secular is neither the natural opposition of space and time, whose contradictions are always other than and opposed to the nature of what the self, both individual and collective, is in itself, nor the dualistic opposition between the self and its appearances in space and time, whose contradictions reduce one side of the dualism to that which is not natural, to nothing natural, to the very nothing from which the secular world of historical space and time is created. The very thought (concept) that nothing exists, the very existence of nothing as a thought, is utterly absent from the world of extra-biblical paganism whose first, indemonstrably certain principle, reflecting its beginning with the law of contradictory blindness and ignorance, is that nothing comes from nothing, the contradictory opposite of which is the first, indemonstrably certain principle that everything comes from everything. The very thought that nothing exists, plus the notion that existence is the very nothing thought, creates not only the freedom to think and to exist but also its dualistic opposition, the idolatry of annihilation, which undertakes to reduce its opposite to nothing, a thought whose existence is inconceivable to extra-biblical peoples. The fearful paradox of the Bible is that, precisely because thought and existence, both divine and human, express creation from nothing—from nothing which, in itself, is subject to the contradictions of nature—they also involve the idolatry of nihilism—the reduction of thought and existence to everything contradictory in nature.

In the extra-biblical world nothing comes from nothing—nothing is not—and everything comes from everything—everything is. Everything both is and is not, simultaneously, both contradicting the law of contradiction and obeying the law of contradiction. That this *aporia* captures the classical opposition between Parmenides and Heraclitus—everything is (nothing moves); nothing is (everything moves)—only shows, in concrete fashion, the ineluctable fate to which all peoples who view themselves in terms of the images of natural generation and destruction are subject. There is no beginning in the world whose thought and existence are forever hidden within the fatal secret of the contradictions of natural space and time, the endless metamorphoses of which reflect the opposed positions that nothing comes from nothing and that everything comes from everything, simultaneously (in the same space and time and thus in no space and time). The opposition between mortality and immortality is but one traditional exemplification of this endless contradiction. In the extra-biblical world each position is always other than and opposed to, both ignorant of and blind to, what it is in itself, and what it is in itself is that, in life, in the beginning, in generation, it is contradictory, and that, in death, in the end, in destruction, it is no less contradictory, for that which is destroyed cannot be "nothing," and thus the end is but the contradiction of the beginning, which is everything.

There is only one alternative to, one choice other than, the extra-biblical law of natural contradiction for which nothing comes from nothing and everything comes from everything. This is that alternative, that choice which is inconceivable as existing (which does not exist as thought) in extra-biblical paganism and which the Bible shows to be that alternative to which there is no alternative, that choice which we cannot choose but choose. There is no alternative to thought and existence as their own alternative. There is no choice which is not its own standard, the standard of both what constitutes choice and what does not constitute choice (evasion, falsehood, deception, lying...). The one, and universal, alternative to the nature of extra-biblical contradiction is the choice to think and to exist, in freedom, equality, and solidarity with others. What the Bible, in so radical, so perplexing, so fateful a way demonstrates to us is that we can begin to think and to exist, that we can establish the principle of thought and existence as the inheritance of all human beings, only if we embrace the paradox of reducing nature—the natural contradictions of space and time—to nothing and of creating our secular world of human relations from nothing, from nothing subject to the natural contradictions of space and time. The "everything" (being nothing) and the "nothing" (being everything) of the extra-biblical world are reversed, but this reversal of the law of natural contradiction can escape the contradictory reversals of nature only if it is a reversal which is irreversible, consequential, and historical, only if it involves and expresses the freedom of thought and existence (what theologians call providence and Kant self-determination).

When the Bible shows that everything is created from nothing so that it can become everything creative, it transforms the opposition of fate into the story of free beginnings. The secular world comes into thought and existence as the history of humankind repeating the story of creation and fall: everything must be revealed to be nothing (in itself) in order for it to become everything (in our human relations). The leap or gap between being and becoming everything is precisely nothing, the fall from the paradise of natural contradiction into the secular world of human relations, the moment of recognition, the revelation, the miracle that we are now free to begin loving God above all others and our neighbor as ourselves. The dialectic of being and becoming, the liberation from the fatal domination of the natural opposition of contradictory space and time, which both is and is not, is the beginning, the irreversible beginning, which must be chosen in order to be chosen. There is no beginning when (where) there is no beginning. We cannot begin in order to begin, except within the paradoxical beginning that we have already begun. There is no history when (where) there is no history. We do not begin outside history and then discover history. Rather, we begin historically and then discover—through the paradox of revelation (the revelation of the paradox)—our non-creative, our non-historical beginning in extra-biblical paganism. We discover that, because history is our beginning, we conjure up—in the paradoxical stories of creation, paradise and fall, and the call of Abraham from the pagan world of the tower of Babel—the world of non-history from which the freedom to think and to exist within the dialectic of creation from nothing is absent. We discover that, where and when the secular does not exist as our sole thought and the thought of the secular is not our sole existence, there is no beginning, no history, no creativity.

Because everything creative comes from nothing, from nothing which is not creative—of human thought and existence—there is nothing which is not creative—of human thought and existence. The dialectic of creation and nothing is precisely that captured by the ontological argument that nothing exists outside (its) thought and that nothing thinks (is thought) outside (its) existence. The ambiguity which the preposition "outside" creates in us—is it spatial or temporal?—properly characterizes the paradox that outside (except for) nothing—in space and time—we should not be able to begin to think and to exist, to exist within our thought and to think within our existence. Outside of nothing we should not be able to think everything as our existence and to exist within everything as our thought. In looking upon everything subject to the natural contradictions of space and time as nothing—in itself—but as everything—in us—the Bible recognizes extra-biblical paganism to be everything creative—for us—but only insofar as it is understood to be nothing—in itself. The natural world of extra-biblical paganism is not the secular world in itself, for in itself it is nothing; it becomes the secular world—for us—when we choose it, when we liberate it from the fatal ignorance and blindness of the law of contradiction, when we begin within it, when we begin thinking and existing within it, something inconceivable and unimaginable within its own terms, which are always other than and opposed to the concept of their existence (the existence of their concept). To begin within the world of extra-biblical paganism is always to begin separate from it in thought and existence, to repeat, ever again, the paradox that history is the eternal revelation within the *saeculum* of the providential story that everything is created from nothing so that it can become everything creative. The secular is everything creatively revealed to human thought and existence, the revelation that it is only that which is not creative in itself, the nature of contradictory space and time, which can become the creation of our thought and existence.

What is so curious—paradoxical, oxymoronic, ironic...—about the creation of the secular world from nothing, from nothing which is natural in itself, is that it must hold within its conception of existence (and within the existence of its concept) the possibility of nothing which does not become creatively everything (or the possibility of everything which does not undergo the creation from nothing). The contradictory world of extra-biblical paganism can be made or becomes creative but only on the terms of the biblical doctrine of creation, not on its own terms of the fatal law of contradiction. In order for the extra-biblical world of paganism to become created it must be chosen, it must begin, something inconceivable and unimaginable in its own terms. The secular must then always preserve the limit of what lies outside its revelation of creation as reflecting the doctrine of opposites, the opposition between nothing and everything, with the middle between them, the secular life of thought and existence, forever excluded.

Precisely because there is no alternative to, no choice other than, beginning with everything created from nothing in itself so that it can become everything which it is in itself, which is that it can be thought only existing, the Bible reveals not only that the dialectic of thought and existence is totally other than the doctrine of opposites but also that it is constantly subject to reduction to the idolatry of dualistic opposites. Once the critical distinction between everything and nothing is revealed to embody the leap of faith and reason from the law of contradictory nature into human thought and existence, the possibility is equally created that the gap between being and becoming, the nothing which extra-biblical paganism forever hides within the fate of contradictory ignorance and blindness, will become the idolatrous dualism of opposites. The idolatry of dualism is truly diabolical or Satanic because it involves the reduction of those opposed to you to nothing, to that which is in itself nothing but the contradictions of space and time, that from which everything is created. Once thought and existence are liberated from the ignorance and blindness of the law of contradictory nature, then human beings find themselves burdened with the fear and trembling of conceiving of themselves as things-in-themselves whose existence must be distinguished from their appearances as the objects of possible experience in natural space and time. With the doctrine of creation from nothing a critical distinction between human life and nature is constituted such that everything can be created from nothing so long as, and only so long as, we relinquish, forever, all possibility of knowing our thought and existence as the natural objects of space and time are known. It is equally the case that, with the doctrine of creation from nothing, the science of nature emerges as the body of natural laws which can explain the phenomena of space and time insofar as, and only insofar as, they are liberated from contradiction, and natural phenomena can be liberated from contradiction only if they are shown to be grounded not in themselves but in the thought and existence of human beings.

The paradox which the science of nature presents to us is the critical distinction between nature as it reflects the doctrine of opposites within the extra-biblical tradition, on the one hand, and nature as it embodies the dialectical distinction between thought and existence (as that which nature is in itself) and the appearances of thought and existence (as the objects of nature), on the other. Within the extra-biblical tradition, nature is contradictory, and what is natural is always ignorant of and blind to its own contradictions. What ultimately represents nature is fate, for which there is no natural representation which is not fatally contradictory, which does not contradict fate. Because nature is both thought and existence (soul and body...) and thus always neither, it endlessly reflects the contradictory doctrine of opposites for and in which there is no beginning. That which is natural can never know itself to be natural, and thus we have returned to the classical *aporia* according to which nothing natural comes from nothing natural and everything natural comes from everything natural.

Within the biblical tradition, however, nature, although it is not contradictory in itself, so readily can and does become contradictory, this second type of contradiction being utterly inconceivable and unimaginable within extra-biblical paganism. The nature of contradiction—the contradiction of nature—within the tradition of extra-biblical peoples does not exist as thought and is not thought as existing. The very ignorance and blindness to which the law of contradiction subjects all those over whom it rules—all extra-biblical peoples—reflect the contradiction that the law of contradiction cannot be thought existing and cannot exist (in or as) thought. Thought and existence are forever subject to the doctrine of opposites, such that each is always other than and opposed to not only its opposite but equally itself. With the doctrine of creation from nothing, however, thought and existence are liberated from the blindness and ignorance of natural contradiction and revealed to be something, and what they are divides into the nature of thought and existence (alike divine and human), on the one hand, and the nature of space and time, on the other: one self (person) in two natures. The paradox which the science of nature must accept is that the certain objects of natural space and time can be preserved from the illusion of uncertainty only if they are not confused with or reduced to the nature, the thought and existence, of human beings. The world of nature can be liberated from the blindness and ignorance of the extra-biblical doctrine of opposites only if it is understood that its appearances are delicately suspended between illusion and reality. But the moment we pretend to know the appearances of things in natural space and time as objects knowable in themselves or to know things-in-themselves—thought and existence, whether divine or human—as the objects of nature, then the heinous idolatry of dualism breaks out as the disastrous confusion between illusion and reality. The science of nature has an enormously significant role to play within the drama of human thought and existence: it provides the eternal limit to any attempt on the part of human beings to go beyond loving God above all things and their neighbors as themselves. The moment they attempt to know God and neighbor as—to reduce their priorities to—things subject to objective or natural manipulation, then the worlds of both human relations and natural science vanish. It is equally the case, however, that, the moment science claims to know things-in-themselves, it turns human beings into natural objects and the science of natural objects into illusion, thus losing both.

We must never forget how apparently easy and comfortable it can become for us to view the paradoxical relationship of human thought and existence in terms of the immediacy and certainty of nature. In the extra-biblical world there is no option or choice of thought and existence, for they remain fatally hidden within the nature of contradictory opposites. But within the biblical tradition thought and existence are revealed to be the choice for human beings. But choice, as always, is paradoxical. Although the choice is eternally for thought and existence, the choice is so easily conflated with and reduced to a choice between thought and existence, this false choice generating the very dualism between thought and existence—alike dogmatic and skeptical—which cannot be conceived to exist within extra-biblical paganism. When choice as the dialectic of thought and existence—we can think only of that which exists and can exist only in our thought—degenerates into the dualism between thought and existence, the dialectic of the thing-in-itself—as that which alone can be thought to exist and exist as thought and which can be known only as it appears in natural space and time—degenerates into the dualism either of reducing one or the other of thought and existence to the contradictions of nature or of elevating the contradictions of nature to one or the other of thought and existence. In either case there is generated the human oppression of arguing from fact to right which Rousseau identifies as the idolatrous chains of slavery. Rousseau shows us that, if we are to become natural, that is, if we are to appropriate our nature as the truth of the *condition humaine*, then we must be liberated from both the contradictory blindness to and the ignorance of the state of nature to which current social relations have been reduced. For, once we become natural—we are born free—we find ourselves enslaved to the chains of sin, idolatry, and oppression. The human task is the historical one, not that of returning to nature, which in itself is fatally contradictory, but that of becoming natural, whereby we judge the objective facts of natural custom by the right legitimating human thought and existence.

The world of pagan nature is so important—for us—to preserve as that which cannot be known in itself without contradiction, for only then are we properly able to distinguish between thought and existence, on the one hand, and the scientific knowledge of nature as that which does not exist in its own thought or think in its own existence, on the other. The thought and existence of nature belong to us, to us who are not natural but who must become natural in our thought and existence. The issue as always is to remain critically alert to the infinitely divers ways in which we can lose a firm grasp on the dialectic of thought and existence, whereby, in giving up one side of the dialectic in dualistic opposition to the other, we lose both, both our thought and existence. The issue is to remain critically alive to the fundamental distinction between dialectic and dualism; and I do not find that this is possible for us moderns unless we confront, in the boldest way possible, the critical difference between the creation of thought and existence from nothing, from nothing subject to the pagan doctrine of natural contradictions, and the extra-biblical doctrine of opposites.

It is only when we really begin to absorb the shock that the law of contradiction, together with the doctrine of natural opposites in which it is reflected, endlessly opposes thought and existence in the tradition of extra-biblical paganism, that we can truly begin to comprehend the fact that the dualisms with which modern (biblical) thought and existence are riven derive from two sources (having a common root): the conflation of thought and existence, alike divine and human, with and their reduction to their appearances in (1) nature and (2) extra-biblical paganism. It is essential, therefore, for us to recognize that, if we are ever to possess a comprehensive conception of secular existence, the secular world of human thought and existence must not be falsely opposed to the religious, human being to divine being, reason to faith. When the secular is dualistically opposed to the religious, then it is inevitably reduced to the contradictory appearances of nature and/or the nature of extra-biblical paganism. But human thought and existence must fall from the contradictory law of nature into the nothing from which everything is created if they are to be liberated from the doctrine of natural oppositions and thus to be critically distinguished from the dualism between thought and existence.

In differentiating the secular from both nature and natural paganism, it is important to comprehend the world of the secular as alike historical and democratic. History is neither empiricist nor rationalist. History can be understood on the model of neither the natural science of appearances nor logical relations, neither on what Hume calls matters of fact nor on what he calls relations of ideas. It is precisely this dualism between sensibility and understanding which, as we saw, leaves Hume shipwrecked between a false reason and no reason at all. In contrast to Hume (and to his dualistic opposite Leibniz), we must learn that whatever is—must be thought to exist. Whatever exists as human being must be thought to exist, with thought and existence freely bound by necessity: the Cartesian *ergo*. Whatever thinks must think its existence as human. Whatever is thought as human being must exist as thought, with thought and existence freely bound by necessity: the Cartesian *ergo*. Whatever is—historical—must be thought—historical. History, as the proper domain of secular men and women, involves and expresses the ontological argument for thought and existence. History is precisely that which can be thought only existing and which can exist only as it is thought. Just as human being is not empiricist or rationalist, except in appearance, so God—the God of the Bible—is empiricist or rationalist only in appearance. God no less than human beings is historical, the historical subject of the ontological argument for thought and existence.

History is so deceptive, as is all human thought and existence, for it seems so obvious that we see (experience) human events in the same way that we see (experience) the events of nature. Yet, when we think about it— when we put our thought into our existence (when we exist in our thought)—we realize that we have never seen a human action. The reader of this essay in thinking, once he thinks about it, sees the words on the page before him; but, when he looks at the literal words on the page, he is no longer thinking about what he is reading. When the reader thinks about what he is reading, he knows that the subject of his reading—as the subject of my writing—is not seen as the objects of nature are seen. We have never seen a human action, either in the empiricist (extrinsic) sense or in the rationalist (innate) sense, for human action is precisely that which embodies the leap of faith and reason whereby everything natural is rendered null so that it may become the matrix for the creation of thought and existence. Historical action—the world as one action—binds our beginnings and ends, our past and future, into the present, into the eternal presence of abiding by the golden rule of doing unto others as we would have them do unto us. The paradox of history is that it takes place precisely in the present, in the presence of human thought and existence, in that gap which is created from nothing when the nature of contradiction is revealed as appearances which are not other than and opposed to but grounded in the history of thought and existence (alike divine and human).

Our history stretches between three and four millennia into our biblical past, a few more thousand years into our non-historical past, many thousands and even millions of years into our anthropological past, and ultimately a number of billions of years into our natural past—to the beginning of the universe. Still, once we confront our beginnings in the Bible—and there are no beginnings outside our beginning with the Bible—we are obligated to recognize that, in studying our beginnings in archeology, anthropology, geology, and cosmology (that of astrophysics and nuclear physics alike), we arrive at, finally, ourselves, at our thought and existence, divine and human. The sole beginning of nature—anthropological and cosmological—is our thought and existence, divine and human. If we do not discover ourselves, in the beginning and in the end, as the principle or ground of nature, then both nature and our conscious existence (the existence of our consciousness) in nature vanish into the illusion of idolatrous dualism. We may prefer, and we are free, to eschew the divine metaphor of creation. But we do so at the risk of reducing the human metaphor to the idolatrous similes of nature, with the result that we are enslaved to a denatured concept of reason as technological and to a denatured conception of humanity as subject to the hierarchies of domination whose grounds we are unable to explore because they are mystified by being hidden in and identified with that which is called natural, a contradiction which extra-biblical paganism, at least, could never have conceived of existing.

The principle, the beginning and end, of nature is thought and existence, both divine and human. Such is the simple, eternal, and paradoxical revelation which the Bible is the first and last text to bring into the world. This principle is history, the recognition that our beginning with self, both divine and human, both individual and collective, both faithful and rational, is always beginning, yet always at its end. History, as the thought and existence which binds together past and future, is always contemporary.

Because thought and existence are eternally bound together—if they are not dualistically opposed to each other—to exist is to find oneself at the (historical) beginning of one's thought, and to think is to begin, once more, to exist (historically). The more deeply and extensively we explore the history of our thought and existence, the more profoundly we confront our beginnings and thus the implications of our history for our future thought and existence. When science becomes cosmology, as its hypotheses become increasingly tentative and finally outright speculative, then cosmology ultimately either becomes dualistic—mystifying, superstitious, and trivial—or folds back into reflecting our beginning with the history of the self, the self both divine and human, both individual and communal. In the beginning is the creation of thought and existence from nothing, from nothing which is found in the spatial and temporal appearances of either the atom or the cosmos. Either thought and existence eternally overcome the contradictions of nature and do not succumb to them—recognizing the critical distinction between the creation of history from nothing (in itself) and the generation (and destruction) of nature as nothing (in itself). Or thought and existence succumb to the contradictions of nature, reducing not only history, as the creation of human thought and existence from nothing, but also nature (nothing), from which thought and existence are created, to the contradictory dualisms of idolatrous nihilism.

Just as it is essential to understand the beginning of the secular world as historical, so it is equally important to understood it as democratic. Democracy is the recognition that it is precisely the city of God, to use Augustine's powerful metaphor, which provides the beginning, the principle, for the city of earth, which otherwise lies hidden within the natural contradictions of the pagan doctrine of opposites. Democracy is the beginning such that it can be repeated by all human beings, without exception, whatever their natural beginnings, so long as they choose to begin, this choice to begin embracing the beginning as the golden rule which is the choice no less for you than it is for me. The democratic choice, the beginning in democracy, is the beginning such that I do not choose between you and me, for that is to falsify choice by choosing to discriminate between you and me on grounds other than our common bond in the golden rule of loving God above all others and our neighbor as ourselves. The only grounds for discrimination—for choice—are those which include both you and me—our self, which cannot be thought except as alike individual and communal existence and which cannot exist except as alike individual and communal thought—within the choice. Democracy as the beginning which liberates the self—of all individuals as of all communities—from the blind contradictions of nature is unthinkable outside the existence of the Bible. Democracy is the beginning of the city of God on earth, whose end is the golden rule freely binding all human beings in thought and existence.

The thought whose existence is democratic and the existence which cannot be thought except democratically are, from the beginning, historical. Democracy is unthinkable outside the existence of history and history is unthinkable outside democratic existence. History is the story of the self, both individual and collective, which comes into thought and existence from nothing, from nothing subject to the contradictory nature of space and time. The selves of all individuals and of all peoples, precisely because their natural differences have been revealed for what they are—nothing in themselves—belong to a common humanity whose history is both one and universal. But democracy, like history, is not, however, immediately or directly one or universal; for it is not the case that the peoples of the world are historical and democratic, in themselves. In themselves, they are blind to and ignorant of what they are in themselves, for the history of their democratic thought and existence is located in fatal otherness whose natural appearances are ineluctably contradictory. The democracy of history—the history of democracy—is not given naturally in itself but in the relationship which each people establishes such that it is accessible to all peoples historically. No individual people can be historical in exclusive isolation from others, but, at the same time, the principle of democratic inclusiveness always involves the principle of exclusiveness. The chosen people are the first and the last democratic people for the precise reason that their history includes all who choose to love God above all others and their neighbor as themselves while excluding not only extra-biblical peoples but, with the constitution of the Common Era, those who twist the dialectic of inclusion and exclusion into the idolatrous dualism of excluding some from the thought and existence of humanity which include all within its democratic history.

History and democracy reveal the anxiety of consequence which burdens the world of the secular. The secular is unthinkable outside the historical existence of democracy, the history of democratic existence. But if the secular is opposed dualistically to the religious tradition which brings it into thought and existence, then both history and democracy are turned into the idols of self-repression and popular oppression. It is equally true, however, that the secular must be eternally vigilant not to allow the tradition of religious (biblical) discourse to claim any priority in beginning. For it is equally true to say that, in the beginning, God creates the thought and existence of the *saeculum*. The secular reminds us that God belongs to the self, both individual and social, both historical and democratic. God is not first religious and then secular. He is religious and secular, from the beginning. Secularization is not a process which sets in subsequent to a religious development. Much of what we call religious in the Middle Ages, for example, has nothing to do with authentic religion (the Bible), just as much that we call secular today has nothing to do with what is authentically secular. That the idols of secularism—reason, progress, individualism, nature, science, technology...—dominate our modern world would allow one to argue for our age being a much more profoundly religious age than the Middle Ages, in which the idolatry is characteristically religious (biblical concepts rationalized in the terms of Greek philosophy). In any case, the Bible is secular from the beginning. For the secular is but the recognition that God creates human thought and existence from nothing, from nothing natural, just as faith recognizes that God and neighbor represent the priorities of life which overcome the oppositions which divide people in the contradictory state of nature.

Today we secularists should be particularly suspicious of the Bible whose rhetoric never appears to put God in question. The Bible appears to privilege God, to put God above criticism (critique), to impute to God, separate from his human creatures, the creation of humanity, the revelation of human history, and, ultimately, the salvation of humankind. Still, when we recall Spinoza's acute observation that the Bible is true only insofar as we recognize that it errs, that the truth of its sovereign doctrine, the golden rule, cannot be equated with any finite combination of words in which it is expressed, not even with that collection of finite words which we call the Bible, then we recognize that we must not conflate the concepts of the Bible with its terms. We must not confuse the concept God (which can be thought only existing and can exist only thought) with the term God, for it is precisely that confusion which reduces God to an idol on which we project, in bad faith, the dualism between our own thought and existence. As we noted in our chapter on the Bible, just as the Bible is subject to truth as its own standard, which is not to be equated with any finite rendering of the Bible, so the sovereign God of the Bible must not be conflated with or reduced to any finite representation of God. God is subject to his own standard and must not be confused with it, just as the Bible is subject to its own standard and must not be confused with it.

Indeed, when we realize that it is the Bible which is concerned, above all else, to repudiate the reduction of truth to error, of thought and existence, whether divine or human, to idolatry, then we see that it is the Bible itself which becomes the greatest idol of all when we fail to distinguish between the Bible as the thing in itself—which exists only in its concept and whose concept cannot be thought except existing—and its finite appearances in language. The Bible becomes the greatest idol of all precisely when we fail to recognize that we have no choice but to choose thought and existence, alike divine and human. If we undertake to distinguish between thought and existence, whether human and divine, on any grounds other than their own dialectic, their relationship in the covenant of the golden rule, the result, inexorably, is the reduction of one of them to the contradictions of nature such that the other is rendered equally contradictory. There is only one distinction to be made in the world of the secular, that between thought and existence, on the one hand, and their appearances in the objects of natural space and time, on the other. There is only one choice which we can make in the world of the secular, the choice of living the dialectic of thought and existence. The moment that we oppose thought and existence such that we choose between them—either between thought and existence or between human thought and existence, on the one hand, and divine thought and existence, on the other—on any other grounds than their own dialectic, then we fall into the idolatrous dualism of reducing one of them and thus both of them to the contradictions of nature.

It is clear, therefore, that to read the Bible within the secular world is to become aware that the fact that its writers ascribe sovereign authority to God represents an enormous paradox. Biblical authors—alike divine and human!—test both God and human readers to see if they will overcome the idolatrous dualism of distinguishing between divine and human sovereignty on any other grounds than their own authority, their sovereign covenant. The Bible is so modern a text—that is, even the Bible is a biblical text constantly to be created by its secular and believing readers alike!—for the very reason that its surfaces unceasingly contradict either thought and/or existence, equally divine and human. The test for readers, as for Abraham, is to see if they can remain steadfast in their love for and trust in God—his thought and existence—without giving up love for and trust in their own creation—their thought and existence (Isaac or the neighbor). The Bible turns its readers and its God into idols the moment readers fail to recognize that the ontological argument applies no less to human than to divine thought and existence. God's story is equally the story of human beings. The authority imputed to God by its authors is no less human than divine. The alternative to the sovereignty of thought and existence—divine and human—is the idolatrous dualism either of reducing ourselves to God, with the result that we are unable to distinguish between divine thought and existence and the contradictions of nature, or of reducing God to ourselves, with the result that we are unable to distinguish between our thought and existence and the contradictions of nature. When we dogmatically reduce ourselves to God, claiming to honor him above all others, what we actually do is to project upon him our all-too-human dualisms, making God into the idol than which none is more perfect. When we skeptically reduce God to ourselves, claiming that all honor is due to man, we rationalize our all-too-divine dualisms as human, making man into the idol than which none is more perfect.

The Bible is the original, and final, enactment of Pascal's Wager. The Bible—divine and human—bets on thought and existence. We have to wager our life in order to win it. When we sit down to play at the gaming table of life, we have already placed our bets. The dice are loaded. We cannot choose not to bet on thought and existence; thought and existence are the very stake that we wager on life. We bet on God no less than on ourselves. He bets on us no less than on himself. How different is the biblical wager of life from Hume's diverting himself from the melancholy of finding himself betwixt a false reason and no reason at all—in not recognizing that whatever is must both be thought to exist and exist as thought—by playing what he calls an innocent game of backgammon.

When we read the great stories of the Bible involving creation, Adam and Eve, Abraham, Moses, David, the prophets, Job, and Jesus and we think about their implications for our existence, then it becomes clear that the sovereignty ascribed to God is, indeed, the test of human authority. The test by which all human authority is tried is to see whether human beings will abide by their faith in thought and existence as alike divine and human. When, in Genesis 22, God calls to Abraham; Abraham answers, here I am; and God tells him to take his son Isaac and to go forth to Mount Moriah and offer him up in sacrifice to God, we normally view this as a test of Abraham. Indeed, the biblical authors say that God puts Abraham to the test. But surely this is a test no less of God. Will Abraham's faith be such that the God in whom he trusts is worthy of the test? If the faith of Abraham in the God who tests him is blind, either blindly certain or blindly uncertain, then the God who tests him is unworthy of human thought and existence. Can or how will Abraham justify the ways of God to man? Can the reader justify the ways of God to the world? What does it mean to sit down to the gaming table of the world where God has stacked the cards against you? The Bible enjoys the sublime privilege of representing God's point of view. But this privilege is both loaded with paradox and ironic. If we take it literally, then we turn God into a cardsharp. If we reject it literally, then we refuse to play the game of life. But it is precisely the relationship of God and human beings which makes the Bible so profoundly a secular work, a work constantly demanding the most intense commitment of our thought and existence, if we are not to turn it into sheer idolatry (which is what naturally happens to it in the hands of both believers and nonbelievers).

The religious idolatry into which the Bible constantly falls emerges from our unwillingness to acknowledge the radical consequences of the doctrine of creation from nothing. If this doctrine is true, if it is the only truth accessible to interpretation, then thought and existence are no more divine than human, no more religious than secular. But it is this very doctrine—expressed through the ontological argument and the golden rule—which shows that truth and interpretation are accessible to all men and women only because their thought and existence have been liberated from the blindness and ignorance of the fatal domination of nature by the law of contradiction. But, just as secularism liberates the Bible from its dogmatic dualisms, so the secular attitude has an equally fatal penchant to fall into the dualism of viewing the religious rhetoric of the Bible—God, revelation, miracle, salvation—as having nothing to do with the secular world or, indeed, as its mystification. But then religious consciousness comes into play and reminds the secularist of the radical consequences of the doctrine of creation from nothing. If this doctrine is true, if it is the only truth accessible to interpretation, then thought and existence are no more human than divine, no more secular than religious. But it is this very doctrine—expressed through the ontological argument and the golden rule—which shows that truth and interpretation are accessible to all men and women only because their thought and existence have been liberated from the blindness and ignorance of the fatal domination of nature by the law of contradiction. The secular stands and falls with the religious, as does the religious with the secular. Either/or. Either embrace the dialectic of the secular and the religious as that which cannot be thought except existing and cannot exist except as thought. Or be offended that you cannot escape the anxiety of consequence that the secular involves the religious as the religious expresses the secular. Either embrace your thought and existence as equally divine and human. Or be offended by the fact that if you oppose either dualistically to the other you will actually lose both and thus be blindly opposing yourself. Either embrace your thought as existing and your existence as thought. Or be offended by the dualism between your thought and existence which puts you in opposition to both.

PART III
CONCLUSION

The Truth of Interpretation and the Interpretation of Truth

I. INTRODUCTION: TO MAXIMIZE OUR THINKING—I THINK, THEREFORE, I AM

The ultimate aim of my essay in thinking is to show that, and how it is that, thinking, all thinking without exception, whatever are the infinite and however infinite are the varieties of thinking, involves and expresses the dialectic of truth and interpretation. I am equally concerned to show that truth and interpretation, in the plenitude of their infinity, embody thinking, the activity of thinking. These aims, and the claims they entail, are, I should think, unexceptionable, at least to begin with. Human beings think, it is clear. Yet, if a friend telephones me and asks me what I am doing, as friends are wont to do, and if I tell my friend that I am thinking, the friend will probably be surprised and feel that I have not answered her question. I myself shall probably feel somewhat uneasy about my answer unless I have decided, in high glee, to put my friend on. If it is not obviously a joke that I am playing on my friend, my friend will probably ask me, quite spontaneously: thinking about what? as if to say: tell me what you mean, for thinking is too generic an activity to be concrete; nobody just thinks; you must be thinking about something, in particular. If I answer that I am reading or cooking or cleaning or writing (common activities for me), my friend will doubtless understand me, although she may well wish to hear more about what I am actually reading, cooking, cleaning, or writing. When we read, cook, clean, or write, concrete things come to mind: books, food, dirt, and ideas (among many others). But what comes to mind when we think, beyond mind and thought themselves? What do we think? Still, it is clear that, if, during our telephone conversation, my friend and I find ourselves talking about a complex and perhaps even difficult issue which involves the two of us quite deeply, one of us may ask the other, in all seriousness: what do you think? Or one of us may say, with or without that particular question having been asked, in all seriousness: here's what I think. That properly subjective question or declaration involves two subjects—my friend and myself. It also involves the subjects which my friend and I are thinking about together in our conversation: our actual conversation. To ask another what she is thinking or to declare what I am thinking indicates that thinking involves both the thinking subject and the subject thought, both thought and existence, both method and content, both self and other, both—as I have indicated in my previous chapters—faith and reason, ultimately (when the ontological implications are pursued) not only human but also divine thought and existence.

Thinking is both commonplace (even trivial) and mysterious (often alienating) precisely because it is so close to us and, for that very reason, it is extremely difficult to think (about). We also wonder, once we begin thinking (about it [thinking]), how or in what way thinking (thought, thoughtfulness) can be understood to cover all intellectual and, ultimately, artistic or even spiritual activity, not to mention the infinite range of human practice, including the life of religion and faith (spirituality) and the affective life of the emotions (love, anger, delight, melancholy, joy...). Still, we doubtless do not want a thoughtless prime minister, a thoughtless pastor or teacher, a thoughtless lover, a thoughtless parent or child, or a thoughtless sales clerk. But how thought informs the life of faith and service or the affective life of practice and emotion often seems mysterious, if not downright contradictory. We also wonder about human negativity. What is the role of thought in human violence (including murder), oppression, repression, ideological distortion or bias, bad faith, cowardice, fear, racism, sexism, and, finally, insanity and suicide? Are aggression towards the self—both individual and social—and irrationality categories of thought? Can violence and irrationality, in other words, be thoughtfully comprehended? What does it mean to think about them?

Truth and interpretation, like thinking, also appear unexceptionable. We may be staggered by the question which Pilate puts to Jesus, when we think about it, and we may prefer not to think about it. Still, we expect others—friends, politicians, lovers, parents, children, teachers, doctors, sales clerks, auto mechanics, judges...—to tell (us) the truth, and, when they do not, we are upset and demand an accounting. The conspiracy of silence surrounding *los desaparecidos* in Argentina remains one of the most chilling events of recent times. When we listen to children, of six or seven years of age, we quickly discover that they have no difficulty in knowing what it means to tell the truth, and they show not only that they understand the concept in their practice but also that they can use it fittingly in their speech if asked about it, just as they also know what it means to love their parents, siblings, playmates, and also God and (Christian children) Jesus. (Children may have somewhat more difficulty in knowing what it means to love themselves.) Concepts such as truth (and love) are by no means abstract to children, although it is also true that children can be superb liars; and the hateful way in which children often treat their peers (not to mention their parents and teachers) shows that Machiavelli is still a child when it comes to analyzing the dynamics of manipulating truth and falsehood (love and hate).

Interpretation also strikes us as a commonplace human activity, something in which we are all involved, although we may not be very clear about the nature of that involvement. But, whereas truth tends to indicate the subject of our thinking, what it is that we think about, interpretation tends to locate thinking in subjects, to describe how it is that individuals think about the truth or what it is that they bring to thinking about the truth. We typically ask: what is that person's interpretation of the truth? How did the jury interpret the facts (the truth) of the situation? Just as thinking about the truth tends to make us skeptical towards dogmatic claims about objective truth—for do not different people have different objects in mind as true?—so interpretation tends to make us skeptics about the relativity of subjective truth—do not different people have different interpretations of the truth? It is also the case that an objectivist conception of truth often emerges in response to the skeptical relativity of interpretation when all truth appears to be a matter of opinion, my opinion and your opinion, my interpretation and your interpretation. There is also an objectivist conception of interpretation, whereby I view my interpretation as objective truth and yours as subjective opinion. It is also commonly held that, whereas science provides us with the most objective truth possible, although certainly nothing involving absolute truth but also minimally involving subjective interpretation, in contrast, politics, literature, religion, life, generally, precisely because they are subjective and relative, unlike objectively certain science, involve interpretation but hardly truth at all. The opposite point of view is also common, that it is religion which possesses the truth of certain objects, while science, politics, life, generally, concern what is merely a matter of uncertain opinion.

I should add that such views frequently bear little relationship to the actual conduct of human beings in their daily lives—at home, at school, in the work place, in running errands, in service and leisure activities...—in which people show an abiding concern to treat others with decency, fairness, kindness, consideration, helpfulness, and caring, which suggests that common citizens, all of us, may be reticent about claiming to possess truth or to know what interpretation is, while embodying the dialectic of truth and interpretation in our relations with others. Indeed, it is characteristic of our age that, as we support and advance the welfare of others (in both the personal and the public spheres), we tend to be skeptical in our verbal rationales about knowing the truth or acknowledging that our thought and existence involve interpretation. It is also characteristic of our age that there is an enormous split between what formal thinkers, philosophers, above all, tell us that we do not know about truth and interpretation in theory and what informal thinkers, above all, people in their daily lives, both individually and collectively, show us that we do know about them in practice. I have always been struck by the observation of Kant, whose powers of ratiocination are incomparable, that in his comprehensive analysis of the groundwork of the metaphysics of morals he simply articulates the principles which people embody in their daily practice. The philosophic owl of Minerva flies only at dusk.

I juxtapose these commonly expressed views about thinking and what we mean by truth and interpretation—while noting their frequent incongruency with our practice—to my presentation in the preceding chapters in order, not to give credence to the conventional notions about the dualism between theory and practice, but to show that we must take exception to the standard conceptions of thinking if we are to be in a position to show how thinking involves both truth and interpretation. I wish to make clear that I choose the term thinking as my medium for exploring thought and existence not for any hidden ideological reason (of which I am aware), although it is true that I do want a term which has universal applicability, enjoys common usage, and is not heavily freighted towards one side or the other of the dualism between faith and reason. We call both theologians and philosophers thinkers, although it would not be so obvious to call Moses or Jesus thinkers, not to mention literary or musical composers like Shakespeare or Bach or visual artists like Rembrandt. Still, we commonly suppose that all human beings, eminent or humble, think, whatever the medium of their thought. More problematic than the incongruity of calling writers, composers, or artists thinkers is the difficulty we thinkers—professional and everyday—have with the vocabulary of what Spinoza calls the *affectus* and what we translate with the neologism "affects" (the rich cognates of *affectus* having been largely reduced to the verb "to affect" ["affected"], although we do have the noun "affection," plus its adjective "affectionate") or with the not very apposite "emotions." To call somebody (in his or her response to a situation) emotional is to say that the person, in our judgment, is not thinking in a careful, cool, clear, or collected manner or is thinking (responding) in a manner which we (men, especially) find to be inappropriate or embarrassing. It is to say that the person is not being rational. We (thinkers) have an enormous prejudice against the language of the *affectus*, against the language of the emotions, against love, above all (and this prejudice is reinforced by the suspicion with which religious or spiritual language is generally viewed). The enormous dualism in our lives between the personal and public realms is reflected in the dualism between the language of emotion (and religion) and the language of reason, which is, in turn, mirrored in the dualism between skepticism and dogmatism. Still, although the values traditionally attaching to the term thinking fail to do justice to the concept *affectus*, thinking is not heavily loaded in one direction or the other with regard to the distinction between the personal and the public realms, between the individual and the collective.

There are, however, more cogent reasons why I have chosen to focus my essay on truth and interpretation in thinking, reasons which take us more directly to the heart of the issues which are involved here. I find that, in the brave new world of North American individualism, the uncritical acceptance of a naive conception of scientific empiricism, with its strong, positivistic emphasis on value-free methodology, remains so pronounced in not only the social sciences but also the humanities (history, philosophy, social and political thought, literature and the arts, and religious studies) that it is important to plump for its dialectical opposite, thinking. In focusing on the subject who thinks, thinking illuminates the subjectivity which lies at the unknowing heart of individualistic empiricism and which doubtless explains its compulsion in insisting upon value-free objectivity (objects free of value). More important, thinking is obviously an activity in which we engage; it is not just passive receptivity (although the opposite problem of innate ideas cannot then be ignored). What or how we think often seems mysterious, as I remarked; but, because thinking is something we do, it is evident to us that it involves not only an agent acting (thinking) but also a context in which the activity of thinking is exercised.

This brings me to the most important reason for using thinking as the way in which to bring into sharp focus the dialectic of truth and interpretation. Thinking is not only a term weighted in various directions, given its linguistic history, but it is also a concept. Indeed, thinking is not only a concept but it is the concept (of concepts), as I have shown in my previous chapters. I do not mean for a moment that thinking is superior to other concepts; what I do mean is that every concept, so long as it is in truth a concept and can be interpreted conceptually—that is, as existing—can stand for or represent all concepts. Every concept is a metaphor, representing the leap between being and becoming, the dialectic of unique and universal, the relationship of self and other. I do not want to be perverse in saying that my choice of thinking is arbitrary, that I could (just as well) have chosen another concept. Still, if our choices lose their sense of what is arbitrary, chancy, serendipitous, idiosyncratic, quirky, whimsical—in sooth, the paradoxical—then necessity as self-determination becomes determinism fatally masking chance. I choose thinking, given the above, but I also want to emphasize, in these preliminary remarks, the fact that my choice, like any choice, must be justified; it must be thought through; it must be demonstrated; it must be shown to embody good faith and to have reasons; it must be shown to support, and to be supported by, the dialectic of truth and interpretation. Every choice, to paraphrase what Hegel says about history, is to render the arbitrary thoughtful, to fill the contingencies of life with our thought. To think is to make our life worthy of human existence. To think is to exist. I think, therefore, I am.

Thinking has been called many things by the most thoughtful among us: essaying by Montaigne; human dignity by Pascal; perseverance (*conatus*) by Spinoza; the social contract by Rousseau; practical reason and will by Kant; reason, desire, and spirit by Hegel; fear and trembling, love, subjectivity, the absolute paradox of faith, and the purity of heart in willing one thing by Kierkegaard; labor by Marx; the will to power by Nietzsche; libido by Freud.... Notwithstanding the superficiality of such a catalogue, it serves to remind us, once again, that we must exercise caution in not confusing the concept with its terms. The very reason that I found it necessary, as I indicated in the Preface, to work systematically through the thinking of Spinoza, Kant, Hegel, and Kierkegaard—or I could equally say that the reason that I find them to be our greatest thinkers—is that, in providing us with the most comprehensive treatment of what it means for us human beings to think, they show us both the range and the depth of human existence which must be accounted for if thinking is to be conceptually adequate and not to be split asunder into the dualistic terms of faith and reason.

This, however, is an essay in thinking, in thinking historically, not an essay in the history of thought, although the difference is, I think, not one of thinking but one of emphasis (presentation). Thinking is history (history is thinking). The thinking of history is the history of thinking. I begin—and end—with Descartes, not historically, but in my thinking, although it is true that Descartes is our first philosopher (and still one of our last philosophers) precisely because he is the first (and also one of the last) to articulate, with superb confidence, that miraculous chain of entailments involving the *ergo* of thoughtful (active) determination which shows thinking to be, not casual or causal, not linear or circular, but dialectical: ...*ergo* I doubt, *ergo* I think, *ergo* I exist (the self exists), *ergo* God exists, *ergo*... I doubt.... (It is precisely because I doubt, because I can doubt nothing but what exists, that my doubt demonstrates simultaneously the existence of thinking and the thinking of existence.) That Descartes appears to put thinking first and existence (the soul's and God's) second must not fool us, just as the fact that I call my presentation of truth and interpretation an essay in thinking and not an essay in existing should not fool us (author or reader). Indeed, the reason that I undertake to have my thinking comport with that of Descartes is because his thought is simple (all that he says of critical importance is found in the four or five pages of Part IV of the *Discourse on Method*) and, therefore, beguiling (having fooled nearly all his successors, including even himself in his appallingly inadequate moral philosophy).

Descartes is reputed by philosophers to have foisted upon modernity all the problems with which its thinking is burdened (although, as we have seen, these problems are due not to Descartes but to philosophers who are blind to the distinction between dialectic and dualism, between the dialectic of truth and interpretation and idolatry, this blindness being rooted in their idolatrous rationalization of Greek philosophy as thinking). Imputed to Descartes are the dualism between subject and object, solipsism (the problem of knowing other minds, as if one could grasp one's own mind separate from or before understanding others' minds), and skepticism (Hume claims, in playing backgammon, to mitigate what he considers to be Descartes' radical skepticism!). He is pilloried for having generated the ghost in the machine by looking upon philosophy as the mirror of nature. He is attacked both for being irreligious (by Pascal) and for bringing God surreptitiously into his thinking (by his theological critics in their Objections to the *Meditations*). His claim to be original in beginning in doubt is scoffed at by his contemporary critics who observe that the ancient skeptics doubt everything (while Spinoza shakes his head in despair, wondering, like so many of Descartes' critics, how his great master could have been so naive as to think that one could begin by beginning in doubt, by doubting one's beginning). He is viewed as reactionary by his philosophical successors for shaping his thinking around the ontological argument for God's existence, the hangover of the Middle Ages from which all enlightened thinkers have had more than sufficient time to recover, thanks to the sobriety of their common sense stand betwixt a false reason and no reason at all (just think of Hume: whatever *is* may *not be*). He is viewed as a great philosopher who simply went wrong, great-mindedness, combined with wrong-headedness, being the philosophical fit to be avoided according to the criterion by which the history of philosophy, at least in the English-speaking world, is written, the criterion of trivial-minded clarity. He is said to be wrong, indeed, foolish, to think that one can prove existence, that one can prove that either the soul (the self) or God exists, let alone both (at the same time), separate from the body. But what else, we ask, can we think of proving—testing, probing, questioning—if not our existence? How, we ask, can we undertake to prove—to test, to probe, to (be)think—our existence, if our existence does not equally involve and express the existence of our neighbor, if our existence, insofar as it is not confused with or reduced to the corporeal world of natural space and time, does not equally involve and express the existence of God? Do we not, like Rousseau, begin our argument, our demonstration, with the ontological right of human beings, in the beginning, to think and to exist?

I have come, clearly, not to bury, but to praise Descartes. Indeed, although I am not primarily concerned here with the historical corpus of Descartes, I am wrestling with the beginning, with the principle and thus equally the end, of what constitutes our human thinking. To the degree that my articulation of thinking as the dialectic of truth and interpretation—my articulation of the dialectic of truth and interpretation as expressly thinking—is successful, to that degree I rightly claim to begin (and to end) with Descartes. It is naturally possible, rather, doubtless likely, that the inadequacy of my thinking will be distinguished from Descartes' greatminded wrong-headedness (it is less likely that I shall be criticized while Descartes is defended, while it is altogether unlikely that I shall be praised while Descartes is damned). Still, we have to begin somewhere, and is it possible to begin anywhere else than in the beginning, in the beginning which, in order to begin, must already have begun mindful of existence and fully existing in mind?

I begin with Descartes. I think, therefore, I am. Descartes begins with the recognition that all beginnings are to be understood as beginning simultaneously with what I thematize in my essay in thinking as the dialectic of thought and existence, with the recognition that to begin to think expresses existence and that to begin to exist involves thinking. What is astonishing about Descartes is that he epitomizes the modernist (biblical) principle that less is more. What he says is minimally true, such that we discover that what is maximally true—the maxim of truth—is but an articulation of his basic principle, of what is traditionally called the ontological argument for the existence of God. I am concerned to show that, in order to understand the full truth comprehended by the ontological argument—in order to expand the ontological argument for God's existence to maximal truth—we must understand it to comprise, in addition to the existence of God, not only the thought of God but also the thought and existence of human beings. With the exception of Spinoza, Kant, Hegel, and Kierkegaard, plus thinkers like Vico, Rousseau, Marx, Nietzsche, and Freud, the expansion of modern thought sees the minimal kernel of truth in Descartes split into the fruitless opposition of its dualistic halves, which creates a situation of melancholy altogether different from the trance-like embrace of fate on the part of Socrates who, following the description of Kierkegaard, hollows out the nut of life only to throw away the kernel. The basic reason that modern thinkers are and remain entranced by the Greeks and, above all, by Socrates—from Erasmus to Arendt—is that so often no truth, an empty shell, seems more attractive than half a truth, half a nut. To live in a world of half-truths generates the *melancholia* of Hume, the depression of the modern world, the split between knowing what you do not know and not knowing what you do know, the very split in personality of which Freud is our great doctor and which is utterly inconceivable and unimaginable outside of modernism (the Bible). The split personality of modernity makes Socratic ignorance attractive (to intellectuals), and it shows how easily we confuse the ancient skeptics' suspension of judgment—the skeptics, following Socrates, know that they are ignorant (they know that they do not know), but they can never conceive of knowing (the existence of) what they are ignorant of (what they do not know)—with Cartesian doubt—whereby we are obligated to know what we do not know: our thought and existence.

We can overcome the melancholy split between our thought and existence, between knowing the existence of the unknown (our existence) and existing unknown in our (known) existence, only if we expand the minimal truth of Descartes to the maximum, while avoiding the pitfalls which line the route of modernity and which are filled with the dualistic *corpora* of our melancholy predecessors. The maximal truth (in one of its infinite guises, that of this essay in thinking) is that truth involves interpretation and that interpretation expresses truth. There is no truth outside its interpretation and no interpretation outside its truth. Truth is infinite, but falsehood is infinitely rampant in the world. Interpretation is infinite, but there is an infinity of false interpretations. These formulations are not in themselves solutions to the basic problems of thinking but invitations to think, to recognize that our task, as always, is to articulate a notion of truth (existence) such that it involves our thinking and a notion of interpretation (thinking) such that it involves the truth (our existence).

Our task is a double one. It is dialectical. We want to show both that the dialectic of truth and interpretation articulates the structure of thinking and that to think—the very nature, process, and activity of thinking—is the articulation of truth as interpretative and of interpretation as truthful. All of this might appear unexceptionable—it's hard to say—were it not for what I have written in the preceding chapters (and elsewhere). What thinking—as the dialectic of truth and interpretation—has shown me and, by now, also the reader, I hope, is that we shall not be able to transcend, overcome, and appropriate the dualisms to which thinking (epistemology and ethics) is prone if, prior to dealing with truth and interpretation, we do not show that there is no thinking outside the ontological argument, the ontological argument for the existence of God, which Anselm is the first thinker to articulate in modern (historical) terms. But the minimal truth of the ontological argument, as conventionally formulated and as conventionally criticized, must be maximally expanded if its truth is to be comprehensively interpreted.

I cite the formulation of the ontological argument with which Spinoza initiates Book I of his *Ethics*, entitled *De deo*, and which, given that it is said by Spinoza to explicate the cause of itself (*causa sui*), is by no means conventional: "By cause of itself I understand that whose essence involves existence or that whose nature is not able to be conceived except existing." As with Descartes, I am not concerned, here, with writing a commentary on Spinoza's philosophy. Still, it is worth noting that, whereas Descartes begins with the ego of the thinker—I think, therefore, I am—Spinoza begins with the cause of itself: God. Descartes begins with the thinker in doubt, while Spinoza begins with God as the undoubted cause of itself whose definition in the terms of the ontological argument is followed by seven more definitions, which are followed by seven axioms, which are followed by the propositions of Book I and their demonstrations and so on to the end of Book V, with definitions and axioms providing the basis for the subsequent propositions and their demonstrations, while the demonstrations are constantly punctuated with the reiterated Q. E. D. (*quod erat demonstrandum*). The classic criticism of Descartes is that, in beginning with the thinking (of the) ego (soul) of the individual thinker, he is unable to escape from egoism and the skepticism (dogmatism) of its subjectivity. The classic criticism of Spinoza is that, in beginning with dogmatic or undemonstrated definitions and axioms, above all, as they relate to God, his demonstrations have no objective validity but are mere (skeptical) assertions. My point here is not to show that such criticisms of Descartes and Spinoza are wrong, although they are (as the general tenor of my essay in thinking indicates and as I show elsewhere in detail). Rather, what I want to indicate is the importance of expanding the minimal (or one-sided) expression of even our strongest thinkers to the maximal strength possible.

Descartes and Spinoza begin, consciously and purposively, as distant from, as alienated from, the immediate givens of our experience, from the concrete appearances of our thought and existence, as it is conceivable to begin (in existence). Descartes begins with the ego of the individual thinker completely withdrawn from the world whose very existence he doubts so very strongly that he is willing to imagine that it is merely an illusion, a dream, or a joke perpetrated upon the thinker by a malicious demon (God other than or untrue to himself!). Spinoza begins with God, with definitions and axioms so austere, so emptied of apparent content that the very thought and existence of the world are called into question. When we think about it, however, do not all beginnings—not only for human beings but also for God—involve doubt, dread, fear and trembling, austerity, or alienation? Do not all beginnings, beginnings committed to the dialectic of thought and existence, repeat Rousseau's quest: given that we are born free, how is it possible to legitimize the bonds to which we are presently enchained? How do we transcendentally deduce—or justify— our thought and existence? Do not Descartes and Spinoza begin with, do they not repeat, the story of Abraham and his God? Do they not submit all that they think and are—their possessions, their history, their children, their very selves, their God—to the supreme proof (demonstration)? Do they not test out whether they can submit to the absolute demand that all be sacrificed—to the soul (Descartes) and to God (Spinoza)—without giving up their love for, their commitment to, both, just as Abraham knows that what is so terrible about God's command that he sacrifice his son Isaac is that he must continue to love Isaac, that he must abide forever in his commitment to the world of human thought and existence?

If Abraham could only stop loving Isaac, then it would be easy to love God. (It would also be easy for Abraham to prefer his love of Isaac to his love of God.) But it is precisely Abraham's love for Isaac, his adherence to the golden rule of human thought and existence, which makes his love for the God who commands him to sacrifice, but not to give up or to relinquish, his love for Isaac, for the world of creation, so absurdly paradoxical. Surely, love for God is but the most austere, the most alienating, the most exalted, the most transcendental, and thus, ultimately, the most human expression possible for our love of the human self, for the neighbor, both you and me. The demand that we love God above all others and our neighbor as ourselves means that there are no other priorities in the world than— that the sole priority in the world for us is—the love of God whose single demand is that we never relinquish but abide forever in our commitment to loving the human self, our thought and existence. In their formulations of the ontological argument, both Descartes and Spinoza represent the minimal (but always absolute) demands of love or of truth in the human self and in the divine self. The point, always, they realize, is to regain the world, to regain Isaac, to recognize that we die, to acknowledge the contradictions of natural space and time without being driven into dualistic melancholy by them. The maximal proof which we can marshall in support of human thought and existence—the love of the golden rule—is the demonstration that the ontological argument for God's existence not only expresses both the thought and existence of God but also involves the thought and existence of human beings.

II. CREATION FROM NOTHING AND THE NOTHING OF IDOLATRY

The burden of my essay in thinking is to show that thinking can be preserved from mere subjectivism (solipsism) or relativity and from mere objectivism (totalitarianism) or absolutism, whether dogmatic or skeptical, only if we are conscious of taking a number of critical steps whose combined effect is to maximize the truth and interpretation of the ontological argument. We can undertake to summarize the steps which we have taken in the previous chapters by enumerating them one after another, although it must be understood that it is only when they are combined together that they express the truth of interpretation and involve the interpretation of truth. (1) Thinking, insofar as it is thinking, involves and expresses existence; and existence, insofar as it is existence, involves and expresses thinking. (2) Thinking and existence each inhere in the self, the self which thinks and exists. (3) The self is equally individual and collective, both personal and communal. (4) The thinking and existence of the self are to be understood in terms equally religious and secular, faithful and rational, and theological and philosophical. Thought and existence are no less divine than human. Or we can say that the self, both individual and collective, is equally divine and human. (5) The self, alike individual and collective, both divine and human, equally thinking and existing, can be known, not in its actual self (not as the thing-in-itself) but only as it appears in the possible appearances of natural space and time. (6) The thought and existence of the self cannot be construed on analogy with, or by representation through, the natural world of finite space and time. Thought and existence are not, in themselves, empiricist (the correspondence theory of truth). The thought and existence of the self cannot be construed on analogy with, or by representation through, any innate faculty of mind or soul. Thought and existence are not, in themselves, rationalist (the coherence theory of truth). (7) What thought and existence actually are in themselves are their relationship. What the self, alike individual and collective, both divine and human, is, in itself, is relationship, the relationship as self, the relationship of selves. Not to know thought and existence in themselves but to engage them dialectically is to articulate the golden rule. I can think (will) the self—the self of my neighbor, the self of others, the self of God, myself—not in itself, for in itself the self is nothing but relationship. Thus, I can think (will) the self only in my relations with the self, as the self of other(s) can know itself only in its relations with the self. There is nothing outside or inside the self to be known—except its appearances in space and time—but only the self, its thought and existence, in its relationships with self. (8) The very beginning of the self is its relationship(s): in the relationship is the beginning. The only possible—that is, actual—beginning is in thought and existence, not in space and time which have no beginning (or end). Without beginning in relationship, without the relationship which is the beginning, there is no thinking, no existence, no self (whether divine or human), no history..., only fate (thought and existence always other than and opposed to what they are in themselves). (9) The beginning, the principle, history, thought and existence... can begin only once, and thus every beginning is eternal. For the self—alike individual and communal—to begin, for each self to begin, it must embody the original and eternal relationship of beginning in the freedom of thinking and existing. (10) The unique and universal model of this beginning, the principle or beginning of this beginning, the beginning which brings beginnings into the world at the beginning is the Bible, than which nothing prior in beginning can be thought to exist in the beginning and that which cannot be thought to begin except by beginning to exist (existing in the beginning). (11) The Bible begins the history of thought and existence, divine and human, by beginning, by revealing that the beginning of the self, individual and collective, is from nothing, from nothing found in the finite appearances of natural space and time. (12) Nothing begins before the Bible, for there is no beginning when (where) there is no beginning. There can be no beginning before the beginning. In the beginning is the beginning (is the beginning...). Nothing begins after the Bible, for there is no beginning when (where) there is no beginning. There can be no beginning after the beginning. In the beginning is the beginning (is the beginning...). (13) Thought and existence begin and end with the Bible. (The Bible begins and ends with [its] thought and existence.) They are found neither before the Bible—for that is inconceivable—nor after the Bible—for that is equally inconceivable. (14) Thought and existence are not found in what I call in my essay in thinking extra-biblical paganism. They are not found outside their beginning and ending with the Bible.

Let me stop here, for this is where my essay in thinking begins and ends. I hope these loaded—dialectical, paradoxical, contentious, controversial—propositions involving thought and existence serve to recall the beginning and end of our discussion. My one point, always, is to show that thinking—the dialectic of thought and existence—is not given to us naturally, either by the senses (empirically) or innately (rationally). It is given to us—and we give it back—as the gift of relationship, in our thought and existence, in the self as relationship and the relationship as self, the self individual and social, alike divine and human. What must be radically eschewed, for all space and time, is any idea of knowing the self—the self of persons, the self of God—as an object of nature, as something we can possess, either in our hands literally (and so empirically), or in our mind or soul literally (and so rationally). Self-knowledge is relational in as radical (and limited!) a sense as is knowledge of God and knowledge of others. Thought and existence are not given naturally to humans in physical birth. Thought and existence do not begin naturally. They do not begin in nature, for it is precisely nature which has no beginning (or end). All peoples who model themselves on nature—extra-biblical peoples—have no conception of beginning to exist (they have no existence in beginning to think).

I argue so vigorously for the absolute distinction between the chosen people of the Bible and extra-biblical peoples, for it is only on the basis of acknowledging, accepting, and embracing—in fear and trembling—this distinction that we can develop a notion of discrimination which distinguishes between truth and falsehood, between freedom and slavery, between discrimination accessible to all and discrimination which is used against some to benefit others. It is only when we distinguish critically between the ignorance of and blindness to beginning in nature on the part of extra-biblical peoples and the revelation of beginning separate from nature—in thought and existence—on the part of biblical peoples that we are then in a position to effect the one distinction that counts, the distinction between what I call the dialectic of thought and existence and their idolatrous reduction to dualistic opposition, such that one or the other side of the relationship is identified as unnatural and thus as ultimately deserving of annihilation (nihilism), something utterly inconceivable and unimaginable in extra-biblical paganism. There is no merit as such in demonstrating, without letup, what must, to begin with, appear utterly alien to those who have not yet begun to think and exist—that thinking is not to be found in the extra-biblical world, that there is no thinking based on nature (extrinsic or intrinsic, objective or subjective), that nobody in the extra-biblical world exists, that extra-biblical texts cannot be interpreted (they have no conception of interpreting existence)....

To note that there is no merit in itself in demonstrating that thought and existence are not to be found in the extra-biblical world is but to remark, indirectly, that there is no concept of merit (merit does not exist) outside the Bible, merit in which all can share equally, the merit flowing from loving God above all others and your neighbor as yourself. Naturally, all extra-biblical peoples have terms, verbal and nonverbal, which indicate what they mean by merit, what merit means in their culture. This is naturally the common sense riposte, that is, evasion, on the part of both scholars and lay people to the awesome demands of thought and existence. What is inadequate—fundamentally wrong—about this response, however, is that it fails to recognize, it represses, the complex oxymoron which is our common sense. Our five senses (what Kant and Hegel call sensibility and Kierkegaard the aesthetic sphere of human existence) are common to all peoples (they are innate). But what the five senses show us, when we have eyes to see and ears to hear, is how particular, subjective, relative, and uncertain and thus how egoistical, certain, and absolutist they are. Since tastes cannot be disputed, they become indisputably absolutist. What makes our senses common in truth and interpretation is not that we all possess them naturally but that we all use them commonly, that we all interpret their truth in our common thinking and existence. What is common in common sense is not given either commonly or in our senses. It is given only when we become responsible for beginning commonly, and we can begin commonly only when we choose to think and to exist in freedom, equality, and solidarity with others as they with us. It is naturally proper for scholars to be scrupulous in detailing what a particular extra-biblical society, say in pre-Columbian America or in antiquity, views as meritorious. But scholars would properly consider it unscholarly if the merit of their scholarship were judged according to the notion of merit which they bring to our attention in their scholarly study.

The only merit to be found in our unforgiving demonstration that thought and existence are not present in the extra-biblical world is that only then can we begin to account for their idolatrously dualistic perversions in our own modern (that is, biblical) world. We can begin to overcome the disastrous dualisms between thought and existence, between faith and reason, between the religious and secular, between theology and philosophy, not to mention those splitting the self between the individual and the collective, only when we recognize (1) that neither is to be found in the extra-biblical world and (2) that both sides of the dialectic come into thought and existence with the Bible from nothing, from nothing subject to the ignorance and blindness of the natural law of contradictory space and time. In terms of practical criticism this means that we have to engage ourselves on three overlapping fronts: (1) extra-biblical paganism; (2) the Bible; and (3) modernity (including the Bible but beginning, universally, with the Common Era and, more particularly, with what we, in the English-speaking world, call the early modern world). Our three fronts overlap or occupy shifting relations not merely or primarily because their content, in part, occupies common ground but, above all, because it is we moderns—biblical heirs—we who conduct the investigations whose content, whose thought and existence, overlaps these three fronts simultaneously. Let us review these three fronts, in preparation for concluding our essay in thinking with the dialectic of truth and interpretation, its real beginning and end.

Whether we begin analytically at the end with our double distinction—first, between the extra-biblical law of contradiction and the golden rule of the Bible and, second, between the dialectic of truth and interpretation, on the one hand, and idolatrous dualism, on the other, which is thus actually only one distinction, that between dialectic and dualism—or whether we begin historically at the beginning by studying the actual texts (both verbal and nonverbal) of extra-biblical peoples, what counts, ultimately, is that we account for our beginning with peoples who have no account of beginning. My experience, as teacher, reader of scholarly and critical works, and interlocutor, indicates that beginning students (whether undergraduate or graduate) and accomplished scholars, critics, and thinkers alike generate enormous resistance to being called upon to account for their beginnings, for their own thought and existence. I am not here concerned with the psychological and/or sociological reasons for this resistance (although they are most absorbing and deeply troubling, in themselves). To account for one's beginning is to learn to view oneself—all selves—historically, to learn to embody the ontological argument in one's life—all life—such that nothing can be thought outside (your) existence and that nothing exists outside (your) thought. I think, therefore, I am. Whatever is, must be. Facts are to be deduced from right, not right from facts. The beginning student senses and the experienced student knows that all the world's problems meet in—are created by!—the demand that we live the dialectic of our thought and existence, that we boldly, forthrightly, bluntly, even rudely, as Nietzsche counsels, think through our existence and exist within our thought, that we account for our existence and exist within (be responsible for) our accounting. This account is history, the common story of our lives, both involving the interpretation of our existence as true and expressing the truth of the interpretation of our existence. The bluntness or even rudeness enters in when we demand that our interlocutors move beyond the standard clichés of our sophisticated culture that we be critical and open-minded like Socrates or that teaching be understood on the model of Socratic dialogue. I come to bear witness to the truth, I say. What is truth? they ask. I write this book. I attempt to maneuver our discussion into what I think may be the more immediately neutral territory of interpretation, knowing all the while that it is not. I ask people to account for their interpretations, for what is presupposed by and implied in the very thought and existence of interpretation in the world. I ask them to reflect on what it means for us that to think and to exist are to interpret, that thought and existence—not separately but only in their unified dialectic—are indistinguishable from interpretation. I come to bear witness to interpretation, I say. What is interpretation? they ask. I write this book.

Thinking, thought and existence, truth and interpretation are so common, apparently, so ubiquitous, so abstractly immediate that we have to make them unnatural, we have to be rude about them, we have to make them alien to ourselves if we are to return to (and with!) them, possessing a refreshed sense of being at home in and through them. The problem is not only that familiarity but also that unfamiliarity breeds contempt. Still, if we are to overcome the contempt of familiarity, we must rudely court the contempt of being unfamiliar. Think of Hamlet! Great philosophers, like strong poets, call upon our contempt of the familiar—our grousing, our cynicism, our melancholy, our alienation, our common sense experience that the more things change the more they stay the same—and then challenge that contempt to see if we are really prepared to overcome our contempt of the unfamiliar by embracing the familiar as the unfamiliar. Their stock in trade is paradox and metaphor by and through which they challenge our common sense evaluation of things such that, in our re-evaluation of them, we discover new value in the old and old value in the new. Recall that Descartes and Spinoza alienate us from what is familiarly contemptible by challenging us with the unfamiliar as contemptible: the individual self withdrawn from all that is familiar to it in the world of experience, in the body, even in its own thought; the cause of itself (substance or God) withdrawn from all that is familiar to us in the world of experience, in our body, even in our own thought. The self of Descartes—which is ultimately the self not only human but also divine—and Spinoza's cause of itself—which is ultimately the self not only divine but also human—is the principle of alienation; the principle with which we must begin if we are ever to begin to think such that the only thing we can think is our existence and if we are to begin to exist such that the only existing thing is our thinking; the beginning; history....

Surely, it is the Bible itself which begins—which provides us with the archetype of beginning—with utter contempt for the world, the world of natural space and time whose thought and existence—as found in both the immortal and mortal beings of extra-biblical peoples—are hidden in the contradictory law of fatal ignorance and blindness. The Bible comes into thought and existence—the thought and existence of both God and human beings—declaring that their creation is from nothing, from nothing to be found prior to them in spatial and temporal nature. The Bible begins as the alien, as declaring itself alien to the common sense world of natural space and time, as alienated from the natural processes of generation and destruction. We can equally say that the Bible declares the world to be alien to itself, its alienation the secret which fate hides within the ignorance and blindness of the law of contradiction. But the paradox of the Bible—its enormous creativity and its enormous danger—is that its creativity is its salvation from contempt. For the Bible shows that God creates all there is, in thought and existence, from nothing, from nothing contemptible in itself.

We must show contempt for our contemporary ignorance and blindness by alienating ourselves from them, by reducing them to nothing, by showing that they are not creative or original in themselves, that in themselves they are nothing. For only then are we free—in our thought and existence—to choose the world, the world of the secular, as the beginning which is accessible to all human beings, without exception, without discrimination based on the facts of natural difference (race, gender, class...), without contempt. We cannot choose what we are, literally or naturally. We can only choose what we are not so that we can become what we are (not). But the rub, as always, is the irreversible paradox that, so long as the world lies under the ignorance and blindness of natural contradiction, it knows no contempt. It knows nothing at all. It neither thinks nor exists. Nothingness—contempt for natural contradiction—must be introduced into the world as the very alienating beginning of its thought and existence if we are, in fact, to be able to think and to exist beyond or uncorrupted by the contempt of alienation, the contempt of nothingness. Oh happy contempt! we can say, paraphrasing Augustine in his recognition of the paradoxical joy of sin: *O felix culpa!* We must have contempt for what is familiar if we are to choose the familiar in good faith as the substance of our thought and existence, as the cause of itself. But it is precisely because contempt, like nothing, comes into the world in the very choice which we make of our thought and existence that it becomes so common to reduce our thought and existence to nothing, to contempt for the familiar. The proverbial saying that familiarity breeds contempt is the cynical idolatry which the Bible engages from beginning to end. The challenge, as always, is how to begin with the familiar, how to live with the familiar, not on the grounds of the familiar in itself, for in itself the familiar is nothing creative of our thought and existence, but on the grounds of choosing the familiar such that we make ourselves responsible for its thought and existence, that we make the familiar our very thought and existence.

In order to begin we have to begin separate from, alienated from, what is immediately given in the nature of space and time, for only then can we choose them as our thought and existence and not find them—that is, ourselves—contemptible. Prophets, however, live as aliens, dishonored in their own country, held in contempt by their contemporaries. To challenge the common sense contempt with which people normally live their lives and thus to challenge them to embrace the unfamiliar, not as the contemptible to which they merely transfer, dualistically, their familiar contempt, but as that which allows them to confront, embrace, appropriate, and overcome their contempt for the familiar is often only to find oneself the familiar subject of contempt, the subject to which familiar contempt has been transferred as that which is unfamiliar (the archetype of the scapegoat). What distinguishes original thinking—whether in formal texts: philosophical, religious, poetic, and artistic; or in the informal texts of our familiar lives—is its very contempt for merely contemptible thinking, for thinking which does nothing but replicate the familiar breeding of contempt in that it does not take us—our thought and existence—back to its beginning in which the familiar is chosen, again and eternally, as the radically unfamiliar, as that which is ever new, fresh, and creative. Original thinking demands, with both rudeness and grace, that we show our contempt for the familiar which breeds contempt by subjecting it to the unfamiliar, by our beginning with it in our thought and existence, by our freely choosing it as that which properly constitutes the human family. The beginning is always original, always creative, always liberating, always revolutionary, always radical, always revelatory insofar as the beginning is constituted—insofar as we constitute the beginning—as our choice of the beginning, as the choice in which we are responsible for our beginning with our thought and existence. In the beginning are thought and existence. The primordially human (if not natural) desire is to think and to exist. Human beings are original—creative—in the beginning. But everywhere they are enchained to contempt for the familiar. How does this contemptible change come about? I do not know. How can the chains of familiar contempt be legitimized as the familiar bonds of thought and existence? That is the question I undertake to answer by showing that it presupposes our comprehending—living—our thought and existence as beginning, eternally, with the dialectic of truth and interpretation.

The only way that I know of to break the chains of familiar contempt—in the tradition of Nietzsche's prophetic image of smashing the idols of *ressentiment* with the insistent hammer of truth and interpretation—is to maximize our alienation from our familiar notions of thought and existence. As I indicated before, we can do this, we must do this, both analytically and historically. Philosophical—and theological—analysis of, say, the problematic of beginning, of nothing, of contempt tends, it is my experience, to arouse polite dismay on the part of listeners (or readers) as if they were in the presence of a precocious child whose cleverness may be as unpredictable and as unfathomable as its temper tantrums. The best thing to do, they feel, is to remain patient, not overreact, say as little as possible, and the outburst will (one hopes to god) pass. Historical analysis—discussion of the thought and existence of actual texts, verbal or nonverbal, or their structure—tends to have the opposite impact, when, that is, the analysis is truly historical and demonstrates that all extra-biblical texts, without exception, have no conception of beginning, of creation, of choice, of freedom, of history, of thought and existence. Such an analysis shows, as we have seen, that extra-biblical texts do not exist in their own conception but are forever blinded by and rendered ignorant of the terms of their discourse whose thought and existence lie hidden within the law of fatal contradiction. To show that extra-biblical texts have no thought and existence—when there they are, reflected in the eyes of the readers beholding them—reflects, unnaturally, back directly on their readers, as it never reflects on their own heroes (Oedipus, Socrates, Pentheus...). The reaction of listeners (or readers) tends to be the adult equivalent of a temper tantrum.

Greek texts—epic and tragic poetry, and also comedy; philosophy, from the pre-Socratics through Socrates, Plato, and Aristotle to the post-Socratic philosophers of Hellenistic Greece, culminating in Sextus Empiricus and Plotinus; and history—are central to maximizing the anxiety of consequence and its contempt for learning to view the familiar in a most unfamiliar (alienating) fashion. The paradoxes of our relation to the Greeks are legion—when they are not, as they normally are, contradictory (idolatrous). It is the civilization of the Greeks (and Romans)—syncretically combined with other elements of the civilizations of the ancient Near

East—which accompanies the Bible in its conquest of the world and in the world's conquest of the Bible. The privilege seemingly bestowed upon the civilization of the Greeks as superior to that of all other extra-biblical peoples leads nearly all thinkers—with very rare exceptions, like Shakespeare and Kierkegaard—to forget that comparisons with that which has no principle of comparison, no conception of beginning and end, are utterly contradictory. Kierkegaard, doubtless the most acute student of Socrates of all time, reminds his readers that from Socrates he learns more than from any other human being, while adding that from no human being can one learn anything. Kierkegaard, like few others, really grasps the principle that we cannot learn—in the strong sense of learning: renewing our beginning; rethinking (reliving), from the beginning, our thought and existence—from one who has no conception of learning, who shows that to seek knowledge is to be ignorant of what you are seeking and that to learn (or to teach) is to find yourself always other than and opposed to what is knowable in itself, the law of contradiction, the fatal teacher of extra-biblical paganism which demonstrates without end that, in seeking to learn and to teach the law of contradiction, what you ineluctably learn and teach is that your learning and teaching violate the law of contradiction.

Kierkegaard understands that we can learn from no human beings, as such. We can learn from no human beings who, as such, are nothing in themselves. We can learn from human beings only when they recognize that they are created from nothing. We can learn from human beings only when they choose to begin, having fallen from the natural paradise of contradiction, when they choose to begin loving God above all others and their neighbors as themselves. We can learn from human beings only when they are our neighbors, when we learn from and teach them as we would have them learn from and teach us. Human beings are not in themselves our neighbors; they only become our neighbors, and, in that radical sense, human beings, when they choose to live by—to invest their thought and existence in—the golden rule of life. Those from whom we cannot learn as such are the extra-biblical peoples of the world. What they have to teach us, and this is why they are so precious to us, is—in inverting Socrates—that we have nothing to learn from them, that they have nothing to teach us. Our responsibility—as thinkers, as thinkers whose thought is our only existence and whose existence is our only thought—is to learn from Socrates in recognizing that he demonstrates to us that to live by the law of contradiction is to be ignorant of and blind to your thought and existence. In learning from Socrates we must not fall into the non-Socratic contradiction, that is, into idolatry, that there is any method or content, any thought or existence, in what we learn from him. The enormity of what we learn from Socrates—as from all extra-biblical peoples—is that their life, as such, is nothing in itself, this nothing being what I call the gap, the leap of faith and reason, the presence including all people within the middle of life, within the beginning, within the choice of beginning to think and to exist freely, within history, within the Common Era of life. The only people excluded from the common middle embracing beginning and end, past and future, in the eternal life of historical thought and existence, are those who refuse—in brazen or cowardly fashion—to choose the golden rule of living within the presence of their fellow human beings.

To comprehend—in fear and trembling—the awesome nothingness of what it is that lies hidden in the ignorance and blindness of contradictory nature, to which extra-biblical peoples are endlessly subject, is the beginning of wisdom whose principle is the fear of—the reverence for and the love of beginning in thought and existence with—the lord God, the beginning than which none other can be conceived as existing. Just as we must learn, negatively, what it means to think and to exist as nothing, within the extra-biblical world of paganism, so we must learn, positively, what this nothing is within the thought and existence of the biblical world. Each step takes dialectical finesse, and each is but the mirror image of the other. With a single misstep we are plunged back into Hume's melancholy slough of despond. The danger from the Socratic side is that we are constantly tempted to identify the fatal absence or lack of thought and existence, the ignorance of and blindness to what things are in themselves, or the nothingness which is hidden in fatal otherness always opposed to its appearance in contradiction, with something, with the very appearances of Greek life, that which all Greeks ineluctably experience as their contradiction. The danger from the biblical side is that the nothing to which the world of natural space and time is reduced and from which thought and existence are created becomes something which is nothing, an idol of nature whose identity is unthinkable and unimaginable as existing within extra-biblical paganism.

Idolatry is the demonic shadow of creation from nothing for the precise reason that it is creation which gives nothing prominence, which shows us that nature is nothing in itself but everything in our thought and existence. Nothing is not present in the extra-biblical world except as the lack or absence which we—we modern thinkers, the heirs of biblical creation from nothing—discern as the presence of fate endlessly opposing beginning and end, excluding the middle from life. In the biblical world, however, nothing becomes the very matrix of divine—and human— creativity. Nothing cannot be thought in itself and does not exist in itself, but there are no thought and existence outside nothing. Nothing is precisely that gap or leap whereby we begin to think and to exist. Nothing is the freedom to think and to exist. Nothing is the recognition that thought and existence are the cause of themselves, that they are their own choice, their own beginning, their own self-determination, that they are the covenant, the social contract, what Kant calls the kingdom of ends. It is precisely because thought and existence—divine and human—are nothing in themselves but everything in their relationship, the relationship of self which is both individual and communal and articulated through the golden rule of life, that not only is nothing creative of everything—to speak hyperbolically—but also nothing can become destructive of everything, something inconceivable and unimaginable to the extra-biblical world. Because everything—in thought and existence—is created from nothing, from nothing found in the world of contradictory space and time—everything can also be reduced back to nothing contradictory, to the contradictions of nature. Because nothing expresses the creative gap or leap—something—between being and becoming, something can also become—be reduced back to—nothing. It is this idolatry of annihilation or nihilism, of claiming to reduce something found in thought and existence to nothing, to nothing (that is, everything) contradictory, which comes into thought and existence with the Bible and is utterly inconceivable in the extra-biblical world.

The Bible is not fundamentally concerned, as the cause of itself, with what lies outside itself and what I call extra-biblical paganism (that which is endlessly caused through another). The extra-biblical world is nothing in itself, doomed without end to pass through the fatal vicissitudes of natural generation and destruction. Yet, that extra-biblical paganism becomes a category of thought and existence is due only to the Bible. In distinguishing itself from what in itself is nothing and without beginning and end, the Bible reduces extra-biblical paganism to the nothing from which it creates thought and existence, both human and divine. We all begin as pagans, like Abraham, in possession of our innate dispositions of sensibility and understanding. We perceive and we understand. But what we perceive and what we understand are but appearance whose metamorphoses are endlessly subject to fatal contradiction until and unless we make the leap out of nature into the freedom to think and to exist, both faithfully and rationally, as the self that is alike individual and communal.

The Bible, however, suffers maximal anxiety of consequence in creating thought and existence from the contradictory nature of space and time, for idolatry then emerges as the contradictory choice of paganism, the contradictory embrace of contradiction, the contradictory claim that, because some contradict nature, they should be reduced to that from which nature comes, to nothing, a claim utterly absent from the extra-biblical world where it is inconceivable that one could contradict the law of contradiction. In the extra-biblical world contradiction is always understood as ignorance or blindness (ultimately, natural death, destruction as the opposite of generation). But in the biblical world contradiction becomes the idolatry of dualistically distinguishing between those who are deemed natural and those who are deemed unnatural, the second group, having been denatured, then being subjected to annihilation, to reduction to nothing, the very opposite of creation.

III. CONCLUSION: THE DIALECTIC OF TRUTH AND INTERPRETATION

It is only in (the revealed) light of the biblical doctrine of the creation of thought and existence from nothing, from nothing subject to the contradictions of natural space and time, that we can develop a universal conception of truth and interpretation. Truth and interpretation are universal, however, not in themselves but only as they are chosen by the self, individual and collective, their choice eternally repeating the story of creation from nothing, the expulsion of Adam and Eve from the garden of natural paradise, the call of Abraham from extra-biblical nothingness into the fullness of thought and existence. We shall never be able to comprehend truth and interpretation as modern and we shall never be able to comprehend modernity as the age of truth and interpretation until and unless we recognize that neither truth nor interpretation can be thought to exist or can exist as thought outside the biblical tradition. The moment we impute truth and interpretation to extra-biblical peoples, we falsify both their lives and ours. We project into their lives our own values, without being fully or properly conscious of either their values or our own, and then we read back into our lives the values which we find there, with the result that, in producing an unholy admixture of both their values and our own, we falsify not only their but also our own values, without even knowing it.

The issue, in itself, is not how we think about extra-biblical peoples. The issue, as always, is how we think, and nothing is more important to our thinking than how we think about that which is utterly different from our thinking. If we fail to come up against the unknown, if we fail to experience the awesomeness of what is unknown, if we simply assimilate the unknown to what we know and thus the known to the unknown, then we shall fail, abysmally fail, to account for the truth of interpretation and for the interpretation of truth. Truth and interpretation (and their infinite versions) are so precious, like thought and existence, for they are all we are. Otherwise, we are nothing, suffering, with Hume, the melancholy of living betwixt a false reason and no reason at all, as we gamble at the playing table of life where all the cards are jokers: whatever *is* may *not be*. In order to establish a comprehensive conception of truth and interpretation we have to understand thought and existence, their unique and universal subject, as created from nothing, from nothing natural. Thought and existence are to be comprehended neither on the basis of natural space and time, according to the methods of scientific verification, nor on the basis of natural humanity, as found in extra-biblical paganism. Thus it is critical to understand both that thought and existence are created from nothing natural and that they are simultaneously religious and secular. The secular no more reflects the world of space and time than it reflects the world of extra-biblical paganism. It is also the case that the religious no more reflects a space and time projected into a space and time after death, a space and time which are no space and time, than it reflects the notion of immortality found in the extra-biblical world.

The only way in which we can protect truth and interpretation from degenerating into dogmatism, absolutism, and objectivism—especially on the side of truth—and into skepticism, relativism, and subjectivism—especially on the side of interpretation—is forthrightly to eschew all dualism between faith and reason, between the religious and the secular realms. Only then are we in a position to recognize that truth and interpretation, like their subject, thought and existence, are created from nothing, from nothing appearing in the contradictions of natural space and time, and thus cannot be located in either the natural realm of space and time or in the extra-biblical world of natural contradiction. What has to be comprehended is the complex truth, which alone is amenable to interpretation, that scientific knowledge of nature as objectively certain can be preserved from becoming illusory (uncertain) only if it is recognized that liberation from the ignorance and blindness of the contradictory doctrine of opposites which rules nature in the extra-biblical world is due to the creation of thought and existence from nothing, from nothing objectively certain or uncertain. In the extra-biblical world subject and object are endlessly opposed to each other in life, while they are at their end and identical with each other in death. Indeed, subject and object together constitute fate, that which is always other than and opposed to itself in the life of appearances and that which is always at its end and identical with itself in the death of appearances. Once, however, the law of contradictory nature is revealed for the contradiction which it is by the creation of thought and existence from nothing, then a critical distinction is introduced, not between the terms subject and object, which are indistinguishable, but between the concept—whether comprehended subjectively or objectively—and the term, which is indifferently subjective or objective. The concept is precisely that which cannot be thought except existing and cannot exist except as thought. The concept is always thought and existence, the subject or self, both individual and collective, alike divine and human, as distinct from the objects of nature, which, if either thought or existence is imputed to them, become idols subversive of not only thought and existence but also the science of nature.

Neither truth nor interpretation is to be found in Greek or in any other extra-biblical texts. It is not that the Greeks, like all extra-biblical peoples, do not have a term which we would properly translate as "truth." It is not that we do not recognize that one of the characteristics of the god Hermes—whence the term hermeneutics—is that he is an intermediary, an interpreter, between immortals and mortals. Rather, what we must recognize is that truth and interpretation are concepts and that, like all concepts, they can be thought only existing and can exist only as thought, notwithstanding the difficulty modern men and women have in breaking with the idolatry of nature (the naturalistic fallacy). Truth and interpretation can be conceived as existing and can exist as conceived only in the context of the ontological argument for thought and existence, which is the sole ground of truth and interpretation, the sole ground of demonstration. That which is ignorant of and blind to truth and interpretation cannot be interpreted as true (or false) and cannot be held to possess (or to falsify) the truth of interpretation. Truth and interpretation are not simply one opinion among other opinions. That alone can be interpreted as true which can be interpreted as true from itself alone, to recall Spinoza's formulation of biblical interpretation. Truth and interpretation, precisely like thought and existence, capture the dialectic of the golden rule. Both truth and interpretation are relationship. Truth and interpretation are no more mine than they are yours. I may well criticize your interpretation of the truth and the notion of truth underlying your conception of interpretation, but I can do this only in presupposing that the truth and its interpretation are equally accessible to the two of us. Indeed, it is only because I presuppose that you are truthful and want to be interpreted as truthful that I can hold you responsible to what you say and do, whether or not what you say and do are truthful and are consistent with the interpretations of what you say and do.

Not only do truth and interpretation hang together, in opposition to any notions of skepticism and dogmatism, but it is also the case that, when taken individually, each must be protected from idolatrous falsification as objects which are knowable only in the space and time of nature. The truth is absolute, the priority beyond which none can be thought to exist or can exist as thought. But the absolute truth is not to be confused with or reduced to the realm of natural certainty whose immediacies inevitably turn into uncertainties. The absolute which is the truth can be known as an object neither in itself nor relative to anything else, not to you, to me, or to anything found within or even without natural space and time, including God. Truth is not knowable any more within the self, whether the self of God or human beings, than it is relative to the self, whether the self of God or human beings. But the truth is known—it is thought and exists—as relationship, the golden rule of loving God as the truth above all others and your neighbor as the truth of yourself.

Truth is not mine as opposed to yours, or yours as opposed to mine. Truth is not God's as opposed to yours or mine. Truth is not one community's as opposed to another community's.... Truth is the self, but not the self viewed in terms of either the appearances of natural space and time or an object knowable as certain in itself. Truth is the self as relationship, the relationship of truth, both individual and communal. I do not possess the truth of myself as I possess certain things. The truth which I possess of myself is my relationship to my self, as I hold myself constantly responsible to the truth of myself, which is traditionally what has been called conscience (knowledge with or in relationship to myself). Conscience is no more interior (intrinsic or innate) than it is external (extrinsic or learned), so long as the opposition between interior and exterior is understood in terms of the spatial and temporal similes of nature. Conscience is my self-relationship, my recognition that I must be true to myself and that I can be true to my relationship with myself only insofar as I eschew all notions of the self as a thing which can be, with certainty, located in natural space and time. When, in good conscience, I am true to myself, I represent myself as I want all selves to represent themselves, in their self-relationships and in their relationships to me. It is conceivable that, in any given space and time, there remains only one person of good conscience, just as audacious theologians in the Middle Ages imagine that only one good person remains pure among human sinners, the Virgin or ultimately only God himself. But, just as it is impossible to conceive that God could stop loving sinful men and women, for his love is absolute and unconditional, which does not mean that God loves the sin of men and women, so it is also inconceivable that the one remaining person of good conscience would have originally been the only person of good conscience in existence. Good conscience comes into thought and existence only in relationship, in that relationship of self which is both self and other. It is equally inconceivable that persons of good conscience, so long as they remained of good conscience, would relinquish their faith in others, however corrupt they were, for persons of good conscience do not forget the common history of all persons, that, in the beginning, they come freely into thought and existence from nothing, from nothing which is not worthy of thought and existence, both divine and human, notwithstanding the fact that everywhere they are in chains.

Interpretation is no less absolute as relationship than is truth. But interpretation is not absolute in itself, as if it could be known as certain things are known, for that would be to fall into the idolatry of turning the subject of interpretation—thought and existence—into a finite object. Indeed, interpretation is the methodological side of truth as thought is the methodological or conscious (thinking) side of existence. What interpretation constantly reminds us of is that, in Hegelian terms, the method is the content. Interpretation is not something we do separate from the ontological argument of thought and existence. Interpretation is the recognition that we interpret others—including ourselves—as we would have them interpret us. To interpret a text, a person, a situation....—as true—is to recognize that my interpretation of the text, person, or situation is no less subject to the truth of interpretation than is the interpretation on the part of the text, person, or situation of me to the truth of interpretation. I cannot interpret something without my thought and existence being implicated in that which I interpret. We may call this subjectivity—interpretation is subjectivity—so long as we recognize that the subject of interpretation is absolute—the absolute relationship—and that it is not to be idolized as a certain object of nature. The subject of interpretation can never become certain (or uncertain) like a natural object of space and time, and this is why it is critically important not to confuse the subjects of thought and existence with the objects of nature. The subjects of thought and existence, what Kant calls things-in-themselves, can be interpreted only as selves in the actualities of their relationships and can be known as objects only in the appearances of natural space and time.

Precisely because truth and interpretation are each the absolute of relationship—the relationship of thought and existence—each is critically important both to creating the significance of the other and to preserving the other from collapsing into the idolatry of dualism. It is critical to recognize that, when we claim to know the truth—as the absolute worth of the self, individual and communal—we also recognize that this claim is always an interpretation, an interpretation of the truth. It is equally critical to recognize that, when we claim to interpret something—and the only significant thing we can interpret is the self, both individual and communal—we also recognize that our interpretation involves and expresses the truth. If, however, we deny that truth is attainable or view it as indistinguishable from the certainty of natural objects, then our interpretation—and whatever activity involving thought and existence we are engaged in is always interpretative—turns into the idolatry of dualism. Equally, if we deny that interpretation is grounded in truth or if we hold that the truth in which interpretation is grounded is that of objective certainty, then our interpretative activity no less becomes idolatrous dualism. All notions of truth outside interpretation and all notions of interpretation outside truth always fall into the dualism between objectivity and subjectivity, alike dog-matic and skeptical. Truth, we must constantly realize, is not an object, on analogy with the objects or things of nature, but the subject of our lives, the self which we share with others as they share it with us. Interpretation, we must constantly realize, is not a method among other methods, but it is the method of our lives, the method by which we engage other selves as they engage ours.

The test of any conception of thinking, of any conception of truth and interpretation, is its capacity to discern, to deal with, and to account for error, falsehood, or deception, that which the biblical tradition com-prehends as sin. Indeed, the paradox of truth and interpretation is that, in order to account for error, in order to provide for a history of error, they must acknowledge themselves as the source or principle of error. In the section of *The Critique of Pure Reason* entitled Transcendental Dialectic, in which the argument of the work reaches its magnificent culmination, Kant recognizes that, if reason fails to account for its own error or irrationality, what he calls transcendental illusion, which I introduced in an earlier chap-ter, then reason will not be truly rational: reason will not embody the prac-tical relationship of thought and existence. Kant undertakes to show that the transcendental illusion into which reason falls results from its thinking that it can know the thing-in-itself (that is, what it is in itself) either as an object appearing in space and time or as a transcendent object existing out-side space and time. That reason falls into error, is the source of its error, must recognize its error, and is responsible for overcoming its error Kant calls reason's dialectic. As dialectical, reason becomes other than itself; it becomes its own opposite; but, as other than and opposed to itself, reason is still itself, however deluded it is about itself. It is still reason in itself. What Kant is concerned to demonstrate is that it is reason alone which is responsible for error. It is reason which errs; it is reason which is constantly subject to the transcendental illusion of conflating the transcendental reality of the thing-in-self, persons in relation, with objects as they are known with certainty either within the natural realm of space and time or in themselves as completely transcending all natural experience. (In Kant's technical vocabulary, "transcendental" illusion indicates that reason is con-scious of and wills to overcome the error for which it is responsible, while reason becomes "transcendent" when it falsely thinks that it can know ob-jects separate from their appearances in space and time.)

If reason (which Kant equally calls practice, will, and even faith) is not dialectical, if reason does not represent the dialectic of thought and existence, then it will have no way of distinguishing between, on the one hand, the ignorance and blindness to which the law of contradiction subjects extra-biblical peoples and, on the other, the revelation to all peoples that they are liberated from the contradictions of nature so long as they choose to create their thought and existence from nothing and do not confuse it with objects either natural or transcendent (the dualism between empiricism and rationalism). In the extra-biblical world, where thought and existence are endlessly opposed to and other than what they are in themselves—their dialectical relationship—all wrongdoing, deception, sin... is ignorance. One cannot knowingly do wrong. Everything wrong is always done in ignorance of the good. It is inconceivable in the extra-biblical world that something could exist in thought or be thought to exist as both good and bad; that someone could—knowingly, purposely, and determinately—will, think, or do something wrong; or that, finally, reason—life as thought and existence—could be dialectical. The opposites of knowledge and ignorance, or of good and bad, are forever excluded from their common ground in the dialectic of thought and existence, whether divine or human. But the moment that thought and existence are created from nothing or, in more Kantian terms, transcendentally liberated from the fatal ignorance and blindness of natural contradiction, error and deception—sin—enter the world in the shadow of thought and existence as transcendental illusion, the idolatry of dualism.

The terrible paradox of idolatry is that we know the contradiction which we are, that we must know and are responsible for the contradiction which we are—which is inconceivable in the extra-biblical world—and then evade, repress, deny, and lie about it. Socrates knows that he is contradictory, but what the contradiction is that he knows—that it is his own self, the dialectic of his thought and existence—slips away from him, fatally, ineluctably, into ignorance, oblivion, blindness, and death. It is inconceivable to Socrates that he could know contradiction, that he could know what contradiction is, for it is precisely contradiction of which he is ignorant. It is contradiction which blinds him to contradiction. We may recall that it is Aristotle who observes that the law of contradiction is the first principle of demonstration for the very reason that it is indemonstrable, without beginning. The law of contradiction is itself ignorant of and blind to the contradictory appearances of its beginning in the world of thought and existence. It is their very contradictory ignorance and blindness, the contradiction of which can never be known.

It is the heirs of the Bible who ineluctably have to confront the fate of knowing that it is they who are contradictory. What they have to know in knowing that they are contradictory is that it is they themselves who are the contradiction, that they are what the contradiction is. This is what Kant means by saying that reason is dialectical. It is reason which must recognize that thought and existence, both human and divine—that is, reason itself: we human beings—become dialectical, contradictory, dualistic, idolatrous, or sinful by being confused with natural objects such that we think we can know thought and existence either as objects of natural appearance in space and time or as transcendent objects beyond space and time. Ignorance of contradiction, in the Socratic mode, is not a choice; it has never been a choice and never will be a choice. Knowledge of contradiction, in the biblical mode, means that reason has the choice of its own dialectic of thought and existence, the choice of living them in the golden rule of relationship and of not reducing them to contradictory (or dualistic) idols. If reason does not look upon itself as dialectical, if reason fails to account for its own dialectic or error, then it will hide the errors of its own self-contradiction under dualistic idols (which, in turn, are often masked by the rhetoric of Socratic ignorance).

If we do not claim error or deception—sin—as our own, then either we shall pretend to live in the extra-biblical world ignorant of and blind to the contradictions of nature—the logical possibility which practical dialectic has eliminated for all space and time—or we shall fall into the idolatry of projecting our errors into idols for which we abjure responsibility. Error is not something which happens to us. Error is not due to nature (or, we might add, to language, the law of contradiction, or extra-biblical peoples...). Error (deception, illusion, falsehood...sin) is not due to our ignorance (of the law of contradiction), as it is in the extra-biblical tradition. Error is due precisely to the fact that the truth has been transcendentally revealed to us—through our eating of the fruit of the knowledge of good and evil—and that we fail to interpret it according to the golden rule of the relationship of thought and existence and thus fall into the transcendental illusion of confusing it with or reducing it to either the objective appearances of nature or transcendent objects outside nature. Whereas, in the extra-biblical tradition, people are naturally born ignorant of and blind to contradiction, in the biblical tradition contradiction is revealed as that from which all people who choose to live the dialectic of thought and existence are liberated for all space and time. It is precisely because we are born free, revealed in the truth which we are responsible for interpreting, that we fall into the transcendental illusion of locating our truth and interpretation, our freedom, in objects, thus contradicting ourselves, something unthinkable in extra-biblical paganism.

It is the Bible, we see yet again, which is the beginning, the beginning (or principle) of error and falsehood, of what theologians call sin. Outside the Bible there is no sin, just as outside the Bible there is no salvation or liberation from sin. Outside the Bible there is only contradiction. Outside the Bible there is only ignorance of contradiction. Outside the Bible there is only the contradiction of ignorance. It is the Bible which brings contradiction, the knowledge of contradiction, the knowledge that it is we who are contradictory, the knowledge that it is we who are responsible for contradiction, into thought and existence from nothing, from nothing contradictory. It is the Bible which brings truth and interpretation into the world from nothing, from nothing which can be accounted the contradictory origin of sin. Any account—text, representation, statement...—which cannot account for its own ignorance, deception, falsehood, contradiction, or sin is not an account which can give an accounting of itself. An account which is ignorant of its own beginning—the extra-biblical world of paganism—is not an account which, in itself, can account for itself. We, equally, cannot account for it; but, unlike the unaccountable account which is ignorant of and blind to its own account, we can—must—account for our not being able to account for it, so long as we do not conflate its lack of account, its ignorance of not having an account of itself, and our lack of accounting for it, our recognition that, compared with what it means to provide an accounting, it cannot be accounted for. An account which recognizes that it must account for itself, from the beginning, must always account for its errors or sin, for the ways in which it constantly falsifies that beginning by conflating it with or reducing it to the contradictory idols of nature which cannot account for their beginning.

There are only two accounts in the world, that which is ignorant of accounting for itself, from the beginning, and that which has the responsibility of accounting eternally, from the beginning, for its beginning and, in light of that account, constantly falsifies its account of the beginning. Once again, we see that it is solely within the dialectic of truth and interpretation that we can account for—narrate the history of—human error, sin, falsification, oppression, repression.... Indeed, it is only within the commitment to absolute truth and to absolute interpretation—which involves and expresses the thought and existence of the self, both divine and human, alike individual and communal—that error, deception, and sin can be revealed for they are, the reduction of absolute truth and interpretation to the relative certainties of idols. Not only does the dialectic of truth and interpretation provide for an accounting of error, but it also brings error, sin, conflict, disruption, revolution... into the world, by showing how any attachment to the relative certainties (and thus uncertainties) of the world are idols which, in themselves, are nothing.

When it is reported in the Gospels that Jesus tells his listeners that they must hate their father and mother, all their loved ones, their friends, and their companions and (that is, in order to) follow him, he does not mean that they are to replace one love with another, the love of human beings with the love of God, following extra-biblical adherence to the law of contradictory opposites according to which it would be inconceivable for one to love two (say, God and neighbor) equally. Rather, in following the law and the prophets, Jesus is demonstrating that love based on natural preference or favor—what Pascal calls the hate which human beings naturally bear for one another and Lactantius the *vitia splendida* of extra-biblical peoples (which are glittering sins not for them but solely for those of us who think that we can be called virtuous on the basis of imitating pagan ignorance of the truth and love of God and neighbor)—must be replaced by love which is unconditional and absolute: the love of God and neighbor. Jesus, in fact, is only repeating the story of Abraham's relationship to his son Isaac. The test for us human beings, eternally, is to love others, including ourselves, such that our human love can stand the test of divine love: that our love be absolute, that it not be conditioned on receiving anything finite, certain, or objective in return. The point is not to give up (on) the world—for that is the sin against the spirit which will never be forgiven—but to regain the world, to love the world, not on the world's terms, but according to the concept which cannot be thought except existing and which cannot exist except as thought.

That truth and interpretation are the absolute relationship of self, both individual and communal, which brings error into the world on its own account indicates that the account given as the dialectic of truth and interpretation is universal history which is accessible to all human beings who choose thought and existence as their eternal way of life. We can account for ourselves historically—and there is no accounting other than history—only if we begin such that all human beings, individual and collective, are equally free to begin in solidarity with us and we with them. The only beginning accessible to all is that which begins with our thought and existence liberated from fatal subjection to the contradictions of nature. The beginning can be true and interpreted truly yet is one whose truth can be interpreted falsely only if the beginning is its own account, if we begin on our own account. If we begin other than with ourselves—and we must always keep in mind that "ourselves" is no more human than divine—then we shall never be able to account for ourselves but shall find ourselves subject to the contradictions of nature for which there is no accounting. It is critically important to understand that both truth and interpretation are fundamentally—radically—historical, but it is equally important to understand that history embodies the absolute relation to the absolute, that relationship of self which is both individual and communal, both divine and human. History is the story of beginning dialectically with truth and interpretation. It is the universal story accessible to all, for no one is excluded on the basis of natural differences (the space and time of birth), and all are included on the basis of their thought and existence which are the universal choice for all. But truth and interpretation equally exclude all who refuse to include themselves within the universal accounting demanded by truth and interpretation. History is the account of all those who account to others as they would have them account to them. It is clear, therefore, that the notion that truth and interpretation are historical has nothing to do with relativity or subjectivism (in opposition to the idol of objectivism); but that truth and interpretation are historical does mean that they are relational and, in that precise sense, subjective, for history tells the story of subjects, selves both individual and collective, in their mutually rich and diverse relations of truth and interpretation.

Just as truth and interpretation are the universal point of view embodying the historical beginning in thought and expression accessible to all peoples, so they are also radically democratic. Truth and interpretation express the rule of all for all by all. The moment that truth and its interpretation become the rule of some for some by some, then they collapse into idolatry such that the self, individual and communal, divine and human, is divided against itself, with one part identified with what is natural and the other part identified with what is unnatural. Democracy is to be understood neither as mob rule nor as the dictatorship of the proletariat (however commonly such idols are conjured up by right wing and left wing ideologues). Democracy is to be understood as the rule of truth which is accessible to all and for which all bear the responsibility of interpreting. Democracy is the truth of all which must be interpreted not by some (who are not democrats) but by all for all.

It is clear that, just as truth and interpretation are radically historical and democratic, they are also secular. The secular, however, as I have argued at length, is to be understood not as natural simile but as the metaphor of thought and existence, alike divine and human, which is expressed solely in the relationship of self, the self of God and the self of human beings, both personal and communal. The secular is to be radically distinguished from both the natural world of science and the nature of extra-biblical paganism. The secular comes into thought and existence as the eternal history of the democratic self from nothing, from nothing which cannot account for its beginning in the world of natural appearances, but as everything which does account for itself as the relationship of loving God above all others and its neighbor as itself. To comprehend truth and interpretation as secular is to appropriate our religious vocation as the history which eternally liberates us from the ignorance and blindness of the contradictory law of nature. But life in the secular becomes undemocratic, unhistorical, unfaithful, irrational, contradictory, illusory, dualistic, and idolatrous the moment it attempts to account for truth and interpretation on any other basis than their beginning, not in the world of space and time, but in the world of thought and existence, which can never be understood as human if they are not equally and at the same time understood as divine (just as the ontological argument is properly subject to philosophers' ridicule if it does not apply as well to their thought and existence as to God's).

When Pilate asks Jesus, who says that he comes to bear witness to the truth, to the truth of the law and the prophets, what is truth?, it is Descartes and his modern successors who silently bear the anxiety of consequence that thinking cannot exist outside the Bible and that existence cannot be thought outside the Bible. To think is to exist within the Bible, and to exist is to think within the Bible. To think is to demonstrate the existence of the Bible, and to exist is to demonstrate that all thought is biblical dialectic. The Bible is the one text which cannot be thought except existing and which cannot exist except as thought. Indeed, the anxiety of consequence is such that there is only one answer to Pilate's question, an answer incomprehensible to Pilate. Pilate's question is rhetorical and sophistical, in the tradition, not of the golden rule of biblical dialogue, but of Socratic dialogue, dialogue whose sole function is to reflect the law of contradiction such that all speech, any human action, is shown to be ignorant of and blind to, both other than and opposed to, what it is in itself, its thought and existence. As a consequence of the Bible, I think and I exist, as you think and you exist. We have no choice—outside the choice of thought and existence.

To be silent or not to be silent is not the question. There is a time to be silent and a time to speak. The issue is how we are silent or how we speak, what it is that we communicate in our silence or in our speech. We may have nothing to communicate, or we may communicate nothing either in being silent or in speaking. In either our silence or our speech we may evade, repress, or subvert our responsibilities to communication. But communicate we must, either in silence or in words, either verbally or nonverbally. We have no choice but to communicate. To communicate or not to communicate is not the question, for the question is not whether we communicate or even why we communicate, but the question is Anselm's: *cur verbum* (*sermo* or *communicatio*) *homo?*—why does (did/will) the word of communication become human flesh?—or Kant's: how is it possible for that which comes belatedly into the world, the synthesis of communication, to be the priority of our thought and existence? Rousseau, after observing that human beings are born free to communicate but are everywhere enslaved to the chains of Babel, asks: how can the chains of our communication be legitimated, how can our communication, the very chains of our slavery, be the concept which can be thought only as existing and which can exist only as thought?

The anxiety of consequence is enormous. It is eternal. It is historical. It is consequential. We are the historical bearers of the consequences of eternity, willy-nilly. We belong to a chain of voices from which there is no exit. Communication is not a choice which we can make, for that choice has already and forever been made for and by us. The consequence of the original choice of communication is that communication is our only choice, the only choice which we can make, forever and historically. We may resist, shirk, repress, or reject communication. We may parody, subvert, deconstruct, or deny the chains of our communication. We may not even be aware that we communicate, or we may distort or even undertake to negate communication through propaganda, double-speak, the big lie, or the annihilating silence of the death camps. But the anxiety of consequence which we suffer as heirs of the Bible, believing and secular, is that there is no act which does not communicate, so long as we survivors remember the thought and existence of our forebears as the consequences for which we bear responsibility unto eternity. For even the ultimate denial of communication, the idolatry of nihilism, we redeem by not forgetting, by refusing, ourselves, to accept nihilism as representing or embodying life, our thought and existence. We continue to bind past and future, whatever the consequences, to our present. To redeem the past does not mean to forget the past. To forgive others does not mean that we forget the horrors for which they are eternally responsible (even as they evade and deny their responsibility). There is one sin only which is unforgivable: the sin against the spirit, the sin of not bearing the anxiety of consequence, the sin of not recognizing that all actions, even those denying life to others, must be judged to be actions which bear consequences, a future, a history, unto all eternity, for us, their heirs. To forgive others their past actions means, simply, that we must become eternally responsible for our actions in the future and not succumb, ever, to their evasion of the anxiety of consequence.

When Descartes formulates his response, the response of modernity, to Pilate's question, what is truth?, he articulates the anxiety of consequence as the recognition that we have no choice but to doubt, to search for that which is first or prior in our lives, to justify our enslavement to the appearances of the corporeal world, to legitimize the world, not on its own terms, but according to the concept which cannot be thought except existing and which cannot exist except as thought. Thinking—Descartes' and my term for the concept of the fullness of human action, will, desire, passion, concentration: *conatus*—is bound eternally—historically—to existence. To think is to discover, indeed, to create from nothing, our existence. But this proposition is true only so long as its dialectical opposite is equally true: we can exist only insofar as our existence owes nothing to anything either extrinsic or intrinsic to itself. Both of these propositions are true, therefore, in their relationship only when we understand that our thought and existence are given solely in the relationship of the self as the cause of itself, not in the relationship of the self to nature (the body) as caused through other bodies. The very relationship of thought and existence is the self, not in itself, but in its relationship, the self which is simultaneously individual and social, both divine and human. It is naturally the case that the self constantly tries to alleviate its anxiety of consequence by finding its relationship not in the other—the neighbor (including itself) and God—but in nature. For the self constantly claims either to be first, in certain, literal, natural, that is, hierarchical domination over others (in the state of nature it seeks to enslave others before it is enslaved by others) or to be last, again, in certain, literal, natural, that is, hierarchical domination by others (in the state of nature it seeks to be enslaved by others before they are enslaved by it). But the anxiety of consequence to be eternally borne is that the self can be first and last only as all selves, individual and communal, divine and human, are first and last, the alpha and the omega.

The anxiety of consequence is enormous. Our thinking, our thought and existence, is the priority which involves the priority of all beings, divine and human. We are first, we can be first only insofar as we put all other human beings first as God is first. The moment we attempt to be first, on our own, without recognizing the priority of all others, we become last. It is equally the case that the moment we attempt to put others first, without recognizing our own equal priority, we merely succeed in reducing their priority to our anxiety of consequence. The anxiety of consequence is enormously increased when we recognize that thought and existence bear the dialectic of truth and interpretation. Thought and existence express the truth, they are the answer, eternally, to Pilate's question. But they are true only in their interpretation. Thought and existence equally involve interpretation, and the consequence of interpretation is that they cannot be interpreted outside their commitment to truth.

The anxiety of consequence is increased yet further when the commitment to the truth of thought and existence as their sole interpretation and to the interpretation of thought and existence as solely the truth involves the recognition that there is nothing which cannot be interpreted as true and that there is nothing which is not true in its interpretation. Truth and interpretation, like their subject thought and existence, bear the anxious consequence of nothing, the anxious consequence of having been created from nothing, from nothing found in the contradictory appearances of space and time, from nothing which does not involve and express the priority of truth and interpretation. To bear the anxiety of consequence in saying I think, therefore, I am, is to acknowledge that I think nothing and that I am nothing except in the relationship of my thought and existence and that this relationship is nothing except insofar as it can be interpreted as the truth of all relationships and as it is the truth by which all relationships are to be interpreted. To bear nothing as the anxiety of consequence is to recognize both that where there is nothing—in extra-biblical paganism—there is no truth or interpretation and that where there is nothing—in the dualistic reduction of the Bible to idolatry—truth and interpretation are repressed through their reduction to the contradictory idols of nature which the Bible demonstrates to be nothing, nothing in themselves worthy of thought and existence, whether divine or human.

To bear the anxiety of consequence is to be haunted by nothing, by nothing which can be interpreted as the truth of everything and by everything which is true in and through its interpretation because it is created from nothing. To bear the anxiety of consequence is to bear witness eternally to truth and interpretation as the communication of thought and existence. To bear the anxiety of consequence is to distinguish between extra-biblical paganism and the idolatry of the Bible, between nothing thought to exist or existing as thought in natural space and time, from which truth and interpretation are created, and the idolatry of the Bible, which reduces truth and interpretation to nothing in thought and existence. Either/or. Either bear the anxiety of consequence that thought and existence are nothing in themselves outside of their truth and interpretation. Or be offended by the consequence that, in identifying your thought and existence with something other than truth and interpretation, they are nothing, nothing at all, nothing but idols. The truth of interpretation and the interpretation of truth bear the anxiety of consequence of undertaking eternally to distinguish between the creation of thought and existence as our choice of history and democracy from nothing and the reduction of our creative thought and existence to nothing historical or democratic. To think is to recognize that nothing can be thought outside the existence of truth and interpretation and that nothing can exist outside the thought of truth and interpretation. In the beginning God creates thought and existence from nothing, from nothing which does not express the interpretation of truth and from nothing which does not involve the truth of interpretation.

BIBLIOGRAPHY

Indications of specific editions and translations are provided only when they have a particular importance or utility.

M. H. Abrams, "Kant and the Theology of Art," *Notre Dame English Journal* (vol.13,1981); *Natural Supernaturalism: Tradition and Revolution in Romantic Literature*

St. Anselm, *Proslogium* and *Why God Became Man*, in St. Anselm, vols. 1 and 3, tr. J. Hopkins and H. Richardson

Philippe Ariès, *Centuries of Childhood: A Social History of Family Life*

Aristotle, *The Complete Works*, 2 vols., the rev. Oxford tr., ed. Jonathan Barnes (Princeton, 1984)

Erich Auerbach, *Mimesis: The Representation of Reality in Western Literature*

St. Augustine, *The City of God; Confessions*, tr. R. S. Pine-Coffin (Penguin)

Owen Barfield, *Saving the Appearances: A Study in Idolatry; Poetic Diction: A Study in Meaning*, 3rd ed. (Wesleyan)

J. H. van den Berg, *The Changing Nature of Man: Introduction to a Historical Psychology*

Peter Berger, *Invitation to Sociology*

Harold Bloom, *Agon: Towards a Theory of Revisionism; The Anxiety of Influence; Kaballah and Criticism; A Map of Misreading*

Martin Buber, "Distance and Relation" [1951], in *The Knowledge of Man. A Philosophy of the Interhuman*, tr. M. Friedman and R. G. Smith (New York, 1966); *I and Thou*

Rudolf Karl Bultmann, *Theology of the New Testament*

Kenneth Burke, *The Rhetoric of Religion: Studies in Logology*

Thomas Carlyle, *Sartor Resartus*

E. H. Carr, *What is History?*

James P. Carse, *Death and Existence: A Conceptual History of Human Mortality*

The Complete Greek Tragedies, 4 vols., ed. D. Grene & R. Lattimore (Chicago)

Harvey Cox, *The Secular City*

Benedetto Croce, *History as the Story of Liberty*

Oscar Cullmann, "Immortality of the Soul or Resurrection of the Dead?", in *Immortality and Resurrection: Death in the Western World: Two Conflicting Currents of Thought*, ed. K. Stendahl (Bison)

Charles R. Darwin, *Origin of Species*

Jacques Derrida, *Of Grammatology*

René Descartes, *Discourse on Method; Meditations on First Philosophy*

John Dewey, *Art as Experience; Experience and Nature; Reconstruction in Philosophy*

Ronald Dworkin, *A Matter of Principle; Law's Empire*

A. S. Eddington, *The Nature of the Physical World*

Paul Eidelberg, *Jerusalem vs. Athens: In Quest of a General Theory of Existence*

Mircea Eliade, *The Sacred and the Profane: The Nature of Religion*

Emil L. Fackenhein, *Encounters Between Judaism and Modern Philosophy: A Preface to Future Jewish Thought; To Mend the World: Foundations of Future Jewish Thought*

Haskell Fain, *Between Philosophy and History: The Resurrection of Speculative Philosophy within the Analytic Tradition*

Stanley Fish, *Is There a Text in This Class? The Authority of Interpretive Communities*

Michael Fishbane, *Biblical Interpretation in Ancient Israel*

Martin Foss, *The Idea of Perfection in the Western World; Symbol and Metaphor in Human Experience*

M. B. Foster, "The Christian Doctrine of Creation and the Rise of Modern Natural Science," *Mind* (vol. 43, 1934); "Christian

Theology and the Modern Science of Nature" (Parts I & II), *Mind* (vols. 44-45, 1935-36)

Sigmund Freud, *The Ego and the Id; A General Introduction to Psychoanalysis; The Interpretation of Dreams*

Erich Fromm, *You Shall Be As Gods: A Radical Interpretation of the Old Testament and its Tradition*

Edward Gibbon, *The History of the Decline and Fall of the Roman Empire*

René Girard, *Deceit, Desire, and the Novel: Self and Other in Literary Structure; Violence and the Sacred*

Michael Goldberg, *Theology and Narrative: A Critical Introduction*

Lucien Goldmann, *The Hidden God: A Study of Tragic Vision in the Pensées of Pascal and The Tragedies of Racine*

Susan Handelman, *The Slayers of Moses: The Emergence of Rabbinic Interpretation in Modern Literary Theory*

G. W. F. Hegel, *Lectures on Fine Art; Lectures on the Philosophy of History; Lectures on the Philosophy of Religion; Logic; The Phenomenology of Spirit; The Philosophy of Mind*

Martin Heidegger, *Being and Time*

Herodotus, *The Persian Wars*

A. J. Heschel, *God in Search of Man: A Philosophy of Judaism; The Sabbath; Who is Man?*

Thomas Hobbes, *Leviathan*

Homer, *Iliad; Odyssey*

Victor Hugo, *William Shakespeare*, in *The Works of Victor Hugo* (The Colonial Press, Boston & New York)

David Hume, *An Enquiry Concerning Human Understanding; A Treatise of Human Nature*

Virginia Hunter, *Thucydides: The Artful Reporter*

William M. Ivins, *Art and Geometry: A Study in Space Intuitions*

Karl Jaspers, *Nietzsche and Christianity*

John Jones, *On Aristotle and Greek Tragedy*

Immanuel Kant, *The Critique of Practical Reason; The Critique of Pure Reason; The Grounding of the Metaphysics of Morals; Religion within the Limits of Reason Alone*

Frank Kermode, *The Genesis of Secrecy: On the Interpretation of Narrative*

Søren Kierkegaard, "The Anxieties of the Heathen," in *Christian Discourses; Attack on Christendom; The Concept of Irony with Constant Reference to Socrates; Concluding Unscientific Postscript; Fear and Trembling; Philosophical Fragments; The Point of View for My Work as an Author; Purity of Heart Is To Will One Thing; Sickness unto Death; Works of Love: Some Christian Reflections in the Form of Discourses*

Alexandre Kojève, *Essai d'une Historie Raisonée de la Philosophie Païenne*: vol. 1, *Les Presocratiques*; vol. 2, *Platon-Aristote*; vol. 3, *La Philosophie Hellénistique. Les Néo-Platoniciens*

Dominick LaCapra, "Rethinking Intellectual History and Reading Texts," *History and Theory* (vol. 19, 1980)

A. Th. van Leeuwen, *Christianity in World History; Critique of Heaven and Critique of Earth*

G. W. von Leibniz, *Theodicy*

Bernard Lightman, *The Origins of Agnosticism: Victorian Unbelief and The Limits of Knowledge*

B. J. F. Lonergan, *Insight: A Study of Human Understanding; Method in Theology*

Niccolò Machiavelli, *Discourses on the First Ten Books of Livy; The Prince*

John Macmurray, *The Self as Agent; Persons in Relation*

Karl Marx, *The Class Struggles in France; The Economic and Philosophic Manuscripts; The Eighteenth Brumaire of Louis Napoleon; The German Ideology*

Angel Medina, *Reflection, Time, and the Novel: Towards a Communicative Theory of Literature*

John Milton, *Areopagitica; Paradise Lost*

José Miranda, *Being and the Messiah: The Message of St. John; Marx against the Marxists: The Christian Humanism of Karl Marx; Marx and the Bible: A Critique of the Philosophy of Oppression*

Michel de Montaigne, *Essays*, tr. D. M. Frame (Stanford)

Frederick Nietzsche, *The Antichrist; The Joyful Wisdom; On the Genealogy of Morals; Thus Spoke Zarathustra*

H. A. Oberman, *The Harvest of Medieval Theology*

Cynthia Ozick, "The Moral Necessity of Metaphor: Rooting History in a Figure of Speech," *Harper's* (April 1986)

Blaise Pascal, *Penseés*

Octavio Paz, "Food of the Gods," *New York Review of Books* (26 February 1987)

Plato, Dialogues and Letters (especially useful are those published by Hackett and the Library of Liberal Arts)

Plotinus, *Enneads*, tr. A. H. Armstrong (Loeb Library)

Brayton Polka, *The Dialectic of Biblical Critique: Interpretation and Existence;* "Spinoza and the Separation between Philosophy and Theology" (forthcoming in *The Journal of Religious Studies*); "The Supremacy of God and the Rule of Law in the Canadian Charter of Rights and Freedoms: A Theologico-Political Analysis" (*McGill Law Journal*, September 1987); "Truth and Metaphor: Interpretation as Philosophical and Literary Practice" (*Diogenes*, Fall 1988)

The Presocratic Philosophers, tr. G. S. Kirk *et al.*

John Rawls, *A Theory of Justice*

Richard Rorty, *Philosophy and the Mirror of Nature*

Denis de Rougemont, *Love in the Western World*, rev. and augmented ed., including new postscript, tr. M. Belgion (Princeton, 1983)

J.-J. Rousseau, *Discourse on Inequality; Emile; The Social Contract*

Oliver Sacks, *The Man Who Mistook His Wife for a Hat and Other Clinical Tales*

Edward Sapir, "Language," *Encyclopaedia of the Social Sciences* (vol. 9, 1933)

H. N. Schneidau, *Sacred Discontent: The Bible and Western Tradition*

G. G. Scholem, *Major Trends in Jewish Mysticism; The Messianic Idea in Judaism and Other Essays in Jewish Spirituality; On the Kabbalah and its Symbolism*

Thomas Sheehan, "The Dream of Karl Rahner," *New York Review of Books* (4 February 1982)

Page Smith, *The Historian and History*

Baruch Spinoza, *Ethics*, in *The Collected Works of Spinoza*, vol. 1, tr. E. Curley (Princeton); *The Theologico-Political Treatise* (forthcoming in vol. 2)

Meir Sternberg, *The Poetics of Biblical Narrative: Ideological Literature and the Drama of Reading*

Leo Strauss, "The Mutual Influence of Theology and Philosophy" [1954], *The Independent Journal of Philosophy* (vol. 3, 1979)

Mark C. Taylor, *Erring: A Postmodern A/theology*

Patrick Taylor, *The Narrative of Liberation*

Thucydides, *The Peloponnesian Wars*

Tzvetan Todorov, *The Conquest of America: The Question of the Other*

David Tracy, *The Analogical Imagination: Christian Theology and the Culture of Pluralism*

Giambattista Vico, *The New Science*, tr. and abridged T. G. Bergin & M. H. Fisch (Cornell)

Michael Walzer, *Exodus and Revolution*

Lynn T. White, *Medieval Technology and Social Change;* "The Significance of Medieval Christianity," in *The Vitality of the Christian Tradition*, ed. G.F. Thomas (1944)

INDEX

337